THE 500 HOME RUN CLUB

*Baseball's 16 Greatest Home Run Hitters
from Babe Ruth to Mark McGwire*

by **Bob Allen**
with **Bill Gilbert**

SPORTS PUBLISHING INC.
www.SportsPublishingInc.com

© 2000 Bob Allen and Bill Gilbert
All rights reserved.

Director of Production: Susan M. McKinney
Production Coordinator: Erin J. Sands
Photo insert design: Terry N. Hayden
Cover design: Terry N. Hayden
Cover photos courtesy of AP/Wide World Photos

ISBN: 1-58261-289-7
Library of Congress Catalog Card Number: 00-101217

www.SportsPublishingInc.com

Printed in the United States.

To my very own Hall of Famer, my wife Ellie, and to my son Tim and daughter Cathi and my lifelong friends, Hank Aaron and Eddie Mathews. And to the baseball greats and not so greats, but major leaguers all, who gave generously of their rememberances of this book.
In many respects, this is their book.
But most of all to my mentor, Bill Gilbert, "My Rembrandt With Words."

— B.A.

To Lillian and Dave and Katy, champions all.

— B.G.

CONTENTS

ACKNOWLEDGMENTS

The contents of this book have been reviewed for accuracy by Bruce Markusen, Senior Researcher for the National Baseball Hall of Fame Library in Cooperstown, New York.

Special thanks to Steve Gietschier of *The Sporting News*, Jim Gates of Baseball's Hall of Fame and Debbie Skalecki, assistant to Bob Allen.

Special thanks are also due to four other people who played key roles in the publication of this book—Andrew Pope, our literary agent at Curtis Brown, Ltd. of New York, and our All-Star team at Sports Publishing Inc.—Mike Pearson, Jeff Ellish and Susan McKinney.

FOREWORD

By Hank Aaron

For almost all of the Twentieth Century, America has had a love affair with home runs. That's why it is so appropriate to publish this book as the century ends.

Although more home runs than ever seem to be flying out of ballparks—and going farther—hitting them is still the most exciting play in any sport, and one of the hardest things to do. Even Mark McGwire, Sammy Sosa, Jose Canseco and Ken Griffey, Jr., who teamed up to make 1998 "The Year of the Home Run," will tell you that hitting home runs is never as easy as it sometimes looks.

I'm flattered to be included in these pages with all-time stars like Babe Ruth, Willie Mays, Frank Robinson, Harmon Killebrew, Mickey Mantle, Ted Williams, my old teammate—Eddie Mathews, and the others, all the way to the newest member of our club, Eddie Murray. To hit 500 home runs is a rare athletic achievement, a baseball Mount Everest, reached by only 16 players out of the 14,500 men who have played in the Major Leagues. But is more than a sports accomplishment. It is also a personal victory in endurance and in a person's ability and willingness to overcome adversity.

From my own experience I know that a player's challenge is made more difficult by the phone calls, the stacks of mail, the constant mobbing by well-meaning fans and the media spotlight that never gets turned away from you. Here's one example: When I was chasing Ruth's record of 714 home runs in a career, I had to stay at a different hotel from the rest of the team when the Braves were on the road. Another example: I was *averaging* 3,000 letters a *day*.

Others in this book faced challenges of their own while hitting over 500 homers. Ruth overcame the effects of his excesses, Mantle played his entire career on two bad knees, Jimmie Foxx developed a problem with alcohol during his playing days, Mel Ott was only five feet, nine inches and weighed only 170 pounds, and Ted Williams missed five seasons—five *prime* seasons—because of military service in World War II and the Korean War. Others overcame different obstacles in their way.

And yet each of them hit more than 5,000 home runs. Another, Lou Gehrig, hit 493 and certainly would have hit over 500 if his career had not been cut short by his tragic illness. When I read of their individual struggles, it made me appreciate their accomplishments even more.

All baseball fans should be grateful to my friend from our days with the Braves in Milwaukee, Bob Allen, and his colleague, Bill Gilbert, because this is more than just a fascinating book. It is also a valuable contribution to baseball history, revealing the stories—many of them never published—behind these men, told in their own words and by the Major Leaguers who played with them and against them.

And who knows? Maybe this book will have to be reissued a few years from now—to include chapters about Sammy Sosa, Jose Canseco and Ken Griffey, Jr.

I hope so.

Ellie and Bob Allen with Hank Aaron

PROLOGUE

When Bob Allen and I started talking about writing this book, it was before all the predictions that some slugger would break the record of 61 home runs in one season, and soon. As fate would have it, we began writing it in early 1998, turning out pages of stories even while Mark McGwire and Sammy Sosa were blasting out home runs.

It was our thought, before the McGwire-Sosa assault on Roger Maris's record began, that a book needed to be written about baseball's most elite group of hitters, the 16 men who hit more than 500 home runs in their careers. Our goal was to record and preserve not only the stories of their baseball feats but also the stories of their lives, their glories and their burdens, as could be told only by themselves and those who played with and against them.

We wanted to do more than just copy a fistful of clippings from various libraries, read shelves of baseball books and then write a perfectly good book about these 16 giants. We wanted to go beyond that , to talk to the 12 living members of this group themselves, and as many of their teammates and opponents as we could catch up with by telephone and in face-to-face conversations at baseball banquets, card shows, other events and in hotel lobbies and guest rooms all over America. In this exhaustive effort, bob interviewed 180 former Major League players about power hitters from Babe Ruth in the teens, 1920s and '30s to Eddie Murray in the 1970s, '80s and '90s. In the process of all these interviews, supplemented by extensive research at the Baseball Hall of Fame Library and through other sources, we were able to reach our goal of telling the reader what made these men succeed, and what made them different.

We are proud to contribute this volume of 16 uniquely American lives and this testimony to their greatness as 16 American heroes.

—BILL GILBERT
October 1998

INTRODUCTION

I was eleven years old in 1942 and World War II was in full swing. The Milwaukee Brewers offered free admission to any child accompanied by an adult who donated an aluminum pot or pan to the war effort. Our American Association entry defeated the Columbus Red Birds that day and my lifelong love affair with baseball was underway.

After that I would clean under the bleachers before every home game to gain free admission. I rarely missed a game. I will never forget the excitement I felt one season when the Brooklyn Dodgers and Chicago Cubs played my Brewers at old Borchert Field.

Later, when the Boston Braves became the first team in 50 years to move and arrived in Milwaukee in 1953, I was the only Milwaukeean to join the club and worked 13 glorious years in the team's publicity office as we won two pennants and a World Series behind Warren Spahn, Lew Burdette and two of the subjects of this book—Hank Aaron and Eddie Mathews. When the team moved to Atlanta 13 years later, I resigned out of loyalty to my city and state. After all, I had my 1957 World Series ring.

For 14 years I have served as an agent to Hank Aaron and since then I have been supplying players for "baseball card shows" throughout the country. For 12 of those years, I served as Stan Musial's agent as well as eight other subjects of this book—Ernie Banks, Reggie Jackson, Harmon Killebrew, Mickey Mantle, Willie Mays, Willie McCovey, Frank Robinson and Ted Williams. During this time, I would meet and visit with Jimmie Foxx and Mel Ott, leaving Babe Ruth as the only subject of this book I have never met.

Now I am the author of this book about my friends and business associates. How lucky can I be! I still pinch myself from time to time. I hope you enjoy reading this book as much as Bill Gilbert and I enjoyed writing it for you.

—BOB ALLEN

1

HANK AARON

Patience

I t is an appropriate coincidence that Hank Aaron is the first player
listed in the records of the 15,000 Major Leaguers whose statis
tics are shown in the Baseball Encyclopedia.

No one can argue that Aaron belongs at or near the top of any list of
players, alphabetical or not, with credentials that qualify him to be ranked
among the greatest players ever and not just baseball's all-time home
run king.

Every fan knows that Aaron broke Babe Ruth's record for the most
home runs in a career when he hit his 715th homer on the night of
April 8, 1974, in Atlanta. However, two other accomplishments are often
overlooked, maybe even unknown, in illustrating Aaron's stature in the
sport's history: He also is baseball's all-time leader in total bases and
runs batted in. He is tied with Ruth for the second most runs scored,
behind only Ty Cobb, and trails only Cobb and Pete Rose for the most
hits in a career.

Another of baseball's greatest hitters, Stan Musial, a seven-time batting champion, remembers that Aaron really didn't look or swing like a
home run hitter at the start of his career. "When he came up (to the big
leagues)," Musial said, "who would have thought he would go on to break
Babe Ruth's record? He hit the ball to all fields, but ... he started pulling
the ball, and by the time he went to Atlanta, he really had his power ..."

Musial elaborated: "He was a deceptive home run hitter. It's just
hard to believe he hit as many home runs as he did. You would have
thought it would have been Reggie or Mickey or Harmon, guys who
were natural home run hitters. It's the trait of a good hitter to be able to
change his style the way he did."

Aaron has his own theory, based on one word—patience.

"The thing I had on my side was patience," he said. Aaron, whose
ancestors were slaves, explained, "Patience—which is really the art of

waiting—is something you pick up pretty naturally when you grow up black in Alabama. When you wait all your life for respect and equality and a seat in the front of the bus, it's nothing to wait a little while for a slider inside."

TWO SANDWICHES, TWO DOLLARS AND A CARDBOARD SUITCASE

Aaron began life in a small, six-room home without lights or windows and an outhouse in the yard. He wanted to be a carpenter when he grew up—until he started playing baseball.

While still a student at Central High in Mobile, he began playing semi-pro baseball as a shortstop with the Mobile Black Bears at three dollars a game. He played only in their home games. His mother, Estella, a homemaker, would not allow her son to travel to the Bears' out-of-town games.

The Indianapolis Clowns of the Negro League offered him the heady sum of $200 a month, but his mother insisted he finish high school. The Clowns agreed to wait. In the meantime, they almost lost him to the Brooklyn Dodgers in the first years after Jackie Robinson broke baseball's "color barrier," followed by Roy Campanella and Don Newcombe. Hank attented a Brooklyn tryout camp in Mobile, but the Dodgers told him he was too small. Besides, he batted crossbanded.

The Clowns later invited Aaron to their spring training camp at Winston-Salem, North Carolina. He went not only with his mother's blessing but with two sandwiches and two dollars from her. He also carried a note for the Clowns' manager from Ed Scott, young Hank's manager on the Black Bears. The note said, "Forget everything about this player. Just watch his bat!"

Aaron made the team, at a salary of $200 a month.

It wasn't exactly big league life. The Clowns stayed in hotels only on Saturday nights. The other six nights of the week, they slept on the bus while riding down the highway to their next town. They also ate most of their meal on the bus, since few restaurants in that part of the country served African-Americans in the early 1950s.

"We didn't have roommates," Aaron remembers. "We had seatmates. We ate and slept on the bus."

The Clowns' owner, Syd Pollock, was always anxious to sell his players. He wrote John Mullen, farm director of the Boston Braves, extolling the virtues of several players on the Clowns and closed with a P.S.: "I've got a kid playing shortstop you've got to see. An exceptional hitter. His name is Henry Aaron."

Mullen dispatched scout Dewey Griggs to take a look. What Griggs saw was Aaron going 7-for-9 in a doubleheader with two home runs. He wrote excitedly to his boss, Mullen, "I would sign him with money out of my own pocket."

In the meantime, the Clowns' owner had agreed to sell Aaron to the New York Giants that same day, but Mullen pleaded with him, reminding Pollock that he had promised Aaron to the Braves. Pollock conceded and Aaron joined the Braves. Without Mullen's powers of persuasion, the Giants would have had a batting order featuring Aaron and Willie Mays batting back-to-back for 20 years.

The future Hall of Famer began his professional career with Eau Claire, Wisconsin, of the Class C Northern League. After only two weeks, he was chosen for the All-Star game. By the end of the season, he was named the league's Rookie of the Year for 1952 with a .336 average, 116 hits in 87 games and 61 runs batted in—but only nine home runs in 345 times at bat.

His manager, Bill Adair, reported to the Braves that Aaron was accomplishing this under difficult conditions, around white folks for the first time and homesick while living at the YMCA. At one time he almost went home to Alabama. His low point came when it rained hard while he was waiting outside for the team bus. His cardboard suitcase, given to him as a going-away present by the Clowns, fell apart, leaving him standing in the rain and holding only the handle.

STRIKE ZONE? WHAT STRIKE ZONE?

Billy Southworth, former manager of the St. Louis Cardinals, was a Braves scout that year. After watching Aaron in several games, Southworth wrote back to his bosses, "I will see the remaining games tonight but will send in this report now, because regardless of what happens tonight, it will not change my mind in the least about this boy's ability."

Aaron was quickly promoted to the Jacksonville Braves, where he destroyed pitching at that higher classification by leading the league in seven departments, including a .362 batting average and 22 home runs. He was voted his league's Most Valuable Player.

He led Jacksonville to the pennant. On the night they won the championship in a game in Savannah, the team celebrated in a local restaurant—except Aaron and his only two African-American teammates. They were forced to hold their own celebration in the same restaurant's kitchen. It wasn't a new kind of experience for Aaron. In Montgomery, African-American players were not allowed to dress for the Braves' games at the ballpark. Instead, they had to dress in their hotel rooms.

His manager at Jacksonville, Ben Geraghty, said Aaron could handle any pitch, and it didn't have to be in the strike zone. "He's a bad ball hitter with very strong wrists," Geraghty said, adding that Aaron's strike zone extended from the top of his head to his ankles.

During a game against Augusta that year, Aaron had six hits, much to the irritation of the opposing catcher, who complained to Geraghty,

"Aaron's lucky. He got six hits, but not one of the balls he hit was in the strike zone."

Geraghty laughed and asked, "What do you mean, 'strike zone?' Henry doesn't know a thing about the strike zone. He hits them no matter where they come from."

Aaron's skipper remembered something else about him in 1953 at Jacksonville, a night when the fans chipped in with $400 in cash for Aaron on player appreciation night, a common practice in the minor leagues in those years.

Aaron told Geraghty, "Split the money among all the players."

Geraghty said, "I've been in baseball a long, long time, but I've never found a more generous and unselfish kid than Aaron."

THE BIG LEAGUES AND THE OUTFIELD

One of the few negatives in the scouting reports on Aaron was his fielding. As a shortstop in Eau Claire, he committed 35 errors. The Braves switched him to second base in Jacksonville, where he made 36 more, the most in the league. When the Braves invited him to spring training before the 1954 season, their major project for him was to convert him into an outfielder.

There was nothing in Aaron's first game in the Major Leagues to suggest he was destined for the Hall of Fame and touched by fate to top the great Babe Ruth. He went 0-for-5. His first hit, a home run, came a few days later off former Yankee star Vic Raschi. His rookie season was a commendable one, with a .280 average, 13 home runs and 69 runs batted in. It ended abruptly and prematurely in early September when he collected five straight hits in a doubleheader in Cincinnati but broke his ankle in the second game and missed the rest of the season.

With his first year under his belt, Aaron took the National League by storm in 1955. He hit .314 with 189 hits, 27 home runs and 106 runs batted in and led the league with 37 doubles and finished second behind teammate Billy Bruton in triples with 14. Before the start of the season, he changed his uniform number from 5 to the now familiar 44.

It was an entirely satisfactory performance for a season that got off on the wrong foot when Aaron and several other Braves were fined $50 each for starting spring training before March 1. He received a telegram from Commissioner Ford Frick about the violation but threw it out. When Manager Charlie Grimm explained the seriousness of the situation, the normally obedient Aaron said he didn't know who Frick was. Grimm convinced the Braves to pay the fine.

Aaron's star rose even higher in 1956. He won the National League's batting championship with a .328 average and also led the league with 200 hits, 340 total bases and 34 doubles. He was the youngest player in National League history to win the batting crown. At six feet tall and 170 pounds, he was becoming a towering figure in baseball. *The Sporting*

News recognized this and named him its National League Player of the Year.

He was still plagued by errors, but he was getting better. He committed 13 in 1956, the most in the league but two less than the year before. Continued hard work brought continued improvement. Only once during the rest of his remaining 20 years did he commit more than seven errors in the outfield. During that same span, he won three Gold Gloves as the best fielder at his position, mostly right field.

The Braves, playing in Milwaukee for their fourth season after moving from Boston for the start of the 1953 season, were also doing well. They finished in second place, only one game behind the champion Brooklyn Dodgers.

The star hitter may not have known who Ford Frick was, but he showed he knew who Lou Perini was. At a baseball dinner in Milwaukee over the winter, Perini, the Braves' owner, lavished praise on his superstar. Aaron leaned over to the person next to him at the head table and asked, "Does Mr. Perini mean all these nice things about me before I sign my contract, or after?"

Shortly after, he signed his contract, for $28,500. Then came the magical season of 1957.

The Braves won their first Milwaukee pennant in '57, led by Aaron's booming bat. He topped his best year—27 homers in 1955—with 44 in 1957, his fourth season in the big leagues, to lead the league. It was the first of eight seasons that he hit 40 or more homers. He was also tops in runs scored and runs batted in and finished fourth in hitting with a .322 average.

The Braves beat out the Cardinals for the pennant by eight games. Aaron won the pennant for them on September 23 in Milwaukee, with a long home run in the eleventh inning off Billy Muffett, the first home run given up by Muffett that year.

The whole baseball world was marvelling at Aaron's achievements and his consistency, including Dick Groat of the Pittsburgh Pirates. "As a shortstop, I never had any idea where to play Henry Aaron," he said. "People don't recall that when he was hitting for a high average, he was hitting from line to line. He drove me insane. Once he decided to go for the home run, then he became a dead pull hitter. That proves how great he really was. He changed his whole style of hitting, made himself a pull hitter, and started hitting a lot of home runs, and yet still hit for average."

Another star whose eyes popped every time he watched Aaron was Mickey Mantle. His teammate on the Yankees, Clete Boyer, said, "Mickey used to tell me a million times—'I don't believe this guy.' I never heard Mickey talk about Joe DiMaggio, Willie Mays or Ted Williams. All he talked about was Aaron."

Dick Stuart said, "The fact that he played in Milwaukee, you hardly knew he was around, and at the end of the season you'd look up and he'd have 40 home runs and 120 runs batted in and a .330 batting average. If he had played in New York, he'd have been the greatest thing since sliced bread."

A WORLD SERIES HERO

The icing on the cake came in 1957, when the Braves upset the Yankees in seven games in the World Series, with Lew Burdette winning his third game of the Series in the final contest on only two days of rest. And Aaron again was a hero.

In his first World Series, the pressure did not bother the 23-year-old Aaron. He dominated the Series by leading both teams in average, home runs, runs scored and runs batted in. He collected 11 hits in the seven games, drove in seven runs, scored five times, hit three home runs and had a .393 average. To the surprise of no one, he was named the Series' Most Valuable Player.

First baseman Frank Torre, a .300 hitter in that World Series himself, attributes Aaron's stardom over the years to his stability and his performance under pressure. "You could never tell by looking at Henry in the clubhouse or in the hotel whether he was on a hot streak or in a slump," Torre said. "He had a very level disposition. That's a great thing, because you play seven days a week, and he didn't have any highs and lows, whether he went 5-for-5 or 0-for-5."

After the Series, Aaron was saluted with "Hank Aaron Day" in Mobile. He was honored with a parade, was presented a key to the city and was the toast of the town. Then things turned sour. He was scheduled to speak at one of the service clubs—a white one. When Hank mentioned that he would be bringing his father, officials of the club said no to the idea.

So Aaron said no to them.

Hank hit another 30 home runs in 1958 and compiled a .326 average, teaming up with Third Baseman Eddie Mathews and his 31 homers to provide one of the most powerful one-two punches in either league.

Their fate in the World Series was different this time, although it was not Aaron's fault. He hit .333, second only to teammate Billy Bruton for the highest average on either team, with two doubles among his nine hits. It was the last time he played in the World Series. His career average for those two Series is .364, the seventh highest in history.

The loss was a bitter one, because the 1958 Braves seemed even stronger than the '57 team. Aaron won his second batting crown with a .353 average, hit 39 homers and drove in 123 runs. Mathews led the league with 44 homers, hit .306 and had 114 RBIs. Warren Spahn, on his way to becoming the winningest lefthanded pitcher in history, won 22 games, with Burdette winning 20.

EMANCIPATION

For the Braves in Milwaukee, their glory days were over. Beginning in 1960, they finished seven, ten and 15 games behind in the next three years. But Aaron continued his assault on the National League pitchers.

In the six years remaining before the Braves moved again, this time to Atlanta in 1966, baseball's future home run king had homer totals of 40, 34, 45, 44, 24 and 32 even though he was playing half of his games in a park considered the toughest home run target in the league except for Pittsburgh's cavernous Forbes Field. He also led the league in total bases three times in those six seasons, RBIs and doubles twice and home runs and runs scored once. He topped off this streak with three Gold Gloves for his fielding.

Columnist William Barry Furlong of the *Chicago Daily News* wrote, "The secret ... seems to be in his supple, powerful wrists. They measure almost eight inches around, about one and a half to two inches more than the wrists of heavyweight champion Floyd Patterson. They allow him to 'crack' the light bat like a buggy whip ... "

Something else good happened in those years. In 1961, Aaron and the other African-Americans on the Braves were "emancipated"—allowed to stay in the same hotel with the white players during spring training. For seven springs, Hank and his minority teammates were assigned to live in an apartment over a garage in Bradenton, Florida, while all the white players stayed at the beautiful Manatee River Hotel. The garage was owned by a woman known simply as Mrs. Gibson.

The following season, Manager Chuck Dressen would not allow the Braves to eat in any restaurant that would not admit minorities, a stance for which Aaron always admired Dressen.

In 1962, Aaron, now known as "The Hammer," hammered the longest home run of his career. In a game at New York's Polo Grounds against righthander Jay Hook and the newly created Mets, Hank became the second player to hit a ball into the center field stands, 470 feet from home plate.

A MOVE TOWARD MORE HOMERS

The Braves moved to Atlanta for the 1966 season, a development at first considered by Aaron to be a sad day. He had played in Milwaukee, the beer city, for 12 years and lived there that entire time. He married a local girl after making good on his promise to hit a home run for her, and raised four children there with her.

Conditions in Atlanta were less than ideal for African-American athletes, even though the city was considered a progressive one in the 1960s. Until the Braves arrived, no black man had played for an Atlanta baseball team. Aaron was forced to live in a segregated part of the city. He received hate mail. On the day of the Braves' first home game, the loudest cheer from the sellout crowd came when the scoreboard flashed a message that said, "April 12, 1861: First Shots Fired on Fort Sumter ... April 12, 1966: The South Rises Again."

But a new role was awaiting Hank Aaron in Atlanta—power hitter. The city had the highest elevation in baseball then, and the hottest. Because of that combination, hitters could hit a ton of home runs if they could get the ball into the air and then see it carried over the fence. After only one turn in the batting cage in his new city, Aaron knew his career was headed in a different direction. He changed his batting style overnight and became a pull hitter.

Hank knew that baseball lore said the first corrosion of coordination for a hitter is a decreased ability to pull the ball—that older players just can't get the bat around quickly enough to hit the fastball. So he simply adjusted his stance, his batting grip and his swing. He brought his hands down on the bat and closer to his body. His idea was to shorten his swing, not lengthen it, to react faster to the pitch and still "pull" the ball with his whole body behind his swing.

During Aaron's 12 years in Milwaukee as a spray hitter with power, he averaged .320. While swinging for the fences in Atlanta for nine years, he averaged .292.

His second homer of 1966, his first season in Atlanta, was the 400th of his career. He didn't know it then, but his Babe Ruth chase was underway. Ruth wasn't on his mind, but something else was: Could he hit 500 home runs? He had just turned 32.

In his first two years in Atlanta, Aaron's experiment with power produced immediate results. He led the league in homers his first year there with 44 and again in 1967 with 39. Then it occurred to him that he might have a chance to break baseball's most cherished record, Ruth's achievement of hitting 714 home runs in his career. His power strategy continued to pay handsome dividends. In the first nine years of his ten seasons in Atlanta, Hank hit 40 or more home runs four times and hit 39, 38 and 34 in three other years.

Ron Swoboda, in the middle of his nine-year big league career, noticed the change. "The first time I saw Henry Aaron," he said, "I couldn't believe hitting was that easy. He'd hit a pitch in any direction. Then I saw him 11 years later, and he would rarely hit a ball to the right of second base. He had decided to pull everything. Most hitters, if they tried to adopt that approach, would not have the discipline and would lose tons of points off their average and probably not produce much more offense. He produced *more* offense and didn't lose any points off his average and became, in the process, the most prolific home run hitter we have ever seen."

Then Swoboda admitted, "He made you feel that you should just walk in and take your uniform off and just confess that you were unworthy, and that you were a fraud."

Aaron continued to put together a star-studded list of hitting achievements. He hit his target, his 500th home run, against San Francisco's Mike McCormick in 1968 at age 34. His home run totals continued to attract attention. Keith Coulbourn wrote in the *Atlanta Journal and Constitution Magazine* in 1969, "He'll probably never surpass Babe Ruth's 714 homers, but it's interesting to note that Babe Ruth had 470 home runs when he was 34. Hank Aaron at the same age had 481."

In 1970, he reached the milestone of 3,000 hits, off Wayne Simpson in Cincinnati's Crosley Field, where he had played his first Major League game 16 years earlier.

That hit placed him in elite company as only the ninth player to accomplish the feat, and the first African-American. He reached the earlier levels of 1,000 hits, then 2,000 and finally 3,000 ahead of Cobb's age in each case. If he had not decided to concentrate on home runs, he might have had more than 4,000 hits and might have topped both Cobb's and Pete Rose's totals.

AARON VS. MAYS

Not long after Aaron collected his 3,000th hit, Willie Mays got his. In Aaron's book, *I Had a Hammer*, he confessed, "It was the first time I had ever reached a milestone ahead of him and, frankly, it felt good. But Willie was still more than 40 homers ahead of me, and that's where the attention was focused. It was still mostly on Willie, and I'd be lying to say it didn't bother me a little bit, because the same thing had been going on for 15 years."

Hank admitted, "I had to work at not being envious of Willie. I always told myself that my time would come. I considered Mays a rival, certainly, but a friendly rival ....I've never seen a better all-around ballplayer than Willie Mays, but I will say this: Willie was not as good a hitter as I was. No way."

In April 1971, Hank, then 37, hit his 600th home run, off Gaylord Perry of the Giants. The Braves lost the game on a hit by—who else?— Willie Mays. But Willie's once-great skills were eroding at age 40. He hit only 18 home runs that year, compared to Aaron's 47, Hank's career high and second in the league, only one behind Willie Stargell.

Hank's homers gave him 639 for his career. Now it was clear that if anyone was going to break Ruth's record of 714 home runs in a career, it was going to be "The Hammer." The chase was on, and the whole baseball world was talking about it.

Aaron closed the gap again in 1972, this time with 34 more homers. He was only 41 shy of Ruth, and he was stimulated by the challenge. "Now I really wanted the record, the recognition and the money," he said in 1994 on the 20th anniversary of the night he broke Ruth's record.

FROM A CHALLENGE TO A CRUSADE

What had been a challenge became a crusade. Aaron now wanted the record more than ever. "If I ever had any doubt, it was erased in late October (1972), when Jackie Robinson died. Just before he passed away, he visited the Oakland A's clubhouse, supported by a cane, and was mostly ignored. He finally left. I felt I owed it to him to break the record. Even to some in the African-American community, it seemed he had been all but forgotten. But not by me."

The closer he drew, the harder the challenge became because of the conditions surrounding him. Aaron was now receiving hate mail among the 3,000 letters a day pouring into him, an avalanche that eventually totalled nearly a million. Every piece of his mail was opened by the F.B.I., at the Atlanta post office. His life was threatened. His parents received calls saying they would never see him again. A plot to kidnap his daughter was uncovered.

On road trips with his team, Aaron stayed at a different hotel, away from his teammates and registered under assumed names. Catcher Paul Casanova went out for all of Aaron's meals and brought them back to his hotel room. In Atlanta, a plainclothes police officer accompanied him everywhere, with his gun and a badge in a binoculars case.

Hank hit Number 700 in late July of the 1973 season off Philadelphia's Ken Brett. By the end of the season he was only one home run behind Ruth at 713. His numbers for that season: a .301 batting average and 40 home runs, at age 39.

His manager and old teammate in Milwaukee, Eddie Mathews, a fellow member of the 500-homer club and a future Hall of Famer himself, wanted to keep Aaron out of the lineup when the Braves opened the 1974 season on the road so he could break Ruth's record before the home fans in Atlanta. But Mathews was overruled by Commissioner Bowie Kuhn, so Aaron, playing under a direct order from the Commissioner of Baseball, homered in the Opening Game—in Cincinnati.

Ron Swoboda remembers Aaron's composure. "When he needed that one home run to break Ruth's record," Swoboda said, "and with all the hoopla, and to hit it almost on demand was simply unbelievable. He managed to stay so cool in the middle of the storm."

"A MAGICAL MOMENT"

Aaron broke one of the most cherished records in American sports against lefthander Al Downing of the Dodgers on the night of April 8, 1974, two months and three days after his 40th birthday, before a national television audience and a sellout crowd in Atlanta. There were 250 reporters covering the moment.

When he stepped into the batter's box for his next turn at bat, only 20,000 fans of the sellout crowd were still there. The rest had left. Commissioner Kuhn was not in the sellout crowd before or after Aaron's record-breaking homer. He elected to speak to a group in Cleveland that night and sent one of his aides, Hall of Famer Monte Irvin, to represent him. Aaron considered it a slight, said so publicly and never forgave Kuhn.

His achievement that night was voted by sportswriters as the greatest moment in baseball history, even ahead of Bobby Thomson's "shot heard 'round the world" in 1951 and Don Larsen's perfect game in the 1956 World Series. The home run also broke Ruth's record for the most homers by a player with one team and gave Aaron and Mathews the record over Ruth and Gehrig for the most home runs by teammates over their careers.

Hank also endured criticism from some fans and certain members of the media who claimed he enjoyed advantages over Ruth—more games on the schedule, more times at bat, a friendly ballpark in Atlanta for homers. But these criticisms overlooked the advantages that Ruth enjoyed—playing all day games, facing only one pitcher a game instead of four or five fresh arms, and Ruth's advantage of playing in Yankee Stadium, where the right field seats that he aimed at as a lefthanded hitter were only 296 feet from home plate, with a low wall in front.

Students of pitching also point out that Ruth never had to worry about the slider, a pitch that always bothered Aaron, but also bothered Ted Williams, another 500-homer hitter, and Joe DiMaggio—and almost every other hitter since the pitch came into widespread use by Bob Feller and others after World War II.

Stan Musial, who hit 475 home runs himself and missed the entire 1945 season because of military duty in World War II, speaks in Aaron's favor. Columnist Bob Broeg pointed out that Musial was a .340 hitter in daytime and a .320 hitter at night. Musial told Broeg, "Ruth played nothing except day games, and take it from me, you see the ball better in the daytime than at night."

Musial added another telling point: "Henry Aaron hit against the best black pitchers of his era, and Ruth didn't. So no one can take anything away from Henry. Not even the Babe."

Downing talks candidly about that moment: "My serving up Number 715 to Hank is part of history. As we get older in life, I think we get a little more tolerant of certain things. You see, I was on the bench when Roger Maris hit his 61st home run. I knew Hank was a tough out. And the one thing about Hank I wanted to make sure was that I don't give him anything he can hit to left center field, because in that point of his career, I knew that if he got the ball airborne, it was gone. So I try to get it down and get that double play. They make a lot of who threw the pitch—like me, Ralph Branca, Ralph Terry—but don't give enough credit to the hitter who accomplished those things. It was a good pitch, but he hit it. To me, the most impressive thing about the record wasn't that he hit 715, but that he hit 40 more after that."

Downing's teammate on the Dodgers, Steve Garvey, remembers that night. "I was playing first base when he broke Ruth's record," Garvey said. "As soon as it was hit, you knew it had a good chance of going out. I remember the anticipation. He just did his normal trot around the bases. I almost wanted to stick my hand out. It was a magical moment, and I was just happy I was there. He stayed within himself that night like he always has. I never saw him get too high or too low."

Before a party at his house that night, Aaron went off by himself, got down on his knees, closed his eyes and said a prayer of thanksgiving. "I had done something that nobody else in the world had ever done, and with it came a feeling that nobody else ever had—not exactly anyway," Hank said in his autobiography. "I didn't feel a wild sense of joy. I didn't feel like celebrating. But I probably felt closer to God at that moment than at any other in my life. I felt a deep sense of gratitude and a wonderful surge of liberation all at the same time. I also felt a stream of tears running down my face."

When Bob Allen was writing a magazine article in 1994 on the 20th anniversary of that historic home run, he asked Aaron's wife, Billye, what Hank said to her after everyone left at the end of the evening and they were all alone.

"Oh, Bob," she said, "you know Henry well enough not to ask that question. He didn't say a word to me about it that night, and he hasn't said a word about it since."

The next day, Aaron came up to Downing at the ballpark and said, "Hey, I've hit you before. Don't feel any disgrace about it. You're a fine pitcher."

And Downing congratulated him.

COMING HOME

Aaron returned to Milwaukee, the scene of many of his favorite baseball memories, for the 1975 and '76 seasons, the last of his career. He was joining an expansion team, the Brewers, owned by Bud Selig, now the Commissioner of Baseball, formed in 1970. He was back where it all started, with the fans who had always been in his corner and where he always claimed he spent his happiest years. In his first time at bat, he was accorded a five-minute standing ovation.

On May 1, 1975, Aaron went 4-for-4 and drove in a run to tie Ruth's RBI record, then broke Musial's league record for most hits in a career. They were the high spots. On the down side, his skills were leaving him. He hit only .234 with 12 home runs and 60 RBIs. The magic in his bat was gone. He needed glasses to read. His back and knees bothered him.

On July 20, 1976, he hit his tenth home run of the season before his fans in Milwaukee. It was the 755th home run of his career, and the last. When he played his final home game in 1976, 40,000 fans turned out. In his last game, against Detroit, he beat out an infield hit, his 3,771st hit, at age 42.

In talking about his brilliant career today, Aaron says, "Frankly, I'm more proud of the fact that, even to this day, I totalled more bases and drove in more runs than anyone else. Any player will tell you that getting on base and driving in runs is what this game is all about. But no, every time I sign an autograph, they want me to write, 'Hank Aaron, 755' or 'Hank Aaron, All-Time Home Run King.'"

As for his home runs, Aaron is candid about them, too. "I look at it this way," he says, "It doesn't make any difference if they were hit in the 1920s and '30s or the '50s or '60s or '70s. Or by Willie Mays or Mickey Mantle or Ted Williams or Reggie Jackson. Or if they were hit at home or on the road or during the day or night. Or at Yankee Stadium, the Polo Grounds, Ebbets Field or Fenway Park. The fact is I hit 755 home runs and nobody else did."

Then he adds, "I'm grateful for all the recognition over breaking Ruth's records, but I would like to be remembered as a player who accomplished other things, too."

Aaron on Aaron

If you were pitching to me, the smartest thing you could do was never throw me the same pitch twice in a row. Seriously, I was very patient at the plate, and after two-three years in the big leagues, I had all kinds of confidence. I studied the pitchers, I really did, and I knew exactly what a pitcher could get me out with. I felt I knew exactly what they were going to throw me in a given situation. I guessed correct 99 percent of the time.

Not only guess, but I would guess what spot it was going to be thrown in because I studied them so good. And you look at my entire career: For the amount of home runs I hit, I don't think there was one time that I struck out 100 times. (His high was 97, and he averaged 60 for his 23 years in the Major Leagues.)

My philosophy was that each time I went to the plate I wanted to make contact. I felt if I did, my chances of getting a base hit or doing something were great. And yes, I did hit cross-handed for a while. And the most amazing thing was that I should have been a switch hitter. Easy, very easy. Because I was hitting righthanded. All I had to do was move over to the other side of the plate.

I did it in my first season in Eau Claire, and the reason I stopped doing it was I was taking batting practice cross-handed and I hit a liner that broke the nose of one of my teammates. I never did it again. Hitting cross-handed, all I had to do was go over to the other side. It would have been easy, really easy, because I was hitting balls out of the ballpark in batting practice while batting cross-handed. But I never did it in a game.

Comparing the home run he hit to win the 1957 pennant and his 715th: The one I hit in Atlanta to break the record was an individual thing, you know. That's your trophy. But the one I hit in Milwaukee was a pennant-winning ball. We had a great team and great fans, and the people of Milwaukee deserved it, and it climaxed my year, because I was voted the league's Most Valuable Player.

I don't really have any more goals. For a boy who grew up in Mobile, Alabama, in the Deep South, and only went through the twelfth grade, and to play as many years in the big leagues, I was extremely lucky. But I don't know if I would have lasted as long if I had to play in New York. Some people say I would have made tons of money in New York, but I don't think I would have lasted.

Milwaukee was made for me. It was my style of town. It was slow. It was a long ways from New York, but yet it was a big city. People there appreciated me. I made a lot of mistakes on a baseball field, especially as a young kid, and all the time I played in Milwaukee I was never booed.

If I ever met Babe Ruth and had to ask him one question. I would ask him if he was proud of me. And I think he would answer, "Yes, yes, I'm very proud of you."

WHAT OTHER PLAYERS SAID ABOUT HANK AARON

Red Schoendienst—One of the best players ever to walk on a diamond. He did it all with no fanfare. He just made everything seem so easy. He did it all at the plate, in the field and on the bases.

Bob Buhl—He had the best wrists in baseball. He was so quick with that bat.

Del Crandall—No question, Hank Aaron was the best player I ever saw play. The yardstick was Willie Mays because of the flair he had. But Aaron could do everything that Mays could do and even more. He was a better hitter and thrower and just as good in the outfield.

Andy Pafko—When I first saw him in Florida, he had a "can't miss" sign all over him . . . . He was just born to play the game.

Mickey Vernon—In my 19th year I played with Aaron in 1959. The first two months, I never saw a guy hit a ball any harder and so consistently like he did. He just tore that ball apart. He hit it hard even when he made an out.

Larry Jansen— When I was the pitching coach for the Giants, I told my pitching staff never to let him hit the fast ball.

Phil Cavarretta—He had unbelievable quickness. He would just wait and wait on the ball and then cream the hell out of any pitch. He could have stolen 65-70 bases if he had wanted to.

Gaylord Perry—Most of the time, I figured I was better off just walking him. He got so many key base hits. In a pressure situation, he was just a great hitter. He waited so long you'd think you got a ball by him and— WHAM!—a base hit.

Bobby Thomson—He hit the ball hard, but he didn't get the ball up in the air. I thought, 'If this guy ever gets the ball up in the air, those are home runs.' And sure enough, he did. And he could do everything else.

Ernie Broglio—My first year at spring training, in 1959, Aaron was the first guy I faced, and he hit a ball out of the catcher's glove and hit it 400 feet over the right center field fence. I said to myself, "Holy Toledo! Welcome to the big leagues!" I'd never seen anyone hit a ball like that. I figured if I had to face a guy like that for a long time, I was going to have a short career. He'd swing at anything. He didn't have a strike zone.

Al Oliver— The best all-around hitter I ever saw. He made hitting look easy. He could wait on a pitch as long as possible, and that's why he hit home runs to the opposite field. Few power hitters could do that.

Frank Howard—He was easily one of the greatest all-around players of all time. Had he not chosen to go for the long ball when he moved to Atlanta with the prevailing winds blowing to left field, he probably would have led the National League in hitting six or seven times.

Lew Burdette—I'm not saying Willie Mays wasn't a great ballplayer, but I just think Hank was a better ballplayer and did everything Willie did but without Willie's flair.

Mudcat Grant—Hank Aaron was the best hitter I have ever faced. Like Williams (Ted), he had the patience to wait for his pitch and then he hit it hard. If you wanted to show a kid the swing of a pure hitter, I think that Aaron was first and Williams second. I think they always saw the bat hit the ball.

Bobby Bragan—His hitting and all-around play kept me in business as his manager for four years.

Chuck Tanner—Hank Aaron, without question, could wait on the ball longer than any hitter I ever saw play in the Major Leagues. In a game in Milwaukee, Aaron had two strikes on him, and umpire Al Barlick raised his hand and said, "Stri — ." He was going to call a strike, and Aaron hit the ball over the right field fence for a home run. His bat was so quick he literally took it out of the catcher's glove.

Willie Stargell—I never saw him fooled at the plate. Home run hitters like me commit themselves, but not Hank. He'd just flick his wrists, and the ball would just take off.

Bob Gibson—The most dangerous hitter between Aaron and Willie Mays was Aaron.

Gil McDougald —Pound for pound, he was the best hitter I ever saw.

Tony Kubek—The last five years I was in New York, I stayed at the same hotel as Mickey (Mantle). Once we were talking about the greatest player, and I told him it might be him. "No, Tony," he said. "All you have to do is look at the record. The best player of all was neither me nor Mays. It was Henry Aaron. Look at his home run record, his doubles. If you need a base stolen, he'd steal a base for you. He could throw. A great base runner with great instincts. He just never played in New York, so he went kind of unnoticed."

Ralph Garr—He'd tell me, "Just do what you can do. Work hard every day. But you got to go get 'em, Ain't nobody going to give you anything. You got to earn what you get." That's the best way to describe him, too.

Robin Roberts—I thought Henry would be the next .400 hitter. When he started pulling the ball, the home runs mounted. His wrist action on the inside ball was remarkable.

Ralph Kiner—He and Stan Musial had the most unusual batting stances I ever saw in that they shifted their weight up to their front foot and their back foot off the ground. Then he found out where the money was—or heard what I had said about home run hitters driving Cadillacs and singles hitters driving Fords.

General Manager Roland Hemond—When he came up, he looked like he would be a player with a high average. There was no way to envision he would become the all-time home run king. Ben Geraghty said at Jacksonville Aaron didn't pay any attention to what bat he used. He'd just go over to the bat rack, grab one and go to the plate. It just proved the type of hitter he was—see the ball and hit it.

Don Newcombe—He sure could hit everything I threw. I told him one day in Milwaukee, "I'm going to throw my shoe next time and see if you can hit that." He just wore me out. He used to laugh at me. He'd hit a double and get to second base and laugh at me. I'd look at him like I was mad, and after the game we'd go and have a few beers.

Alex Grammas—I don't know what kind of adjectives I can add to his greatness. Hank is one of those rare individuals who come along once in a lifetime. It was a pleasure to play against him and to manage him in his last year in the game at Milwaukee.

Ernie Johnson—One thing about Hank: When the game was over, you never knew if he was 4-for-4 or 0-for-4. He was always the same.

Maury Wills—I think Hank Aaron could have stolen as many bases as he wanted. But when you're a home run hitter and a good hitter like Aaron, it's not a good idea to steal a lot of bases and risk getting hurt. He got the biggest lead of anybody I ever saw and still could get back on the pickoff earlier than I did.

Ed Kranepool - What I liked about him was that he was personable to the opposing players. Some players with that standing can be a little standoffish, but he was always available to anybody, willing to talk to you or offer advice or words of encouragement.

Don Zimmer—When I saw Hank Aaron as a young guy with the Milwaukee Braves, he wasn't a home run hitter. He was just an exceptional hitter who would hit a home run now and then . . . . I would say Hank Aaron would have probably won five-six-seven batting titles if he had wanted to. He could have probably been a .340-.350 hitter all the time. I guess he realized he could win batting titles or hit home runs. It's unbelievable—he could have probably done either one. But with the power he had, he chose after a few years to be a home run hitter. A phenomenal hitter who could have done anything he wanted.

Gorman Thomas—I only played with him at the tail end of his career, but you could only imagine what this guy could do . . . . Even at his age, you could still see the intensity and the commitment. Guess why I wore number 44 in Milwaukee.

Umpire Doug Harvey—The toughest thing about Henry Aaron was his half-swings. He would get the bat so far toward swinging and not swinging it was unbelievable. I've never seen any other batter who could take the bat through as far as Henry could and then stop when he realized it was out of the strike zone and not go through with it . . . . I was always afraid he was going to fall asleep between pitches. You'd swear his eyes were closed.

Gene Conley—Lew Burdette always said if Hank hadn't been so competitive with his teammate, Eddie Mathews, about hitting home runs and just stuck to his line drive hitting, he might have finished with a lifetime .330 or .340.

Harry "The Hat" Walker—I think he was a little better all-around player than Willie Mays. Don't get me wrong. I'm not downgrading Willie, but he'd get a little careless, kind of nonchalant on things. With Aaron, it was business, business, business.

Umpire Shag Crawford—All the time I umpired against him, he never said a word. His wrists did all his talking for him.

Walter Alston, during Aaron's playing career—Forget statistics. It's just the conviction of most managers that Aaron wins more games than any guy since maybe Rogers Hornsby in his prime. More times than anyone else, he's made me wish I wasn't a manager.

Frank Robinson—He really played the game the way it was supposed to be played. And that is you go out and do the job without any fanfare and trying to call attention to yourself. He just went out and did things the good old fashioned way. In other words, he'd get a base hit and run hard to first base, round the bag just in case and hurry back to first. Hit a home run? He'd run around the base without drawing attention to himself like he wanted to get off the field before he embarrassed the pitcher anymore. A tremendous all-around ballplayer and never got credit for it. He wasn't flashy. He made all the plays in the outfield, had a terrific arm. He stole bases when the team needed him to steal bases. He didn't steal bases to steal bases. He was an outstanding base runner. What I'm trying to say is that he was the complete player and a guy you would not want to be at the plate if you were on the other team with the game on the line. I admired him for that. I looked up to him for that. And, he made me a better player. I chased Henry from the time I was in the minor leagues. At Columbia, all I ever heard was Hank Aaron, Hank Aaron. He did this. He did that. Right there, that's where he hit a ball in this ballpark. And I was always trying to say, he I can do better cause you only want to measure yourself by the best. Everyone said he was the best player to ever come through that league. And when I got to the major leagues, there he was. I always wanted to try to outdo him. He hit a home run, I wanted to hit one. If he hit two, I wanted to hit two. That type of thing. I always respected him as a person and a player.

Ted Williams—I remember one spring training I was sitting in the dugout and there was this crack of the bat on the ball and I said, geez, someone hit that one on the nose. I peered out and there was this skinny kid I had never seen before in the batter's box. It was my introduction to Hank Aaron.

Harmon Killebrew—When they talk about Hank Aaron, they naturally talk about his home runs, but to me he was a great player. Not only was he a great home run hitter who hit for average, he was an excellent outfielder and a really great base runner. Hank could do everything that was called for on the field, and those are the things they don't talk enough about. He was the complete ballplayer.

Eddie Mathews—He was one of the best all-around ballplayers I ever saw. He never got the publicity, but he got it all done and in a way hardly anyone knew he was doing it. I'd like to see him in a foot race with someone like Mays. I'd bet you he'd give him a damn good race. He was fast, and he could steal bases when asked to do so, but we just weren't that type of club to run a lot.

Pete Rose—Henry is up there among the best who ever played the game...I got a big kick out of the way they were talking all year about Mark McGwire and Sammy Sosa...this and that...and this and that...and Babe Ruth. But the truth of the matter is that the home run king is Henry Aaron....You can't take that away from him. And no one's going to beat it. If he had played in New York, he would have been just as popular as Willie (Mays).

Joe Garagiola—I don't think he got enough credit for what he did. I think his record is one that will never be broken. I don't think people realize what he did. You almost have to explain it to them. What I liked was the way he just kind of sauntered into the batting box and as much as said, "Well, that ball is going to be thrown and I'm going to hit it." He had such a quick bat. He'd wait...and wait...and then all of a sudden there would be a lot of activity in the strike zone. He exuded confidence. He could hit it with a ballpoint pen.

Steve Carlton—His hands were so incredibly quick—to flick that bat at the last moment and put the ball in play. He hit some monster home runs off me. I struck him out a few times, but he was just an incredibly difficult out.

THE AARON FILE

Full Name: Henry Louis Aaron.

Date and Place of Birth: February 5, 1934, Mobile, Alabama.

Nickname: "The Hammer"

Position: Right field, left field, first base, second base, third base, designated hitter.

Major League Career: 23 years, 1954-1976.

Home Runs: 755 (1st).

Runs Batted In: 2,297 (1st).

Runs Scored: 2,174 (2nd).

Lifetime Batting Average: .305.

Number of Hits: 3,771 (3rd).

Walks: 1,402.

Strikeouts: 1,383.

Records: Most home runs in a career, most runs batted in, most total bases, most hits in a career in the National League.

Other Highlights:

— Sporting News National League Player of the Year, 1956 and 1963.

— National League's Most Valuable Player, 1957.

— National League batting champion, 1956 and 1959.

— National League home run champion four times.

— Hit 40 or more home runs eight times.

— Runs batted in champion four times.

— Led league in doubles four times.

— Played in 100 or more games in 22 straight seasons.

— Third most games played, second most times at bat.

— Seventh highest career World Series batting average (.364).

Elected to Baseball Hall of Fame: 1982 (with Frank Robinson).

2

ERNIE BANKS

"Let's Play Two!"

E rnie Banks is remembered as much for his bubbling personality as for his 512 home runs.

His enthusiasm for baseball—and everything else—was personified in his battle cry every day at the ball park: "Let's play two!" It was an urging that was no mere slogan. Ernie Banks really wanted to play two. His love for the sport, and for playing it, was unmatched by any other player of his time, according to those who played with and against him and the broadcasters and reporters who covered him during his nineteen years as the Chicago Cubs' shortstop and first baseman.

Banks retained his enthusiasm despite playing on chronic losers and was destined to become the only player among the 500-homer hitters who never made it to post-season play. Losing bothered him, but it never detracted from the joy he found in playing baseball.

"I don't clown around about losing," he told Dave Condon of the *Chicago Tribune*. "I'm really baseball's worst loser. But baseball can be fun, even when you're not on a championship club. Being with the Cubs has been fun for me. Do you know of a better way to earn a living than playing baseball? Baseball isn't work to me—it's a game. If I was with the Yankees, I couldn't play any more innings than I do for the Cubs."

A highly publicized encounter with Willie Mays typified the Banks attitude. He predicted to Mays, "No kidding—the Cubs are going to win the pennant this year."

With mock sarcasm, Mays asked, "What league?"

"The National League, of course. The big leagues!"

At the time of their conversation, the Cubs were 35 games behind, and it was September. But Mays couldn't discourage Banks. No one could.

Just how bad were the Cubs during most of Ernie's career, while he was earning his nickname, "Mr. Cub"? In his first 14 seasons, the Cubs finished last or next to last ten times. They averaged 90 losses a year over that stretch, the worst in the major leagues, and never finished in the first division.

Jimmy Dykes, who managed six teams over 21 seasons, was once asked where the Cubs would finish. "Without Ernie Banks," he answered, "the Cubs would finish in Albuquerque."

PICKING COTTON AND BREAKING WINDOWS

Ernie Banks was introduced to baseball through his father, a chain store warehouse employee who spent his spare time catching for the semi-pro Dallas Black Giants for eight years. When Ernie turned eight, his father bought him a baseball glove for $2.98, a sizeable amount in the late 1930s during the last years of the Depression.

The two played catch every evening after the elder Banks returned from work, but the purchase of the glove looked like a bad investment. The son showed little interest in baseball. His father was forced to resort to bribery, giving little Ernie nickels and dimes to keep him playing catch. But the trademark Banks enthusiasm kicked in when he began breaking windows in the neighborhood with long fly balls. Baseball became fun.

Fate played a trick on Banks early in his life: His high school, Booker T. Washington, an all-black school, didn't have a baseball team. He starred in football, basketball and track. He was the captain of the football team, and averaged 20 points in basketball, attracting the attention of the Harlem Globetrotters, who gave him a tryout later. In track and field, he ran the quarter-mile in a swift 52 seconds and cleared five feet, eleven inches in the high jump.

At the same time, young Ernie was learning the life of the working man, especially as a black kid in the Deep South or the Southwest. At 14, he began picking cotton with his father. A truck picked them up at five in the morning and drove them 40 miles to the cotton fields of Mosquito, where they filled 300-pound sacks. He spent the day kneeling under the broiling Texas sun on knee pads, suffering from cramps and a sore back.

A local resident named Bill Blair spotted Ernie playing in a pick-up softball game when he was 17 and was impressed enough to arrange a tryout for Banks with a traveling Texas semi-pro baseball team, the Amarillo Colts. His salary: a percentage of the gate receipts, which reached the dizzying amount of $20 after a game in Hastings, Nebraska.

Fortune smiled broadly on Banks when he was spotted by a "birddog" scout—a part-timer—Barney Serelle, who recommended the young slugger to scout Dizzy Kismukes of the Kansas City Monarchs in the Negro Leagues. Ernie signed a contract for the staggering sum of $500 a month, plus room and board.

In his first year with the Monarchs, he hit .305, but the frosting on the cake came after the season ended, when he played on a barnstorming team of major leaguers, including Jackie Robinson, Roy Campanella and Larry Doby, three black stars who were thrilling black Americans two years after Robinson broke baseball's "color line." Those times were especially exciting for an eighteen-year-old black kid from Texas with a burning desire to join Robinson, Campy and Doby in the major leagues.

But then Uncle Sam threw Banks a curve ball. This was 1951, the sixth year of the Cold War and the first full year of the Korean War— "World War Two and a Half." The whole world feared that "the Russians" might expand the Korean action into World War III.

The military draft, discontinued only five years earlier, had been reinstituted, and Banks did not escape the call. He was drafted into the Army on March 1, 1951 and served in an all-black unit in Germany for two years. Inevitably, he soon began playing baseball for his post's team instead of peeling potatoes on K.P. He hit .305 with 15 home runs, but said modestly, "I went in as a private and came out as a private."

When he did, he returned to the Monarchs, and his timing was perfect. With more and more blacks breaking into the major leagues, scouts were eagerly mining the newest mother lode of talent, the Negro Leagues. Two teams—the Cubs' cross-town rivals, the Chicago White Sox, and the Yankees, completing their record streak of five pennants and five World Series championships in a row from 1949 through 1953—were ideally positioned to sign the young shortstop. Both teams blew their opportunities.

Banks was on display right under the noses of the White Sox every time the Monarchs played in Chicago. And the Yankees had open access to him every time the Monarchs played at home in Kansas City because it was also the home of their triple-A farm team in the American Association.

One of the White Sox pitchers, Connie Johnson, tipped off the manager, Paul Richards, about Banks, but Richards ignored him. He needed pitching, not another infielder, even though Johnson told him Banks was ready to play in the majors at that moment.

While Richards procrastinated and the Yankees ignored the bright young prospect, the Chicago Cubs made their move. The business manager of their farm team in Macon, Georgia, Tom Gordon, is given the credit for discovering Banks for the Cubs. Ironically, he had no experience at all in evaluating baseball talent. His job was on the business side, not the baseball side. But on an open date, he drove to Columbus, Georgia, to see the famous Monarchs and couldn't take his eyes off Banks. He promptly called the Cubs' director of player personnel, Wid Matthews, admitted he was no expert on the subject, but said a kid named Banks on the Monarchs looked sensational and could solve the Cubs' long-standing problems at shortstop.

Matthews checked his book of minor league prospects, but Banks wasn't listed. There were two good reasons for that: He had been in the Army for two years, and besides, the team he was playing for, the Monarchs, weren't a minor league team anyhow. The Negro Leagues were an independent operation, not part of the minors.

Fortunately for the Cubs, Matthews followed his baseball instincts instead of the minor league directory. He dispatched a scout, Ray Hayworth, to follow the Monarchs, but didn't tell him why. Without being influenced by any glowing reports from Matthews, Hayworth reported back with high ratings for the prospect. Matthews then sent two other scouts, Vernie Helms and Jimmy Payton, to evaluate Banks. They came back with equally impressive reports. Finally, the extra-thorough Matthews assigned one of the Cubs' coaches, Ray Blades, to watch Banks in action. The result was the same—another dazzling rating.

Almost convinced, Matthews conducted the next round of evaluation himself. He checked Banks out at the Negro Leagues All-Star game at Comiskey Park in Chicago, the home of the White Sox. The Sox, including Paul Richards, knew Banks was playing in the game, but they were intent on landing pitcher Fran Herrera and paid no attention to Banks. Their rating of Banks: Good field, no hit. The Cincinnati Reds and the Yankees were also unimpressed.

Matthews needed only one look. Then he rushed over to the hotel room of Tom Baird, the owner of the Monarchs. His heart sank when Baird told him he owed the White Sox and the Yankees first crack at Banks, even though they had not shown the enthusiasm for him that Matthews was exhibiting.

On the spot, Matthews made Baird a take-it-or-leave-it offer. Baird said he needed $15,000 for Banks. Matthews quickly agreed, and even tossed in another five for a pitcher. Baird grabbed the offer, and the Chicago Cubs grabbed Ernie Banks.

He joined his major league team without a glove. Second baseman Eddie Miksis gave him one. Blades, an outfielder for ten years with the St. Louis Cardinals in the 1920s and early '30s, gave him a book—on how to play major league baseball.

A QUIET ERNIE BANKS, BUT THEN ...

Every player interviewed for this book who remembers Banks as a rookie agreed that he was not the Ernie Banks we know today. He was actually quiet, which no one else would believe, but the reason was the atmosphere surrounding the 23-year-old future Hall of Famer. He was the only black player on the Cubs, and he roomed alone. He kept to himself, went to the movies, watched television in his room and slept for ten or 12 hours every night. Only gradually did he start to open up. But when he did, he became a chatterbox—and one of baseball's greatest goodwill ambassadors was born.

From that time to this, Ernie Banks is the epitome of what owner Phil Wrigley, the head of the chewing gum family, and the family members who have succeeded him with the Cubs have always wanted Cubs baseball to be: clean, enthusiastic, a sign of what baseball players used to be like.

Ron Santo, Banks's teammate in the Cubs' infield from Santo's arrival in the big leagues in 1960 until Ernie retired in 1971, said, "I've never heard him say a bad word about anyone—player, manager, writer, fan—anyone."

Santo remembers when someone asked Ernie if there was one person in the world he didn't like. Banks thought for a long time and finally said, "Oh, maybe Mao Tse-tung," the ruthless dictator of China during the tensest years of the Cold War.

"He cares about life," Santo says today. "He cares about people. In the many years I have known him, he's never changed a bit. He's always the same. Home run or strikeout—nothing ever gets to him. He's so clean inside. He's uncomplaining, always happy. He's predictable. He doesn't smoke, doesn't drink. No dirty jokes. No night life."

Pete Reiser was even shorter and to the point: "He does more good without trying than any man in the game."

But despite their admiration for the immensely popular and respected Banks, his old teammates and opponents are not reluctant to give him a good going-over on the subject of his love for talking ... and talking ... and talking.

His fellow Hall of Famer on the Cubs, Pitcher Fergie Jenkins, nicknamed him "AM-FM." Jenkins says, "He was real personable and loved to talk. You couldn't turn him off. Turn off AM and he'd start talking on FM. You turn off FM and he'd be talking on AM. 'Let's play two!' And, 'It's a great day for baseball!' And, 'The friendly confines,' meaning Wrigley Field."

Another fellow Hall of Famer on the Cubs, Billy Williams, said, "Ernie is the most energetic, positive person I've ever met. He played heads-up baseball. He was an inspiration to me. I roomed with him for three weeks, and I had to get out of there, because he'd talk baseball after the game for so long I couldn't get any sleep."

Base-stealing champion Maury Wills of the Dodgers remembers that there was an ulterior motive behind Ernie's non-stop chatter. Wills says Banks was trying to distract opposing base-runners. "Ernie was always saying, 'Hey, Maury—a great day for baseball! Let's play two! How's the family, Maury?'

"I told him, 'You don't even know my family. Let me concentrate on the pitcher.' And sometimes I had to ask him, 'Hey, Ernie—will you please shut up?'"

Ron Swoboda, the Met's outfielder, has both great respect for Banks' ability and appreciation for his enthusiasm. "He had a lot of Hank Aaron in his swing," Swoboda said—"a pretty swing. He had a timing mechanism in there. And like Aaron, he had great hands. His 'pop' through the strike zone was so impressive."

A STAR AND A REVOLUTION

Banks served notice immediately that he was destined for stardom. With the Cubs' front office still hoping that Roy Smalley was the answer at shortstop, Banks played in the team's final ten games of the 1953 season, hit two home runs, compiled a .314 batting average and was impressive at short. He hit the first of his 512 home runs on September 20 off righthander Gerry Staley of the Cardinals.

The Cubs were quick to determine that Banks had a long future ahead of him. During spring training before the 1954 season, with Banks still having played in only those ten games, the Cubs traded Smalley to Milwaukee. Banks proceeded to justify their judgment by playing in 424 straight games until he fractured his wrist halfway through the 1956 campaign.

Banks continued to win high marks for his play, right from the start of his big league career. Long-time catcher Clyde McCullough called him the greatest shortstop to come into the National League in McCullough's time. Manager Phil Cavarretta was surprised that Banks, with a wiry build at six-feet, one-inch and 180 pounds, generated so much power. But a teammate offered at least one explanation, saying Banks had "wrists right up to his armpits."

The only fault that veteran observers could spot was Ernie's arm. Almost everyone agreed that Banks had the best hands in the sport, but his arm was another story. He "cheated" in semi-pro ball and the Negro Leagues by playing a shallow shortstop, but in the big leagues, he had to play deeper and make longer throws. He combined three qualities to offset the lack of power in his throwing arm: the surest hands anyone could ask for, a fluid motion in fielding ground balls, and the ability to get rid of the ball quickly.

Having compensated for his throwing arm, Banks made a discovery late in his first full season, 1954, that immediately propelled him into superstar status and even forced a revolution in the philosophy of hitting among many major league players, managers and coaches.

He picked up a bat used by future Hall of Famer Monte Irvin of the Giants, another former Negro Leagues star, and noticed that it weighed only 31 ounces. He said in later years that it felt like a toothpick compared to his much heavier 35-ounce bat. Ernie switched to the lighter model for the 1955 season and began blasting his way into the headlines. He hit five grand slam home runs that year, breaking a record held by Babe Ruth, Lou Gehrig, Ralph Kiner and Hank Greenberg. By the end of the season he had blasted 44 home runs, hit .295 and had 117 runs batted in.

He also led all National League shortstops in fielding, topping such veteran stars as Pee Wee Reese, Dick Groat and Alvin Dark.

In proving the value of bat speed with Irvin's light bat, Banks was verifying the principle long espoused by Ted Williams, who swung a 32-ounce bat when he hit .406 in 1941, while other hitters were using bats that weighed 35 and 36 ounces. Williams contended that by using a lighter bat, hitters could wait longer before beginning their swing. This would give them a longer look at the pitch and increase their chances of recognizing what kind of a pitch it was. Then they could adjust their swing accordingly.

So Banks was giving himself the same advantage that no less an authority than Ted Williams had as a hitter.

Ernie shared another advantage with Williams—keen eyesight. Williams was considered to have the sharpest vision of any hitter of his time. Ernie, it turned out, did, too. The Bausch and Lomb Optical Company tested his eyesight as 20/13, meaning he could see objects at 20 feet that a person with normal eyesight could see only at 13 feet.

With the lighter bat and his 20/13 vision, Banks hit 40 or more home runs in five of the next six seasons, establishing himself as the hardest-hitting shortstop in major league history. He hit more home runs over that six-season span—248—than any hitter in either major league including Willie Mays, Ted Williams, Mickey Mantle and Duke Snider. From 1955 to 1960, he averaged 41 homers, 116 RBIs and a .294 batting average. Meanwhile, his team never climbed out of the second division, the bottom half of the league standings in the pre-expansion era when each league had eight teams and the second division was regarded as the league's slums.

Two of the seasons in that six-year streak were the zenith of Banks's career. In 1958, he hit .313 and led the National League with 47 home runs and 129 runs batted in. He won the league's Most Valuable Player award over Willie Mays in a landslide, 283 points to 185. He topped himself in '59 with 45 homers, one behind Eddie Mathews of Milwaukee, and winning the RBI championship of both leagues with 143.

Banks also led the league that year in the number of games played. And to complete his career year, he set a major league record for shortstops by fielding .985 and leading the league in assists. Banks won the MVP award again, this time over Mathews and Mathews's Milwaukee teammate, Hank Aaron.

The Banks popularity was demonstrated by two incidents during that 1959 season, one of which Banks still considers among the greatest thrills of his career, maybe *the* greatest.

While the Milwaukee Braves and the Los Angeles Dodgers were going head-to-head in the National League pennant race, Banks was hit in the leg during a game against the Dodgers. The word went out: Banks would not be able to play the next day.

But when the word got to Banks himself, he vetoed everyone else. He said the pennant was on the line, and it would be unfair to the Braves for him not to try to play against the Dodgers. He wasn't able to start the game, but he was available for pinchhitting.

Late in the game, he was sent up to hit. As he limped to the plate, the Cubs' fans began to cheer loudly for him. Banks popped up, but as he limped back to the dugout, the fans rose in unison to applaud his courage and sense of fair play.

Banks later said that, because it was so unexpected, it was like winning his back-to-back MVP awards.

The other incident was more of a non-event, something that didn't happen. During his torrid six-year streak, the Cubs proposed in 1959 to stage a "day" for Banks, those festive occasions where the players, especially in those years, were showered with acclaim and gifts. But Banks declined. With his typical modesty, he said he hadn't been in the major leagues long enough to be honored like that.

So the day didn't happen. Not that year, anyhow. In 1964, the idea was put forth again. This time Banks agreed, and Ernie Banks Day was held at Wrigley Field after all.

WITNESSES TO GREATNESS

Gaylord Perry testifies to the Banks greatness in those years, and to his courage and determination: "One thing you didn't want to do with Ernie Banks was knock him down, because he, more than anyone else, would really accept the challenge. If you knocked him down or hit him, he was really tough on you the rest of the year."

Clete Boyer, then the Braves' third baseman, said, "He'd beat you, but he didn't scare you like Hank Aaron. He was just so relaxed. I never saw a guy like him. He would just walk up there loosie-goosie and hit a home run."

Hall of Fame Pitcher Robin Roberts has painful memories of Banks: "He hurt me more in close games with home runs than any other batter."

Gene Oliver goes beyond the nice-guy image associated with Banks and describes him as a clever, even a scheming opponent. "Banks was one of the few guys truly capable of setting up a pitcher," Oliver claims. "He would purposely look bad on a pitch, figuring he was going to get it again..."

SCARES AND TRANSFERS

Health problems twice threatened Banks' career and his journey toward the Hall of Fame in Cooperstown, New York. One involved his eyes, the other the possibility of leukemia.

In 1961, Banks got off to an uncharacteristically slow start. An examination revealed eye problems, even with that 20/13 vision. Spasms of the muscles that control the inner rotation of each eye caused a lack of coordination between his eyes. A brief spasm would cause his eyes to pull toward each other, resulting in a small, fleeting but periodic blind spot in the left eye. His depth perception was also affected.

After that scare, his eyes responded to a therapeutic combination of rest and daily eye-strengthening exercises. After his return to the lineup, he finished the '61 season with 29 home runs, an entirely respectable total but a drop from 41 or more in each of the previous four seasons.

But that wasn't Banks's only problem in 1961, The Cubs brass, never totally satisfied with his fielding, especially his throwing arm, talked to him about moving to left field, where players can get by with a weaker arm than at short, third or the other two outfield positions. Banks disagreed with the idea.

He argued that playing shortstop helped his hitting because he was so busy fielding, making cut-off plays, handling relays from the outfield, holding runners on and being more involved on every pitch than is demanded at other positions that it helped to keep his mind off his hitting between at-bats. This, in turn, he argued, made him a better hitter.

In presenting that logic, Banks was ahead of his time. Since the American League introduced the designated hitter eight seasons later, various players have complained that the DH role is difficult because it leaves them too much time between trips to the plate to dwell on their last time at bat.

But the Cubs were determined to make the change. They transferred him to left field, but he lasted only 23 games there. It became apparent that he did not have the arm for left field either. Base runners were taking extra bases on him. So he was transferred again, this time to first base. He lasted there for only seven games before returning to shortstop for the remaining 104 games of the '61 season. They were his last games at that position.

In 1962, Banks played virtually the entire season at first base, filling in at third base for three games. The adjustment caused no apparent ill effects on his hitting. On the contrary, he bashed 37 homers and drove in 104 runs.

As he adjusted to his new position, the popularity of Banks continued to grow. On August 27, new proof of his hold on Cubs' fans surfaced.

A crowd of 7,500 mobbed a men's clothing store in downtown Gary, Indiana, just outside Chicago. Twenty-three persons, mostly children, were injured when the crowd began to surge toward Banks to get a closer glimpse of "Mr. Cub." The fans accidentally smashed through a large plate-glass window. No one was injured seriously.

The response by Banks was perfect, new evidence of why he was, and is, held in such high esteem. He signed as many autographs as he could under the circumstances, then hurried to the hospital where he signed more autographs for the injured and visited with them.

By season's end, Banks was a fixture at first base for the Cubs. He told reporters he discovered two things about his new position: "Get your body out of the way of the runner or he'll break you apart. And get your feet out of his way or he'll carve them off with his spikes."

After overcoming his eye problems in 1961 and being transferred to first base in '62, Banks looked forward to a healthy and successful 1963, and it showed in his performance. He slugged 13 home runs by June 9. But then his production fell dramatically. During the rest of June and throughout July and August, Ernie hit just five home runs. He didn't play at all in September.

Serious concerns about his health were again being heard around Wrigley Field. Banks thought he had leukemia, the dreaded blood disease that often proves fatal in adults, even more so in those years before recent advancements in the treatment of the illness.

He tired more easily. He admitted that he was worried. When his doctors discovered a minor blood infection, his fears multiplied. A thorough examination at the famed Mayo Clinic in Rochester, Minnesota, revealed a case of mumps. His five-year-old son, Jerome, had come down with mumps early that season. Since facial swelling and other symptoms did not develop in Ernie, he had overlooked the possibility that mumps might be his problem.

After learning that mumps was indeed the culprit, Banks was able to relax over the winter and look forward with more enthusiasm than usual to the 1964 season.

HAPPY DAYS ARE HERE AGAIN, SORT OF

A relieved Banks returned to the starting lineup as optimistic as ever, especially in the knowledge that Billy Williams and Ron Santo now had a few seasons under their belts. The Cubs and their loyal fans were looking forward to a major improvement over their usual second division finish of 1963—in seventh place.

Instead, the baseball gods still refused to smile on them. For the next three years, the Cubs wandered lost in the National League's desert. Banks hit 23 home runs in '64, Williams hit 33 and Santo hit 30, but the Cubs were worse than ever—last place. The slugging threesome continued to power baseballs over the National League's outfield fences, but the result was the same—last place again in 1965.

In '66, with Banks slipping to only 15 home runs, but with Santo and Williams hitting 59 between them, the Cubs hit rock bottom—tenth place. They lost 103 games, only the second time in their history that they lost 100 or more games.

It added up to a demonstration of futility and failure that stretched over season after agonizing season—four straight years in next-to-last place, followed by three straight seasons in last place.

One of the solutions, according to new manager Leo Durocher, could be a change at first base. Banks, Durocher reasoned, was over the hill. His meager total of only 15 home runs in 1966 proved it. Durocher handed the first baseman's mitt to various candidates, who managed to play themselves out of the job one by one over the next two seasons. Each time, Banks was given his old job back, and each time he responded the way great athletes always seem to respond in the face of formidable challenges.

Aging Ernie hit 23 home runs in 1967 and drove in 95 runs as he helped to spark the Cubs to an impressive comeback, from last place all the way up to the rarified atmosphere of third place.

History repeated itself in '67. Near the end of spring training, with no better prospect on the horizon, Banks won his old job back almost by default. His production continued to improve, with his homers up to 32. The Cubs finished third again.

In 1969, while Durocher grew more disbelieving with each passing year, Banks, 38 years old and playing on arthritic knees, played in 155 games, belted 23 home runs and drove in 106 runs. He lifted the Cubs to second place, their highest finish in 24 years. It was his last hurrah.

There was one more highlight in his future, in the career than ended in 1971 after 19 years and 2,528 games. It happened at Wrigley Field on May 12, 1970 when Banks became the ninth player to hit 500 home runs. He belted the most historic homer of his brilliant career off Pat Jarvis of the Atlanta Braves on a one-and-one count in the second inning with the bases empty. It was a line drive to left.

Ron Santo wasn't surprised that the homer was a line drive. "He wasn't the kind of guy who took the ball 500 feet out of the park," Santo said. "He hit nothing but line drives, and any place you played, he could take it out of the ballpark. He was a pure wrist hitter."

Threatening weather that afternoon held the crowd to only 5,264 fans. Ernie could still find a smile and a laugh, even in such a momentous achievement. He flashed his famous ear-to-ear grin as he enjoyed the irony of it all. "Old Man Banks," he told reporters, "hits his 500th on Senior Citizens Day!"

With all of his success, his Hall of Fame acclaim and his enormous popularity with fans everywhere—not just Cubs' fans—Banks was also called on to endure some of baseball's biggest disappointments. There were those 14 straight years in the second division, those finishes in next-to-last or last place in ten of those years, an average of 90 losses a year, the worst in the major leagues. He is the only member of the 500-homer club who never got to play in a playoff or the World Series.

But things like that never discouraged Ernie Banks. As he ended his career, he looked back in his usual joy and said, "I was thinking about my mother and dad, about all the people in the Cubs' organization who helped me, and about the wonderful Chicago fans who have come out all these years to cheer me on."

BANKS ON BANKS

All of us (the 500-homer hitters) had many things in common—the passion for the game, loving the game—the challenge of facing solid pitching every game, day or night. Durability. I guess we all felt that hitting a home run would give our local fans, and especially those who drove so far to see us play, a thrill and the feeling that they had a connection with the game.

Individually, we had different styles. If I could choose one thing we all seemed to have in common it was quick hands. If someone would ask me what it takes to be a good, consistent hitter with power, I would say quick hands. I was always trying to strengthen my hands.

Each had his own style, but the hands were always there to create the power. All of us had a natural desire and ability to do what we did. It was like we didn't think about it, we just did it. I once asked Willie Mays what was his secret about hitting the ball, and he said, "Man, I don't think about anything when I get up to the plate but the ball. That's it."

The focus is not thinking about where are my hands, how am I standing, how am I gripping the bat? You just go out and do what you do best—and that is hit the ball.

I think most of us had humility. When we hit a home run, we didn't try to show up the pitcher, except maybe Reggie (Jackson). To hit a home run to win a game, that's the ultimate. A home run hitter has to deal with a lot of envy on the team, because the rest of the players would like to be like him. So you have to show humility in front of them.

One of the things I like about sports and what I accomplished by hitting 512 home runs is that you can look it up. Most things you do in life you can't look up. And pretty soon, you know it's all over. You know, and the people around you know—the scouts, the managers, your team-mates—they start whispering and talking, and you start to realize it's all over. One day you realize you have to step aside and pass the baton to someone else, that you'd had your day in the sunshine.

When people ask me if I would rather hold the all-time home run record or the RBI record, I tell them I'd rather have been in one World Series. I guess I was the only one of the 500 home run hitters that didn't, and it hurts.

I did it, I enjoyed it, and I'm moving on with the rest of my life....You just don't have to do one thing with your whole life. If I have a goal in life now, it is to be the poor man's philanthropist. I think it's the greatest joy in the world to give money or help to those who need it. And some day I'd like to be an abstract painter.

It was May 12, 1970 at 2:03 p.m. in the afternoon on a Monday. The game started at 1:30 and I was hitting fifth in the lineup playing the Atlanta Braves and Pat Jarvis was pitching. My daughter was telling me all along, "Dad, would you please hit number 500 so we can get some rest and the writers won't be around?" And I said I think today I'm going to do it. I was in my forties and when I rounded third base and touched the plate and after the game was over I felt like I was 22 years old. It was just one incident but it brought so much joy into my life.

WHAT OTHER PLAYERS SAID ABOUT
ERNIE BANKS

Billy Williams—Ernie helps everybody he can. He helped me. I roomed with him the year I came up. I was one scared kid. Ernie relaxed me. He said I was trying to crush the ball. He said timing and coordination —that's what counts.

Phil Cavarretta—He had the quickest bat speed I had ever seen. This kid was unbelievable. He creamed it all over and I just couldn't send him out (to the minors). I moved Gene Baker over to second base to make room for Ernie at short.

Alvin Dark—He hit them everywhere. You could knock him down. It wouldn't make any difference to him. He would say, "Boy! That guy is wild, isn't he?"

Bobby Thomson—He used to needle me every time I saw him. "Are you the Thomson with the p or without the p?" The other Thompson, of course, was a black guy.

Don Kessinger—Ernie was something special. You know, sometimes when the club isn't going well and you're down and the end of the season is nearing, here would come Ernie, the same way before every game: "It's a great day for baseball! Let's play two! This is the Cubs' day today!" You'd think, "Ernie, what are you doing?" But he'd get you up. At first base, you couldn't throw a ball by him in the dirt. He had wonderful, wonderful hands.

Al Oliver—Ernie loved to talk. He'd be at first base and I'd be at the plate, and he's talking to Fergie Jenkins about how to pitch to me. "Throw him a slider. Throw him a fast ball, Fergie." I could hear him. I think he was playing mind games with me.

Dick Groat—Ernie was always blabbing. He never shut up. "A beautiful day! We ought to play two!" If I heard it once, I heard it a million times.

Mudcat Grant—Ernie was a kind of a fun guy to pitch to. He would lull you to sleep. He was always humming, tapping his thumb on the bat. He was always trying to get in your mind, and you thought, "Here's a guy who loves the game. He's just a nice man who's not going to hurt you." And before you know it—BAM!

Ron Santo—In my second year, I batted fifth in the lineup, and he batted fourth. He hit 44 home runs, and I spent 44 times in the dirt. I kept asking him, "Why do they knock me down when you hit home runs?"

Bobby Bragan—He got a kick out of playing. He was really serious when he said, "Let's play two!" He'd rather play two every day.

Chuck Tanner—They would take films on guys hitting. The normal was eight frames. Ernie's was six. That's how quick his bat was. They talk about Ernie hitting in hitter-friendly Wrigley Field, but a lot of other guys played there and didn't hit them.

Willie Stargell—Ernie just had so much ability, but the thing everybody always remembers is a man who talked a lot of trash. He never shut up. "I hit that ball hard, didn't I? Yes, sir! I tell you, I can hit a baseball!" Then he ended up at first base when I came along. "Man, you're young and strong. You're going to be a good hitter! You're going to hit a lot of home runs! They're going to get you out, but you're going to hit home runs! Come from a big family?" He never stopped.

Bob Gibson—I didn't particularly care for him talking all the time. I never talked to the other guys too much any way. I would never talk to him. He would ask me, "Are you pitching tomorrow?" All that stuff. And I just wouldn't answer him. And he'd say, "Billy Williams is going to hit a home run off you." One day I told him, "Ernie, you'd better stop messing with me." I hit him in the ribs. He stopped messing with me. I was just really serious about my work. Ernie and a lot of others thought I was just mean. But I was just serious about my work. I didn't think being friends with the guys on the other teams was a very good idea.

Bob Rush—He reminded me of Hank Aaron in that it seemed the ball would be almost by him before he committed. They both had such quick wrists.

Orlando Cepeda—At the All-Star game in Washington, he asked me to come to the park early and give him some tips on how to play first base because they had switched him to first. It was a shock—the great Ernie Banks asking me for advice.

Duke Snider—Most of the conversations with Ernie were nodding your head or smiling, because he did all the talking. He would ask a question and answer it, too.

Ed Kranepool—If there was anybody you wanted to see get in a World Series, it was Ernie. Everyone felt sorry for him in that regard. He gave his all to baseball and never got that ring.

Roger Craig—He had the greatest swing of any righthanded hitter I've ever seen.

Don Zimmer—You know Wrigley Field. I always called them Wrigley Field One and Wrigley Field Two, because when the wind is blowing out, all you have to do is hit a pop fly. When it's blowing in, you have to hit with a cannon. When I was with the Dodgers, the wind would be blowing in like a gale and I'd see Gil Hodges or Campy (Roy Campanella) hit balls into left center—a definite home run—and the left fielder goes back to the wall and then comes in to make the catch. Ernie Banks, on the same day, could hit the ball and you'd say, "If Hodges' didn't go out, or Campy's didn't go out, Ernie's ain't going out." But Banks had such a carry on the ball it was unbelievable. He'd hit it and he had some kind of backspin that would just cut into the wind. Along with his great wrists, out it would go.

Al Downing—Ernie always had that bat. Everyone would say he's got quick wrists, but Ernie was a big man with a big chest, big arms and legs. He was a very strong man, and when you hit 500 home runs, I don't care where you played. I was surprised when I met him that he wasn't this skinny guy people talked about.

Juan Marichal—I tell you, I used to like to watch Ernie Banks. He'd wiggle his thumb. He was a smooth hitter with a beautiful swing. I don't ever see Ernie Banks get in trouble with a pitch. He was so perfect swinging at the ball, so beautiful timing. He was beautiful to watch.

Gene Conley—I always felt he was swinging with a switch he was so quick.

Harry "The Hat" Walker—He was the kind of guy if it had to go 310 feet, it would go 320. If he needed 400, it would go 410. He looked like he wasn't going to give it any more than was needed. We used to laugh about it. He'd just make it.

Bill White—He and Hank Aaron had the quickest wrists I ever saw.

Carl Erskine—Ernie Banks would hypnotize you. Any pitcher will tell you he had these long, thin fingers, and the thumb on the top would just start to circle as you got into your windup. As you went further into your windup, his thumb would go faster—faster—faster. It was his peculiar little way, unconsciously I'm sure, to time the pitch. You could see that from the mound, so you would almost think, "This guy's hypnotizing me."

Umpire Doug Harvey—He was the best I ever saw at getting a man home from third base with less than two outs. I swear he could hit a sacrifice fly any time he wanted to.

Randy Hundley—He was a lot like Hank Aaron. He didn't hit tape measure jobs, but he was just able to get the square part of the bat on the ball, and the ball would just keep carrying for him. He was also a very smart hitter. When a pitcher made a mistake against him, he was able to take advantage of it. A lot of guys foul those pitches straight back or pop up or something, but Ernie would have that one spot on the bat, and that is where he would hit the ball all the time. He didn't have scuff marks from the label to the end of the bat.

Ron Swoboda—I went to Vietnam with Ernie Banks in 1968, and he talked from the time we left until the time we got back. He exuded this tremendous love for being out there and playing the game. He'd talk to you in the dugout. He'd talk to you on first base. "You love the game of baseball don't you? I love to play baseball! I could play all day!" It was all this enthusiasm for baseball and people just bubbling over.

Frank Robinson—The type of guy who made things look easy. Nice easy swing and at the last moment the wrists would pop in there and the ball would fly off the bat and he would run around the bases like he wasn't movin' but he was movin'. He wasn't the flashy type at shortstop but he made all the plays. Then he moved over to first base and it was like he'd been there all his life. Ernie played the game and had fun playing the game. Winning the Most Valuable Player award two years in a row for a last-place ballclub showed you the kind of player and competitor he was.

Harmon Killebrew—Ernie could hit anywhere. He was a great hitter. One of the knocks about him was he didn't play on winning ball clubs, but it sure wasn't his fault. It's just a shame he didn't get to play on some really good ball clubs.

Eddie Mathews—He never got the publicity he should have. He played in a fairly small ballpark, but like Mark McGwire, he hit them...I don't know how he hit them...or where he hit them...The fact is, he hit them!

Hank Aaron—If anybody was made to hit in Wrigley Field, it was Ernie Banks. And I don't know, in any era, if there was a shortstop who could hit like him. It was a shame he never got in a World Series, but it just shows you that back in those days, if you got stuck with a bad ball club, it could stay bad for a long time...Players didn't move from club to club like they do today and almost dictate a championship team they want to play on.

Joe Garagiola—When he came up, I batted sixth, right behind him. I remember that Gerry Staley struck him out on a high knuckleball, and when he came back to the bench, I told him, "You're going to hit one. He's going to hang one." Next time up, he hit a homer, and when he came back to the dugout, he grinned and said, "He hung one." And I said, "Hey, this kid is going to be all right!"

THE BANKS FILE

Full Name: Ernest Banks.
Date and Place of Birth: January 31, 1931, Dallas, Texas.
Nickname: "Mr. Cub"
Positions: Shortstop and first base.
Major League Career: 19 years, 1953-1971.
Home Runs: 512 (tied for 12th with Eddie Mathews)
Runs Batted In: 1,636.
Runs Scored: 1,305.
Lifetime Batting Average: .274.
Number of Hits: 2,583.
Walks: 763.
Strikeouts: 1,236.

Other Highlights:
— Led National League in home runs twice.
— Led National League in runs batted in twice.
— National League's Most Valuable Player twice (1958 and 1959).
— Along with Mel Ott, one of only two members of the 500-homer club who never played in the minor leagues.
— Including brief terms at third base and in left field, played four positions in the major leagues.
— Averaged 27 home runs per year for his career.
— Missed two years because of Army duty in 1951 and '52.

Elected to the Hall of Fame: In 1977, his first year of eligibility.

3

JIMMMIE FOXX

Triumph and Tragedy

When Ted Williams ranked Jimmie Foxx as the greatest righthanded hitter of them all, trailing only lefthanders Babe Ruth and Lou Gehrig, such praise from the master was evidence enough of the remarkable abilities and achievements of "Double X."

In his book, *The Ted Williams Hit List*, the last man to hit .400 wrote, "If you asked the baseball gods to design the perfect power hitter, they would probably just point to Jimmie Foxx and say it's already been done. When you talk about power, you start with Foxx and Ruth. Foxx carried on where Ruth left off. He inherited the long ball mantle that the Bambino created. If anyone was ever capable of actually tearing the cover off the ball, it would be Double X, my teammate when I first came to the Red Sox."

Compared to the other 14 sluggers who smashed more than 500 home runs, Foxx's accomplishments more than hold their own in such a rarified atmosphere. He was the only one of the fifteen to hit 30 or more home runs twelve years in a row. Only Ruth ranks with Foxx as the two men who 13 times drove in 100 runs. Among the 500-homer hitters, only Williams and Ruth topped his .325 lifetime batting average, a dazzling combination of power and high average. And only the all-time home run champion, Hank Aaron, and Williams topped Foxx's slugging average of .609.

His accomplishments were not limited to power and average. He could run, too, with 125 triples, eight inside-the-park home runs and 88 stolen bases. Such numbers, impressive as they are, become even moreso when placed in the context of playing time: Among the 500-homer hitters, only Williams played fewer games, and only Williams and Mickey Mantle had fewer plate appearances.

When it came to hitting under pressure—what baseball people called a "clutch hitter" in Foxx's time—Double X was never found wanting. In three World Series, he hit .350, .333 and .343, a career average of .344, topped only by Aaron and Reggie Jackson among the sluggers.

Hall of Fame Pitcher Lefty Grove testified to Foxx's power. "He was the only hitter I ever saw who could hit balls on his fist and still get them out of the park," Grove told Ed Rumill of the *Christian Science Monitor.* "He has muscles in his muscles."

Another Hall of Fame pitcher, Lefty Gomez of the Yankees, put it another way: "He has muscles in his hair."

Standing only six feet tall and weighing between 185 and 190 pounds during his peak years, Foxx won his league's Most Valuable Player Award three times and the batting championship twice. He led the league in home runs four times and in runs batted in with numbers hard to believe today, even with the longer schedules—175 RBIs, 169 and 163.

As one writer put it, "Could Foxx hit? Could Rembrandt paint?"

FOXX INSTEAD OF MARIS?

It could have been—make that *should* have been—Foxx instead of Roger Maris who broke Ruth's record of 60 homers in a season, and by plenty.

Foxx homered 58 times in 1932, five years after Ruth set the record with 60. Two of Foxx's home runs in '32 came in the early innings of games which were rained out before they became official, so the homers were washed out. That happens, and it no doubt happened to Maris, too, but in the case of Foxx, fate, not just the Weatherman, also stepped in.

Alterations to three ballparks cost Foxx at least nine more homers. Three times he hit balls into a new screen at Sportsman's Park in St. Louis that stretched from the right centerfield pavilion to the rightfield foul line. All three were ruled ground rule doubles.

In his own park in Philadelphia, the A's slugger hit three more into a screen placed above the rightfield fence to keep kids from climbing the fence and sneaking into the park free. They were also ruled ground rule doubles. And Foxx hit a new screen in Cleveland three times, for three more ground rule doubles.

All three of the screens were constructed after Ruth's record year in '27 and before Foxx's blistering pace in 1932.

Foxx remembered a different total for his St. Louis experiences. "That year I hit that screen twelve times," he recalled in later years. Al Horwitz, the old Philadelphia baseball writer, figured out that with those twelve 'homers' and a few other things, the least I'd have hit would have been 72 home runs." Then the easygoing, philosophical Foxx added, "But I didn't, so what?"

To add to the odds against him, Foxx broke a bone in his left wrist in August trying to break up a double play and went 20 days without a home run while playing despite excruciating pain.

But fate wasn't finished with Double X.

He was en route to baseball's coveted Triple Crown—leading the league in batting average, home runs and runs batted in—with a .364 average, his 58 homers and 169 RBIs. But Dale Alexander edged him out by three points with a .367 average while playing in only 124 games for Detroit and Boston and coming to bat only 392 times. Foxx, in contrast, played in all 154 games and had 585 at-bats. Under today's criteria, a hitter must have at least 477 at-bats to qualify for the batting title. With that rule, Foxx would have won the batting championship and the Triple Crown.

He won it the next year anyhow, with a .356 average, 48 homers and 163 RBIs. With today's criteria, he would have equalled Williams as the only players in history to hit 500 home runs and win the Triple Crown twice.

That year—1933—was the second baseball season of the Great Depression. With attendance down because fans simply didn't have the money to spend on ball games, owner Connie Mack asked Foxx to take a pay cut, even with the triple crown. He asked him to take a cut from $16,333 to $12,000. The slugger said later, "I had a helluva time settling for $16,000."

Another triple crown eluded him in 1938, when he led the league with a .349 average and 175 runs batted in. He hit 50 home runs too, but Hank Greenberg hit 58.

Foxx, who finished his career second only to Ruth and tops among righthanded hitters with 534 home runs, was often compared to the Sultan of Swat. Although he stood two inches shorter than Ruth and was some 20 pounds lighter at 195, he was as much of a power hitter as the immortal "Sultan of Swat."

Their styles, however, were different. Ruth took powerful, sweeping swings with a 42-ounce bat. Foxx swung a bat that was six ounces lighter and took short, quick swings to generate peak velocity, much like Hank Aaron and Ernie Banks.

Most experts agree with historian Ira Smith, who compared the two sluggers by saying, "I loved the Babe, but for sheer power I think Foxx had the edge. A baseball never came off anybody's bat like it did off Jimmie's. The Babe hit a lot of high, looping flies that went for home runs. Foxx put them into the seats like they'd been shot out of a cannon."

His massive shots and brute power earned him the nickname "The Beast," and won him recognition among many as the most menacing hitter of his time. Maybe an even higher compliment came in his other nickname—"the righthanded Babe Ruth."

At the plate, he looked even stronger and huskier—sturdy, broad and appearing to be much heavier. Some said the bat looked "like a toothpick" in his hands. He gripped the bat at the end and stood deep in the batter's box, using a straddle stance and a full stride into the pitch. His bare biceps bulged from sleeves cut deliberately short to intimidate opposing pitchers, and his arm muscles flexed visibly—maybe intentionally —before he swung. Like Ruth, he even looked good striking out, which he did 1,311 times, 19 times fewer than Ruth. Jimmie led the league in that department seven times.

TAPE-MEASURED HOMERS BEFORE MANTLE

No hitter in history, including Mantle, hit more tape measure shots than Foxx. Most were classic in their Bunyonesque distances. "The Boston Strongboy," another nickname he earned with his brute strength, hit the first ball ever to sail over the centerfield wall at Chicago's Comiskey Park. It landed well into the bleachers atop the wall. But that was nothing compared to another bash in the same park that witnesses said cleared a 92-foot high wall at the 352-foot mark and landed on a playground across the street. It was estimated to have traveled 550 feet.

In an exhibition game in Cincinnati, Foxx blasted what is considered the longest ball ever hit at Crosley Field, the home of the Reds until 1970. Those who were there claimed the ball hit the top of a beer sign on a laundry building across the street, then bounced so high it landed on the roof of another building.

Many claim it was Foxx, not Mantle, who hit the longest home run in the history of Yankee Stadium. Mantle's hit the facade at the top of the triple-tiered roof in right field. But the stadium is much deeper in left field, and Foxx hit a ball that came back to earth three feet from the top of the third deck in left. Twenty feet to the right and it would have been the only fair ball ever to sail completely out of Yankee Stadium during a Major League game.

Lefty Gomez, who threw the pitch, simply could not believe it. After the game, he walked to the spot where the ball landed. Later he told reporters it took him twenty minutes to get there.

It seems appropriate that Gomez was the pitcher for that eye-popping blast. Gomez was Foxx's "cousin," the baseball term for a pitcher against whom a particular hitter enjoys frequent success, and Foxx was consistently successful against Gomez.

Two stories illustrate the point: In one game against Foxx, Gomez kept shaking off Bill Dickey until the exasperated catcher finally trotted out to the mound and demanded, "What do you want to throw?"

Gomez answered, "If it's all the same with you, I'd rather not throw him anything."

Foxx hit the next pitch out of the park, prompting Gomez to yell into Dickey, "See what I mean?"

On another occasion, the same sequence unfolded, with Gomez continuing to shake Dickey off until the catcher again went to the mound and demanded to know what Gomez wanted to throw. Gomez said, "Let's not throw him anything. Maybe he'll get a phone call."

Another Yankee Hall of Fame pitcher, Waite Hoyt, gave up a homer to Foxx that enabled his Philadelphia A's to beat the Yankees in the ninth inning. On the train out of Philadelphia that night, a rookie asked the ace pitcher what happened to Hoyt's fast ball he'd heard so much about.

"If you'd really like to know," Hoyt said, "it's in the upper deck in left field in Shibe Park where Foxx hit it this afternoon."

Then there was the time that Dario Lodigiani was playing third base for the A's and Foxx had moved on to the Red Sox. Foxx ripped a sizzler down the line. The ball hit the bag, broke the strap, tore the bag loose and ripped it apart as if it had been hit by a shotgun blast. Then the ball continued screaming its way into left field for a single, while Lodigiani gave thanks that he was still alive to tell about it.

THE FARMER'S SON

James Emory Foxx was born October 22, 1907, in a farmhouse just outside Sudlersville, Maryland, on the state's Eastern Shore, fifty miles from where Babe Ruth was born in Baltimore twelve years before. His father, Sam Dell Foxx, was a Protestant Irish farmer.

Jimmie was short and stocky with shoulders as wide as a barn and arms like the village blacksmith. Like most boys on a farm, he had a hearty appetite, shoveled out the barns, milked the cows and did his other daily chores. He filled out so robustly that at the age of ten, remembering his grandfather's tales of being a drummer boy in the Confederate army, he ran away to join the Army during World War I, convinced he could pass for someone much older.

The Army didn't need 10-year-old drummer boys in 1917, so young Jimmie was sent back home, where he immediately took up sports and dreamed of becoming the next Charlie Paddock, then the world's fastest human. As a high school freshman, Foxx broke the state record for 80 yards. As a sophomore, he won the state 220-yard dash and high jump and was named Maryland's outstanding high school athlete. But then he discovered baseball.

At the age of 12, Jimmie began playing in a local county league as a catcher. His father, denied a promising baseball career when he had to give up the sport to support his mother and five sisters after his own father's death at an early age, was a pitcher on the same team. The pitcher-catcher combination of father and son made them local favorites.

At 14 and now weighing 160 pounds, Jimmie was catching for his high school team and the local Goldsborough semi-pro club, for which he was paid a dollar a game. He was moved to catcher shortly and was given a whopping raise to 12 dollars a game.

Enter Frank "Home Run" Baker.

Baker owned a farm in nearby Trappe. He led the American League in home runs for four straight seasons from 1911 to 1914. The most he ever hit in one season was 12, but that was the "dead ball era," when home runs were shorter and less frequent. He won his nickname in the 1911 World Series, when he hit game-winning homers in back-to-back games against two future Hall of Fame pitchers, Rube Marquard and Christy Mathewson, to lead the Philadelphia A's to the championship over the New York Giants.

Baker was managing a team in neighboring Easton in the Eastern Shore League. He heard about this talented and powerful kid and mailed him a penny postcard with a message in pencil inviting Jimmie to come to Easton for a tryout.

Foxx got to Easton as fast as he could, got his tryout and won a contract for $125 a month. Wanting to look older around his senior teammates, Jimmie started chewing tobacco and smoking cigars, habits he continued for the rest of his life. At the same time, he quit high school and began his professional career. He was 16 years old.

Late in Foxx's first season, Baker hurried up to Philadelphia on an open date in the Easton schedule to shop his young prospect to Baker's old team, the A's, and the Yankees, who were in town for a series against Connie Mack's team. Baker had played six full years with each team.

Baker visited the Yankees first, and told Manager Miller Huggins and Babe Ruth about Foxx in glowing terms. They laughed, thinking he was exaggerating. Baker, disappointed, walked across the field and talked with Mack.

After the Yankees' rejection, Baker pleaded with Mack. "Please take him," he told his old manager. "He can hit with more power than any hitter I've ever seen, including Ruth. You'll find a place for him somewhere."

The A's owner told Baker if he was that high on the kid, Mack would take him sight unseen because Baker's word was good enough for him. For $2,000, one of the greatest future stars of the game joined the Athletics. The Yankees? As Foxx tore up the American League for the A's and later the Red Sox, the Yankees were left to ponder how much more explosive the "Bronx Bombers" would have been with a batting order that would have featured Ruth, Gehrig and Foxx in the third, fourth and fifth spots — all of them in their prime.

Mack's plan was to let Foxx play the rest of the season in the minors, then report to the A's spring training camp at Fort Myers, Florida, in 1925. But Jimmie got off to such an impressive start in the minors that he made the All-Star team. He was playing in the game in Martinsburg, West Virginia, when he received a phone call in the dugout. It was "Mr. Mack." The A's owner-manager told Foxx to report to the big league team the next day at Shibe Park in Philadelphia. "Don't worry about your clothes," Mack added. "We'll buy them for you when you get here."

Foxx sat on the bench for the rest of the A's season, learning from Mr. Mack. And Mr. Mack was doing some learning of his own, learning just how good his prospect was. He told anyone who would listen that he had never seen a young player with such potential.

After returning to high school for the winter, Foxx reported to spring training and immediately discovered his competition—the veteran Cy Perkins, in his tenth season and his fifth as the A's starting catcher, and a 22-year-old rookie named Mickey Cochrane, destined to make the Hall of Fame.

Foxx announced his arrival by belting the longest home run anyone could remember at the A's training grounds, a 468-footer that veterans believed would have cleared the centerfield wall at Shibe Park. He made the team as its third-string catcher. His roommate: Cochrane.

He recorded his first big league hit while pinch-hitting for Lefty Grove at Griffith Stadium in Washington, against Vean Gregg, a veteran lefthander. Jimmie singled to left, the first of 2,646 hits. In the 1926 and '27 seasons, still only in his late teens, Jimmie hit .313 and .323. In 1927, with Ruth hitting his record 60 homers, Jimmie hit the first of his 534 homers, off a spitballing righthander, Urban Shocker, in the second game of a Memorial Day doubleheader in Philadelphia.

When he left his teen years in 1928, the 20-year-old began to mature and increase his run production. In 118 games, he drove in 79 runs while hitting .328 with 13 homers. He was versatile, too, playing third base, first and catching. Mack spoke in glowing terms about his new star. "He is the easiest boy on the team to handle," he said. "He does whatever I ask. He plays any position and never complains."

Double X made 1929 a breakthrough year for himself and for his team, too. Mack's A's were poised to put together three of the greatest years achieved by any team. Finally breaking the Yankee domination, the A's won three straight pennants and two World Series.

Throughout spring training in '29, Foxx played third base, but just before Opening Day, Mack asked him if he had a first baseman's glove. When he said no, Mack told him he'd better get one because he was going to be the A's first baseman from then on. Foxx finally had found a permanent home. Although pressed into service at other positions in emergencies—as a third baseman, shortstop, catcher, outfielder and even ten times as a pitcher—Foxx was primarily a first baseman for the rest of his 20 years in the Major Leagues.

Having turned 21 the previous October, and fortified with a raise of two thousand dollars to a cool $5,000, Foxx began the 1929 season with a bang and never looked back. At the halfway point he was hitting over .400 and gracing the cover of *Time* magazine. He finished with a .354 average, 33 home runs and 117 runs batted in. The A's left the Yankees in the dust, finishing 18 games ahead of the Ruth-Gehrig machine, the one which only two years before was called—and still is—the greatest team in the history of baseball.

In his first World Series, Double X became an immediate hero, then played a key role in one of the most memorable comebacks in any sport. Foxx broke a scoreless tie in the seventh inning with a home run off Charlie Root of the Cubs to win the first game, 3-1. Then he hit a three-run blast and powered his team to a 9-3 victory, giving the A's a commanding 2-0 lead in the Series. The Cubs narrowed the gap with a 3-1 win in Philadelphia, and the stage was set.

The Cubs held an presumably insurmountable 8-0 lead in the bottom of the seventh inning of the fourth game, with their pitching ace, Root, a 19-game winner that year, on the mound again. No one got excited when Al Simmons opened the inning with a home run and Foxx singled. But then Bing Miller, Jimmy Dykes and Joe Boley singled too, and the A's suddenly had three runs.

The barrage continued—a single by Max Bishop, an inside-the-park home run by Mule Haas when Hack Wilson lost his routine fly ball in the sun and before long it was 8-7. Foxx got his second hit of the inning, and the A's went on to win, 10-8. The Cubs, still in a state of shock the next day, lost the Series in five games.

DAYS OF WINE AND ROSES

The A's were world champions for the first time in 16 years, and Foxx was their leader with a .350 batting average, two home runs, five runs scored and five driven in. His World Series share was $5,620.57, more than his salary for the entire year.

Foxx joined a "barnstorming" team of stars and picked up another $5,000 by playing games in minor league cities and small towns around the country, an annual rite of autumn that gave baseball fans outside Major League cities their only chance to see big leaguers in those years before television and expansion.

The money kept pouring in. Mack rewarded Foxx with a three-year contract for $50,000. For the farm boy from Maryland, these were days of wine and roses. As he reached new heights in baseball every season, he began making poor business decisions with his money and turning to alcohol in both good times and bad. The combination of bad business and booze led him eventually to bankruptcy and alcoholism.

Foxx and his A's delivered a repeat performance in 1930. He continued his assault against the American League's pitchers and the outfield fences behind them, hitting .335 with 37 homers and 156 runs batted in. Against the St. Louis Cardinals in the World Series, he enjoyed another memorable Fall Classic, hitting .333. He hit only one home run, but it was both dramatic and decisive, a two-run shot in the ninth inning—the only runs of the game for either team—to win the fifth game. The A's closed out the Cards in the next game.

That home run was the most satisfying of his career, and not just because it won a World Series game for his team. Jimmie hit it against the most successful spitball pitcher of all time, future Hall of Famer Burleigh Grimes, but there was more to it than that. As Foxx told his story later, "Grimes was quite a bench jockey. I didn't mind him getting on me, but when he got on Mr. Mack, that was against all the rules."

Grimes struck out Foxx on spitballs twice in the first game of the Series and again earlier in the fifth game. He told Foxx later that by the top of the ninth, with the A's coming to bat, "He had thrown only two curve balls all day—one when he struck me out in the seventh."

As Foxx stepped into the batter's box, he was trying to out-think Grimes. "I thought, 'I wonder if he'll do it again.' Sure enough! Instead of that great spitball, here it came (the curve ball)—and there it went." Foxx always said it was his greatest thrill in baseball.

THE DEPRESSION AND MR. MACK

The A's made baseball history in 1931, becoming the first Major League team to win 100 or more games three years in a row. After a slight dip at the plate—a .291 average with 30 home runs and 120 RBIs—Foxx and his teammates were defeated by the Cardinals, but that was only the start of a long slide that never really ended for "Mr. Mack" and his team.

What should have been Mack's greatest triumph—four straight pennants for the first time in American League history—never happened as a revenge-seeking Yankee team jumped off to a quick start and left the A's 13 games behind by the end of the 1932 season. But more than the season ended. An era did, too.

In the same October when the Yankees were defeating the Cubs and Babe Ruth was hitting his "called shot" home run off Charlie Root, the depression was entering its fourth year. Like so many other companies and their executives, the A's and Mr. Mack were reeling under financial problems. Saddled with the highest payroll in baseball because of his team's on-field successes, his problem was compounded by the plunge in attendance in ballparks all over the country caused by the staggering amount of unemployment. To make matters worse, Mack had borrowed huge sums to renovate Shibe Park, and those payments were still due.

The respected owner-manager had no choice: He had to break up his team and sell his stars for cash. Al Simmons, Mule Haas and Jimmy Dykes were the first to go, sold to the Chicago White Sox in September 1932 for $100,000. How much of a loss was that three-man departure? Simmons hit .322 the year before with 35 home runs and 151 runs batted in. Haas hit .305. Dykes drove in 90 runs.

The A's slipped to third in 1933, the first sign of the inevitable decline, but it was no fault of Foxx. He almost equalled his great 1932 season. This time he hit .356 with 48 home runs and 163 RBIs—and won his first Triple Crown.

He reached a personal high in a game in Cleveland when he drove in nine runs. In successive trips to the plate, he rapped out a two-run triple, a grand slam home run, an RBI double and a two-run single. In his last trip to the plate on his explosive day, Foxx added the perfect Ruthian touch—he fanned magnificently. His own fireworks show topped one of the year before, in an 18-inning game, also in Cleveland, when he smashed three home runs and three singles and drove in eight runs.

Mack continued to dismantle his team for urgently needed cash. He sold Lefty Grove, the finest pitcher in the game, to the Red Sox for $125,000. Grove had averaged 25 wins a year for the previous seven seasons. All-Star catcher Mickey Cochrane, a .322 hitter, went to Detroit for $100,000.

For the A's, their ranks depleted through the cash transactions, the 1934 season was all Jimmie Foxx. The team dropped to fifth place, but it wasn't Jimmie's fault. He hit .334 with 44 homers. At the same time, Ruth drove in under 100 runs for the first time in nine seasons and would leave the game a year later.

By now, just about everyone was agreeing with Mr. Mack that Jimmie Foxx was the preeminent slugger in the game.

The A's continued their downward spiral in 1935, hitting the bottom of the American League standings with only 58 wins. The slide continued almost without interruption over the next 20 years, until the team was sold and moved to Kansas City in 1955, then to Oakland.

But Foxx continued his heroic efforts in 1935 despite his team's problems, with a .346 average and another 36 home runs.

After that '35 season, Mack dropped a bombshell. He sold Double X and John Marcum, a 17-game winner, to the Red Sox for $150,000, veteran pitcher Gordon Rhodes and a minor leaguer. It was his last act in dismantling a World Series championship team 62 years before the Florida Marlins did the same thing.

By this stage in his career and his life, Foxx had earned a reputation. He was said to own a wardrobe second to none. He was also said to be drinking heavily and giving away money as a soft touch for anyone who was down and out and needed a buck. After a raise of $7,000 to $25,000 —a fortune in the depths of America's worst depression—Foxx became even more vulnerable.

His teammate and fellow Hall of Famer, Second Baseman Bobby Doerr, said recently, "Jimmie was a big spender. He would always be the one to pick up the tab whenever we went out for steaks. It was not unusual for him to call out, 'The drinks are on the house—Ol' Double X is here!'"

Tom Yawkey brought Foxx to Boston for two reasons: To tatoo the Green Monster in left field and to lead his team to its first World Series in eighteen years. Foxx did his part in his first two years there, with 41 homers, 143 RBIs and a .338 average in 1936 and 36 roundtrippers and 127 RBIs in 1937. But the Bosox finished in the second division both years.

Just before the '37 season, Foxx began suffering from severe sinus headaches, attributed partly to a beaning the year before. His batting average dropped to .285, his first sub-.300 season after averaging .350 over the previous four years. Late in the season, his headaches grew so bad his vision became impaired and he was fitted for glasses, although he dropped that experiment in short order.

The Boston Strongboy bounced back with a vengeance in 1938, leading the Red Sox to second place and becoming the first righthanded hitter to hit 50 or more home runs twice. He led the league in hitting for the second time with .349 and in RBIs for the third time with 175. Only Greenberg's 58 homers kept him from his second Triple Crown, but they didn't keep him from winning his third MVP award.

It was to be his last monster year, those seasons when he dominated the league in all three Triple Crown categories.

He was now one of the highest paid players in the sport, and deservedly so, but those headaches, his heavy drinking and abusive living habits began to take their toll. He hit .360 in 1939 with 35 homers, but his production dropped with only 105 runs batted in. In 1940, he still managed to wallop 36 homers and drive in 119 runs, but his average dropped under .300 for only the second time, to .297.

In 1941, with Greenberg and others being drafted into military service as the war clouds grew darker, Foxx hit an even .300 with 19 homers and 105 RBIs. Even though he played three more seasons during the wartime manpower shortage, 1941 was Foxx's last as a full-time player.

Ted Williams remembers Foxx's last full-time seasons. "The Splendid Splinter" was a rookie in 1939 and was Foxx's teammate into the 1942 season, two members of the 500-homer club on the same team. The combination was broken up on June 1, when Foxx was sold to the Cubs on waivers. At the end of the season, less than a year after America entered World War II, Williams left for military duty and became a pilot in the Marines.

In his autobiography, *My Turn at Bat*, Williams wrote, "Foxx was getting toward the end of his career then, but he had switched to a lighter bat, maybe 35 or 36 ounces, and he was hanging in, getting a lot of blunk hits and every now and then really crashing one."

Ted has specific memories of Foxx's power. "I remember on a road trip that year," he wrote, "Jimmie hit three balls like I never had seen before. The first one was a real ripper in Chicago, over the left field bleachers, and in Cleveland I was on second and Mel Harder was pitching when Foxx hit one over the 435-foot sign. Then in Detroit, right after that, he hit the longest ball I'd ever seen—way up into the bleachers in left center. Just hard to believe."

Williams was frank in admitting his respect for Double X. "I truly admired Foxx," he wrote. "He was older, of course, and he and I were a generation apart, but he was such a good-natured guy. Always a giggle and a 'Yeah, sure, sure.'"

Williams remembered another side of the Foxx personality as well. "He never made any bones about his love for Scotch. He used to say he could drink 15 of those little bottles of Scotch, those miniatures, and not be affected. Of course, nobody could do that and stay healthy, and it got to Jimmie later on."

When he joined the Cubs in '42, Foxx told reporters he couldn't raise his arms over his head and couldn't hit his weight, but he would do his best. His best was a saddening .205 average and only three home runs in 70 games. At the end of the season, he called it quits and worked as an oil salesman in 1943. Jimmie's life continued its downward spiral. His wife divorced him that year, claiming he drank to excess and was abusive during his drinking binges.

The Cubs, desperate for players during the manpower shortage, talked Foxx into a comeback in 1944, but after only one hit in 20 at-bats, the end to his playing career seemed undeniable. The Cubs sent him to Portsmouth to manage there, but Foxx disliked the move. He told reporters later he had no desire to manage, that it was a lot easier to hit home runs than to manage 17 players who thought they were home run hitters.

The Phillies talked him into giving it one more try, in 1945, the last year of the war. He surprised most observers with a creditable performance, hitting .268 in 89 games, 26 of them as a pinchhitter, and hitting the final seven home runs of his career at age 37. He played three different positions for the Phillies—third base, first base and pitcher.

"The Beast's" last big day came in a Sunday doubleheader in Pittsburgh on September 9, seven days after General Douglas MacArthur and his Japanese counterparts signed the peace treaty ending the war. Double X hit a two-run homer in the first game, and in what sportswriters used to call "the nightcap," he walked, singled twice, doubled and hit the 534th and last home run of his power-filled career.

In the final days of the season, Foxx took the mound against Cincinnati, his ninth appearance that year as a pitcher. Easily the most versatile player of all the 500-homer hitters, he played every position in his Major League career except second base. He pitched five hitless innings that day against the Reds before surrendering a hit in the sixth and was the winning pitcher, giving him a perfect 1-0 record for the season and an earned run average of only 1.57 in 23 innings.

Foxx never played in another Major League game.

THE DOWN SIDE

His years after his playing days were marked with one setback after another, financial disasters on business deals, illnesses and finally the cruelest blow of all: He choked to death on a piece of steak while having dinner with his brother in 1967, at the age of 59. His plaque in the Hall of Fame was draped in black.

From the end of his playing days, nothing had been heard from or about Jimmie until he appeared on the Today show in 1958 and told host Dave Garroway that after making a quarter of a million dollars in salary as a player, he was broke. With his characteristic honesty, he said, "The money I lost—and blew was my own fault, 99 percent of it. Suddenly you're 50 years old and nobody wants you."

Then he sounded a warning that has even more applicability today in this era of seven-figure salaries. "So athletes," he told Garroway, "have to put something away. You only stay up there so long. It's always nice to have the crowds on your side, but it doesn't last long once you stop producing."

As he spoke to Garroway and the show's nationwide audience, Foxx was three months behind in his rent, and his telephone had been disconnected. He had held jobs driving a coal truck, pumping gas part-time and selling bakery products, paint and sporting goods.

In the saddest blow of all, a pension fund for Major League players was established, but only for those who played in 1946 and beyond. If Jimmie had retired after the '46 season instead of 1945, he would have been eligible for a lifelong pension based on his 20 years as a player.

Foxx was candid in discussing his plight, with a wife and three kids depending on him. "Funny thing," he told a reporter, "but my best years were the Depression years. You didn't make much on the outside then as the players do now. I had only one contract that I remember, with a cereal company for $1,000...You made appearances on the banquet circuit all right, but most of the time for free."

His personal manager and friend, Jimmy Silan, said offers for help poured in following Jimmie's TV appearance. He showed Jim McCulley of the *New York Daily News* a sheaf of papers and said, "These are all offers for jobs. They come from all over the country."

"Anybody from baseball?"

"Nobody from baseball," Silan said, "and that's what he'd like to do."

A year later, living in Phoenix with his brother, Foxx was interviewed by the Associated Press. His condition was no better. "I'm broke," he admitted, "and guess I always will be. When you get 51 years old, nobody wants you. There's nothing tougher than doing nothing. I've had a lot of experience recently at doing nothing. If my brother Sam wasn't working, we wouldn't be eating." Then he added poignantly, "I heard a man down at the service station say he might need a helper. I could pump some gas. A few dollars are better than nothing."

People tried to help. The Boston baseball writers honored him at their annual dinner. The general manager of the Red Sox, Joe Cronin, gave him a job as a coach with their Minneapolis Millers, but Jimmie was frequently ill and reportedly continued his heavy drinking. The Red Sox released him. In 1961, he filed for bankruptcy.

Throughout his career and his life, Jimmie had only one weakness —that one drink too many. People remember that about him, but they remember other things about him, too. They remember that he was a general, personable and kind man to everyone, and he could hit a baseball harder than any man who ever walked to the plate.

Sportswriter Al Hirshberg expressed the feelings of everyone in baseball:"His personality was one of the gentlest in the game. Foxx hated no one and no one hated him. From the day he first went into the Major Leagues, he was pleasant to everyone, never impatient with fans or admirers, always, always accessible to anybody who appreciated him."

However, it is also true that Jimmie's number has never been retired by either the Red Sox or the Athletics.

Foxx never allowed the cruel downward spiral of his life to change his disposition and attitude. "This much I know," he said as he tried to cope with the reverses which haunted his later years."Whether they ever call me back to the game or not, I'll always have my memories. Of Mr. Mack and the World Series. Of nice guys like Lefty Gomez. Of 534 kicks watching that ball sail out of the park. Of being elected to the Hall of Fame."

Then he concluded simply and eloquently, "I'm glad I was a ballplayer."

WHAT OTHER PLAYERS SAID ABOUT JIMMIE FOXX

Bobby Doerr—I was just like a little kid in awe ... I can remember my first trip around the league. In Chicago they said Foxx hit one over the left-center field—over the whole ball park ....Then we went to Detroit and they said he hit another one over there that is still going. One time we're playing in Cleveland—about '39 or '40—it was cold and the rain was blowing in. We stood there in the runway and someone said, "There won't be anything hit out of here tonight." It think it was the first or second time Foxx went to bat—he hit a line drive up in leftfield. There was no stopping that one! ...I have to think Foxx was the greatest I saw, and almost everyone else I know agrees.

Birdie Tebbetts—He didn't take time off from having fun. A happy-go-lucky guy. He was just the greatest guy there ever was ....Life was just one big good time for Jimmie.

Mickey Vernon—In my rookie year with Washington, Rene Monteagudo, a little lefthander from Cuba, struck Foxx out and strutted around the mound. On his next time up, Foxx hit one three rows from the top. As he rounded first, he looked at Rene and said, "How did you like that one, little guy?" Someone would hit one in Detroit or someplace and everyone would talk about it, but one of our old coaches, Nick Altrock or Clyde Milan, would say, "If you think that was long, you should have seen where Foxx hit one." They were always comparing where Foxx hit one.

Mel Harder—He hit eleven off me. He was the most powerful hitter I ever saw. Babe Ruth could hit them far, but when Jimmie Foxx hit one, it was like a golf ball. When he hit one, it took off. Distance to the fences didn't make any difference to him. Ballparks didn't mean anything to him. He could hit it out of anywhere. He hit some balls that would run out of sight. Later his drinking hurt him a lot. But he had a lot of friends.

Bob Feller—He could hit a ball farther than Joe DiMaggio or Ted Williams. He hit balls that were floaters because he didn't get that backspin like Babe Ruth did. The trouble with Jimmie was he had a blind spot—high and tight—and that's why he struck out a lot . . . . He had great wrists and was a wrist hitter like Hank Aaron.

Lou Boudreau—Foxx was the strongest guy I ever saw on a baseball diamond. He handled the bat like a toothpick. He tried to hit it out on every swing. He wasn't the type to hit and run or hit behind the runner to the opposite field.

Cecil Travis—This is one guy who would scare you at the plate. Big muscles. Especially if you were playing on the left side of the infield like I was at short or third. You didn't have to worry about Ted Williams hitting over to that side, but Foxx was a different story. You had to really be on your toes he hit them so hard. Most don't realize he was really a good all-around player who could play several positions. The fallout was his drinking. There's no telling what he could have done if it hadn't been for that. He wasn't one of those stars who wouldn't talk to you, who thought they were higher than anybody else. Just an ordinary guy.

Eddie Yost—When I was with Washington, we would go into these parks—Washington, Cleveland, Yankee Stadium, Chicago— and our coaches would point and say, "There's where Jimmie Foxx hit one." It would be a mile away from home plate. I couldn't believe it!"

Elmer Valo—He could hit a ball a country mile. I saw him hit a couple of balls out of sight. The only one I ever saw who could remind me of Foxx was Mantle. A big, strong young man, you know. It was so sad to read in later years all the things that happened to him. I think everyone who ever saw or knew him was really touched by it all.

Joe Garagiola—I never saw him play. As a kid I saw him come out of a restaurant one day and thought he was the biggest guy I ever saw. Lefty Gomez said guys would tell him what a hell of a pitch he made to Foxx, and Lefty would say, "Yeah, for three-quarters of the way, and then Foxx took charge."

THE FOXX FILE

Full Name: James Emory Foxx.
Date and Place of Birth: October 22, 1907, Sudlersville, Maryland.
Date and Place of Death: July 21, 1967, Miami, Florida.
Nicknames: "Double X", "The Beast", "The Boston Strong Boy".
Position: First base. Also third base, shortstop, catcher, left field, center field, right field and pitcher.
Major League Career: 20 years, 1925-1942, 1944-1945 (20 years).
Home Runs: 534 (9th).
Runs Batted In: 1,921 (6th).
Runs Scored: 1,751.
Lifetime Batting Average: .325
Number of Hits: 2,646.
Bases on Balls: 1,452.
Strikeouts: 1,311.
American League Most Valuable Player: Three times — 1932, 1933 and 1938.

Other Highlights:
—Hit 30 or more home runs 12 years in a row.
— Led American League in home runs four times, including 58 in 1932, and runs batted in three times including totals of 163 RBIs, 169 and 175.
—Won American League batting championship twice.
—Hit over .300 14 times including averages of .364, .360, .356 and .354.
—Averaged .344 for three World Series.

Elected to the Baseball Hall of Fame: 1951 (with Mel Ott).

4

REGGIE JACKSON

Mr. October
(Also September and Other Months)

Reporters started calling Reggie Jackson "Mr. October" after he hit three home runs on three consecutive pitches to power his New York Yankees to the 1977 World Series championship over the Los Angeles Dodgers. But the nickname wasn't originated by the press, and it didn't even start as a compliment.

When the Yankees' manager, Billy Martin, in another of his many personality snits, benched Jackson for the decisive fifth game of the American League championship Series against the Kansas City Royals, Catcher Thurman Munson, their team captain, said, "I guess Billy isn't aware that Reggie is 'Mr. October.'" Munson, no Jackson admirer, said it with heavy sarcasm.

After Jackson performed his now-historic feat against the Dodgers, Munson walked over to Jackson in the dressing room at Yankee Stadium and said, "See? I knew what I was doing when I gave you the nickname, you big —— ." This time, there was no sarcasm.

Reggie Jackson led the American League in various categories over his Hall of Fame career. He also led the league in adjectives. Writers, broadcasters, fans, other players—everyone had an adjective to describe his opinion of the controversial slugger: impulsive, driven, misunderstood, inconsistent, complex, controversial, charming, friendly, intelligent, generous to friends, available for kids, physically and mentally tough, egotistical, outspoken, emotional, insecure, lonely, troubled, confused, haughty, demanding, uncompromising, occasionally mistrusting, rude, seemingly indifferent.

One of his teammates on the Yankees, Mickey Rivers, taunted him once about his heritage, and may have struck closer to home than he realized: "Your first name is white, your second is Hispanic, and your third belongs to a black. No wonder you don't know who you are." (Jackson's full name is Reginald Martinez Jackson).

An opponent, first baseman Mike Hegan, may have described Jackson best by saying he defied description. Hegan said, "He is the most complex man I ever met. Is there anybody who really knows him? Does he really know himself?"

AN 11-YEAR-OLD PROSPECT?

Whoever heard of an 11-year-old kid being scouted by the Major Leagues? Reggie Jackson was. The second youngest of six children born in 1946 to Martinez and Clara Jackson in Wyncote, Pennsylvania, a suburb of Philadelphia, he obviously inherited at least some of his genes from his father, a semi-pro player.

He began playing softball when he was seven. By 11, while playing sandlot baseball, a scout for the New York Giants, Chick Genovese, handed him a business card and told him to look him up in a few years. By the time the Jackson kid was a senior at Cheltenham Township High School, other scouts were following him too, lured to his games by his .500-plus batting average and three no-hitters.

Reggie liked playing football better, became an All-American high school running back and selected Arizona State from among a ton of scholarship offers. But when Coach Frank Kush tried to convert Jackson into a defensive back, Reggie moved over to the university's baseball diamond and teamed up with future big leaguers Sal Bando and Rick Monday, who were destined to become Jackson's teammates with the Oakland A's.

He became the first college player to hit a ball out of Phoenix Stadium, then followed that achievement by being named College Player of the Year by *The Sporting News*. He was rewarded with a signing bonus of $85,000 after being drafted by the Athletics, playing their final years in Kansas City before their move to Oakland. The Mets, who had since replaced the Giants in New York, had the first pick in the baseball draft that year. Instead of Jackson, they chose a catcher named Steve Chilcott, who never made it to the majors.

After a one-year apprenticeship in the minors, Jackson was called up to what baseball people call "the big club" late in the 1967 season. He announced his arrival with considerably less fanfare than he became known for later. He hit only one home run in 35 games, drove in only six, hit a meager .179 and struck out 46 times in only 118 times at bat, hardly the credentials of a future Hall of Famer.

The A's moved to Oakland for the 1968 season, and the brash 22-year-old with all those strikeouts and the anemic batting average promptly told the world the A's would become baseball's next dynasty, succeeding the Yankees, and they would be led by—who else?—Reggie Jackson.

He played in 154 games, hit 29 home runs and had 74 runs batted in. He led the American League in two departments, neither of them good. He struck out a hard-to-believe 171 times, only four shy of the Major League record, the first of five times he led the league in that negative department, and committed the most errors among the league's outfielders with 12.

He also led the league in temper tantrums, thrown bats and slammed helmets. Pitcher Darold Knowles, said, "There's not enough mustard in the world to cover that hot dog."

The A's seemed unable to do anything about his personality, but they tried to do something about his strikeouts and his atrocious fielding. Owner Charlie Finley went all the way—he hired Joe DiMaggio as a coach to work with Jackson.

DEMONS

The world knew only what it saw in Jackson's flamboyant behavior. What the world did not know what that Jackson was fighting demons inside himself, the result of his parents' broken marriage when Reggie was only six, orders from his college coach to stop dating white girls, criticism from his fellow blacks for spending what they considered too much time with too many white friends, and for his shortcomings at the plate and in the field.

Jackson was able to overcome the demons in his second full season, 1969. By mid-season, he had 30 home runs, one more than his whole rookie year, and was the leading vote-getter among American League outfielders for the All-Star game in Washington. On July 29, he had 40 home runs and was 23 games ahead of Babe Ruth's pace in 1927, when he set the then-record of 60 homers in one season.

He finished with dramatically higher numbers than his rookie season—47 homers, 118 RBIs and a .275 average. The American League's pitchers were acquiring respect for him already. They walked him 114 times. But he led the league again in strikeouts—142—and errors with 11.

His manager that year, the only year he managed Jackson, was Hank Bauer. When author Maury Allen wrote his book, *Mr. October: The Reggie Jackson Story*, Bauer told him, "I never had any trouble with the kid. He played hard for me. I told him if he played hard, hustled, gave me everything he had, I'd be his best friend. Then he started making big money later on. Changed him a lot, I hear. But in 1969, in the only year I had him, he was one hell of a baseball player."

Early in his Oakland years, the young home run specialist began feuding with his owner, the equally explosive Finley, a sales and marketing genius who knew little about baseball and had a reputation for treating his players like serfs. Mostly they feuded, publicly, about money and Finley's constant public statements about Jackson's deficiencies in striking out so often and making so many errors.

The feud reached an early peak in 1970, when Jackson hit a grand slam home run, then saluted Finley with an obscene gesture as he crossed the plate. Finley demanded an apology from his employee, and got one.

Along the way, however, things were changing in Oakland. Bauer was replaced by John McNamara near the end of the 1969 season, and McNamara was succeeded by Dick Williams in 1971. At the same time, the A's were putting together a solid lineup of Jackson, Sal Bando, Bert Campaneris, Joe Rudi, Rick Monday and Gene Tenace, with a strong pitching staff of Vida Blue, Ken Holtzman and future Hall of Famers Catfish Hunter and Rollie Fingers.

Over the next five seasons, beginning in 1972, Jackson's prediction of a dynasty came true, and so did his prediction about who would lead it. The A's won five consecutive divisional championships and three straight World Series. In four of those seasons, Jackson led the A's in home runs, twice leading the league too. In 1973, he also led the league in runs scored and runs batted in.

In 1973, he was voted the league's Most Valuable Player award. He earned the same recognition in the World Series that year against the Mets, with the game-winning home run in the seventh game and a .310 average. The MVP award included a new car, which he gave to a Chicano and Yaqui Indian community organization in Tempe, Arizona.

One of his managers with the A's, Dick Williams, said of Reggie in those years: "I never had any trouble with Reggie. He played like hell for me. He was a leader on that ball club. You could count on him. I'm proud to have had Reggie."

Changes were in baseball's winds after a banner year by Jackson in 1975. He led the league with 36 home runs, but the A's lost the American League pennant to the Boston Red Sox. On April 2, with talk stirring about "free agency," Finley traded Jackson to the Baltimore Orioles. Reggie, anticipating free agency, openly admitted that he had no intention of remaining in Baltimore, that he was headed for the big markets and the big bucks. He said with his characteristic bluntness, "The trouble with Baltimore is it's in Baltimore."

After missing a month when a fast ball hit him in the face, Jackson came back with a respectable year—27 homers, 91 runs batted in and a league-leading slugging average of .502 while the Orioles were finishing second behind the Yankees.

NEW YORK: IF YOU CAN MAKE IT THERE...

Jackson was in the right place at the right time. Free agency was now a fact, allowing players to change teams at the end of their contracts, something they had never been able to do. They had always been bound by baseball's "reserve clause," a standard provision in every player's contract which specified that the player remained the property of his team even if he didn't want to sign the contract offered to him. In other words, if you didn't play for that team, you didn't play for anybody.

With the arrival of free agency, players could shop their talents to other teams, which is exactly what Jackson did. The timing was perfect for Reggie. He had been one of the best players in baseball for five years, and now he was going to capitalize on it after the 1976 season ended.

He visited one team after another, where he was wined and dined and made to feel he was the incarnation of Babe Ruth. The bidding started at $2 million, and quickly escalated to twice that amount.

George Steinbrenner of the Yankees offered less, only $3 million, but he emphasized to Jackson that he was giving him the opportunity to be a Yankee, with their pinstripes and the tradition of Ruth and DiMaggio and Mantle—and now Jackson. Reggie was alert enough to know there was even more in New York—all those Madison Avenue types waving endorsement money, big money, at him.

After meeting with four other teams in Chicago the next day, Jackson told Steinbrenner he would sign with the Yankees. He would be a Yankee in the goldfish bowl that is New York City, with all those writers and radio and television reporters. And some of the toughest fans in baseball, fans who had booed DiMaggio and Mantle. But he had what he wanted —a five-year contract calling for $3 million, making him the highest paid player in the game.

With his contract placing pressure on him, Jackson had to deliver. Unlike the Frank Sinatra song, "New York, New York—if you can make it here, you can make it anywhere," Jackson had no such luxury. In his case, it wasn't *if* you can make it here. He *had* to make it.

He arrived for spring training in Fort Lauderdale, Florida, with his black bat, the one he called his "Dues Collector." He explained to his teammates and the writers and broadcasters covering the team the bat would intimidate every other team in baseball, and no team would ever embarrass the Yankees in the World Series as long as he was carrying his Dues Collector.

Jackson immediately applied for the role of team leader, and when Munson, as captain, expressed disagreement with that prospect, Jackson took him on. He told *Sport* Magazine, "I am the straw that stirs the drink. It all comes back to me. Maybe I should say me and Munson. But really, he doesn't enter into it. He's being so damned insecure about the whole thing. I've overheard him talking about me. Munson's tough, too. He's a gamer, but there is just nobody who can do for a club what I can do. There is nobody who can put meat (fans) in the seats that way I can. That's just the way it is. Munson thinks he can be the straw that stirs the drink, but he can only stir it bad."

The Yankees, already beset by internal unrest, exploded now. The battle lines were drawn, with Munson, Sparky Lyle, Graig Nettles and any Yankee with an opinion on one side and Jackson and reserve catcher Fran Healy, the only Yankee to befriend Reggie from the start, on the other. Munson's teammates supported him as their avowed leader—quiet, determined, a battler and a clutch player who led by example rather than his mouth. But he also was saddled with a sulking disposition that caused problems. And he was not a favorite with autograph seekers, who complained that he treated them like the plague.

Even so, Jackson was the one getting the silent treatment from his teammates in the dugout and the clubhouse. Early in the season, that treatment ended temporarily when Martin accused Reggie of loafing on a base hit to right in Boston. He told Jackson his casual approach in fielding the ball allowed the Red Sox to turn a routine single into a double. Then Martin, whose solution to many problems was to start a fight, tangled with his right fielder, on national television. Coaches Yogi Berra and Elston Howard had to pull them apart.

Things approached a climactic point when Munson and veteran Lou Piniella met with Steinbrenner and Martin. They stunned their manager by asking him to move Jackson into the prestigious cleanup spot in the batting order—the fourth position—recognition and status which Jackson coveted. He felt Martin was humiliating him by hitting him fifth, sixth and even seventh.

Martin agreed, and the results were electrifying. With his Dues Collector, Jackson drove in 50 runs for the Yankees in their last 49 games, the Yankees won 41 of their last 54 games and captured the 1977 American League East championship by two and a half games. Jackson drove in 50 runs in their last 49 games and drove in the winning run in 20 of those 41 victories.

Just as he had boasted, Reggie was now the straw that was stirring the drink.

With all of his heroics, Jackson remained the Yankees' lightning rod, the one in the middle of almost any storm involving his team. He continued to be one of the hottest topics in New York and in baseball. He fanned the flames of the controversies surrounding him with his life style, flaunting his wealth by driving a six-figure Rolls Royce to Yankee Stadium, flashing large bills and openly dating white women.

OF HATE AND HOMERS

Behind Jackson and his Dues Collector, the Yankees were now champions of the American League East. The only team between them and a spot in the World Series were the champions of the AL's West Division, the Kansas City Royals, the new team that had replaced his rookie team, the A's, after the Athletics moved to Oakland.

In the first four games of what sounds like a government agency—the ALCS, meaning the American League Championship Series—the two teams split. Jackson's bat wasn't collecting much of anything, with just one single in 14 times at bat. Then, with their whole season riding on the fifth game, Manager Martin made a shocking decision. He benched Jackson.

Did Martin really believe his team had a better chance of winning with his team's leading run producer on the bench? Or was he actually willing to risk defeat to prove before Steinbrenner and everyone else in Yankee Stadium that Billy, not Reggie, was the man in charge?

Elston Howard, the respected Yankee catcher and later one of their coaches, may have given the answer in later years when he described the Martin-Jackson relationship: "Billy was jealous of him." He said Martin "hated the attention Reggie got, couldn't control him. That was part of it. The other part, the big part, was Reggie's black. Billy hated him for that. I believe Billy is prejudiced against blacks, Jews, American Indians, Spanish, anything, if you don't bow to him. He can get along with blacks if they don't challenge him. But Reggie challenged him in every way. Billy was always hostile to him. Did everything to make him unhappy. Went out of his way to see him fail."

Then Howard said something that may bear directly on Martin's decision to bench Jackson in that fifth game of the 1977 ALCS: "I think Billy wanted Reggie to fail more than he wanted the Yankees to win."

But Reggie didn't fail, and neither did the Yankees—or Martin. In the eighth inning, Martin sent Jackson up to pinch hit against a righthander, Doug Bird, and Reggie delivered a run-scoring single that narrowed the Kansas City lead to 3-2. The Yanks went on to score three more times in the ninth inning and won the game and the pennant, 5-3.

Then Reggie blasted his way into the history books.

After the first five games of the World Series against the Dodgers, the Yankees held a 3-2 lead. In Los Angeles, Jackson homered in the fourth game into the left field pavilion off Rick Rhoden and again in the fifth game against a fellow future Hall of Famer, Don Sutton, both times with the bases empty. His second homer became a link to history in the sixth game, when the Series moved back to New York.

On his first trip to the plate, Jackson was walked by Burt Hooton on four pitches. In the fourth inning, with the Dodgers leading, 3-2, and Munson on first base, Jackson whipped his Dues Collector into action and hit the first pitch he saw from Hooton, an up-and-in fastball, on a line into Yankee Stadium's right field seats for a two-run homer that put the Yankees ahead, 4-3.

In the fifth inning, with Elias Sosa now pitching for the Dodgers, Jackson again hit the first pitch, and again for a home run into the right field seats, deeper than the one before, for another two-run homer. Now the Yankees were leading, 7-3.

The score became secondary as Jackson came to bat in the eighth, the Yankees still ahead, 7-3. Now he was facing the toughest kind of pitcher to hit a home run against, a knuckleballer. Charlie Hough was on the mound, and his "butterfly pitch" floated toward the plate like all other knuckleballs—with no speed at all. If Jackson was going to hit this one out of the park, he was going to have to generate all the power himself from his 6-foot, 195-pound frame.

He did. With the crowd of 56,407 fans chanting "Reggie! Reggie! Reggie!", Jackson unleashed that powerful yet smooth lefthanded swing of his and hit Hough's first pitch, that dreaded knuckler, to dead center field. His blast cleared the fence 450 feet from home plate, longer than either of his other two shots. Jackson hesitated at home plate before beginning his trot around the bases, so he could admire his latest triumph.

He wasn't the only one caught up in awe. Down at first base, Steve Garvey of the Dodgers, who hit 272 home runs himself plus nine in postseason play, applauded quietly. "When I was sure nobody was looking," he said, "I applauded in my glove."

Manager Tommy Lasorda of the Dodgers called it "the greatest single performance I've ever seen."

Even George Steinbrenner, Jackson's most vocal critic, joined in the praise. "Reggie is a presence," he said, "the definition of a star. There's one word that describes him: winner. That says it all."

Reggie had his own explanation about the Yankees' victory. "Winning teams just seem to follow me around."

His performance stretched back to Game Five, when Jackson hit that home run on his last trip to the plate. Adding that to his three-homer performance in the next game and even allowing for that walk on four pitches in the first inning, Jackson had hit four home runs on four swings off four different pitchers—under the pressure of the World Series and the added pressure created by his controversial personality. Not even Babe Ruth himself could come close to equalling that kind of performance.

Lost in all the acclaim about his home runs were other achievements by Jackson in the World Series: He led all starters on both teams with a .450 batting average, including five home runs, eight runs batted in and ten runs scored.

His teammates were quick and candid in their praise. After the game, Munson put his arm around Reggie and claimed credit for knowing what he was doing in giving Jackson his nickname. Second Baseman Willie Randolph told reporters, "You heard what he said. He said he was the straw that stirs the drink. He believes that. It keeps him going. He believes he's the leader, and that's the way he carries himself. He leads by example, by going out and coming through."

Even Nettles, an avowed Reggie hater, gave Jackson his due. "He's awesome," he said. "It was a very impressive performance under pressure."

And what did Reggie say? He said the way he was treated during most of the season made him cry. One account quoted him as saying, "The Yankee pinstripes are Ruth and Gehrig and DiMaggio and Mantle. I'm a nigger to them. I don't know how to be subservient."

Speaking of his performance itself and his ability to deliver in such grand style, Jackson said, "I love competition. It motivates me, stimulates me, excites me. It's almost sexual. I just love to hit that baseball in a big game."

MR. OCTOBER'S ENCORE

The treatment by Martin that distressed Jackson so much continued in 1978, aggravated when his team and Jackson got off to a poor start. The manager continued his ranting and raving, and Steinbrenner was adding his part even in the clubhouse, usually forbidden territory for owners. Steinbrenner was telling his players they were an embarrassment to him and to the city and fans of New York, that he could get rid of all of them if they didn't start winning. His chewing outs produced only one result: They made matters worse by adding to the tension. The Yankees dropped fourteen games out of first place before the season was half over.

The latest explosion was detonated on July 17, with the Yankees at home against Kansas City and locked in a 5-5 tie in the tenth inning. With Jackson up and a man on first, Jackson bunted a two-strike pitch and popped it up to the catcher. As he left the plate, he carefully took off his dark glasses to prepare for what he considered the inevitable.

Martin had wanted Jackson to bunt, then took the bunt sign off later in the at-bat. Jackson ignored the latest sign and tried to bunt again when he was supposed to hit away. This upset Martin.

Martin didn't say a word, but he took his star hitter out of the game. In the clubhouse after the game, the manager threw a radio against a wall, followed by a beer bottle. Then he suspended Jackson for five days.

When he returned from his suspension almost a week later, Jackson told reporters he had simply been trying to move the runner into scoring position. Martin exploded again, saying Steinbrenner and Jackson deserved each other. He said Jackson was "a born liar" and called Steinbrenner, his own boss, "a convicted felon," a reference to a controversy concerning Steinbrenner's campaign contributions to Richard Nixon's presidential campaign.

To no one's surprise, Martin "resigned" a week later.

Bob Lemon took over the manager's job, and Reggie took over the team. "Mr. October" came alive again in September, hitting eight of his 27 home runs and driving in 26 of his 97 runs to power his team from that distant standing behind the Boston Red Sox into a one-game playoff for the championship of the American League East.

In only the second playoff game in American League history, Jackson rapped out a home run, to lead his team to a 5-4 victory and a repeat appearance in the ALCS. Their opponents were the Kansas City Royals again, and it was October again.

In the years when the championships of the two leagues were decided in best-of-five series instead of the present best-of-seven, the Yankees disposed of the Royals in four games, with Jackson hitting two home runs, driving in six runs and hitting .462.

In the World Series, against the Dodgers again, "Mr. October" gave an encore performance to his 1977 heroics. This time, as the Yankees defeated the Dodgers in six games again, he launched two more home runs, hit .391 and drove in eight runs in what may be baseball's greatest display of pressure hitting in back-to-back post-season performances. His "Dues Collector" was doing just what Jackson had predicted when he reported to spring training the year before.

Things began to change in 1979. There was no "3-peat" for New York. Jackson was hobbled by injuries, Martin returned as manager in mid-season and resumed his feud with Reggie, and Munson was killed on August 2 while piloting his small airplane near his home to Canton, Ohio. The Yankees won eleven fewer games and finished in fourth place in the American League East, 13 and a half games behind the champion Orioles. Through it all, Jackson managed to slug out another 29 homers, drive in 89 runs and finish with a .297 average.

STEINBRENNER CONCEDES

In 1980, the Yankees won their fourth divisional championship in five years, helped in large measure by the highest batting average of Jackson's career—an even .300—and his league-leading total of 41 home runs, plus 111 runs batted in. Steinbrenner, obviously feeling better about his team and his star, said, "It took some time, but Reggie has finally become the leader of the ball club, as I always expected. He understands his role now. The magnitude of being a Yankee has superseded the magnitude of his being Reggie Jackson."

But then the script changed. The Yankees were swept in three games by their post-season rivals, Kansas City. Jackson was not much help. He did not hit a home run or drive in a run.

In '81, the bottom fell out of things for Jackson. The team won the pennant, but Jackson hit only .237 during the season, with 15 home runs and 54 RBIs. The Yankees won the first two games of the Fall Classic at home, but embarrassingly lost four straight to the Dodgers, with the Series ending back at Yankee Stadium. Jackson played in only three games and hit .333 in the Series in 12 at-bats with one bases empty home run. It was his only run batted in.

When Reggie left Yankee Stadium after the loss to the Dodgers, he knew it was the last time he would wear the Yankee pin stripes. He could look back on a five-year run in New York when he owned the town. He led the most famous team in American sports to four pennants and three World Series. He thrilled fans everywhere with his homer heroics, battled the equally controversial Billy Martin and accomplished something in the 1977 World Series, in "the house that Ruth built," that no one has before or since, not even the Babe himself.

Reggie may have described his wild ride in the Big Apple, and his entire career, better than anyone else. "I get booed everywhere," he said. "I might lead the league in home runs and RBIs and still get booed. But I get cheered at the bank. It's 'Mr. Jackson' there."

New York writer Dick Young, who covered the Yankees, offered his own description of the Jackson personality: "Reggie Jax had the most amazing set of ears. Fifty-four thousand people can be at a ball game cheering him, but if one guy calls him a bum, Reggie will hear it, and it will upset Reggie something awful. Reggie wants it to be unanimous. He wants the whole world to love him . . . ."

Hall of Fame Pitcher Jim "Catfish" Hunter, Jackson's teammate both in Oakland and New York, offered this description of Reggie's makeup: "Reggie's really a good guy; down deep he is. I really like him. I always did. He'd give you the shirt off his back. Of course. he'd call a press conference to announce it."

Jackson proved repeatedly that he had a keen understanding of the most powerful medium in American life today—television. Catcher-turned-broadcaster Joe Garagiola witnessed this key to Jackson's success. "Reggie was made for television," he told us in an interview for this chapter. "He probably handled the camera better than anybody I knew."

Garagiola described one example that made a lasting impression on him: "I'll never forget—I had an interview before the Game of the Week with Reggie in Yankee Stadium about the troubles he was having with George (the Yankees' owner, George Steinbrenner). It ran rather long, and our producer said Reggie had to do it shorter so we could run it as he went up to the plate the first time.

"Reggie said he couldn't do it shorter, but to begin running it as he left the dugout and that I should stand in the broadcast booth. When I sat down, that would be the signal for him to step into the box. He said to trust him.

"Well, he did everything you could do—go back for the rosin bag, smooth out the dirt, take his batting glove off and put it on again, swing the bat 5,000 times, you name it. I can't think of another player who would have such command of himself. But he knew the power of television, believe me."

On November 13 the Yankees made Jackson a free agent. In January he returned to California, this time with the Angels, at the age of 36. On his first return to Yankee Stadium, he hit a home run off one of the best lefthanders around at that time, his former teammate, Ron Guidry. As he rounded the bases, the Yankee fans shouted a derisive chant against Jackson's old boss, Steinbrenner.

Reggie's career was clearly on the downhill side. But he could find comfort in many places and forms, including the 120 vintage sports cars he owned. He favored a Rolls Royce and his black Porsche Carrera, the one with the MVP 73 license plates. Years later, most of that collection was destroyed in a fire.

There was still some life left in Jackson's Dues Collector. He swung that famous black bat of his for 39 more home runs in 1982, the fourth and last time he won the league homer title, to lead the Angels into the

American League playoffs. But his bat was almost silent, with only a .111 average, one homer and two RBIs as the Angels lost the playoffs for the American League West championship to the Milwaukee Brewers.

Over the next five years, his homer totals remained consistently respectable—14, 25, 27, 18 and 15—but his batting averages were pathetic—.194, .223, .252, .241 and .220. In 1986, at the age of 40, he still stroked 18 home runs and drove in 58 runs. Then he left the Angels and rejoined the Oakland A's for his swan song, the last of his 21 years in the big leagues.

When he laid down his Dues Collector for the last time, Reggie could look back on a career that included 563 home runs, more than anyone except Hank Aaron, Babe Ruth, Willie Mays, Frank Robinson and Harmon Killebrew, and more than Mickey Mantle, Jimmie Foxx, Ted Williams, Willie McCovey or Joe DiMaggio. Only Ruth and Killebrew hit more homers in the American League, and only Mays and Aaron of the 500 homer hitters stole more bases than Reggie's 228. Only Jackson, Aaron, Mays and Frank Robinson hit more than 500 home runs and stole over 200 bases. And only Mantle and Ruth drove in more runs in the World Series.

It is also recorded that Jackson is the strikeout king of baseball. He has the most strikeouts in history—2,597, compared to 1,330 times for Ruth—the most years (18) with 100 or more strikeouts, and the most consecutive years (13). But, like the mighty Ruth, even a Jackson strikeout was almost as majestic as his home runs.

As controversial as he was, and unpopular too, when it came to acknowledging his greatness, Jackson was given the highest kind of recognition from baseball's writers. They elected him to the Baseball Hall of Fame in his first year of eligibility. With a 75 percent margin of the votes required, Jackson pulled in 93.6 percent, reminding some of another Jacksonian observation about himself: "Sometimes I just can't understand the magnitude of me."

When he was inducted into baseball's hallowed hall in Cooperstown, New York, on August 2, 1993, 37 other Hall of Famers sat behind him as he delivered his induction speech. Jackson said, "I know I wasn't the best. All I have to do is look behind me. But it's nice to know when they have roll call, sooner or later they've got to mention my name."

Despite the controversies, the feuds, the booing and all the other turmoil, Jackson is happy to admit he thoroughly enjoyed his career. "My career was a dream. A fantasy," he said when it was over. "Think about it. Playing for the Yankees, and walking down Fifth Avenue in New York. I had a Rolls Royce. And a girl on each arm. What more could you ask?"

My dad got to see a lot of my games. He would fly to the East Coast cities and toward the end of my career when I Dh'd a lot, he would sit in the clubhouse and watch the game and I could hit and go in and watch the game on television with my Dad and then go back out and hit. He was fading toward the end and died three months after Cooperstown. But he got to be the mayor of Cooperstown for one day when his son was inducted into the Hall of Fame. I really thank God for him being able to live long enough to share that moment with me.

WHAT OTHER PLAYERS SAID ABOUT REGGIE JACKSON

Al Kaline—That was just amazing when he hit those three home runs on three pitches in the World Series. That's one of those highlights you'll see forever, as long as baseball is played.

George Brett—He had the knack of doing something very dramatic. A very exciting guy to play against. He always got his team so excited.

Robin Yount—Reggie had charisma. It seemed every home run he hit was a Hollywood script. He was as exciting a player as you would want to watch. Everyone stopped and watched—he was that type of player. You always had the feeling something was going to happen, be it a home run or a strikeout.

Dave Winfield—He understood the value of promotion. He could promote himself. He was an intelligent guy who didn't mind putting the pressure on himself. He was up to the task. People would come to see Reggie Jackson because he wanted to be at the center of the universe in baseball.

Fergie Jenkins—I thought at one time he would never hit 400 home runs because he swung too hard. I changed speeds, fed him slow curves, changeups, sliders down, brush him back. He hit his first home run off me. He would always say, "I'm going to get you tonight—I'm going to get you tonight." And it just didn't happen because he swung too hard.

Gaylord Perry—If I was a manager, I'd want Reggie Jackson playing for me, because everybody on the team tried to do better than Reggie. If he got two for four, Graig Nettles wanted to get three for four. If he hit two home runs, Chris Chambliss wanted to get three home runs. He got everybody playing trying to beat Reggie.

George Kell—He was so determined. He just intended to hit home runs. He asked me how many home runs I hit. I told him 78, and he said, "How did you get in the Hall of Fame?" I think he figured if he hit enough homers, they would have to put him in the Hall of Fame. He really wanted to be in the Hall of Fame.

Tony Oliva—The only hitter I saw who never had a cheap home run. Every home run was 400 feet or better. He was not a great hitter, but he hit it a long, long way.

Joe Rudi—He always had the ability to raise himself to another level in big games. The every-day, run-of-the-mill average games, I think he lost interest, lost focus. But when it was the Game of the Week, he could rise to the occasion. In his heart, I think he was a performer. I'm close to Reggie, and when you are alone with him, he's just an average guy. But you get him in a group of three-four people or more, and all of a sudden the switch goes on and he becomes the center of attention—the performer. That's just his personality.

Graig Nettles—He was a good teammate. A very hard worker who worked as hard as anybody I ever played with. He took a lot of pressure off his teammates because he liked the spotlight so much. A lot of guys who didn't like the spotlight could just do their job and not worry about the pressure of the press.

Goose Gossage—When the game was on the line, he was a different player. There was a different approach to his at-bat. More intensity. It was just incredible. His practice swings were more precise. The intensity, the whole at-bat was different. Forget the showboating, forget the fans for the moment. He was total concentration on that pitcher. When the game was on the line and he could win it, he was just a different presence at the plate.

Joe Pepitone—A lot of people misunderstood Reggie. He met my wife just one time at the airport about 20 years ago, and 15 years later he comes up one day and says, "How's Stephanie?" He still remembered.

Luis Tiant—He used to like it when I threw my "hesitation pitch." Like I stop, and then release the ball. He used to laugh. He would swing, miss, he looked at me and laughed. He got two home runs against me, but he never hit my hesitation pitch.

Don Zimmer—Even today, if he went up to take batting practice, other players would watch him swing.

Whitey Herzog—He came out with the Reggie candy bar, and you expected the bar to jump right out at you and tell you how great it was. That's the kind of guy he was. But you had to give him credit—he was a hell of a clutch ball player.

Phil Rizzuto—On our trips, he'd get on the plane, and he'd take over the whole plane. He'd talk to everyone. What I like about him was that he knew he was good and could back it up.

George Bamberger—I was with him at Baltimore, and I always thought he was one of the best hitters I ever saw from the seventh inning on. When something meant something, I don't care if it was TV or whatever, he became better.

Chris Chambliss—The thing I remember most about Reggie was the time he was with the Yankees and said that sooner or later they would name a candy bar after him, and one Opening Day they distributed Reggie Bars to everyone, and in his first at-bat he hit a home run, and everybody threw their Reggie Bars onto the field. It was a pretty wild scene.

Leo Durocher—He couldn't shine Willie Mays's shoes. Jackson never hit .300 (yes he did). He's a butcher in the field, and he's got a big mouth. I wouldn't pay him eight dollars a week.

Claudell Washington—I don't think he means to hurt people, but he talks so much, he can't help it.

Bill North—He could carry the team for weeks. In big games, the real big ones, he was cash, money in the bank. He could do some unbelievable things with that bat. If the Brooklyn Dodgers were the Boys of Summer, Reggie Jackson was the Boy in October. Nobody could play better in a big October game than Reggie Jackson.

Ed Lopat—He was such a wonderful young kid, that's what I really liked about him. A gentleman. Soft spoken. Pleasant. Very bright. Very professional. Then Charley Finley started to mess with him, push him, fight with him. It completely changed his personality.

Bobby Winkles—I remember when I was fired as the California manager. The first call I got was from Reggie. He reminded me that life had peaks and valleys. This was one of the valleys. "Go home and stay with your family. They still love you." Imagine a kid counselling me like that.

Catfish Hunter—The difference with the Yankees is guys paid attention to what he said. At Oakland, nobody listened to him. We just watched him hit. Reggie's really a good guy, down deep he is. I really like him. I always did. He'd give you the shirt off his back. Of course, he'd call a press conference to announce it.

Dave Duncan—Some guys didn't like him, sure, but hell, we all knew he could carry the club for a month by himself. Who the hell else could do that? There was only one big home run guy, one big hero. That was Reggie. He was born to the job."

Billy Martin—You know why I kept things stirred up with Reggie? I wanted to help him and the Yankees. I had to motivate him. That's how I did it.

Frank Robinson—Reggie loved the spotlight, that's all there was to it. Reggie was a great promoter of himself. He made it fashionable to stand at the plate and watch your home runs. He'd hit them so high he knew they were gone and he'd stand there and admire them and then trot around the bases. But the pitchers respected him enough not to get angry at him for doing that. The tougher the situation, the better Reggie liked it. That's why he would rise to the occasion in playoff and world series games, cause he loved the spotlight and loved to be on stage. But he was the type of guy who could carry a ballclub for a lot of days and months and he could make his teammates better than they were because he would show them how it was supposed to be done. His teammates would say, if Reggie can do that, if he plays that hard, if he dives for a ball, slides into second base to break up a double play I can do it, too! I think that's what it was. He just made his teammates rougher. And he showed they could still win no matter what the situation. You don't give up until the game is over.

George Steinbrenner—It took some time, but Reggie finally became the leader of the ball club as I always expected. He understood his role. The magnitude of being a Yankee superseded the magnitude of his being Reggie Jackson.

Umpire Don Denkinger—Reggie was a legend in his own mind. His attitude was almost always positive, and he had a great arm from the outfield. And we all know what a "gamer" he was.

Gary Carter—Reggie was a full swinger. He hit the home run or struck out. He was really something. He was the all-or-nothing type of guy.

Jim Palmer—Of all the guys I played with, he played the game as hard as anyone...He had trouble hitting Scottie McGregor, and one night in New York Scottie came in to relieve and Reggie was on deck. He looked over at me...and gave me a wink and pointed to right field like he was going to hit a home run—like Babe Ruth did—and he hits a home run. As he comes around third, he looks at me and I've got a big smile on my face and he just gives me a wink as he trots home with the winning run.

Bill Virdon—He knew when to get them. He knew when to hit them. He hit them in important times.

Harmon Killebrew—Extremely tough in tough situations...That's the thing that impressed me about him the most.

Ernie Banks—Reggie established the "hit a home run and then come back and take a bow" thing. Not that he was a showoff or anything—he just knew the people enjoyed it. The way he swung at the ball, the way he connected, the way he played to the fans was something.

Bert Blyleven—He knew he could strike out, but he also knew if you made a mistake, he could hurt you. One time he hit a breaking ball low and away the other way, and he just lifted it into the stands. You just had to tip your hat to him and say he hit the hell out of a good pitch. He struck out with grace, and he hit home runs with grace.

Joe Altobelli—He was the kind of guy who liked the limelight. He liked to talk. If he could find a listener, he'd talk to you. He liked to talk baseball, but he could talk anything really.

Hank Aaron—Reggie had that magic. He talked a lot, and he said a lot of things, but he backed them up. He struck out a lot, but he played on a lot of championship ball teams. He did some great things. He's easy to like and easy to dislike.

Pete Rose—Reggie was tremendous. Reggie was a promoter for both himself and the team he played for. What I liked about Reggie is that he always promoted baseball. He always tried to sell the game of baseball, not necessarily himself. He always talked very positive about the game of baseball. He was a lot like Banks, but he had a greater platform, being in all those World Series and playoffs.

THE JACKSON FILE

Full Name: Reginald Martinez Jackson.
Date and Place of Birth: May 18, 1946, Wyncote, Pennsylvania.
Nickname: Mr. October.
Position: Right field.
Major League Career: 21 years, 1967-1987
Home Runs: 563 (6th).
Runs Batted In: 1,702.

Runs Scored: 1,551.
Lifetime Batting Average: .262.
Number of Hits: 2,584.
Bases on Balls: 1,375.
Strikeouts: 2.597 (1st).
American League Most Valuable Player: 1973.
World Series Most Valuable Player: 1973 and 1977.

Other Highlights:
— Third most home runs in American League, behind Babe Ruth and Harmon Killebrew, second among lefthanded hitters behind only Ruth.
— American League home run champion four times.
— American League leader in runs batted in once and runs scored twice.
— Led American League in slugging average three times.
— Hit 23 or more home runs 13 years in a row.
— Fifth most World Series home runs (10), third among 500-homer hitters.
— Second highest World Series batting average among 500-homer hitters (.357).
— Third most stolen bases (228) among 500-homer hitters, behind only Willie Mays and Hank Aaron.

Elected to Baseball Hall of Fame: 1993.

5

HARMON KILLEBREW
The Popular Killer

Ask Harmon Killebrew which of his many records he's proudest of and he'll tell you it's being the leading righthanded home run hitter in the history of the American League. Only the lefthanded Babe Ruth hit more baseballs out of American League parks than the still-popular Killebrew, the Hall of Fame slugger they called "Killer."

But Killebrew accomplished more than that. Like champions in all fields, not just athletics, he overcame adversity, and few successful men or women had more of it in their lives than Killebrew—managers who didn't think he'd make it in the Major Leagues, financial problems, family ordeals and three brushes with death.

As a bonus rookie with the Washington Senators in the mid-1950s, the raps against Killebrew were that he couldn't run, he was a defensive liability wherever you played him, and he struck out too much. His early managers with the Senators didn't do much for his confidence. His first skipper, Bucky Harris said, "He throws like a girl." His second, Chuck Dressen, asked, "How can they expect me to win with players like Killebrew?"

When he retired after 22 seasons, Killebrew had helped several managers to win, even if Dressen wasn't one of them, and stood fifth on the all-time home run list, ahead of the next five—Reggie Jackson, Mike Schmidt, Mickey Mantle, Jimmie Foxx and Ted Williams.

ONE SENATOR SCOUTS ANOTHER

After Killebrew's father bought him a baseball glove when the boy was eight years old, the senior Killebrew enjoyed games of catch in the front yard with Harmon and his three older brothers when Dad came home from his job as a house painter. When his mother complained that they were ruining the lawn, Killebrew's father had a ready and convincing answer: "We're not raising grass here—we're raising boys."

Harmon was a 12-letter man and an honor student at Payette High, lettering in football, basketball, baseball and track and winning high school All-American honors as a split-T quarterback. His number 12 was retired when he graduated.

He attracted as much attention in baseball as in football, with a .500 batting average. One of those caught by Killebrew's baseball feats was a Washington Senator, the elected kind, Herman Welker, who represented Idaho in the U.S. Senate and was a family friend. A frequent visitor to Senators' games at Griffith Stadium, Welker tipped off the team's owner, Clark Griffith, about this slugging Idaho boy whose grandfather was considered the strongest man in the Illinois brigade of the Union Army in the Civil War.

Senator Welker had certain credentials of his own as a judge of baseball talent. Only a few years earlier he had tipped off singer Bing Crosby, one of the owners of the Pittsburgh Pirates, about a star lefthanded pitcher back home named Vernon Law, who won 162 games in 16 years with the Pirates in the 1950s and '60s, and Rudy Regalado, who made it to the big leagues as an infielder with the Cleveland Indians in the 1950s.

This was in the era of "bonus babies," when Major League teams signed kids just out of high school for what was then big bucks and jumped them right to the big leagues. Griffith, a 240-game winner as a pitcher in the majors, was usually strapped for money as an owner, but he dispatched his farm director, Ossie Bluege, to Idaho, to scout Killebrew in a local semi-pro league. In his heart, Griffith may have been hoping to strike gold in the same country where another Washington Hall of Famer, the sainted Walter Johnson, was discovered a half-century earlier.

When Killebrew was inducted into the Hall of Fame exactly 30 summers later, he told the crowd at Cooperstown what happened after Bluege landed in Idaho:

"Mr. Bluege flew to Boise," Harmon said, "rented a car and drove 60 miles to Payette. It had rained hard all day, and it didn't look as if the game would be played. We sat in his car, and he asked if I would come to Washington and work out with the Senators. I told him I had already accepted a football and baseball scholarship to Oregon. While we talked, the skies cleared and the townspeople, knowing that a Major League scout was there, hurriedly got the field in order and we played that ball game...

"I happened to hit a ball over the left field fence. No one had ever done that before. Mr. Bluege went out the next morning with a tape measure and measured the drive at 435 feet. It landed in a beet patch."

The teenager slugger went four-for-four that night, but that's not all. Bluege found out he was in a 12-for-12 streak in the three-game series, including four home runs and three triples. He was hitting .857.

In those days before long distance phone calls became commonplace and the world began communicating by faxes and e-mail, Bluege sent a telegram to Griffith saying he couldn't believe what he had seen in this kid, that he had Mantle power and the Senators should offer whatever it might take to sign him.

Griffith authorized a bonus of $30,000, a fortune in those days. Only one other team made an offer, the Boston Red Sox, who offered $6,000 with the explanation that they could send Killebrew to the minor leagues for seasoning. Otherwise, under the rules of the day, if he signed for more than that, the big league team would be required to keep him on its roster for at least two years.

A third team, the Brooklyn Dodgers, was also heard from, sort of. One of their scouts, Bill Smulich, contacted Harmon, then sent him a Christmas card. But all it said was "Merry Christmas."

On June 22, 1954, seven days before his eighteenth birthday, Griffith's big gamble joined the Senators in Chicago during a Midwestern swing. He appeared in his first big league game that day—as a pinch runner, an ironic debut for a player who some said couldn't run. In his next three games, his role remained the same, as a pinch runner.

He got his first start two months later and jumped all over the opportunity with three hits and two runs batted in against the A's in Philadelphia. For his rookie season, he played in nine games as a second baseman, pinch hitter and pinch runner, finishing with four hits in 13 at-bats for a .308 batting average.

THAT FIRST HOME RUN – THANK YOU

His first home run didn't come until his second season, 1955, and then it was thanks in part to the charity—some would call it the foolishness—of catcher Frank House of the Detroit Tigers.

In a game at Griffith Stadium, Killebrew stepped into the batter's box to face lefthander Billy Hoeft with the Tigers pounding the Senators, 13-0. House told him, "We're going to give you a fast ball, kid." He wasn't kidding, and neither was Killebrew, who hit that fast ball over the left center field fence, 420 feet away and 24 rows into the bleachers.

As he crossed home plate, House said to him, "That's the last time we'll tell you what's coming, kid."

After a few more home runs and reassignment to the Senators' minor league team in Charlotte, North Carolina, following his two years on the Washington roster, Killebrew appeared ready to make it in the majors as the 1957 season began. He had raised eyebrows and hopes at Charlotte with 15 home runs and 63 runs batted in just 70 games, plus a .325 average.

Things kept coming his way in the first nine games of the season —two home runs and five runs batted in—but then came the surprise of his young life. While sitting on the team bus after a series in Detroit, en route to a series in Cleveland, the team's traveling secretary, Howie Fox, was called off the bus to take an important phone call.

When he reboarded the bus, it was Fox's unpleasant duty to tell Killebrew he was being farmed out again, this time to the Senators' top farm team, the Chattanooga Lookouts in the Southern Association. It was raining and Killebrew, still only 20 years old, decided to walk to the train station instead of trying to hail a cab. His teammates on the bus watched the sad sight, the kid walking in the rain, carrying a suitcase as he walked up a hill, shocked to be heading back to the minors, all alone after such an encouraging start.

At Chattanooga, Harmon did what he did so often later in his career and in his life—he fought back. He tore up the Southern Association by leading the league in home runs with 29, drove in 101 runs and hit for a .279 average.

But things went south for him again, figuratively if not geographically, in 1958 after the Senators promoted him from Chattanooga at the Double-A level to Indianapolis in the fast American Association, a Triple-A league, the highest level of the minor leagues.

He never got untracked there. In 38 games, he hit only two home runs and showed an anemic .215 average. He was demoted back to Chattanooga. He staged another of his many comebacks with the Lookouts, clubbing 17 home runs and driving in 54 runs in only 86 games. His batting average attracted attention, too—.308.

What followed in 1959 was one of the greatest turnarounds in any sport.

Clark Griffith died in 1955, the year after he signed Killebrew, and Senator Welker passed away the following year. Griffith's nephew, Calvin Griffith, succeeded him as president of the Senators. He made a decision before the '59 season that proved fateful in Killebrew's career.

Griffith was tired of the Senators' hapless performances as one of the worst teams in either league. In Killebrew's five years, the Senators finished sixth once, seventh another time and last three times. But he thought that two of the young players on his team, Killebrew and outfielder Bob Allison, who joined the Senators as a rookie in 11 games in '58, could lead Washington out of the depths and into better times.

He ordered his manager, Cookie Lavagetto, to put Killebrew and Allison into the starting lineup and leave them there. He promised Lavagetto he would stand behind him if the two flopped and the fans and media began complaining.

Lavagetto followed orders, but not without reservations. Word got back to Killebrew that Lavagetto confided to at least one insider, "The two of them together aren't worth a bucket of warm spit."

SECONDING THE MOTION

Killebrew, as if to second Griffith's motion, hit a home run on Opening Day. Going into May he was hitting only .225, but then he exploded for two home runs in one game and did the same thing the next day. In 17 days he connected twice in a game five times. By the end of May, he had walloped 18 homers. By mid-season, he was leading both leagues.

Shirley Povich of *The Washington Post* wrote: "It is not necessary to measure him in terms of a threat to Babe Ruth's record of 60. If he fails that goal, he will still be a considerable personality."

Povich went on: "This lad has been an exciting ballplayer. He doesn't have to break Ruth's record or come very close to give Washington fans a remarkable show. He has done that already. Those muscles have been exciting. He doesn't have to hit the ball on the nose to get a home run. Just a piece of it is often sufficient. It may be said simply that Harmon gives Washington fans a lot to look forward to."

His torrid pace was attracting attention everywhere, including the White House. President Eisenhower, a frequent fan at Griffith Stadium, asked and got to meet Killebrew. His fame was spreading to the other league as well. The Cincinnati Reds offered Griffith $500,000, a staggering sum in 1959, but Griffith answered, "You can't play $500,000 at third base."

Pitchers resorted to their time-honored practice of throwing at him, the hallmark of respect for a hitter. When Frank Lary of the Tigers did it, Killebrew got up out of the dirt, dusted off his uniform and hit Lary's next pitch for a three-run homer to win the game.

Killebrew, now feared around the league and known as "Killer," hit his 42nd home run on the last day of the season to tie Cleveland's Rocky Colavito for the American League home run championship, the first of six titles for Killebrew. He finished second in the league in total bases and third in runs batted in. He also walked 90 times, another compliment from the pitchers.

Allison became the American League Rookie of the Year with 30 home runs of his own. Another outfielder, Jim Lemon, hit 33, and outfielder-first baseman Roy Sievers connected for 21. Still, the Senators finished last again.

Killebrew's homers continued in 1960, with 31 of them, 80 RBIs and a respectable .276 batting average. Lemon bombed away for 38 homers and 100 RBIs and the Senators, lo and behold, finished fifth in the eight-team league.

But the team wasn't the big news in 1960—the front office was. After writing in a by-lined article in the *Washington Post* the day before Opening Day that "the Washington Senators will never leave Washington in my lifetime," they did. Calvin Griffith did what Clark Griffith never would have done—he moved the team to Minnesota after being thwarted in earlier attempts to move to California before the Giants and Dodgers.

Killebrew, who maintains that Washington's fans had their teams "stolen" from them twice, the second time by owner Bob Short, benefited from the move. No longer would he have to clear the distant fences at Griffith Stadium, one of baseball's biggest parks, where the left field wall in many seasons was more than 400 feet from home plate. Pitcher Mickey McDermott described the cavernous distances when the Senators acquired him in a trade with the Red Sox. "I'm going to love pitching in Griffith Stadium," he said. "From home plate to the left field wall is a three-dollar cab fare."

"Killer" celebrated his arrival in the land of 10,000 lakes in 1961 with 46 home runs and 122 runs batted in and the best batting average of his big league career, .288. He was overlooked somewhat, however, because Roger Maris and Mickey Mantle maintained a season-long assault on Babe Ruth's record of 60 home runs in one season, with Maris breaking it in the last game of the season.

Despite his production, Killebrew's team—the Twins, as in "Twin Cities" of Minneapolis and St. Paul—finished in seventh place in the expanded 10-team American League, two places ahead of an expansion team in Washington, the new Senators, who tied with the Kansas City A's for ninth place.

The Twins finished that low only one other time in Harmon's remaining 13 years with them. They finished in the first division ten times while winning three divisional championships and one American League pennant.

Killebrew made another move in 1962, not to a new city but to a new position, left field, his third position in three seasons. That didn't stop him. He established himself firmly as a superstar by leading the league with 48 home runs, 126 runs batted in, 126 runs scored and a home run average of one every 11.5 times at bat. The Twins vaulted from seventh to second place.

Attendance in Minnesota jumped to a million and a half. Killebrew was exciting more than just the fans in the Twin Cities. On the road, his drawing power nearly equalled that of Mickey Mantle as fans flocked to every American League ballpark to see baseball's newest power star.

Killebrew continued his assault on American League pitching with 45 home runs in 1963 and reached his personal high in '64 with 49. He equalled Ruth by leading the league with 40 or more homers for three straight seasons. Without Maris and Mantle's league-leading totals in 1961, Killebrew would have become the only hitter to lead the league with 40 or more homers for four straight seasons.

People were talking about Killebrew, and not just the fans. Respected veterans with the knowledge and wisdom accumulated over decades in baseball were hailing his feats. The veteran manager, Paul Richards, quipped, "Harmon Killebrew could hit the ball out of Yellowstone Park."

CHUCK DRESSEN AGAIN

Chuck Dressen, the same Chuck Dressen who said he would have trouble winning with young players like Killebrew, said later, "He hits home runs like Babe Ruth. The two hit fly balls so high they didn't look like they would go out of the park, but the ball just carried and carried and carried—over the fence . . . .The outfielder always started back to the fence because a ball hit so high couldn't possibly go that far."

Killebrew had his own thoughts on hitting. He told an interviewer, "I'm not so sure that ballplayers who are called natural hitters really are natural hitters. Hitting is not something a person learns to do and then never forgets, like riding a bicycle. Instead, it's a constant challenge . . . Nobody does this consistently well without working at it all the time. Making contact with the baseball is something I think about constantly. The game of baseball is a child's game against a demanding background of higher competition. It's adults' work—a job."

He has always disagreed with that age-old advice, "Just meet the ball." He says he tries to do that, but he also tries to hit the ball hard. "You try to hit the ball hard," he says, "and the home runs will take care of themselves."

Johnny Sain, winner of 139 games and a pitcher in four World Series, hopped on the Killebrew bandwagon, too. "You don't challenge him right away," said Sain, who later became a big league pitching coach. "You must constantly change pitches. You try to finesse him—anything to upset his timing."

Hall of Famer Al Lopez, catcher and manager, saw Killebrew's improvement. "It used to be you could count on him to strike out on a bad pitch. Not any more."

He made a believer out of righthander Milt Pappas of the Orioles, too. On May 24, 1964, he hit a 471-foot drive over the hedge in left center in Baltimore's Memorial Stadium, one of the longest in its history.

In 1965, with Lyndon Johnson serving the first year of his new term as president and the national debate over America's presence in Viet Nam growing louder, the Twins staged one of baseball's greatest turnarounds. After winning only 79 games in '64 and finishing 20 games behind the Yankees in a tie for sixth place, they won the franchise's first pennant since the Washington Senators in 1933. They topped the magic 100-win mark with 102 victories.

For Killebrew, the season was a bittersweet experience, filled with both accomplishment and disappointment. He delivered one of the key hits of the entire season on July 11, a home run to beat the Yankees in the bottom of the ninth to give his team a five-game lead over New York. Many observers said later that Killebrew's pressure blow broke the Yankees' spirit and was the deciding moment in the race to win a World Series berth.

Two days later, Killebrew thrilled Twins fans again with a two-run homer before the hometown faithful as the National League defeated the American, 6-5, in the All-Star game in Minneapolis.

Everything was pointing toward another 40-homer season when Killebrew injured himself while playing first base on August 2. He was stretching for a throw from third baseman Rich Rollins when he collided with Baltimore's Russ Snyder and dislocated his left elbow. He missed the next 48 games.

Killebrew returned to the lineup in time for the Twins' stretch drive to the pennant as Minnesota beat out the White Sox by seven games. Even though he missed one-third of the season, Killebrew still managed to post 25 home runs and drive in 75 runs. In the only World Series of his career, while still feeling the effects of his injury, Killebrew nevertheless hit .286 in the seven games as the Dodgers beat the Twins. He had one extra base hit—a home run.

Another member of the 500-homer club, Frank Robinson, joined the Baltimore Orioles in 1966 and personally took charge of his new team's drive to win the pennant and the World Series. He won the Triple Crown by leading the league in home runs, runs batted in and batting average and was a key factor as the Orioles swept the favored Dodgers in four games.

That didn't take anything away from Killebrew's year in '66. He hit 39 more homers, drove in 110 runs and hit .281, then topped that in '67 by leading the league in home runs in '67 with 49. He also led the league in walks. The Twins tied Detroit for second place, only one game behind the Boston Red Sox.

His Hall of Fame career almost came to an abrupt halt in 1968 as a result of a freak injury during the All-Star game in Houston. With 17 homers and 40 RBIs already in the book for '68, he slipped on the slick artificial turf in the Astrodome and ruptured his left medial hamstring muscle. The Twins' team doctor called it the worst injury he had seen in ten years.

While others feared an early end to a brilliant career, Killebrew was putting himself through seven months of rigorous rehabilitation. By the start of spring training for the 1969 season, he was still in considerable discomfort but he worked his way back into the starting lineup by Opening Day.

NO. 500—AND COMMEMORATIVE MUGS

His reward was what is now called "a career year," his best ever. With 49 homers and 140 runs batted in, he led the Major Leagues in both categories while hitting .276. His home run total matched his personal high mark, and his RBIs broke the team record. He accomplished all this while also leading the league in walks with 145, 20 of them intentional.

It came as no surprise, then, when he was voted the American League's Most Valuable Player by both the baseball writers and *The Sporting News.*

The Twins lost to the Orioles in history's first American League Championship Series, but Killebrew could look back on that banner season and remember other accomplishments as well. One was finishing only one home run short of becoming one of the few sluggers to that time to hit 50 or more home runs in one season.

After the season, he remembered the last game: "The funny thing was that I had more good pitches to hit than I'd seen in a long time. I just got under the ball too much."

Another, maybe more meaningful, memory was knowing that he drove in the winning run in 20 games. "I could cut my strikeouts a lot more," he said, "and maybe draw more walks, but I think I help the club more by swinging. You've got to swing to make contact. The way I feel is to take a good rip."

He found some baseball "cousins" in Oakland in 1970, when he hit .435 against the A's while leading the Twins in 13 wins in 18 games. His production included eleven home runs and 34 RBIs, prompting Reggie Jackson to remark, "If Harmon Killebrew isn't this league's number one player, I've never seen one. He's one of the greatest of all time."

There was another note of personal satisfaction to Killebrew that year. Even with bruised ribs, a pulled muscle, a banged-up knee and a swollen arm and elbow, he never missed a game.

His Hall of Fame career reached another high point in 1971 with his 500th home run, making him only the tenth slugger in the game's history to reach that level by that point. A month after winning his last All-Star game with a two-run homer, "Killer" got his memorable hit on August 10 off Baltimore's Mike Cuellar, under even more pressure than might be expected.

After he hit No. 498, the Twins, never passing up a promotional opportunity, announced that commemorative mugs would be given to fans attending the Twins' game against the Angels on July 6, confident Killebrew would hit his 500th by then. But they didn't reckon with the injury bug. He sprained his right big toe, missed some games and couldn't swing well when he was in the lineup. It took him more than a month to reach 500.

After he did, he said, "I didn't feel much pressure, if that's what you want to call it, until they passed out those mugs. Then it seemed everyone started asking about it and talking about it, and I tried a little harder to hit it."

When he did, on one of Cuellar's famous slow curves, the 15,881 fans rose for a standing ovation. Third Base Coach Frank Crosetti escorted him down the line toward home plate.

Killebrew expressed his gratitude the best way he knew how—with another home run off Cuellar later in the same game, this time on a fast ball.

When he returned to the clubhouse after the game, he found a path of white towels leading from the door to his locker. On one side was a bottle of grape juice in a bucket of ice and a champagne glass, a congratulatory gesture from Calvin Griffith.

After hitting only five home runs in 1973 during an injury-plagued season and connecting for only 13 in '74, Killebrew, now 38 years old and a Major League player for 21 seasons, was given his choice by Griffith. He could stay with the Twins as a coach and batting instructor, manage Minnesota's Triple-A team at Tacoma or take his release. Harmon took his release and signed with the Kansas City Royals, where he hit 14 more home runs but recorded a batting average of only .199. He retired following the 1975 season.

WHEN LIFE GETS HARD

Killebrew's election to the Hall of Fame in 1984 was the brightest spot in his after-baseball life, but the '80s were often painful for Killebrew, who remains one of baseball's most popular players to this day, with fans, players, the media and everyone else.

From 1976 through 1988, Killebrew was an announcer on the broadcasts of the Angels, A's and Twins games while also operating an insurance business and a car dealership back in Idaho. In 1982, personal tragedy struck when his son, Ken, the second of his five children, was arrested for robbing a bank.

Another bombshell exploded in Killebrew's life only two years later when the *Minneapolis Star-Tribune* reported that he was more than $700,000 in debt because of bad investments and personal debts.

On the heels of such steep financial setbacks, Killebrew developed lung and stomach problems and underwent major surgery three times. He was confined to a wheel chair for a time.

Killebrew explained his plight to the *Star Tribune*: "In baseball, you pack your uniform in the clubhouse after a ball game and you see it hanging up in you locker when you get to your next city. You pack your bag and your bag gets in your room when you get to the hotel. They pay for your meals, your hotel. When you're out there on your own, it's a different situation."

He admitted, "It's been a living hell. You have a lot of those days when you feel you're at the bottom. You get to feeling that sometimes you're out there by yourself. I don't feel anger—more frustration and sadness. Loneliness is another one. Stressful? That's an understatement."

With his finances back in order and his health restored, Killebrew is enjoying life in his sixties, one of the most sought stars at baseball card shows and in his other personal appearances and still one of the most respected figures associated with baseball.

"He's one of the real gentlemen in baseball," according to fellow Hall of Famer Early Wynn, a former teammate and opponent. "He is a big help just being on the team with his attitude and leadership. He's simply one of the great ones."

Killebrew himself seemed to describe his career and his life perfectly in a comment to Steve Simmons of the *Toronto Sun* in 1990: "I struck out a lot—1,699 times. And I always bounced back."

KILLEBREW ON KILLEBREW

Hitting over 500 home runs means more to me now than it did at the time, because now they're making a big deal about it. It's a real exclusive club. The way things are today, there may never be another one. Who knows? I just feel honored to be a part of that group of guys.

Most guys are high fast ball hitters, but when I came up, I was a low fast ball hitter. I had to learn to hit the high ball and then most breaking pitches eventually. I think the best advice I got that helped me a lot was from Ralph Kiner. As a youngster, I hit the ball all over the park, and then I developed into a guy who had some power. And I was talking to Ralph when I was about 18, and he said, "Kid, it looks like you're going to have a lot of power, but to hit home runs, you're going to have to learn to pull the ball." You have to remember—I was just a kid.

He suggested I move up a little at the plate and work at pulling the ball. So I tried it, and I guess it worked out pretty well. The most important thing I had going for me at the plate was patience. I learned to develop a pretty good strike zone, and I learned to put the pressure on the pitcher more than on myself.

The toughest guy I ever faced was Stu Miller. I couldn't hit him. I got two hits in five years off him. The good pitchers always tried to challenge you. Any pitcher who is great is going to give you his best pitch and try to throw strikes. If I had the choice of having the most home runs or driving in the most runs, I would take the latter. Home runs drive in runs, but RBIs win games. They always talk about the guys who hit the home runs, but to me, driving in runs is easily more important.

On the road, I was an old movie buff and liked to watch television. I tried to stay away from superstitions. In fact, I asked Hank Greenberg about that one time, and he joked and said his only superstition was that every time he hit a ball out of a ballpark, he made sure to touch each base.

I decided to retire when my knees got so bad. I just couldn't play any more because of them. My hobbies are cooking and playing golf. I'm involved in a hospice program and visiting a lot of terminally ill people. It's heartwarming to work with the nurses, who are the real care-givers. I've been doing that for quite a while, and it's a heartwarming experience.

WHAT OTHER PLAYERS SAID ABOUT HARMON KILLEBREW

Rollie Fingers—Harmon Killebrew gave me more fits than anyone. He was a fast ball hitter and had a short, quick stroke. He could turn real quick and was strong enough to hit it out. In 1969, I was a rookie, just a young kid, and I kept trying to run fast balls in on his hands, and he just kept hitting them. In his first nine at-bats against me, he hit four homers, two doubles and a single. I finally figured out I'd better either pitch him out and away or, maybe even better, walk him.

Al Kaline—I'll never forget the day he broke in at Tiger Stadium. I went out early to watch Harmon hit, and boy, I saw him pounding the ball into the right field seats. And he was a righthanded hitter. In those days, power hitters didn't go to the opposite field like they do now. He had one of the greatest strokes in all of baseball. He had one of the shortest, quickest swings you would want to see for a power hitter . . . . Unfortunately he couldn't run or he would have been a .300 hitter as well as a 40-home run guy every year.

George Brett—His home runs were always so high. And he used a real small bat. Every home run I ever saw him hit just went a mile up in the air.

Robin Yount—What I remember of Harmon was just raw, strong-as-a-bull power. I always wondered how many home runs he would have hit in Fenway Park . . . .The power he had—wow!

Dave Winfield—When I was a kid, he was one of the guys I would imitate. Arms straight back and his bat straight up. The classic power swing. And he wasn't that big a guy.

Birdie Tebbetts—He hit a ball so damn far it was unbelievable. And in the early years he played half his games in Washington. The only guy who could hit in that park like he did was Mantle.

Mickey Vernon—I was there in Washington when we all watched this 17-year-old kid take batting practice for the first time. He hit some balls half way up the bleachers. We were all amazed at a young kid with such power.

Steve Garvey—I saw him as a kid and tried to pattern myself after him. He put the bat flat on his shoulder, lifted it up and swung. I tell kids, "You don't have to take the big swing. Just turn the shoulder like he did."

Brooks Robinson—His home runs were spectacular. He hit 70 against us, and I got tired of seeing him run around third base. He had the nicest, sweetest stroke you would want to see for a home run hitter. He just rested his bat on his shoulder, just took it back and—WHAM! No extra motion, no hitch or anything. He just muscled it out.

Enos Slaughter—Funny how pitchers kept throwing where he was hitting.

Gaylord Perry—Pitchers just kept challenging him. Most didn't realize he was a tremendous off-speed hitter. You try to curve him and make him look bad and he would hit a home run.

George Kell—The most determined player I ever saw. He could hit with anybody. He hit the most towering home runs I ever saw. He seemed like Babe Ruth—they (his home runs) would never come down. But they did—in the seats.

Hal Newhouser—Nobody ever hit a ball over the left field wall in Detroit, you know, because it's got two decks there. I was scouting and sitting with the umpires before a game and one said, "Hal, look at that guy. This is the new power hitter in the Major Leagues—a guy named Killebrew. He really has some kind of power. If anybody is going to hit a ball out of this park, it's going to be Killebrew." I sort of laughed and said to myself, "I don't think anybody can do it." By gosh, about the sixth or seventh inning he hit one over the roof.

Mel Parnell—Harmon had a little bit of an upward stroke. And making contact, he would get backspin on the ball and it would really carry. He always seemed to get the bottom part of the ball, and for that reason got the spin that carried the ball much farther.

Milt Pappas—Harmon was a mistake hitter…. Making a mistake to Harmon Killebrew was death. The last one he hit off me was a dandy. He dropped his bat and watched it sail out of the park. As he was rounding the bases, I told him if he ever did that again and tried to show me up, I would drill him. The next time up, I drilled him.

Lew Burdette—I was practicing my knuckleball, trying to come up with a new pitch. And I threw Harmon one. He swung and missed. So I threw him another one. The wind was blowing out and he hit a towering fly ball. It was one where they painted the seat and put a plaque on it. You should have heard Jack Sanford. He was cracking up in the dugout. He yelled, "Nice going, Lew—you just gave up the longest homer in the history of the park." The next day Harmon hit one off Sanford in the upper deck just three rows below mine. I wish I could tell you what I told him!"

Tony Oliva —A real gentleman, He was so good a home run hitter it was unbelievable. Every year he smashed the ball. The pitchers would be so careful of him, but if they missed, it was goodbye. Forget it, it was going.

Jim Piersall—One thing about Killebrew—he was a wonderful guy, a class guy, and he still is. He wasn't an exciting player, but he was an exciting hitter.

John Blanchard—He was a hell of a guy. To know him was to like him. And, boy, did he have power! Holy cow! A nice guy, but when he put that uniform on, he was dead serious.

Mudcat Grant—When I was traded to the Twins, it was like going to heaven because I knew he was going to hit a lot of home runs, some with men on, and he was going to put some runs up on the scoreboard for me. It sure gave me an advantage when the game was tight and he was up at the plate.

Hank Bauer—When Harmon came up, he had trouble hitting Bob Turley. Turley would throw him nothing but high fast balls, and Harmon would chase them. Eventually, he didn't chase them. He was known as a pure power hitter. I didn't think Harmon was a good hitter, but he was a damn good power hitter.

Chuck Tanner—He was like a bull in the ring. You'd look at him and figure just get the ball up and in on him. And that rascal, he would just outmuscle you. He hit a ball as hard as anyone could hit a ball.

Walt Dropo—He had that uppercut swing like Ralph Kiner. A classic home run hitter. He had that swing that put that ball high in the air and it carried a long distance.

Tony Kubek—What needs to be said other than he hit more home runs from the right side than anyone in the history of the American League?

Graig Nettles—I played with Harmon. He was a classy guy who really treated the rookies great. That's the thing I remember the most about him.

Sal Bando—Harmon wore us out at Oakland. He hit everything we threw up there, and after a while we just started pitching around him. He was a money player and the key to whatever success the Twins had.

Tommy John—After he hit five home runs off me, I decided that most of the time I would walk him and take a chance on Tony Oliva. There aren't many guys who would say that, but that's the respect I had for Harmon Killebrew.

Clete Boyer—He didn't have God-given ability. He wasn't a good fielder. He wasn't fast, but he was best under pressure .... He just kept beating you. People had to see him to believe him. He couldn't go from first to third or second to home and never made outstanding plays, but he beat you. You'd look up and Killebrew's got four RBIs ...

Jim Lonborg—Harmon was probably the best fast ball mistake hitter I ever saw.

Ryne Duren—He remembers me every time the weather changes. I hit him in the elbow and dislocated it. He hit two off me in Minneapolis in one game—one of them almost went out of old Met Stadium.

Goose Gossage—He's the ultimate professional, the consummate pro. If you wanted to pattern yourself and conduct yourself (like a real professional), you could try to emulate Harmon. He was a very humble person. I didn't pitch to him in his prime, but he still struck the fear of God in you.

Bill Freehan—When you made a mistake, someone got a souvenir. If you didn't get the pitch where you wanted it or hung a breaking ball, sayonara. No one hits good breaking balls—it's the mistake breaking balls you hit. Harmon got better and better at it, especially the ones that hung a little bit. They became history, too.

Don Zimmer—He had great strength. He just overpowered the ball. One of the nicest guys in the whole world.

Stan Musial—He would have hit more if he hadn't played his early years in that big Washington ballpark.

Whitey Ford—The first time I saw Harmon I was pitching in the old ballpark in Washington and the score was 0-0 after 13 innings and we got a run in the fourteenth. In the bottom of the fourteenth, I was still pitching. I got two out and here comes this young kid—he couldn't have been more than 19 or 20, and I get behind him 2-0 and I threw him a fast ball down the middle. He hit a shot straight up in the air. If he had hit it a quarter-inch up on the bat, it would have been gone. I said, "Who the hell is that?"

Whitey Herzog—A Mark McGwire type of guy. When he hit a ball, it would go sky-ing and just carry. Just a raw power guy. He made a lot of his abilities. He worked hard at his game.

Charlie Maxwell—I saw a lot of him, and any home run he hit, there was no cheap one. He was so powerful he could hit them anywhere.

Phil Rizzuto—Oh, he was great. I remember when he came up with Washington. I felt so sorry for the kid because he was a little overmatched. But man, when he would hit the ball! He had arms like Dick Butkus.

Dick Radatz—When he came to the big leagues, he was a low-ball hitter. I think he had such a diet of high fast balls that he became a pretty good high ball hitter. He was one of the strongest players I ever saw play the game. Harmon was not a wrist hitter. He was more of a sweep hitter. His wrists didn't break much—he more or less muscled the ball out of the ballpark.

Randy Hundley—What a great guy he is. Just a great person. You're talking about someone with a short, quick swing. And I mean the ball just jumped off his bat.

U.S. Senator Jim Bunning—When he came into the league, he was a low fast ball hitter, so he was easy to pitch to. Then all of a sudden, when he started hitting all those home runs, where we were pitching him became his power. We started pitching him up, and he started hitting that pitch. After that, it seemed we didn't know what to do with him. He made himself a great hitter because he overcame his weaknesses. Somebody taught him how to hit the high fastball.

Ken Sanders—I played with him, and he has always been one of the nicest human beings you could ever meet. He wasn't very big, but he had that patented home run swing. If you got the pitch in the middle of the plate inside, forget it. It was gone.

Ralph Houk—Killebrew was just an unbelievable power hitter. He was just a great hitter and beat our club many a time.

Elmer Valo—I played with him in Washington and Minnesota. The ball just jumped off his bat. And he was so consistent.

Boog Powell—Killer was the most favorite opponent I played against. The absolute nicest man, the finest gentleman I think I ever met on or off the field—he and Brooks Robinson. Killer never had anything bad to say about anybody. He hit the highest home runs I ever saw. He took Jim

Palmer over the hedge in Baltimore one day, about 460-470 feet, one of the damndest shots I ever saw. With the game on the line, I hated to see him up there. One of the nicest things that happened to me in baseball was after the '69 season. I had a heck of a year but Harmon was the MVP. The next year, on the first day of spring training, Harmon came to me and told me I probably should have won it. Which is really a pretty cool thing to say. Then I won it that year.

Dick Williams—I remember—it was the last game of the season, and I was managing Boston and Harmon was one home run behind Carl Yastrzemski. Jim Lonborg had a pretty good lead and I went out to the mound and told him not to walk anyone, to play it safe. Well, he did. He threw one in there on a 3-2 pitch, and Harmon hit it nine miles to tie Carl. I'll take the responsibility for that.

Sam Mele—He was a complete gentleman, and a hell of a ballplayer. He was a better fielder than people think. His first moves were pretty quick for a guy his size. He could play third or first base and had good hands. And he was a threat to hit any ball out of any ballpark. None of them could hold him.

Eddie Yost—I was traded from Washington because Harmon was ready to come up and take my place at third. That's when I went to Detroit. A wonderful guy. Strong upper body and strong arms. A nice compact swing. He could hit the ball a mile.

Jim Palmer—Dave Boswell was with the Twins, and he hurt his arm and came to us. And he came in one night and it's a tie ball game, and he gets two quick strikes on Harmon, and he looks over at Brooks Robinson and says, "Double heat" —you know, a really good fast ball—and he threw him a good fast ball, and Harmon hits it into the upper deck in left field.

Bert Blyleven—It was a thrill for me as a rookie to be on the same team with Harmon, the classiest guy I ever met, along with Willie Stargell. He had that short, compact swing that could lift a ball out of any ballpark. It was great pitching and knowing that, with him in the lineup, you just tried to hold them to a run or two, knowing Harmon could get that many with just one swing.

Hank Aaron—I didn't see that much of him, but he was probably the greatest threat to hit a home run of anyone in my era. They talk about Mark McGwire, but I don't think he could hit a ball farther than Harmon Killebrew. They painted a lot of seats in ballparks because of him. When he hit them, they were gone.

THE KILLEBREW FILE

Full Name: Harmon Clayton Killebrew, Jr.

Date and Place of Birth: June 29, 1936, Payette, Idaho.

Nickname: "Killer"

Positions: First Base, Second Base, Third Base, Left Field, Designated Hitter.

Major League Career: 22 years, 1954-1975.

Home Runs: 573 (5th).

Runs Batted In: 1,584.

Runs Scored: 1,283.

Lifetime Batting Average: .256.

Number of Hits: 2,086.

Walks: 1,559.

Strikeouts: 1,699 (10th).

Records:

— Leading righthanded home run hitter in American League history.

— Second leading home run hitter in American League history, behind only Babe Ruth.

— Third on all-time list of home run percentage per times at bat, behind only Ruth and Ralph Kiner.

Other Highlights:

— Voted American League's Most Valuable Player in 1969.

— Named to American League All-Star team thirteen times.

— Led American League in home runs six times.

— Led American League in runs batted in three times.

— Hit 40 or more home runs eight times.

— Led American League in walks four times.

6

MICKEY MANTLE

Never Only One

When you conduct exhaustive research on the life of Mickey Mantle going back over all of his 63 years and interview 65 former Major League baseball teammates and opponents, you learn there was never only one Mickey Mantle.

There was the Mantle the fans cheered, and the one they booed, the one they felt sorry for because of his injuries, and the one they criticized when he was declared 4-F—physically unfit for Army duty—during the Korean War. There was the one who appeared to be the picture of health, and the one who was haunted by the knowledge that his father, his grandfather, his father's two brothers and his own son all died before their 40th birthdays.

There was the one with the captivating smile, and the one with the ferocious temper. There was the one who drank too much for too long, and the one who checked himself into the Betty Ford Clinic for treatment. And, in the merger of all these dimensions, there was the Mickey Mantle who died a national hero.

SPECIAL MEMORIES

When one of his closest teammates, First Baseman Moose Skowron, was interviewed for this book, the memories came back, special ones. "Not long ago," he said, "when I was going through my double bypass, he called me up every day. Every day. He called me the day I was operated on and said, 'Moose, I love you' .... He called me up every day after the operation.

"I got home. He called me and said, 'Boy, you really sound good.' I said I felt great, and he said, 'All those guys who sound good die two days later.' I told him not to make me laugh or the stitches will break open. He called me every day to see how I was doing. I'll never forget him .... He did a lot of things for his teammates. That's one thing—he never forgot where he came from. He never forgot his teammates."

Opponents voiced the same kind of admiration for Mantle, the star. Infielder Rico Petrocelli, who hit 210 home runs for the Red Sox, said, "He was my idol. I was in awe of Mickey Mantle .... There was just something about Mickey Mantle—a mystique about him that will last forever. When you talk about legends, you can put him up there with Babe Ruth, Ted Williams and those people."

His teammate and drinking partner, Whitey Ford, remembered Mantle's leadership role—and his temper. "He was really the leader of our team," Ford said. "He was quiet and didn't like to hear that, but the guys really felt like he was the leader .... He had a terrible temper. He'd kick water coolers, tip them over, break bats, and he never really got over it."

Ralph Houk, Mantle's manager with the Yankees beginning in 1961 after Casey Stengel was fired, called him "the best player I ever managed." Houk agreed with Ford about Mantle's leadership role. "He was the leader of our club," Houk said flatly.

He also wanted to set the record straight about Mantle's drinking. "He didn't drink as much as people said he did while he was playing," Houk said. "That mostly happened while he was out of baseball. There's a lot of stories, and he never denied them. He was such a humble-type person. He couldn't have done the things he did if he had drunk like some people seemed to think he did. You'd like to have him as your son. He was just that kind of guy. He gave you 125 percent every day he went on the field."

MUTT AND MICKEY

Mickey Mantle became a baseball player because of his exceptional talents, and because the main goal in life for his father was to see Mickey make it to the big leagues. He even named his son after his own favorite player, Hall of Fame Catcher Mickey Cochrane of the Detroit Tigers.

The father, "Mutt" Mantle, a former semi-pro player, introduced his son to baseball when the boy was still in the toddler stage in Spavinaw, population 300, in the upper righthand corner of Oklahoma about 40 miles northwest of Tulsa. When Mickey was four, the family moved to Commerce, another 40 miles northwest, touching the borders of Kansas and Missouri, where Mutt worked in the town's lead and zinc mines.

From the beginning, Mutt taught Mickey, a natural righthander, how to hit from both sides of the plate. The result: One of the most prolific switcher-hitters in the history of baseball, with Eddie Murray and Pete Rose.

THE INJURIES BEGIN

Mantle began his baseball life as a 10-year-old Pee Wee League catcher weighing under 100 pounds. But the boy was soon switched to shortstop—sporting a new Marty Marion glove that cost his father $22, almost a third of his week's pay. As he grew older, Mickey expanded his horizon and began playing basketball and football, a prospect which held no appeal for his father because of the possibility of injury.

Mutt's worst fears exploded into reality in Mickey's high school football career, when a vicious hit to his left shin caused osteomyelitis, a dangerous cancer of the bone marrow. The doctors spoke darkly of amputation. But two weeks of penicillin shots worked a miracle, one that was repeated four times over the next two years. During each flare-up, the young star athlete was hospitalized for two weeks.

The injury haunted Mantle throughout his career. And fate wasn't finished with Mantle's legs.

When he was playing right field as a rookie for the Yankees in the 1951 World Series, another rookie, Willie Mays of the Giants, hit a sinking line drive to right center. Joe DiMaggio called for the ball, and when Mantle pulled up, he accidentally stepped into a drainage ditch in the grass and went down in a heap. He had torn ligaments and cartilage in his right knee, while his father watched from the stands.

Mantle was admired throughout his career for achieving more on one healthy leg than others did on two, but the truth is that he accomplished what he did without even *one* healthy leg.

Another home run hitter, first baseman Boog Powell of the Orioles, said when he was interviewed for this book, "I played one All-Star game with him, and it was just amazing to watch him dress and see how much tape they put on him. His legs were wrapped up from his ankles straight up to his chest."

COMMERCE...JOPLIN...KANSAS CITY...NEW YORK

People who write about legends sometimes get it wrong. In writing the Mantle legend, it was frequently said that he was discovered by a Yankee scout, Tom Greenwade. But Greenwade attempted to dispel that myth.

"Baseball scouts are tipped off to 99 percent of their discoveries," he said. "I never signed a boy without first being steered to him by some other source."

Mantle revealed the identity of who discovered him: Kay Jacobson of Joplin, Missouri, who was umpiring in the Ban Johnson League, who tipped off a friend, former Yankee First Baseman Johnny Sturm, then a scout for New York.

On the June night in 1949 when his classmates received their high school diplomas, Mantle was playing baseball for the Baxter Springs Whiz

Kids against Coffeyville under Greenwade's experienced eyes. "I think I put on a little show for Tom," Mantle said. "I got four hits and did pretty well in the field, too."

Mantle's performance that night was one of the earliest examples of his ability to deliver under pressure, with high stakes on the table. His reputation for hitting "tape measure home runs" was matched by his reputation for getting the big hit or making the big catch with the game, sometimes even the pennant or the World Series, on the line.

His reward for being equal to the challenge that night was $1,500, plus $140 a month to play for the Yankees' farm team in Independence, Kansas, 75 miles from home, in the Kansas-Oklahoma-Missouri League at baseball's entry level in those years, Class D.

After a promising beginning, he was promoted to Joplin, only 30 miles from home, for the 1950 season. There he crushed the pitching in the Class C Western Association, won the batting championship with a .383 average, scored 141 runs, collected 199 hits in only 137 games, hit 26 homers and drove in 136 runs. At shortstop, he was, well, awful. He committed 55 errors, many of them on wild throws to first base.

His education into the life of a professional baseball player continued at the end of that season, after the Yankees called him up to "the big club" for their final western swing. He traveled with them to Detroit, Cleveland, Chicago and St. Louis, with the stars he yearned to join for real —Joe DiMaggio, Phil Rizzuto, Tommy Henrich, Allie Reynolds, Yogi Berra.

He found himself broke from all those travel expenses and attending movies for two weeks, unable to pay for his trip back home. He was saved when the Yankees' traveling secretary, Frank Scott, asked him how much the team owed him for meals. Mantle was delightfully shocked. He couldn't believe that the team was actually paying for his meals. Now he could get home to Oklahoma.

NEW YORK, NEW YORK

The kid was invited to the Yankees' spring training camp at Saint Petersburg, Florida, before the start of the 1951 season, and his reputation got there before he did. By now the whole baseball world was talking about this spectacular "phee-nom" who might be the next Joe DiMaggio —or the next Phil Rizzuto.

"I read so much about him," Rizzuto said for this book. "I thought, 'What chance do I have?' Here I was the MVP the year before, and I figured this kid was going to take my job, since he was a shortstop, you know. I read all this stuff about him, and then I saw him.

"I'm serious—I didn't even unpack my bag in spring training until we started playing the games. But then I watched him field and throw. He had a strong arm, but when he threw, he would clear everybody out of the first base area. They put him in the outfield real quick."

That's where Tommy Henrich entered Mantle's life. The one they called "Old Reliable," the Yankees' rightfielder next to DiMaggio since 1937, retired as a player after the 1950 season and was now a Yankee coach. His assignment from Manager Casey Stengel: Convert Mantle into a big league outfielder.

"That first year," Tommy said recently, "he was very shy, and anything I said to him, he believed. He was so quiet. He didn't have that drive in his early years, but he learned. He grew into it. But DiMaggio had that pride from day one."

Mantle again proved himself equal to the challenge. With all the publicity surrounding him, compounding the usual pressure on a rookie trying to make good, the kid from Oklahoma turned in a torrid spring training season. He became the talk of the camp, the 19-year-old who wasn't even on the Yankees' roster and had only a year and a half in the low minors as his total professional experience.

In an exhibition game against the University of Southern California, which had beaten the Pittsburgh Pirates, Mantle drove in seven runs on two homers—the first one went 430 feet—a triple, a single and a walk. By the end of spring training, he was a regular in the outfield, with a .402 batting average and 32 runs batted in.

Stengel told reporters, "This is a kid which is going to be tree-menjois." Even DiMaggio called Mantle "the greatest prospect I can remember. Maybe he has to learn something about catching a fly ball, but that's all. He can do everything. If he's good enough to take my job, I can always move over to right or left."

Branch Rickey, considered by many the greatest judge of talent in baseball history, said "He's the finest prospect I have ever seen. He's the kid I always dreamed of finding. He has that flawless, level swing, and the fastest break from the plate I have ever seen."

Mantle's ability under pressure, and his flair for the dramatic, surfaced again when he played in Yankee Stadium for the first time, in the team's last exhibition game of the spring training season. He got four straight hits, including a home run, against the Brooklyn Dodgers.

New York, New York—the kid had arrived.

A DIFFERENT SCRIPT

The story line for this script changed immediately. With the start of the season, Mantle's fortunes nose-dived. He wasn't hitting, especially after the word flashed around the American League via the pitchers' grapevine that he was a sucker for an inside fast ball above the belt. His relations with reporters became strained, with his short, abrupt answers caused by his shyness and discomfort around people being mistaken by the New York media for arrogance and conceit.

As if all this weren't enough, public resentment over his military draft status increased so much the Yankees asked the draft board's doctors to examine him again. His case went all the way up to the Surgeon General, where he was again declared unfit because of the seriousness of his osteomyelitis.

At times, the kid was reduced to tears because of his slump and the boos he was hearing from the New York fans. After he struck out five times in a row in a doubleheader, the team farmed him out to Kansas City, then a top Yankees' minor league team. Even there, he couldn't do anything right.

The emotional burden became too much for the kid, so he called for his father. Mutt arrived in Kansas City to help. He applied a tough-love strategy, telling Mickey if he didn't have the guts and courage to face adversity and conquer it, he should come back home and go to work in the mines.

After Mutt left Kansas City, Mickey caught fire, slugging 11 home runs and driving in 50 runs in only 34 games. He was soon back with the Yankees and finished his rookie season with a respectable .267 average in 96 games, with 13 homers and 65 runs batted in.

After the Yankees defeated the Giants in the 1951 World Series, DiMaggio announced his retirement. For the first time since Babe Ruth arrived in New York in 1920, the team did not have a dominant star in the Ruth-DiMaggio mold. All eyes turned to Mantle.

Despite the disappointments and the controversies, the slumps and the injuries, the record on Mantle was clear: In just two and a half seasons, he had made a mockery of minor league pitching, become an overnight sensation in his first big league spring training camp and jumped all the way from Class C to the bigs, the first Yankee to do it, and established creditable credentials while playing next to the one Hemingway called "the great DiMaggio." And all this by the tender age of 19.

Now, with DiMaggio taking off the Yankee pinstripes for the last time, Mickey Mantle stood on the threshold.

Despite his advance billing, Mantle was not the Yankees' centerfielder when the 1952 season began. Jackie Jensen was. But Jensen was traded to the Washington Senators a month later and Mantle moved into center field, where he remained for 15 years, until his worsening legs forced him to move to first base.

"The Mick" was among the American League's leaders in one department that year—strikeouts—tying Larry Doby with 111. But he also hit .311 with 23 home runs and 87 RBIs and powered his team to its fourth straight pennant and a spot in the World Series against Brooklyn, the fabled Dodgers of Duke Snider, Jackie Robinson, Pee Wee Reese, Roy Campanella, Carl Erskine and Joe Black. Mickey was third in the league in hitting and second in total bases, slugging average and doubles.

In the Series, with his team down three games to two and the score tied, 2-2, Mantle hit a home run in the eighth inning off Billy Loes to win the game. In the decisive next game, he homered in the sixth to put the

Yankees ahead, 3-2, then singled in another run in the seventh to ensure a 4-2 win. He had the third highest average in the Series for the Yankees.

Now the kid from Oklahoma found himself playing a new role—the toast of Broadway—with a salary to match—$18,500 for 1953. And the whole team stood on a new threshold: The chance to become the first team to win five straight World Series.

THE 565-FOOTER, AND A BUBBLE GUM INCIDENT

Mantle proceeded to make the 1953 season a memorable one before it was even a month old. He hit a home run off Chuck Stobbs in Washington's cavernous Griffith Stadium that was measured at 565 feet, the only ball ever to fly over the left field wall and all the way out of the ballpark, into a backyard across the street.

It was the birth of the Mantle legend as baseball's new Paul Bunyan. Other monumental blasts solidified the legend—one off Pete Ramos of the Senators on Memorial Day in 1956 that hit the facade atop Yankee Stadium, something he also did against Kansas City's Bill Fischer.

Mantle hit .295 with 21 homers. The Yankees made history by winning their fifth straight World Series, defeating the Dodgers in six games. Mantle struck out five times in a row, but he hit two home runs, one a grand slam that propelled his team to victory in the fifth game.

Still, there were rumblings that Mantle could be better, that he didn't seem to give maximum effort all the time. It was a criticism that found new fuel when a photographer noticed Mantle blowing bubbles while playing center field. Today the incident might pass. But this was 1954, and Mantle's picture appeared in papers across the country. Stengel called him into his office and read the riot act to him about professionalism. Mantle promised he wouldn't do it again, but he did—that afternoon.

STENGEL LOOKS BACK

As the 1950s reached their midway point, Stengel began to feel vindicated. Mantle was now an established star, even what we call today a "superstar." The Yankees won 103 games in 1954, but they lost the pennant to the Cleveland Indians and their 111 wins, then the American League record. The Mick hit an even .300, including 27 homers and 102 RBIs and led the league's centerfielders by throwing out 25 base runners.

In 1955, he continued his charge toward immortality, hitting .306, and leading the league in homers in 1955 with 37, 11 triples, 113 walks and a .611 slugging percentage. By now Stengel was feeling justified in his early decisions on Mantle.

"Maybe I rushed him along too fast," he confessed to reporters, "but I had no options once DiMaggio announced it was his last year (1951). You saw what I saw. Would you do anything different?"

Almost as if to underline his boss's comments, Mantle went out in 1956 and conquered one of baseball's highest mountains, the "Triple

Crown." He sparkled as one of his sport's brightest stars, leading both Major Leagues in batting average with a hefty .353, home runs with 52 and runs batted in with 130. He became only the ninth player to accomplish the feat since 1900. He won the first of his three Most Valuable Player Awards.

His power was becoming as consistent as it was awesome. Manager Bill Rigney, who managed the Angels in the second half of Mantle's career, remembered, "He had such power, and he had it both ways. I remember making a pitching change, and I kind of looked back at the plate, and Mantle, an incomparable switch-hitter, was leaning on his bat at the plate as if to say, 'Hey, Rig—whichever way you go, you're going to get the worst of it.'"

Something else developed in Mantle over the 1950s, and Rigney saw evidence of that, too. "He took the responsibility of being Mickey Mantle of the New York Yankees in the ball game, and he carried it off real well. This great home run hitter was the leader of those great teams and probably never said two words all the time he played. A lot of guys shuck that responsibility."

SAVING PERFECTION

Mantle's big-play abilities were never more prominent than in Don Larsen's perfect World Series triumph over the Dodgers on October 8, 1956. The Mick gave Larsen the only run he needed with a bases empty home run, then saved Larsen's perfection with a remarkable catch, the combination of both speed and ability, on a long line drive to deep left center by Gil Hodges. Mantle raced to his right and stretched his left arm all the way to make a perfect backhand catch going away from home plate.

He continued his blazing pace into the history books with another MVP season in 1957—a .365 average, 34 homers, 94 RBIs—and the lofty total of 146 walks. On the down side, if there was one, he was now the most feared slugger in the league, and the pitchers were pitching him outside. He became impatient, as many hitters do, and began swinging at bad pitches. Result: He led the league in strikeouts in 1958 with 120 and again in '59 and '60 with 126 and 125.

Enos Slaughter, Mantle's teammate in the mid-1950s, a lifetime .300 hitter and a fellow Hall of Famer, was talking about Mantle's strikeouts not long ago. "I think Mickey got down on himself more than anything else. He would always swing hard, and he struck out a lot, and I think he would brood over striking out."

Tony Kubek, the Yankee shortstop, offered some food for thought on Mantle's homers and strikeouts, then and now. "Righthanded," Kubek said, "he had the perfect swing. There was no way to get him out. Lefthanded, if you could throw fast balls up, you could get him out. When we played, the strike zone was between the arm pit and the knees. The strike zone today has gone to about belt high down to just below the knees, and if Mickey had today's strike zone batting from the left side, he would have hit a lot more home runs because he wouldn't have had to worry about that high pitch."

OF LOYALTY AND KINDNESS

As he achieved stardom, Mantle was becoming the most popular Yankee among his teammates. Catcher Johnny Blanchard says today, "He was, without a doubt, the best teammate you could have. In all the years I knew him, and it was a lot, never once did I ever hear him say a derogatory word about a teammate. Not one time .... Not one bad word would come out of his mouth."

Mantle extended the hand of friendship to Blanchard when the catcher had a bad game early in his rookie season. "I was sitting in front of my locker, lower than low, and he came over and tapped me on the shoulder and said, 'You come with me tonight.' So, Number 7 took me out for the biggest steak in New York City—the great Mickey Mantle. Heck, I couldn't wait to get to the park the next day. I felt like a million bucks. And I saw him do it for Phil Linz, too. What a guy! I could never say enough about him as a person, a friend, a teammate. He just meant the world to me."

As Blanchard stood beside his dying teammate during Mantle's last day in this life, Mickey put his hand out and said, "John, you take care of yourself." Blanchard says, "He was always thinking about you. It was touching."

Joe Pepitone, the Yankees' colorful first baseman, offers the same kind of testimony about Mantle's generosity toward his teammates. "When I joined the Yankees," he says today, "I was having problems, getting separated and divorced from my second wife, and Mickey said, 'You come and stay with me.' He had a two-bedroom suite at the St. Moritz, and I stayed with him two months."

THAT SPECIAL SERIES, AND THAT SPECIAL SEASON

One of the most lopsided of all World Series was played in 1960, when the Yankees clobbered Pittsburgh pitching for 91 hits and 55 runs in only seven games and whipped the Pirates by scores of 16-3, 10-0 and 12-0. But the Pirates won the Series, decided by Bill Mazeroski's home run in the bottom of the ninth in the seventh game.

Mantle was still a hero. After leading the league in home runs for the fourth—and last—time with 40, he hit .400 in the Series with three home runs and 11 RBIs.

That special Series was followed by a special season, 1961, when Mantle and his next-door neighbor in right field, Roger Maris—"the M&M Boys"—combined in some slugging dramatics that made America forget about Khrushchev's threats and the newest symbol of the Cold War—the Berlin Wall—which went up on August 13, while Maris and Mantle were chasing Babe Ruth's record of 60 home runs in one season.

Mantle was the sentimental choice of the New York fans, a legitimate home run hitter with 52 in 1956, compared to Maris's best total, 39, in 1960. But the injury jinx struck Mantle again, this time in the form of an abscess on his right hip. He was hospitalized. His part in the chase was over. When Maris broke Ruth's record on the last day of the season, Mickey, with 54 homers of his own, watched it on TV in the hospital.

Outfielder Bob Cerv was an eyewitness to history. He roomed with Maris and Mantle that year. Later he told *Sport* Magazine how the relationship between the two was able to endure during their marathon race against Ruth and against each other.

"They both admitted many times that while they wished the other fellow luck, this was competition for the greatest honor in baseball, and Mickey was rooting for Mickey and Roger was rooting for Roger. But that had nothing to do with the respect they had for one another."

The injuries were coming more often now. On May 18, 1962, he suffered a seriously pulled muscle in his right thigh and was out of the lineup for a month. In 1963, he broke his foot in Baltimore. After both injuries, he returned as a pinchhitter. He hit a home run both times.

For Mantle, 1964 was his last big season—a .303 average, 35 home runs, 111 runs batted in. He topped off the year with three home runs against St. Louis in the World Series, even though the Cardinals won.

By now, the end was in sight. Over the last four seasons of his brilliant career, Mantle averaged 20 home runs and only 53 RBIs. In his last two years, he played first base after an operation on his throwing shoulder.

When his time came after the '68 season to "hang 'em up" as the players say, Mantle was candid, as always. "I'm not going to play any more baseball," he said on March 1. "I just can't play any more, and I know it . . . I've had three or four bad years in a row, and as a result, I received the greatest disappointment of my career by falling under .300 lifetime."

His retirement marked the end of the longest-running success in American sports history. After Ruth joined the Yankees in 1920, the team of Ruth-Gehrig-DiMaggio-Mantle won 29 pennants and 20 World Series in 38 years.

The fans honored their now-beloved hero with "A Day To Remember" on June 8, 1969, when more than 60,000 of them gave The Mick a standing ovation when his number was retired by the Yankees. The ovation lasted seven minutes.

After it died down enough so he could be heard over the public address system, Mantle said, "I didn't know how a man who knew he was going to die could stand here and say, 'I am the luckiest man on the face of the earth.' Now I know how Lou Gehrig felt."

MANTLE'S DRINKING: HOW BAD WAS IT?

In the first years after his retirement as a player, Mickey Mantle tried to cope with his deep disappointment over not achieving a lifetime .300 batting average. And he was surprised that he missed the camaraderie of his teammates so much—Billy Martin, Whitey Ford, Moose Skowron, Hank Bauer and others. They had been his life for 20 years. Now they weren't around.

That's when his drinking moved from the laughing, back-slapping and partying phase into the far more serious, even deadly, stage of outright alcoholism. He began to drink heavily. He had drunk too much during his playing years too, especially after his father died and when Mickey suffered all those injuries. But it became worse, much worse, in retirement.

Mantle began to believe that drinking was enjoyable, especially on the road to while away the time. He and Martin began drinking even more. It became a game with them, to see who could drink the other under the table. The void in his life merely opened the door wider for still more drinking.

As baseball card shows became popular in the early 1980s, Mantle began spending more time on the road, and by himself in hotel rooms. When he drank with others, he frequently became loud, boisterous, rude and nasty. He drank day and night, often unable to remember what town he was in. None of this came as a surprise to Hank Bauer.

"Mickey was a lonely man," he said in an interview for this book. "He was well known throughout the world, and anywhere he went he got bothered. As a result, a lot of time, Mickey didn't go anywhere. He'd stay in his room and evidently the four walls closed in on him and the outcome was the bottle."

He traveled so much he never really got to know his sons. When they did get together, he took them out to drink, more like buddies getting together than a father spending time with his sons.

In his final days, he publicly admitted that he had not taken care of his body, unlike Pete Rose, Hank Aaron, Stan Musial and other greats. He said that when he was in his starring years, he thought they would last forever. In his opinion, he said, he had only 12 good years out of his 20-year career.

At the same time, he appealed to the public, especially young people, to avoid abusing themselves the way he confessed he had done. He said with his typical candor, "It was just stupid of me."

THE DEATH OF A CHAMPION

Mickey Mantle's final days were watched by the entire nation, befitting his status as a national celebrity and an immense public favorite. His drinking notwithstanding, Mantle was enormously popular by the time he was found to have a diseased liver in late May of 1995.

He had been sober for a year and a half, his latest big win, but he was bothered by a persistent pain in his stomach. A checkup revealed cancer of the liver. His doctors moved swiftly, located a new liver, and performed a transplant on June 8.

After extensive chemotherapy treatments, a routine examination revealed the cancer had spread through his body, attacking both lungs, his heart and his new liver. The doctors told him he had a week to live. Mantle, ever thoughtful of others, swore everyone to secrecy, asking his doctors only that they relieve his pain to whatever extent they could.

In a national news conference, The Mick told his fans only that his cancer had returned and he was fighting it, not revealing the death sentence pronounced by his doctors. He urged young people not to look to him as a role model, and he begged them not to drink.

Whitey Ford called to say he was flying in that night and would come to the hospital the next morning. But the hospital staff told him to come straight to the hospital. Mantle was so buoyed by the arrival of his best friend that he was able to leave his bed and reminisce with Whitey. The next day, Skowron, Bauer and John Blanchard came by. All of them saw only a shell of the Mickey Mantle they once knew.

The last teammate to visit was Bobby Richardson, nicknamed "The Milk Drinker" by Mickey during their playing days. Richardson was a minister now, and Mantle asked him to preside at his service.

Mickey Charles Mantle died just after midnight on Sunday, August 13, 1995. As promised, Bobby presided at his funeral.

That afternoon, the American flag flew at half-staff at Yankee Stadium. Before the game, the monstrous scoreboard in centerfield listed the batter for the Yankees—Number 7.

But the batter's box was empty.

WHAT OTHER PLAYERS SAID ABOUT MICKEY MANTLE

Al Kaline—I always thought he was the best player I ever played against, one of the few you would go out early to watch take batting practice.

Manager Birdie Tebbetts—There was only one Mantle. In spring training one year, Johnny Mize, a hell of a home run hitter, hit one out, and the Yankees sent some young kid up to pinch hit, and he hit one twice as far. It was my first look at Mantle.

George Kell—If he hadn't been hurt, Mantle just might have been the best ballplayer who ever lived.

Bob Lemon—He was pretty easy starting out with. He crowded the plate and gave up on the sinker inside. When he started backing away a foot or so, he was tougher than hell.

Sparky Lyle (before becoming a Yankee)—He hit a rocket to short-stop Jerry Adair, and he just had time to throw his glove up. He came in and called time. That was my rookie season, and he said, 'Hey, I got a wife and three kids. You'd better bear down out here!"

Johnny Podres—I only pitched against him in the World Series in '55. He hit a low, outside changeup off me in Ebbets Field into the centerfield upper deck. I had better luck with him in the seventh game because he didn't play."

Jimmy Piersall—From the waist up, Mickey Mantle was the strongest hitter I've ever seen in my life. If he had wanted to be a better fielder, he could have been . . . . He wasn't lousy, but he wasn't as good as he could have been.

Tom Tresh—He was my idol when I was growing up. When the Yankees came to Detroit, I would sit in centerfield and watch him play. A few years later, I was on his team, my locker was next to his, I played the outfield next to him and went out to dinner and breakfast with him, things like that. It always seemed so unreal to me. I would say to myself, "I don't believe this."

The public rarely got a chance to see him the way he really was. He valued his time alone. He had kind of an air about him that kind of scared people off from talking to him. That wasn't him. That wasn't the real Mickey Mantle. He was really just a shy country boy who wasn't comfortable meeting people.

Joe Rudi—He was my idol growing up. I read every book I could ever find on him. My biggest thrill in baseball was in '68—my first year and his last. I was playing first base one day and he walked and came down to the bag. I'm just 21 and my knees are shaking, and I say, "Hi, Mick." And he goes, "Hi, Joe." I almost had a hot flash. He actually knew my name!

Chuck Tanner—He hit his 500th home run over my head in Cleveland. I was happy. I said, "I'll tell my grandkids about it."

Dean Chance—He would only bunt with two strikes on him, and when he drag-bunted from the left side, I never saw him foul one off. It was an automatic hit every time.

Dick Radatz—I had great luck with him. The only hit he ever got off me was a home run. I gave Mickey a steady diet of inside fast balls and just kept "moving up the ladder" with him. He had problems with my high, inside fast ball. I didn't mess around with throwing him anything but that. I faced him 63 times and he got one hit—that home run—off me. Believe it or not, I struck him out 47 times.

Ken Sanders—I picked Mickey up one time at the Milwaukee airport for a golf tournament, and I told him, "Mickey, you probably don't remember this, but you were my first strikeout in the big leagues." He said, "Big deal, kid—you and a thousand other guys."

Dick Williams—In '68, I was managing the American League in the All-Star game in Houston, and we lost, 1-0. Mantle didn't start the game, and late in the game he went up and struck out on three pitches and said, "You mean I traveled 2,500 miles just to do this?"

Boog Powell—There wasn't anybody who ever hit a ball harder than Mick. I was more impressed with that, I think, than his long home runs. There's only one guy I can think of who hit the ball maybe as hard as Mick did, and that was Frank Howard. In my first game, they played me in left field, and Mickey hit one of those line-drive knuckleballs at me that hit me about four times—bounced off my arm, hit me in the chest, hit me in the chin and it just tore me up. He was very, very impressive. Later on, when I played first base, I used to beg our righthanded pitchers, "Please don't pitch him inside." I didn't want him pulling any of those inside pitches at me.

Denny McLain—Mantle was tied at 534 home runs with the great Jimmie Foxx, and it was near the end of what looked like his last season. It was the year I won 31 and lost four (1968). I was ahead, 6-1, in the ninth with two outs and no one on when up comes Mantle.

I figured, the great player that he was, that I would lay one in there and let him break the tie with Foxx. I figured, "What the heck, he deserves it." I threw one down the middle on an arc at about half-speed, and he took it for strike one. I guess I kind of surprised him. I lobbed another at about the same velocity and he took it for strike two. Another one and he fouled it off. He was trying to figure what was going on. I grinned at him and he got the message.

Then he put his hand out over the plate and let me know, "Here's where I want it."

I threw it right where he wanted me to, and he hit it five miles. They tell me he later felt a little sheepish about topping Foxx's mark in such a fashion. Fortunately, he hit one more—the last of his career—and that one was legitimate.

Frank Robinson—I used to look at Mickey and say, boy, I wish I could be built like Mickey Mantle. He had what I considered the ideal build for a baseball player from the top of his head to the bottom of his feet. It looked like he was sculptured. The greatest switch-hitter of all time. He didn't have a weakness. An outstanding centerfielder and, boy, could he run down the line. With two strikes on him against a tough pitcher he would drag bunt between first and second and beat it out for a base hit. Every time. You loved him on your team cause hey, you bring in a left hander, he'd switch and hit one out.

Harmon Killebrew—One of my favorites. On Opening Day in 1956 in old Griffith Stadium in Washington, he hit two over the center field fence into a tree. It was about 426 feet to center with a fence about 30 feet high. It was unbelievable. I was playing second base the day in Yankee Stadium when he almost hit the ball out—up on the facade about three feet from going out. That was unbelievable, too. But I saw him hit so many. To me, he had more physical ability than any player I ever saw.

Hank Aaron—I think Mickey could have been a lot better than what he was, which was a lot. I know he's no longer with us, and he played on a lot of championship ballclubs, but I think that if Mickey was living today, he'd tell you he was disappointed he didn't finish his career with a .300 batting average.

Joe Garagiola—Whenever you bring up the name of Mickey Mantle, I say, "How good could he have been," because he was so good as it was. I remember the first time he faced Don Drysdale in spring training. Drysdale was a pretty good hitter, and Whitey Ford struck him out on a 3-2 count with a curve ball and Mantle later beat out a bunt off him on another 3-2 pitch, and Drysdale said, "What kind of a league is this? They curve you on 3-2 and bunt on 3-2!" Another pitcher once said his biggest thrill was when Mickey bunted him, too, on a 3-2 pitch in Yankee Stadium. The pitcher said if Mantle would do it every time, he'd send a car for him.

THE MANTLE FILE

Full Name: Mickey Charles Mantle.
Date and Place of Birth: October 20, 1931, Spavinaw, Oklahoma.
Date and Place of Death: August 13, 1995, Dallas, Texas.
Nickname: The Mick. The Commerce Comet.
Position: Center field.
Major League Career: 18 years, 1951-1968.
Home Runs: 536 (8th).
Runs Batted In: 1,509.
Runs Scored: 1,677.
Lifetime Batting Average: .298.
Number of Hits: 2,415.
Bases on Balls: 1,734 (5th).
Strikeouts: 1,710 (8th).
American League Most Valuable Player: 1956, 1957, 1962.
Other Highlights:

— Led American League in home runs four times and runs batted in once.
— Led the League in walks and strikeouts five times.
— Hit more than 50 home runs twice—52 in 1956 and 54 in 1961.
— Played in second most World Series games (65) and has second most times at bat (230) and second most hits (59).
— Has most World Series home runs (18), runs scored, runs batted in walks, strikeouts and tenth highest home run percentage.
— In 18-year career, led his team to 12 pennants and seven World Series championships.

— **Elected to the Baseball Hall of Fame: 1974.**

7

EDDIE MATHEWS

The Classic Hard-Nosed Player

Q uestion: What two sluggers formed the most powerful one-two punch in history?

Answer: Babe Ruth and Lou Gehrig.

Right?

Wrong.

The correct answer is Hank Aaron and Eddie Mathews, who hit 863 home runs as teammates, more than Ruth and Gehrig.

"The poor pitchers," First Baseman Frank Torre groaned while talking about Mathews and Aaron for this book. "When Eddie hit third and Hank fourth, the pitchers went from the frying pan into the fire." Torre, the brother of Yankees' manager Joe Torre, should know. He was their teammate on the Milwaukee Braves for five of his seven years in the majors.

Mathews came by his power honestly. His grandfather was a folk hero back in the early years of this century as the local Babe Ruth on the sandlots around Texarkana, Texas. Eddie's father became a baseball player too, as a semi-pro infielder.

In 1936, in the depths of the Depression, Eddie's father moved the family to Santa Barbara, California, as wire chief of the Western Union office. One of his jobs was as the telegrapher for the games of the Santa Barbara team in the California State League.

During their early years in California, he bought a dime-store bat, glove and ball for his five-year-old son. Mathews surprised his father by picking up the bat and swinging it lefthanded, even though he did everything else righthanded. His father made no attempt to change him, a wise decision in view of later events and achievements.

His father pitched to his son often. The whole activity became a family affair, because Eddie's mother would track down her son's long fly balls and retrieve them so her two men wouldn't have to use up valuable time going after the balls themselves. And some of those shots were on the long side, the result of encouragement from Eddie's father to do pushups and chinups every day to strengthen his arms and wrists.

Athletic success came early to young Mathews—All-Southern California running back in high school football, heavily recruited by Southern California, UCLA, California, Washington, Oregon and Stanford. Word of his football talents got all the way across the country to the East Coast, and Eddie received another scholarship offer, this one from the University of Georgia.

But a serious injury pointed him away from football, a brain concussion that hospitalized him for two weeks with chronic head pains. He also developed a cyst on his left knee and back problems which bothered him throughout his baseball career.

Eddie received an offer of $40,000 from Branch Rickey to sign with the Brooklyn Dodgers, but he and his father turned it down and signed with the Braves, before their last year in Boston, for only $6,000. The reason: Talent-rich teams like the Dodgers, Yankees and St. Louis Cardinals offered big bucks, but they also had so many good players in their farm systems that a prospect like Eddie could get lost. The Braves, however, did not have a rich farm system and their third baseman, Bob Elliott, was 33 years old and starting his eleventh season in the National League.

The Mathews formula was simple: Sign with the Braves for less money but get to the Major Leagues a whole lot faster. There was a second advantage in signing for a much smaller amount. In those years, "bonus babies" who received large signing bonuses were frozen to the major league team's roster for two years. With the smaller amount, Mathews could break into the majors sooner and start making larger salaries anyhow.

As his high school graduation night neared, a feeding frenzy of scouts developed. Contracts could be signed at midnight. As the magic hour neared, scouts from several big league teams were taking no chances. They were shadowing Mathews and his date at their graduation dance at Santa Barbara High School. Several other scouts camped outside the front door of his house.

The Braves' scout, Jeff Jones, employed a different tactic. He rented a room in a downtown hotel. Just before midnight, young Eddie slipped out a side door at the dance and drove to Jones's hotel. He signed a contract with the Braves at one minute past midnight. The next day, the rival scouts screamed foul, but Mathews was a Boston Brave.

HEY, COMMISSIONER—LOOK OUT!

Mathews' first day in a professional environment could have broken a lesser man. He was to meet the Braves at their hotel in Chicago. He arrived just in time to board the team bus for Wrigley Field, where Manager Billy Southworth, his coaches and officials of the front office would work him out and decide which of the minor league teams he should join. In his haste to catch the bus, the kid pulled his glove and spikes from his luggage and shoved them into a paper bag.

When the innocent 17-year-old rookie emptied his paper bag in front of his locker, Bob Elliott, the veteran he was destined to replace as the greatest third baseman in Braves' history, told him he was in the big leagues now—he didn't have to bring his lunch.

Eddie climbed up the minor league ladder in a hurry—Evansville, High Point-Thomasville, Atlanta, Milwaukee, all minor league cities at the start of the 1950s. Home runs kept exploding off his bat until he career was interrupted when the North Koreans invaded South Korea on June 25, 1950. Mathews, then nineteen and a prime target to be drafted into the Army, put his baseball career on hold and joined the Navy.

Midway through the 1951 season, his father developed tuberculosis. Eddie became the sole support of his parents and was given a dependency discharge.

After playing the second half of the '51 season at Milwaukee and Atlanta, Mathews reported to the Braves' 1952 spring training camp at Bradenton, Florida, where the team's long-time equipment manager, Shorty Young, grabbed a uniform out of a stack and handed it to him. On its back was an unlikely number for a third baseman—41. Regardless of his number, the kid became the talk of the camp—for his fielding, or the lack of it.

His reputation preceded him. The Braves knew he had booted 21 balls in just 63 games in '51, so they recruited Billy Jurges to work with Mathews. Jurges was an All-Star shortstop for the Cubs and Giants for 17 years in the 1930s and '40s.

Jurges taught the bright prospect to relax at third base and to keep his weight forward when prepared for a ground ball. He also showed Mathews how to bend his whole body rather than just his knees while going after a ground ball.

By the time the Braves headed for Boston to open the season, Mathews had the third baseman's job, and Bob Elliott was traded to the New York Giants and transferred to the outfield.

Mathews made the headlines for a second reason in spring training that year—he almost got the Commissioner of Baseball killed.

As a contingency plan in case Mathews couldn't make it in the infield, the Braves also tried him in the outfield in the early days of spring training. In a pre-game workout, the rookie was in left field when a long fly ball came his way and began tailing toward foul territory. Mathews, anxious to impress his bosses, was in hot pursuit.

Meanwhile, Commissioner Ford Frick was enjoying a leisurely chat in the outfield during those lazy days of spring training with the Braves' publicity director, Billy Sullivan, and a nationally prominent baseball reporter, Whitney Martin.

Sullivan was standing with his back to home plate when Mathews, running at full speed, backhanded the drive and crashed into the three men. Sullivan was knocked unconscious and went smashing into Frick, knocking the Commissioner to the ground, too. When Frick went down, he took Martin with him.

Frick and Martin were able to shake off the effects of the four-way collision. Mathews and Sullivan were taken to a local hospital for X-rays, with Eddie bleeding from his nose and mouth.

FIRST A BLIND SPOT, THEN THE LIGHT

Mathews was no immediate hero as a rookie with the Braves. After hitting the first home run of his Major League career, a three-run shot in Eddie's fourth game in the bigs, he went into a tailspin and was hitting an anemic .167 several weeks into the season.

The fans were letting him have it with their boos, reminding both the rookie and the front office that the Braves had traded away an established slugger with 100 or more runs batted six times in the past nine seasons for this 21-year-old kid with too many strikeouts.

But then Eddie made a magical discovery, on his own. He noticed he had a blind spot in his swing, the result of employing a "closed" stance with his feet close together, the front foot closer to the plate than his back foot. It worked for Ted Williams and Stan Musial, but it was causing Mathews to miss the high, inside pitch. The National League's pitchers, through the players' grapevine—a better intelligence network than the C.I.A.—spread the word: You can get this kid out with something up and in. As a result, that's all Mathews was seeing.

After opening his stance so his feet were equally distant from the plate instead of putting his front foot closer, Mathews began to hit considerably better. By the end of the season, he had 25 home runs—and 115 strikeouts, a record for a rookie. He certified his credentials as an established big leaguer by becoming the first rookie to hit three home runs in one game, on September 27 at Brooklyn's Ebbets Field.

A MOVE WEST FOR THE TEAM, A MOVE UP FOR MATHEWS

The Braves stunned the baseball world on March 18, 1953, by becoming the first Major League team to move to another city in over 50 years, leaving Boston for Milwaukee.

Mathews began his first season in Milwaukee almost the same way he started in Boston the year before—with too many strikeouts. With the Milwaukee fans screaming in ecstasy over the thrill of seeing their very own big league team, Mathews struck out his first three times up.

But then he hit six home runs in his next seven games, and set himself on a course toward a starring season. He led both leagues in home runs with 47, hit .302, drove in 135 runs and finished second to Roy Campanella, the Dodgers' catcher, in the voting for National League Most Valuable Player.

Along the way, he became one of America's newest fan favorites. For the All-Star game in Cincinnati, he was selected by the fans as the youngest starting infielder in the history of the midsummer classic.

His dream season was not without one serious bump in the road, when he was chosen by *Look* magazine to receive a watch as its All-American third baseman. He was to receive his award between games of a doubleheader, but in the first game he committed two errors that became factors in a Braves' loss and was booed by the Milwaukee fans.

Sulking and hurt, he refused to accept the watch at home plate in front of the fans. Instead, he received it in the dugout. When the fans read about the incident in the papers the next day, Eddie took a beating, charged in the court of public opinion with being a temperamental brat.

He won the fans back to his side the best way any baseball player can—by continuing to have a banner season. His home run total broke Ralph Kiner's streak of leading the National League in homers for seven straight years. His numbers for both home runs and RBIs were records for the Braves. On the down side, his 30 errors were the most by a third baseman in either league.

The excitement caused by the good-looking slugger with the booming bat reached dramatic dimensions with two months remaining in the season. Mathews stood tied with Babe Ruth's pace when he hit his record 60 home runs in 1927. At this point, it was still considered one of baseball's "unbreakable" records, along with Joe DiMaggio's 56-game hitting streak in 1941. Ruth's record was twenty-six years old by 1953, and many fans, players and members of the media said it would last forever.

That's why excitement reached fever pitch when Mathews stood tied with Ruth's pace with 59 games to play. His pace dropped off, but he still could tie Ruth in September if he hit 17 home runs, a daunting challenge since the record for the most homers in any month was still 18 by Rudy York.

Eddie told the writers he'd be happy to hit 50, a rare number itself. But he continued to cool off and settled with his 47 to top both leagues. Other comparisons with Ruth lay in Eddie's future.

Vinegar Bend Mizell, a hard-throwing lefthander for the Cardinals, told us recently, "He was the one we all thought was going to break Babe Ruth's record if anybody did. He had that good, quick swing and had that kind of power, but injuries cut his career short."

The euphoria over Mathews's home runs was exceeded by the euphoria over the team itself. After winning only 64 games in 1952, their last season in Boston, the Braves finished in seventh place. In '53, their first season in Milwaukee, the transplanted Braves won 92 games, finished in second place, and set a National League attendance record by drawing 1,826,397 fans.

The best was yet to come, because a rookie scheduled to join the team for spring training was said to be another potential star—Hank Aaron.

BACK TO HIS ROOTS

At the end of that bright 1953 campaign, when Mathews's season-long performance made him a legitimate star, the folks back home in Santa Barbara happily proposed an Eddie Mathews Day. But the town's newest hero turned them down politely and opted instead for a small dinner.

He was a national celebrity now, with fan mail to prove it. Letters and cards poured in by the bushel from all over the country. His father answered every piece of it, while Eddie, still only 22 years old, went back to delivering orders for a friend's liquor store and delicatessen.

ROUGH SPOTS

Eddie's stardom, combined with his tender age and shy personality, produced some rough spots early in his career, including a police chase and arrest for a traffic violation. It started innocently enough, with dinner at the home of a teammate, pitcher Bob Buhl.

As he was driving home in the early morning hours, which is not really late for professional baseball players accustomed to being up well past midnight because of all their night games, a police officer in a cruiser spotted Mathews speeding and began to chase him. Mathews, hoping to avoid publicity, turned off his headlights and tried to speed away. He was caught, but then he compounded his offense by saying the wrong things to the officer, whereupon he was taken to the nearest police station, booked, fined and released.

The incident made the headlines the next day. He was in the big bold letters again shortly after when he had a brief marital spat and moved out of his home for a few days.

All of this was hard on the young star, who leaned toward being an introvert, demanded his privacy and tried hard to protect it. In Boston, he could probably have walked down Commonwealth Avenue in his Braves uniform and not have been noticed. But Milwaukee was different, with no place to hide. Not like in New York, Chicago or Los Angeles, or Boston. He wasn't used to being mobbed every time he went out in public, and having everyone in town know his business. They knew where he went to socialize, what he liked to drink, what girls he might be dating. Many believed he was a small town boy for whom Milwaukee seemed to be a big city and so he was using brashness as a defense against things he didn't understand.

It didn't help when the Milwaukee baseball writers voted him their "Most Temperamental" award. Many of the fans agreed, saying they felt

Mathews was aloof. Eddie admitted he was a difficult person to know, that he chooses his friends carefully.

He added that he simply wasn't the type to show a lot of emotion on the field, causing many fans mistakenly to feel he didn't care. He said, "I hustle, but in my own way. I'm not a rah-rah guy. I'm not the type to make a big production out of everything I do. I think it's a joke when a guy strikes out and throws his bat. If I have to do that to show the fans I'm mad, to heck with it. They should realize I'm mad at myself. I shouldn't have to fling bats or kick water coolers."

Mathews went on: "Hustling to me means taking the extra base, beating out the slow roller, breaking up a double play, knocking the ball out of the catcher's glove, backing up throws and keeping my mind on the game at all times. But now I realize I'm in a goldfish bowl and am trying to adjust to that fact. Actually, maybe it was best some of those things happened. I feel, as a result of it all, that I have matured a great deal."

Mathews continued to encounter bumps in the road but was able to keep his star on the rise. His father's health deteriorated rapidly during the 1954 season, forcing Eddie to leave the team and fly home to California, the first games he had missed as a Brave. A week after his visit, his father died, on the day before Father's Day, never having seen his son play a game in the major leagues because he had always been too sick to travel. Later in the season, his mother flew to Milwaukee to visit and for her first chance to see Eddie play in the majors. He provided the highlight of his mother's trip by hitting two home runs for her.

Back problems and a split finger, plus his father's illness and death, caused Mathews to miss 16 games that year. Through it all, he still put together a better all-around season than his rookie year two seasons before —40 home runs, 103 runs batted in and a highly respectable .290 batting average.

Other numbers told the story of another positive development in his career—he was becoming a good third baseman. He cut his errors in half, from 30 to 15, and led the league's third basemen in fielding average. To top it all off, the Braves again set a National League attendance record, this time with over two million fans, giving them a record attendance in both of their two years in Milwaukee.

The frosting on the cake came when he was the cover photo for the premier issue of America's newest sports magazine, called *Sports Illustrated.*

New health problems challenged him in 1955, when an emergency appendectomy forced him out of the lineup in May after a miserable start. The slugging star went 0-for-April, failing to homer in his first 15 games. The appendectomy was expected to knock him out of the lineup for at least a month, but true to his fiercely competitive nature, he was back in uniform in less than two weeks.

The Dodgers ran away with the pennant after one of history's most explosive starts with 22 wins in their first 24 games, but the Braves finished second. Mathews continued to put up impressive numbers, with 41 home runs and 101 RBIs. Still only 24 years old, he already had 153 homers, the youngest slugger in history to reach that total. Mel Ott, who previously held the record, needed eight years to reach the total. Mathews made it in half that time.

THE POWER AND THE GLORY

As Mathews continued his stardom, he was joined by Hank Aaron, baseball's future and current home run king. By 1957, if ever there was a team of destiny, it was the Braves. That year they excited not only Milwaukee but the entire nation by sweeping their way to the pennant and conquering the mighty Yankees in the World Series.

With Mathews and Aaron hitting in the third and fourth spots in Manager Fred Haney's batting order, the Braves won 95 games and captured the pennant by eight games over the Cardinals. Aaron, who achieved stardom as quickly as Mathews, won the league's batting championship in '56, and in '57 he swept the long-ball categories by leading the league in home runs with 44, runs scored with 118 and runs batted in with 132 while hitting .322. The world was discovering what became baseball's all-time one-two punch. Mathews was fifth in homers with 32 and fourth in runs scored with 109, plus 94 RBIs and a .292 average.

Mathews figured in one of the most exciting games ever played in the World Series. After the Yankees captured two of the first three contests, they fell behind, 4-1, in the fourth game but tied it in the ninth inning on Elston Howard's home run and took the lead in the top of the tenth on a single by Tony Kubek, a Milwaukee boy, and a triple by Hank Bauer.

As if an extra-inning game in the World Series isn't enough excitement, things became even more nerve-wracking in the bottom of the tenth. Nippy Jones was sent up to pinch hit to lead off the tenth for the Braves and backed away from a close pitch by the Yankees' lefthander, Tommy Byrne. Home plate umpire Augie Donatelli started to rule it a ball, but Jones showed him black shoe polish on the white baseball and Donatelli award him first base, ruling he had been hit by the pitch after all.

Mathews jumped all over the opportunity by hitting a home run for a 7-5 victory to tie the Series at two wins each. But the drama wasn't finished, and neither was Mathews.

Although he was not having a good Series at the plate, he continued his trade mark bear-down style of play, and it produced the Braves' third win of the series in the next game, before the Milwaukee fans.

Righthander Lew Burdette, who won three games in that Series, shut out the Yankees, 1-0. The day's only run came when Mathews hit a high chopper to Jerry Coleman at second base. The Yankee scouting report had made no mention of Eddie's speed, even though some scouts had rated him one of the ten fastest players in the league. Coleman, instead of charging the ball because of Eddie's speed, waited for the high hop. Mathews beat his throw in a bang-bang play. Aaron and Joe Adcock followed with base hits to score Mathews and win the game.

Roland Hemond, one of baseball's most popular and respected front office executives and now a senior official with the Arizona Diamondbacks, remembers the Mathews play vividly: "What a hustler! In the '57 Series, he hit a high chopper like an automatic out to Jerry Coleman and he beat the throw. Coleman was shocked. I guess he hadn't seen enough of him, and scouting reports aren't what they are today. The play led to a big run and turned out to be one of the big plays of the Series. But it was normal for Eddie to go down the line the way he did. It wasn't that he didn't hustle but then turned it on. He did it all the time. In my opinion, that play turned the Series around."

Mathews still wasn't finished. He had one more spectacular contribution to make to his team and its fans, and this time he did it with his glove. Burdette was pitching, trying to become only the second pitcher in history to win three games in one World Series. That seemed to be enough of a challenge, but there was one more: Burdette, who won 17 games that year, was working with only two days of rest because the scheduled pitcher, Warren Spahn, had the flu.

With the bases loaded and two outs in the seventh game, the Braves leading 5-0 and only one out away from a shocking upset, Moose Skowron lashed a screaming ground ball down the third base line.

Mathews, the third baseman once maligned as a defensive liability, the one who broke his nose three times while learning to field ground balls, flagged it down in a flash with a spectacular backhanded stop. The ball was hit with such force by the powerful Skowron that it almost spun Mathews around, but he stayed with it and in one motion tagged the bag for a force play that ended the Series and preserved the victory that delighted the entire nation.

Reporters asked Fred Haney after the game if he was surprised by Eddie's outstanding pressure stop, and Haney said no, that he had seen Eddie make that play hundreds of times in games and practices.

Mathews had a different answer for St. Louis sportswriter Bob Broeg. "That Series was my greatest thrill to that point, and that play ranked right up there with breaking the 500-homer barrier. It was because I'd had a time shaking what was really a bum rap about my fielding. I'd made better plays. In fact, Casey Stengel raved about one on a slow-hit ball by Jerry Coleman earlier in the Series, but that big one in the spotlight stamped me the way I wanted to be remembered."

MORE SLUGGING, OF BOTH KINDS

The Braves repeated as National League pennant winners in 1958 on the strength of the slugging by Mathews and Aaron. Together they hit 61 homers, but then lost the Series to the Yankees in seven games. In 1959, Eddie led the league in home runs for the second time with 46 and drove in 114 runs while Aaron led the league in batting average with .355 and 123 RBIs. Spahn and Burdette, the Braves' one-two pitching punch to go with their one-two slugging punch, both won 21 games.

Mathews continued to hammer the ball in 1960 with 39 homers and 124 RBIs. He clubbed something else that year, too—Frank Robinson.

Robinson, now a fellow Hall of Famer and member of the 500-homer club, was in his fifth year with the Cincinnati Reds, dividing his time between first base and the outfield. But he was something more, a hard-nosed player, cut from the same mold as Mathews, two of a kind who knew only one way to play the game—hard.

He had a habit of sliding into bases with his spikes high. He tried it on Mathews once and was told in no uncertain words that if he did it again, he would pay a heavy price.

Despite that warning from Mathews, Robinson came sliding into him in the first game of a doubleheader in Cincinnati, swinging his arm up as he hit the bag, catching Mathews on the side of the head. Before peacemakers could intervene, Mathews pounced on Robinson and landed several hard blows that cut both of Robinson's eyes and sent him sprawling in the dirt. Mathews, who hurt his right hand while delivering the punches, was ejected from the game.

Robinson earned Mathews's respect in the second game. Despite having to wipe blood from his eyes periodically, he hit a home run that won the game for the Reds.

INJURIES AND GOODBYES

While the first two expansion teams in baseball history played their first season, the new Washington Senators and the Los Angeles Angels, Mathews registered the second .300 year of his career in 1961 with a .306 average and 32 homers. He ignited a power parade during a game on June 8 against the Reds at their old home, Crosley Field. He led off the seventh inning with a home run, and Aaron followed with one of his own, not the first time the one-two punch had hit back-to-back home runs. But then Joe Adcock also hit one, and so did Frank Thomas. Four home runs in a row.

The Braves lost the game, 10-8, which may be a commentary on that season and that period. The Braves slipped to fourth place that year after finishing first or second for six straight seasons and seven out of eight. Attendance also dropped, by 400,000 fans down to 1,100,000.

In 1962, Eddie's roommate for nine years, Bob Buhl, was traded to the Cubs, following the departure the year before of three Braves mainstays—Second Baseman Red Schoendienst, also a future Hall of Famer, Center Fielder Billy Bruton and Eddie's best friend on the team, Shortstop Johnny Logan.

The team wasn't winning, attendance was dwindling and his best friends were gone. For Mathews, nothing was the same. Then an incident occurred that was to affect his ability to swing a bat for the rest of his career, costing him uncounted home runs.

The National League expanded for the first time that season, with the addition of the New York Mets and the Houston Colt .45s, now the Astros, and it was in Houston where Mathews fell victim to a critical quirk of fate. He injured himself not by getting hit by a batted ball or tearing up his knee or throwing out his arm or by colliding with another player. He hurt himself by swinging at a pitch and missing.

Mathews stepped into the batter's box in the first inning against Dick Farrell, a hard-throwing righthander who was making one of his rare starts. Farrell served up a high forkball. Mathews swung mightily with that home run swing of his and fouled off the pitch. In doing so, he tore all the ligaments in his right shoulder.

He missed several weeks of action. When he returned, he began holding his right arm closer to his body to protect his shoulder. The result —he became a defensive hitter and developed bad habits at the plate, a combination that spells doom for any hitter.

Mathews didn't go into any steep decline, but he was unable to maintain his heavy hitting. His home run total told the story. He hit 29, a respectable enough total for other hitters but below his usual total, the first time in 11 years he had not hit at least 30 homers.

That 29th home run came in the last game of the season. In the same game, his new "roomie," Catcher Bob Uecker, another one of Milwaukee's native sons like Tony Kubek, hit his first roundtripper. On the banquet circuit over the winter, Uecker told his audiences that he and his roommate had 400 career home runs between them—Mathews 399, Uecker one.

THE BEGINNING OF THE END

Even with his bad shoulder, Mathews continued to hit home runs, maybe not as many, but enough to maintain his reputation as one of Major League Baseball's feared hitters. He hit 23, 23 and 32 homers in his team's last three seasons in Milwaukee, while talk grew louder during the mid-1960s that the team, saddled with a continued decline in attendance, was going to be moved to Atlanta.

The famed Milwaukee one-two punch kept hitting baseballs out of National League parks right up to the end in Milwaukee and into the team's first season in Atlanta, their last year together. By that time, 1966, Mathews and Aaron, the Braves' two-man murderers' row, had hit 863 home runs between them, breaking the record of Ruth and Gehrig. Neither man carried the other. They split their contributions almost equally, with Aaron hitting 442 homers and Mathews 421. Mathews called the feat the greatest thrill of his career.

In Bob Buege's book, *Eddie Mathews and the National Pastime,* he quotes Mathews' memories of Aaron: "I enjoyed Hank Aaron. I hit it off with him right away . . . . He was the best. He wasn't flashy like Willie Mays, but he did everything well. I never saw Aaron throw to the wrong base, never saw him overthrow the cutoff man, but he did (everything) so easily that nobody noticed. Maybe because his cap didn't fly off," a thinly veiled reference to the Mays trademark.

Mathews headed to Atlanta with his teammates for the team's first year in Atlanta and his last season with the Braves, the only man to play for the team in Boston, Milwaukee and Atlanta. His production dropped steeply, with just 16 home runs and only 53 RBIs and a .250 average.

Then he was treated the way too many other stars have been treated by too many teams. The Braves traded Mathews to Houston after the 1966 season—without bothering to tell him. He found out he wasn't a Brave any more on New Year's Eve in a phone call from a Milwaukee sportswriter. No one with the Braves bothered to phone him and thank him for his loyalty and outstanding performance over 15 years.

Number 41 wasn't finished yet. While playing for Houston, Mathews hit a home run with two on off another future Hall of Famer, righthander Juan Marichal, the star from the Dominican Republic, "the Dominican Dandy" who overpowered National League hitters for 16 years with his blazing fast balls and his high leg kick.

The homer was special for two reasons: Mathews always said Marichal was the pitcher who gave him the most trouble, and it was Eddie's 500th homer. It made him only the seventh slugger in the history of the game to reach that number. Only Ruth, Foxx, Ott, Williams, Mantle and Mays had accomplished the superhuman feat by 1967.

Mathews was traded to Detroit in August and finished his career by playing for the Tigers in the balance of the '67 season and in 1968, when the Tigers won the pennant behind Denny McLain's 31-win season and then defeated the Cardinals in the World Series.

He was a part-timer at first and third base, appearing in only 31 games and hitting three home runs. In the Series, he got into only two games, collecting a single in three times at bat, but he got to go out on top —playing for a World Series champion.

Another nice thing happened to Mathews in 1968. In a sweet touch of irony, the Tigers played a regular season game in Milwaukee, part of an effort to lure big league baseball back to that city to replace the Braves. A local group headed by Bud Selig, now the Commissioner of Baseball, talked the Chicago White Sox, only 90 miles away, into playing one game against each of their American League opponents in Milwaukee to convince baseball's brass that the town would support big league baseball again.

In late August it was the Tigers' turn, and Mathews came back to his baseball home, welcomed and saluted on Eddie Mathews Night. Even more important, the Selig group flew his mother in from California along with Eddie's wife and kids and many of his old Braves teammates.

The game was a sellout. No one could blame Mathews when he told the crowd, "All the good things that happened to me in baseball happened here in Milwaukee."

THE ONE-TWO PUNCH: AN ENCORE

After his playing days, the Braves offered Mathews a job as a coach. He was promoted from that position to replace Luman Harris as the Braves' manager in 1972. He was fired two years later, but not before he teamed up with Aaron for an encore performance of the famed one-two punch in one of baseball's most historic achievements, although Aaron was the only one still swinging a bat.

Going into the 1974 season, Aaron had hit 713 home runs in his career, only one less than Ruth's total. At that time, Ruth's record of 714 homers in his career stood as the most famous record not only in baseball but in any sport. And now Aaron was only one away from reaching one of the pinnacles of American sport.

The Braves opened their season in Cincinnati, and Aaron belted Number 714 off Jack Billingham in his first time at bat for the season. Mathews held his old teammate out of the next game and planned to keep him out of the lineup on Sunday as well so he could break the record in Atlanta, where the Braves were scheduled to open an 11-game home stand.

But Commissioner Bowie Kuhn ruled Aaron had to play Sunday. He did, but Mathews replaced him in the seventh inning. The press corps, by now swollen to 300, then followed Aaron and his team to Atlanta to await the record breaker. Every baseball fan in America was following the news, and so were millions more who weren't even fans. It was the biggest story of American achievement since Neil Armstrong walked on the moon five years earlier.

In his first game back in Atlanta, Aaron broke the supposedly unbreakable home run barrier with a home run off lefthander Al Downing before a sellout crowd and a national television audience. From the stands, 53,775 fans cheered madly, with some of them leaping onto the field to accompany Hank around the bases.

From the dugout, Eddie Mathews applauded, maybe with more enthusiasm than most and surely with more inner emotion. After Aaron passed the immortal Bambino, making himself immortal in the process, the size of the crowd dropped to 10,000. The fans had come to see Aaron break the record, and after he did, they left.

In 1978, Eddie was married again, to Elizabeth Busch, the daughter of the owner of the St. Louis Cardinals and the world's largest brewery.

The 500 Home Run Club

Minor leaguer Henry Aaron in 1952.

(Courtesy of Bob Allen collection)

Young Hank Aaron, his teammates, and Braves publicist Bob Allen (on Aaron's right) listen intently during a visit from immortal Ty Cobb.

(Courtesy of Bob Allen collection)

The 500 Home Run Club

Babe Ruth initially made his mark as a pitcher for the Red Sox. During those five seasons with Boston he hit a total of 49 home runs.

(Courtesy of Boston Red Sox)

Babe Ruth (left) and **Lou Gehrig**, who belted 493 career homers, combined to form the heart of the great Yankee teams of the 1920s and '30s.

(Courtesy of Bob Allen collection)

The 500 Home Run Club

In 1965, **Willie Mays (left)** hammered 52 homers, joining **Babe Ruth, Jimmie Foxx, Ralph Kiner** and **Mickey Mantle** as the only players with more than one 50-home run season.

(Courtesy of San Francisco Giants)

During their careers, **Harmon Killebrew (left), Willie Mays (center)** and **Mickey Mantle** hit a cumulative 1,769 home runs.

(Courtesy of Bob Allen collection)

The 500 Home Run Club

Cincinnati's Frank Robinson, shown here as a rookie in 1956, hit 38 home runs in his first major league season.

(AP/Wide World Photos)

Frank Robinson, a member of the World Champion Baltimore Orioles in 1966, became the first player to ever win Most Valuable Player balloting in both the National and American Leagues.

(AP/Wide World Photos)

The 500 Home Run Club

(Bob Schutz, AP/Wide World Photos)

At age 31, Minnesota Twins' outfielder **Harmon Killebrew** had hit 380 home runs, more than Babe Ruth at the same age.

The 500 Home Run Club

Reggie Jackson hit 267 of his 563 career home runs as a member of the Oakland A's. His very first blast came in 1967 with the old Kansas City A's.

(AP/Wide World Photos)

Jackson earned the nickname "Mr. October" for the New York Yankees.

(AP/Wide World Photos)

Mike Schmidt failed to hit 30 home runs or more in only three of his 16 full Major League seasons.

(Courtesy of Philadelphia Phillies)

An eight-time winner of the National League's home run crown, Mike Schmidt clubbed 548 career round-trippers.

(Rusty Kennedy, AP/Wide World Photos)

The 500 Home Run Club

Even though he was not quite 5'11", Mickey Mantle's mammoth blow reached the facade that hangs from the Yankee stadium roof an amazing five times.

(Courtesy of Bob Allen collection)

When he retired in 1968, Mantle held the World Series record for home runs with 18.

(Courtesy of Bob Allen collection)

In 1932, Jimmie Foxx hit 58 home runs. He might have hit more than 60 if not for a spell in August when he suffered from an injured wrist.

(Courtesy of Detroit Tigers)

Foxx of the Red Sox and **Hank Greenberg** of the Tigers often battled each other for the American League home run lead.

(Courtesy of Detroit Tigers)

The 500 Home Run Club

The soft-spoken but powerful **Willie McCovey** was overshadowed by teammate Willie Mays during his career in San Francisco.

(Jeff Robbins, AP/Wide World Photos)

McCovey belted more home runs than any other National League left-handed hitter.

(AP/Wide World Photos)

The 500 Home Run Club

Ted Williams lost nearly five years of his career to military service in World War II and Korea, but still managed to hit 521 home runs.

(Courtesy of Boston Red Sox)

Author Bob Allen (left) and The Splendid Splinter.

(Courtesy of Bob Allen collection)

The 500 Home Run Club

Ernie Banks, the Chicago Cubs' first black player, hit his 500th home run on May 12,1970, at the friendly confines of Wrigley Field.

(Courtesy of Bob Allen collection)

From 1955-1960, "Mr. Club" hit more homers than anyone in the majors, including Mickey Mantle, Willie Mays and Hank Aaron.

(Courtesy of Chicago Cubs)

The 500 Home Run Club

Of his 512 career home runs, Eddie Mathews hit 486 as a third baseman.

(Courtesy of Bob Allen collection)

Milwaukee's No. 41 led the National League in home runs in 1953 and 1959.

(Courtesy of Bob Allen collection)

The 500 Home Run Club

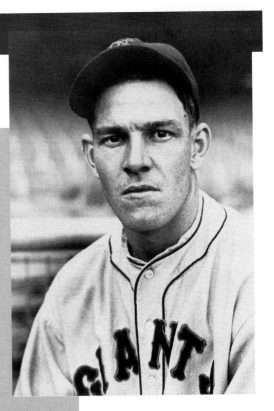

Mel Ott's left-handed power was perfectly suited to the Polo Grounds' inviting right field fence, only 257 feet from home plate.

(Courtesy of Bob Allen collection)

Ott's classic foot-in the-bucket stance helped him become the first National Leaguer to hit 500 home runs.

(AP/Wide World Photos)

The 500 Home Run Club

(John Mummert, AP/Wide World Photos)

Eddie Murray, who played most of his career for the
Baltimore Orioles, was the last player to reach the
500-home run plateau.

The 500 Home Run Club

(Courtesy of Bob Allen collection)

Mark McGwire (left), almost certain to be the next member of baseball's 500 Home Run Club, clowns around with author Bob Allen.

Later that evening, his mother called from California. Why would a man's mother interrupt him with a phone call on a wedding night? To tell him he'd been elected to the Baseball Hall of Fame.

A CLUE TO A MAN'S MAKEUP

It may be that the best clue to the makeup of Eddie Mathews was found not in his 15 years with the Braves but on the first day of his one-plus season with the Detroit Tigers.

An anonymous teammate remembered: "His first day with us, Mathews dressed and headed down the tunnel (toward the playing field). Someone had written on the wall in chalk that the Tigers could win the pennant without Mayo Smith (who was still their manager). Eddie got a wet towel and wiped it out. Then he went to the perpetrators, who defended themselves by saying that's the way they felt.

The unidentified teammate said Mathews answered, "Well, that's not the way I feel."

The teammate continued, "I can't think of anybody on the team who was more respected than Eddie. I don't know exactly what it was about him, but he commanded respect. You could see it from the first day he joined the club."

Today Mathews is just as hard nosed as ever. It shows when you talk to him about the sport he loves and the people who play it. "I don't think much of the way they play the game," he told Joe Turner in *LifeStyle West* in 1998. "I don't think much of their attitudes. There's no loyalty to the fans, no loyalty to the team, no loyalty to the city."

He told Turner that seven-figure salaries and frequent moves by players from one team to another in the era of free agency don't change the basic nature of baseball. "It's a bat and a ball," he said. "You hit it square and run like hell."

The Mathews personality and his abiding love for his sport obviously made a sharp impression on Turner, who wrote, "If you sense a passion in Mathews when it comes to baseball, it's because he has a passion that runs as deep as the red lettering on a Braves uniform."

MATHEWS ON MATHEWS

When I started out, I never thought about hitting 500 homers or 400 or anything. Then once I hit 500, I realized it was quite a milestone. But there was no "500 Home Run Club" then. But once they started that, it became a lot of fun and important to me that I was a member of that, because there are just a few of us. And there weren't 15 when I got in.

On how to pitch to him: I'd throw off-speed stuff—junk. No fast balls. I was a fast ball hitter. Just try to keep me off-stride and get me guessing.

On the best thing he had going for himself at the plate: Reflexes, hand-to-eye coordination, reflexes in that once you see the ball, do something about it. Of course, I had a pretty good build and quick wrists, but I would say the reflexes.

The toughest pitcher for him: I would say the most consistent pitcher who was tough on me was Juan Marichal. He had all the pitches and a rather odd delivery with a high kick—his combination of pitches and delivery—but I hit my 500th off him.

The best parks to hit in: Cincinnati (Crosley Field) and Wrigley Field.

Cooperstown was very important to me. It took me five years to get in after I was eligible. Banks, who went in the first year he was eligible, has a record almost identical to what I had, so that was a little disturbing on why, but I'm in. It's a hell of an honor, and I'm real proud of it.

In 1957, I had a good Series defensively. And when I made that last stop, I think a lot of people thought, "He's come around a bit and can play third base now (laughter). What a thrill that was—making the last out, and we were world champions!

I went from Boston to Milwaukee to Atlanta with the Braves. When they traded me to Houston I cried like a baby. I'm not ashamed of crying. I had totally wanted to play with the Braves, period. But . . . they traded me.

On Hank Aaron: We got along just great. We'd play cards before every game. We did some socializing, not a lot. We've been friends ever since we met, and still are. We broke Ruth and Gehrig's total, but didn't get much publicity for it. We had a certain amount of friendly competition. And I don't think the Atlanta ballpark was that big a help to Hank. Hell, he hit them everywhere!

WHAT OTHER PLAYERS SAID ABOUT EDDIE MATHEWS

Red Schoendienst—He could hit, run and had a great arm. What more could you ask? When he walked into that clubhouse or on that ballfield, he was all business, a bear-down guy, an outstanding competitor. He knew what he had to do and could do it.

Del Crandall—One of the real pure power swingers. No question, he was the leader of our team. Everyone really appreciated his toughness.

When he got hurt, he continued to play or got back in there as soon as he could. He threw his shoulder out later in his career, and if he hadn't, he would have hit 600 homers. We all looked up to him.

Andy Pafko—He was just a so-so third baseman when he came up, but he took a lot of ground balls and made himself into a fine fielder. A tough individual—boy, he came to play. Nothing took him out of the lineup. I think if he had a broken leg, he would still be out there.

Gaylord Perry—What an aggressive hitter he was. At Candlestick Park, the wind was blowing to right field with center field 400 feet away. He tried to pull everything, so I set him up for an outside fast ball. It was probably two inches outside, and he hit it over the centerfield fence. I didn't try to pitch him there any more.

Warren Spahn—He came to play every day. He played hurt. There was just no way you were going to get him out of the lineup. When he came up, he couldn't stop a ball with his chest. He took thousands of ground balls until he made himself into a fine fielder. He asked no quarter and gave none. Throughout the league, Eddie was respected as a hard-nosed ballplayer. He wouldn't take anything from anyone. I'm glad he was on my side.

Frank Howard—A great swing. One of the finest swings of all time. Had he not gotten hurt, he would have approached 700 home runs. A marvelous, letter-perfect swing from a mechanical standpoint.

Lew Burdette—Eddie, Warren Spahn and Bob Buhl were my best friends on the Braves, and after I was traded he got me a couple of times. He was my friend. I had to take good care of him. But he didn't beat me with it. I felt sorry for Eddie, running around with three pitchers. We had more time between starts than he did.

Johnny Podres—Man, being a lefthanded hitter and my being a lefthanded pitcher didn't mean a damn bit of difference. If you made a mistake on him—it was unbelievable.

Bob Purkey—He was a tough out. He was big and strong, and I really didn't have a great strikeout pitch for lefthanders other than a knuckleball. That's what I would throw him. It was not a pitch that would fool anybody unless it broke. He hurt me, because if it wasn't working good, he would let me know quickly.

Wally Moon—The purest, sweetest home run swing of all the guys I saw. He was built to hit home runs. A beautiful hitter to watch, with extraordinary power. He would have reached 600 homers if his injuries hadn't forced him out of the game.

Frank Torre—The unsung hero of all of them. He probably hit as many home runs as Hank did when they batted back-to-back all those years. If he hadn't played his entire career just about in Milwaukee—a tough home run park—he would have gone well over 600. He was one of those rare guys who got few cheap home runs.

Bob Friend—Eddie hit more home runs off me than any other hitter. I had a real tough time with him. He beat me a lot of ball games. He wouldn't brag to the press about how well he hit me, but he'd tell them I was one of the toughest pitchers he ever faced. He had me set up pretty good.

Chuck Tanner—There's nobody who played harder or loved the game more than he did. I played with him, and he was my idol. When we went on that field, you got everything he had inside. If he wanted to, he could have stolen 50 bases a season. He could fly. He had one of the quickest bats that has ever been in the game. He played every game like the world was coming to an end tomorrow.

Monte Irvin—One of the strongest men I saw in baseball. When I first saw him, I knew he was going to be a star because not only was he strong, but he had that home run swing. Mathews followed by Hank Aaron in the lineup was unbelievable.

Roland Hemond—Rogers Hornsby saw Eddie play in Atlanta on the way up and, being the outspoken guy he was, said, "He might hit 500 home runs, but he'll only field .500," meaning he's a bad fielder, but Eddie became a real fine fielder with a tremendous amount of work on his part. He made that great backhanded stab on Moose Skowron's sizzler down the third base line with the bases loaded to end the World Series.

Don Newcombe—Another guy I couldn't get the ball by. In fact, I couldn't get the ball by that whole Milwaukee lineup. Eddie Mathews was one of the best lefthanded batters I ever faced. He sure could hit that low fast ball.

Gene Oliver—I'll never forget when Frank Robinson cut up Roy McMillan at second. Eddie came to the dugout and was watching them sew up McMillan and he said, "I'll get that (deleted) before the game is over," and little did we know Robbie was going to hit a triple and come sliding high with his spikes into third base, into Eddie. It was going to be a close play, but Eddie didn't even try to tag him. He just stepped out of the way and let him have it. He really drilled him, and as Robbie was getting up, he hit him again. He was bleeding profusely, but he came back all stitched up and beat us with two homers in the second game.

Don Blasingame—He and Willie McCovey, being lefthanded hitters, hit the ball as hard to me at second base as anybody. Eddie hit the ball so hard it would actually hook.

Vernon Law—I'll tell you, boy, there was a fierce competitor. I mean, he was tough. There are some guys you don't throw at, and he was one of them. If you threw at him, on the next pitch you couldn't breathe for five minutes because he would swing so hard it would take all the air out of the ballpark.

Don Zimmer—When he came to the big leagues, he couldn't catch a ball. I remember in Milwaukee one night, he booted two or three balls and Jackie Robinson hollered out at him, "Put the glove on your foot!" Eddie was a tough son of a buck. He'd fight you at the drop of a hat. But every time we played in Milwaukee, I'd see him out there catching 50 to 100 balls, to where a year and a half after, he became one of the best fielding third basemen in the league. Another thing people don't give him credit for—he could run. I mean, if he hit a ball to deep short, he was going to beat it out.

Stan Musial—I was surprised that Aaron and Mathews broke Babe Ruth and Lou Gehrig's record for home runs as teammates. Ruth and Gehrig were big, bulky guys, and Aaron and Mathews were skinny guys compared to them. It seemed unlikely that they would be the pair. In fact, it's hard to believe.

Whitey Herzog—He was as strong as a damn ox, and as tough, too.

Carl Erskine—Mathews had a unique style. The first time I faced him, he did something that totally surprised me, and I had been in the league a while. You throw a fast ball to Mathews and it would pass a point where most hitters had already started their swing. But Mathews hadn't started his swing, so you figure he's going to take the pitch. And then, at the very last part of the pitch, here comes this quick bat. He had the quickest bat. He would start his swing later than almost any other hitter. And that's how he generated all the power. He had a really quick bat. He could delay longer and still get that full, quick swing. He was tough to pitch to because he waited so long to pull the trigger.

Umpire Doug Harvey—I really had a lot of respect for Eddie. I'll never forget when I was a young umpire, I made a call and all hell broke loose and I had to eject a couple of guys. At the end of the inning, Mathews came out to third base, and I asked him why he didn't charge me too, and he said because he thought the ball was in the strike zone and I had made the right call. I always respected him for that. He had complete control of himself at all times.

Ron Swoboda—Eddie was all anger and in your face. Every game was like a street fight to him. That's the way he played baseball. That's the way he walked up to the plate. That's the way he did everything.

Gene Conley—Years ago I was talking with Roy Campanella, and he told me that of all the hitters he ever caught behind when Don Newcombe and other flame throwers were throwing fast balls that really popped in his glove, Eddie had the quickest bat of anybody. I told Eddie that, and he just kind of smiled.

Don Mueller—One day I slid into third base, and he had the ball. And I kicked him in the wrist and kicked the ball out of his glove, and he came up and drew his arm back. He wanted to go at it. He was a rough and tumble guy. I just said, "Now wait a minute, Eddie. We're out here to play ball, not fight." He just cooled down and everything was fine.

Umpire Shag Crawford—He was my favorite of all the guys I umped against. One of the great guys in baseball, and a hell of a fielder. He was a hard-nosed ballplayer. He'd give you that old 110 percent. He was the type of guy, if he had a beef, he gives it to you and then forgets about it.

Frank Robinson—Eddie played the game hard. The era we came along in was kinda no nonsense. If you were the opposing player you were the enemy and that's the way Eddie Mathews played it. He was a tough out and he played a very good third base and never really got a lot of credit for it. He was a tough, tough out. He complemented Hank (Aaron), Joe Adcock and those other big bombers in their lineup. He was a lefthand hitter in a predominantly righthand lineup but he didn't have to take a back seat to anybody.

Bill Virdon—Eddie always hurt us as much as Aaron did. Eddie wasn't as good a hitter as Hank as far as consistency is concerned, but when he hit the ball, he hit the ball pretty much to right field while Aaron sprayed the ball in his early years. Eddie would hit the ball out of anywhere, and he played every day. He was tough, and you'd like to see him on your side.

Hank Aaron—Eddie was one of the finest hitters I ever saw. He was very strong and much better than people thought he was. I hit behind him for years. The thing I liked about him was he hit the ball hard all the time. For a guy who hit a lot of home runs, he didn't strike out that much. Pitchers would think they had something by him or could pitch him in a certain place, and—BAM!—he could hit it out of the ballpark. He ran better than people gave him credit for and won a World Series game for us. He wasn't a Brooks Robinson in the field, but I'll tell you one thing: He could play third base about as good as anybody. We got along just great, and I'll always consider him one of my dearest friends. Above all, Eddie was a team man. He was high-strung and if you got into any kind of a fight or scrap, you would sure want him on your side.

Pete Rose—What I remember most about Eddie was the fight he got into with Frank Robinson. Eddie didn't ask any questions—just bip, bop, bip, bop and it was all over. Boy, he was a tough player and a tough guy.

Harmon Killebrew—Eddie was just a great competitor and a great third baseman, too. Great power and, I'll tell you, he didn't want to lose. He was the kind of guy I would like to have on my club.

Ernie Banks—Eddie wasn't just a home run hitter, he was a clutch home run hitter. When the game was on the line, or men on base, Eddie would inevitably come through, especially against the Cubs.

Joe Garagiola—I think Eddie and Henry (Aaron) were such great hitters that the other things they could do on a ball field were overshadowed. He was way above average as a fielder. Of course, he had that real quick bat. Boy, he was a good-looking hitter. No wasted motion. He was a tough guy, a quiet guy. A tough guy and not just because he got into fights. He was tough, a no-nonsense player.

THE MATHEWS FILE

Full Name: Edwin Lee Mathews.
Date and Place of Birth: October 13, 1931, Texarkana, Texas.
Position: Third base.
Major League Career: 17 years, 1952-1968.
Home Runs: 512 (13th).
Runs Batted In: 1,453.
Runs Scored: 1,509.
Lifetime Batting Average: .271.
Number of Hits: 2,315.
Walks: 1,444.
Strikeouts: 1,487.

Records: When he retired, Mathews held Major League records for third basemen in games played, assists, fielding chances and home runs — both season and career.

Other Highlights:
— Holds National League record for most consecutive years with 30 or more home runs—nine.
— Hit 40 or more home runs four times.
— Led National League in homers twice and in runs batted in four times.
— Hit 23 or more home runs 14 straight times.
— Hit three home runs in one game, September 27, 1952, the first rookie to do it.
— Led league in bases on balls four times.
— Named to *The Sporting News* Major League All-Star teams four times.
— Played in third fewest games of 500-homer hitters, behind Williams and Foxx.
— With Mantle, retired earlier than any other 500-homer hitter, both at age 36.
— Named to National League All-Star team ten times.

Elected to Baseball Hall of Fame: 1978

8

WILLIE MAYS

"Say Hey!"

When you talk to his former teammates and opponents about Willie Mays, you're surprised at how many of them call him the greatest baseball player they ever saw, maybe the best ever. That's what many of those interviewed for this book said — people who should know like Al Kaline, Alvin Dark, Gaylord Perry, Frank Howard, Billy Williams, Ron Santo, Bill Mazeroski, Don Newcombe, Don Zimmer, Juan Marichal, Whitey Herzog and Leo Durocher.

Kaline, a fellow Hall of Famer, said, "Willie Mays might have been the greatest player who ever lived." Umpires were just as willing as the players to nominate Mays as the greatest of all time. Doug Harvey said flatly, "Willie Mays was the greatest ballplayer who ever walked on this earth."

GREATNESS AND OBSTACLES

Such high praise is justified in the record book: In 22 years in the Major Leagues, Mays accomplished a lifetime batting average over .300, was the National League's Most Valuable Player twice, played in four World Series and 24 All-Star games (more than any other player), collected over 3,000 hits including 660 home runs—the third most in history behind only Hank Aaron and Babe Ruth—and won 12 straight Gold Glove Awards as the best center fielder in the league.

Like those born to greatness in other fields, Mays knew success unattained by others, but he also knew tragedy, setbacks, family difficulties, health problems, depression and controversy. Some of these elements stalk him even today.

As with so many other minority athletes who reached stardom in their sports, the sting of prejudice always lurked in the background, especially since Mays broke into the big leagues only four years after Jackie Robinson. Even later, during his years in San Francisco, the Giants and their managers were called "Rigney's jigs," "Sheehan's shines" and "Dark's darkies."

Mays accomplished everything with his trademark enthusiasm, his rallying cry of "Say Hey!" and his unabashed love for baseball. Born into the sport as the son of a semi-pro center fielder nicknamed "Kitty Kat," he told Milton Richman in *This Week* magazine, "I remember the biggest surprise of my life, when I found out folks paid my father money to play. That seemed to me just about the best idea that anyone ever thought up—like getting paid to eat ice cream."

Willie Mays was born in Westfield Alabama in 1931, the same year as Mickey Mantle. For his first birthday, his father, Willie Sr., gave him a ball, and it quickly became Willie Jr.'s favorite toy.

For Mays, his first setback in life came early, at age three. His parents, Willie Sr. and Annie, divorced and Willie Jr. was sent to live with his Aunt Sarah while his father worked in one of the many steel mills in the area and starred for Fairfield in the local semi-pro baseball league.

Some of Willie's happiest days were when he accompanied his father to his game and got to sit on the bench with the team.

His father picked him up at Aunt Sarah's place almost every afternoon during the baseball season and the two would go to a game or head for a nearby vacant lot to practice. Occasionally they would drive the short distance to Birmingham to see the Birmingham Barons of the Southern Association or the Birmingham Black Barons of the Negro Leagues.

Joe DiMaggio was Willie's favorite player. He tried to imitate the Yankee Clipper's wide batting stance and his grace in center field, the position of his father and his own position when he grew up.

Fairfield Industrial High School didn't have a baseball team, so Willie contented himself by starring in football and basketball. For a trade, he studied to be a clothes presser. No steel mills for Willie. After high school, maybe he could go to college on a football or basketball scholarship. But what he really wanted to do was play baseball.

Even a part-time after-school salary, for washing dishes in a restaurant, didn't derail his ambitions. He quit after only a few days because he couldn't concentrate on his job when all he wanted to do was play ball.

The Black Barons solved all that by calling Willie after his sophomore year in high school in 1948 and offering him a tryout even though he was only sixteen. He made the team, and his high school days were over.

The Black Barons traveled the eastern half of the United States, most of it on buses that were more like school buses than the comfortable coaches of today. But Willie, in his youthful enthusiasm, enjoyed the travel and the camaraderie of his teammates. The Barons played in different parks all over the East including, as fate would have it, the Polo Grounds in New York, where Willie was destined to reach stardom only four years later, at the still-tender age of 20, with the Giants.

Ironically, the Polo Grounds were Willie's favorite ballpark because it was so big, with an outfield where he could roam far and wide and make exciting catches before he ever heard of a player named Vic Wertz.

His salary wasn't much better than that dishwasher's job—$75 a month—but he picked up more pocket money after the 1948 season by playing on a barnstorming team put together by Roy Campanella. There was another, bigger advantage to playing with the Black Barons—the scouts for the big league teams paid close attention to the Negro Leagues now that Robinson had broken Major League baseball's "color barrier" with the Brooklyn Dodgers only one year before, in 1947.

Under baseball's rules at that time, big league teams had to wait for a prospect's high school graduation before they could sign him. Willie wasn't in high school any more, but the rule said you had to wait until the player's class graduated anyhow. In Willie's case, that meant June, 1950.

Strangely enough, Willie signed with one of the few teams that appeared to know nothing about him. The New York Giants were interested in a husky first baseman named Alonzo Perry on the Black Barons, and Farm Director Jack Schwarz dispatched scout Eddie Montague to evaluate him.

Montague, however, couldn't take his eyes off Mays, so he signed him on his first day of eligibility for $5,000.

The budding star was assigned to the Giants' farm team in Trenton, New Jersey, because their owner, Horace Stoneham, wanted Mays close enough so he and his scouts could monitor his development, so convinced were they that the kid was destined to become what today is called a "superstar."

It would be nice to report that Mays was an instant sensation, but the truth is that he didn't get a hit in his first 22 times at bat. But then he exploded, finishing the season with a .353 average with 108 hits and 55 runs batted in over only 81 games.

This was enough to earn Mays a quick promotion the next season all the way to the top of the minor league classifications to the Triple-A level, a leap of three rungs up the ladder, to the Minneapolis Millers in the American Association. He continued his sensational play, raising his high average of his first season by another 124 points, to an eye-popping .477. He had eight home runs and 38 runs scored in the first 35 games.

Willie didn't just hit the ball *over* the fence. He hit it *through* the fence, too. He hit one of his line drives so hard it went straight through the wooden fence in the outfield. Instead of repairing the hole, management painted a circle around it and left it there as a conversation piece. The hole was still there when they tore down the ballpark several years later.

Willie was averaging almost two hits a game when the Giants decided that a performance like that over 35 games meant Mays was worth another look. They sent another scout, Hank DeBerry, to watch him closely and determine if he was ready for the big leagues after such a short time in the minors.

DeBerry sent back what may be the greatest rave review in the history of scouting:

"Sensational. Is the outstanding player on the Minneapolis club and probably in all the minor leagues for that matter. He is now on one of the best hitting streaks imaginable. Hits all pitches and hits to all fields. Hits the ball where it is pitched as good as any player seen in many days. Everything he does is sensational. He has made the most spectacular catches. Runs and throws with the best of them. Naturally, he has some faults, some of which are: charges low-hit balls too much, runs a bit with his head down. There have been a few times when his manager needed a rope (to control over-eagerness as a base runner). When he starts somewhere, he means to get there, hell-bent for election. Slides hard, plays hard. He is a sensation and just about as popular with local fans as he can be—a real favorite. The Louisville pitchers knocked him down plenty, but it seemed to have no effect on him at ball. This player is the best prospect in America. It was a banner day for the Giants when this boy was signed!"

With a review like that, the Giants did the obvious. They wasted no time and called Mays up to the parent team in New York after only 35 games.

The fans in Minneapolis were so incensed over the departure of their new sensation that Stoneham was forced to take out a full-page ad in a Minneapolis paper to apologize for taking their new favorite away from them.

For Mays, his scouting reports were notable for another reason as well. "I think just about all the Negro players who came up to the majors before I did had the same scouting report," he told an interviewer. "First, they said the player was a Negro, and then they said he was great. With me, they said great. Then they said Negro."

WELCOME TO THE BIG LEAGUES

On May 25, 1951, just 19 days past his twentieth birthday, and with only the clothes on his back, Mays reported to the Giants in Philadelphia, where they were playing the Phillies. He was greeted with open arms, for two good reasons:

1. He had starred for both of his minor league teams.
2. The Giants had lost five of their last six games.

New York sportswriter Barney Kremenko described Mays's debut:

"Willie, with a mob of reporters looking on, was a smashing success in the pre-game workout. Wearing uniform number 24, he sent batting practice pitches all over the lot. He whistled line drives in all directions and ripped screamers into the upper deck of left and centerfield.

"Then he went to the outfield and started winging the ball in from deep center to third and the plate without a hop. It was a tremendous exhibition and impressed one and all.

"When the game began, however, Willie's tightness showed. In his first at-bat, he was called out on strikes. Then in the outfield he let a first inning fly ball by Dick Sisler drop behind him for a triple."

Mays went hitless in five times up in his debut and in 12 times up in his first three games. After Willie's third game, Durocher found him crying in front of his locker. The distressed rookie told his hard-nosed manager he couldn't hit Major League pitching and wanted to go back to Minneapolis.

Durocher, who quickly became a father figure to Mays and remained so the rest of his life, wouldn't hear of it. He told the kid he was his center fielder as long as Durocher managed the Giants. He told Mays to go home and get a good night's sleep.

Sure enough, when the Giants returned to New York, Mays hit a home run in his first time at bat before the Polo Grounds fans, over the left field wall, against the Boston Braves. The Braves' pitcher was Warren Spahn, destined to win 363 games, more than any other lefthander in history.

But another drought set in and Mays went hitless in his next 13 at-bats. Now he was one-for-26 and hitting a barely visible .039. The Philadelphia scene was reprised, with Willie telling Leo again that he wanted to go back to Minneapolis. The determined Durocher said no again, that Willie was his centerfielder, sink or swim.

Mays made Durocher look like a genius by the time the season was over. He rebounded, and this time his recovery was permanent. He hit 20 home runs and compiled a decent .274 batting average. While he was swinging his hot bat, Frankie Frisch, the manager of the Cubs, put in a hurry-up call to Charlie Grimm, who had managed against Willie while Mays was playing for Minneapolis.

Frisch wanted to know, "How should we pitch to this kid?"

Grimm answered, "How the hell should I know, Frankie? He hit .580 against us!"

Willie had proved he belonged. But that wasn't the end of the excitement in Willie's rookie season. This was 1951.

THE "SHOT HEARD 'ROUND THE WORLD," AND WILLIE'S PRAYER

That was the year of the Giants' fabled comeback, when they wiped out a lead of thirteen and a half games by the Dodgers and won the National League pennant on Bobby Thomson's home run. For Willie, it was his dream come true, playing in the World Series in his rookie season, destined to be voted Rookie of the Year and playing in center field opposite his idol, DiMaggio.

Students of baseball history know that when Thomson hit his "shot heard 'round the world," producing "The Miracle of Coogan's Bluff," Mays was in the on-deck circle as the Giants' next hitter. What is not so well known, even by most historians, is that Mays was scared stiff. He wasn't itching to get up there and try to win the game and the pennant for his team. Contrary to what we're told about great athletes in pressure situations, he wasn't thinking, "C'mon—lemme at him!"

Ten years later, he told columnist Dick Young of the *New York Daily News* that he was praying as he knelt in that on-deck circle. Praying for a hit? No. Praying he wouldn't come to bat.

In the last year of Mays's career, Young wrote that Mays told him that as he watched Thomson at the plate, he was saying to himself, "Please, Lord—don't make me get up there. Let him end it right now."

And lo, the Lord did.

YOU'RE IN THE ARMY NOW—AND IN CONTROVERSY

With the Korean War still in its red-hot stages amid fears that it would erupt into World War III, Mays, now 21, was drafted into the Army after one month of the 1952 season, and controversy went with him. When he applied for a deferment as the supporter of 11 dependents, Selective Service officials turned him down. In the Army, he was assigned to Fort Eustis, Virginia, where he played baseball—180 games. Some people complained, and a Congressional committee launched an investigation into the possibility that Mays was being "coddled" by the Army. Mays was absolved of any role in whatever treatment he might have received.

When Willie exchanged his Giants' uniform for a khaki one, the Giants had won 27 of 34 games and were in first place. Without him, they finished second, four and a half games behind the Dodgers.

Durocher was keeping close track of "my boy." When he heard that Willie had stolen a base with his Army team leading by a dozen runs, Durocher scolded him for risking injury. When word got back to Leo that Mays was playing basketball and had injured his ankle, Leo laid down the law—no basketball. Meanwhile, the Giants finished fifth and lost 44 of their last 64 games.

WHEN WILLIE COMES MARCHING HOME AGAIN

Just before spring training began for the 1954 season, Mays completed his Army hitch and was discharged. When he reported for spring training, Durocher took one look at his young star and said, "Here comes the pennant." Mays justified the prediction from the start, with a home run on Opening Day.

By the end of May, he had 14 homers. The Giants, who finished the '53 season 35 games behind the Dodgers, were solid contenders for the National League pennant.

By mid-season, Mays was hitting over .300 and had almost 30 home runs. Life was fun again. Willie was back, even playing stickball again with the kids in his neighborhood on St. Nicholas Place in Harlem and buying ice cream for them and reminding some people of Babe Ruth in his love for the kids and his inability to remember names, greeting everyone with his trade mark, "Say Hey!" And his admirers in the Polo Grounds were dreaming of another National League pennant.

Then tragedy entered Willie's life. Aunt Sarah died, and Willie took it so hard it affected his play. As it did, the Giants' hold on first place began to slip.

Then Mays, as he did so often, rebounded with a vengeance, leading the Giants with a dazzling season as they fought off the hated Dodgers. Facing Major League pitching for the first time in almost two seasons, Mays won the National League batting championship with a .345 average and also led the league in triples. He was fourth in home runs with 41, second in total bases behind only Duke Snider, third in hits, third in runs scored, first in slugging percentage and fourth in home run percentage. Small wonder that the Giants won the pennant over the Dodgers by five games.

The powerful Cleveland Indians awaited them in the World Series, winners of 111 games, a new American League record and armed with such stars as batting champion Bobby Avila, sluggers Al Rosen and Larry Doby and a pitching staff with four future Hall of Famers—Early Wynn, Bob Feller, Bob Lemon and Hal Newhouser, plus 19-game winner Mike Garcia, Art Houtteman and ace relievers Ray Narleski and Don Mossi.

THE CATCH AND THE CAP

The Giants shocked the baseball world by defeating the Indians in a clean sweep of four games. Mays contributed with a .286 average, reaching base eight times on four hits and four walks, scoring four runs and driving in three. But he contributed something else—what may be the most memorable catch in the history of baseball, and some say even the greatest.

With the score tied, 2-2, in the top of the eighth, righthander Sal Maglie walked Doby, and Rosen followed with a single. Durocher called in lefthander Don Liddle to face Vic Wertz, a lefthanded hitter. The move was justified. Wertz became one of the hitting stars of the Series with a .500 average and eight hits in the four games including two doubles, a triple and a home run.

He connected sharply and sent a long, towering fly ball to deep center field. Mays spun quickly, took off full tilt—with his hat flying off— his back to the infield and made a sensational catch over his left shoulder as he reached the cinder path in front of the centerfield wall, 440 feet from home plate. Then he pivoted immediately and made a strong throw back to the infield to prevent Doby from scoring and holding Rosen at first base.

It was a critical play in the game and the Series. The catch enabled the Giants to stay tied with the Indians and extend the game into extra innings, when Dusty Rhodes won it in the tenth with the first of his three key pinch hits in the first three games. This one was a home run off Lemon with two men on base to give the Giants a 5-2 win.

For Mays, the game and the Series were the end of a perfect season after coming back from military duty. He was named the National League's Most Valuable Player and the Major League Player of the Year.

For the millions of fans who have seen photographs of Mays dashing after Wertz's long drive, his back to the plate, his number 24 showing clearly and his cap flying off, Mays made a confession in later years. He told an interviewer, "I was a creator. I did something different each day. I wore my hat a size too large so it would fly off . . . I created the basket catch . . . I felt that I was on a stage all the time, and I had to create something, like a guy singing a song."

ENDS AND BEGINNINGS

The Giants didn't win the pennant again for another eight seasons. In the meantime, they moved from New York to San Francisco before the 1958 season. During their last three years in the Polo Grounds, they finished third in 1955, then sixth in '56 and '57.

Mays continued hits exploits with batting averages of .319, .296 and .333 and home run totals of 51, 36 and 35. In 1955, he demonstrated that he had that rare combination—power and speed—by becoming the first player in National League history to steal 20 bases and hit 50 home runs. Durocher remained his biggest booster. He told reporters, "If he could cook, I'd marry him."

But Leo wouldn't be around to marry Willie or manage him either. He was fired after the '55 season and replaced by Bill Rigney. For Mays, it was another harsh blow. His father figure, the man he always called "Mr. Leo" or "Skip," the players' title for the skipper of the team, was gone, and many said a little bit of Willie went with him.

This was the man Willie always turned to, going back to his arrival with the Giants in 1951, when he took Durocher's advice and signed his first Major League contract without even looking at it, because Mr. Leo said it was okay.

The change in managers didn't help the team, but it didn't hurt Willie. Even with the whispers that the Dodgers and Giants were playing footsies with some persuasive folks in California, Mays continued his slugging and running in 1956, leading the league in stolen bases for the first of four straight seasons with 40 and hitting 36 home runs. In '57, he finished second in batting average behind Stan Musial with a .333 mark and led the league with 20 triples and 38 stolen bases and added 35 homers.

In between the '56 and '57 seasons, Mays became a married man, wedding Marghuerite Wendelle, who became known as Mae Mays.

In 1958, Mays took his act to San Francisco after Horace Stoneham and his fellow owner with the Dodgers, Walter O'Malley, teamed up and moved their teams to California, the first big league baseball teams to move west of the Mississippi. By now Mays was acknowledged as baseball's most exciting player—attacking the ball at the plate, making his patented "basket catches" with his glove at his waist, his cap flying off while chasing down fly balls, his dashing boldness on the base paths and his rifle throws to cut down enemy base runners.

In his first year in his new city, Mays was voted by the baseball writers as the most exciting player in the game for the second straight season. Bob Wolf of the *Milwaukee Journal* expressed his feelings: "Willie Mays gets my vote as the most exciting player in the Major Leagues today. He is an outstanding hitter, runner, fielder and thrower. More than that, he is the type of player who brings fans into the ballpark. His flair for the sensational, his ability to do things with that little extra flourish that sets him apart from the average player are unmatched in modern day baseball."

Despite the acclaim, and to his great surprise and distress, Mays was booed in his first days in Seals Stadium, the Giants' home in San Francisco until Candlestick Park was completed two years later. When he confided his confusion to a writer, he was told that the San Francisco fans considered him an interloper, a big star from New York City who was playing in the same ballpark and position as their greatest hero—Joe DiMaggio. It took Mays years to win over the local fans even while adding to his Hall of Fame credentials every season.

His struggle to gain acceptance became still harder in that same season in the person of a rookie named Orlando Cepeda. While Mays hit from .308 to .347 in his first four years in the Bay Area and slugged from 29 to 40 home runs, Cepeda matched him with averages from .297 to .312 and homer totals from 24 to 46. From the start, Cepeda was heavily engaged in civic affairs and had a friendly personality that made him even more popular.

PRIVILEGE AND PROBLEMS

Alvin Dark became the Giants' manager in 1961, and one of his first actions was unheard of, a letter to Mays saying, "Knowing you will be playing for me is the greatest privilege and thrill any manager could ever hope to have."

Mays justified every word of that unusual tribute the following season, when history repeated itself. The two transplanted teams, the Giants and the Los Angeles Dodgers, tied for the pennant again, just as they had eleven years earlier in 1951. Again the Giants won a three-game playoff and headed for the World Series, against the Yankees again. Mays showed the way by leading the league with 49 home runs and 382 total bases while also scoring 130 runs and driving in 141. Cepeda backed him up with 35 homers and 114 RBIs.

In the midst of all this success, physical problems surfaced for Mays in 1962, while his marriage was breaking up. He had experienced dizzy spells from time to time, starting on a hot, muggy night in Birmingham many years before when he hit an inside-the-park home run and became dizzy as he crossed home plate. It happened again at the Polo Grounds in 1954, also after an inside-the-park homer.

In 1962, he found himself lying on the floor of the dugout in Cincinnati, eyes open but unable to see anything. Somebody yelled, "Get that damn stretcher!" Willie knew what it was—the same thing it always was —he was exhausted mentally, physically and emotionally.

Back in San Francisco, Mays said later, rumors were flying—it was a heart attack. He was an alcoholic. He was an epileptic. The most popular columnist in San Francisco, Herb Caen, wrote that one of Willie's teammates might have slugged him.

"So," Mays said, "a friend of mine later summed it up—I was an epileptic alcoholic, being hit by a friend while in the midst of a heart attack."

Another reason for Willie's spells may have been stress over his finances. He was baseball's highest paid player, but he was on the verge of bankruptcy until he met the founder of a new bank, Jacob Shemano, in late 1962. Willie admitted, "Jake, I've been advised to file for bankruptcy."

Shemano wouldn't hear of it. "If you do file for bankruptcy," he told Mays bluntly, "I want nothing to do with it. You're a baseball player, not some slick corporation executive, living off stock options and pension plans and all the other stunts. Kids look up to you."

He gave Mays more food for thought: "You made $90,000 last year. You'll make better than $100,000 next year. What does it look like to a kid who finds out that Willie Mays, his idol, makes $100,000 and can't pay his taxes?"

Shemano worked with lawyers, accountants and tax authorities and developed a plan for Mays to work his way out of financial trouble, pay off his debts and meet his tax obligations.

The Giants battled the mighty Yankees of Maris and Mantle and Ford and Berra through six games in the '62 Series. They lost it only when Willie McCovey smashed a screaming line drive right at second baseman Bobby Richardson with two men on and two out in the bottom half of the ninth inning. Richardson and the Yankees hung on for a 1-0 win and the Series.

The Giants fielded what may be one of the greatest middle-of-the-order lineups in 1963, yet finished third. McCovey led the league with 44 home runs, drove in 103 runs and hit .280. Mays had 38 homers, 103 RBIs and hit .314. McCovey hit 34 balls out of the park, drove in 100 runs and hit .316. They added pitching support with Juan Marichal's 25 victories.

Willie's dizzy spells returned when he went to the plate to hit, bent over and became dizzy again. Teammates escorted him back to the dugout and Willie was sent home for three days to rest.

The Giants' decline to third place in '63 continued in '64 when they dropped to fourth even though Mays hit 47 homers to lead the league. A critical change occurred when Cepeda injured his leg and was traded to the St. Louis Cardinals, finally relieving Mays of the 600-pound gorilla on his back. But the relief was only temporary. Giants fans switched their allegiance to McCovey, who began pumping homers into the San Francisco jet stream with regularity en route to his own future date at the Hall of Fame.

Mays continued his starring ways, regardless of who might be winning the popularity contests. In 1965, with Cepeda gone and McCovey attracting new attention, Willie smashed 52 home runs, the most in his career, leading the league for the fourth time.

He added a .317 average, 118 runs, 112 RBIs and led the league in slugging for the fifth time. He was again named the National League's MVP, topping the Dodgers' 26-game winner Sandy Koufax.

He made the year complete on September 13 with his 500th home run, off a Don Nottlebart fast ball in Houston. The blow made Mays only the second National Leaguer to reach 500 homers, joining another Giant, Mel Ott.

Over the years, some thought they detected changes in Mays' personality. He had been so fun-loving, with those stickball games with the kids of Harlem, the life of the team on the buses, the road trips, the clubhouse and on the field. He was one of them, popular with his teammates, often the butt of jokes, playing "pepper" games with his teammates and running up debts of thousands of Cokes.

As the years passed, though, Mays became more of a loner. Once, during a marital disagreement, he moved back home to Birmingham for a month, but stayed in a hotel all alone instead of moving in with his family.

SUMMONING HIS GREATNESS AGAIN

That season in 1965 wasn't Willie's last great year. He had another left in his 35-year-old body, hitting 37 home runs in 1966 and driving in 103 runs and reaching another milestone. On May 4, he hit his 512th homer, passing Ott's total on a change-up from the Dodgers' Claude Osteen.

He moved up to fourth on the all-time list, and now he was passing milestones as if they were Burma Shave signs along the highway. On June 23 he equalled Ted Williams with his 521st home run, and on August 6 he hit number 534 to tie Jimmie Foxx for second place on the all-time list. Now only Babe Ruth had hit more home runs.

After 13 years of playing in 151 or more games and reaching the age of 36, the marvelous skills began to erode. He struck out four times in a row in one game. The handwriting was on the wall, and Willie could see it. Still, Mays summoned his greatness to the surface again and again, averaging 21 homers and 70 RBIs over the next five seasons.

He realized another moment of glory in 1968 when he was named the MVP of the All-Star game for manufacturing the game's only run. He singled off Luis Tiant, moved to second when Tiant threw wild trying to pick him off first base, then to third when Tiant made another wild throw, this time trying to pick him off second. Mays scored on a double play ball, still intimidating pitchers with his speed on the bases at the age of 37.

He approached and passed another milestone in 1969 with his 600th home run as a pinch hitter in the seventh inning against rookie Mike Corkins of San Diego. The blow won the game and placed Mays in an exclusive club of sluggers that still includes only Hank Aaron and Babe Ruth.

Just as everyone was writing him off, Mays rebounded with seasons at 39 and 40 that would have put younger players to shame with 28 homers in 1970, a .291 average and 83 RBIs while playing in 139 games. In another 136 games in '71, he hit 18 homers, drove in 61, hit .271 and led the league in walks with 112.

Another honor came Willie's way in 1969. In the hundredth anniversary year since professional baseball began, Mays was named one of baseball's greatest living players, and his father-manager, Leo Durocher, endorsed the selection wholeheartedly.

"He could pick up a team and carry it on his back," he said. "Maybe it was a hit, maybe it was a catch, maybe it was the way he ran the bases. Every day he came to play. Every day he'd do the unexpected."

Even at his advanced age, Mays could still get the job done, Durocher said. "He still can do it all whenever he wants to. Even today, this minute, he's more exciting than anybody who ever played this game."

NEW YORK AGAIN

The 1972 season was barely underway when Stoneham called a press conference on May 11 and announced he had traded Mays to the New York Mets for $50,000 and pitcher Charlie Williams. It was a trade of necessity for Stoneham, who lost a million dollars in 1971 and was facing heavy losses again in '72. He was paying Mays $165,000 a season, plus a commitment to pay him $50,000 a year for ten years after he retired to do promotion work for the Giants. He simply traded his obligations to the Mets, enabling Willie to return to his devoted fans in New York—and to play in his fourth World Series—before ending his career.

On September 26, 1973, the Mets honored the Say Hey kid with Willie Mays Night. His first baseball hero, Joe DiMaggio, was there, and so were Stan Musial, Bobby Thomson, Pee Wee Reese, Vic Wertz—the man whose fly ball led to *the* catch by Willie 19 years earlier—and Duke Snider, Willie's rival, along with Mickey Mantle, for top honors as the best centerfielder in New York in the 1950s, during those by-gone days of Willie, Mickey and The Duke.

Arthur Daley of *The New York Times* remembered those times. "It was a night for memories," he wrote, "and they kept rumbling in like distant memories from the past, the men and the events that provided flashbacks or illuminating glimpses of a spectacular career. The occasion was supercharged with emotion. This was an outward manifestation of the unashamed love affair that has lasted for 22 years between Willie the Wonder and the New York fans."

In the 1973 Series, the Mets faced the powerful Oakland A's of Reggie Jackson, Bert Campaneris, Joe Rudi, Gene Tenace and Sal Bando, plus a pitching staff that included three 20-game winners—Vida Blue, Ken Holtzman and Catfish Hunter. The Mets lost in seven games. Mays, playing in three games, committed an error that led to an unearned run in the first game, but collected two hits in seven at-bats for a .286 average, scored a run and drove in another.

Today Willie earns a comfortable living at card shows and in other personal appearances after he and Mickey Mantle suffered a temporary reductions in their incomes when Commissioner Bowie Kuhn banned them from baseball for their appearances as greeters at Bally's Casino in Atlantic City.

BITTERSWEET MEMORIES

Mays enjoys the fruits of his success and popularity—homes in San Francisco, New York, Reno, Phoenix and Birmingham. A Mercedes roadster, an Audi, a Lincoln Town Car, a king-sized BMW, a midnight blue Lincoln convertible, with license tags numbered from Say Hey 1 to Say Hey 7.

Still, the contradictions in the Mays makeup continue to surface. The man who remains the symbol of enthusiasm and fun can also contradict his own personality. In 1991, the Mets suggested a 40th anniversary celebration of the Giants' historic comeback when they beat the Dodgers on Bobby Thomson's home run. But Willie, one of that team's leaders in his rookie season, killed the plans by demanding to be paid for showing up.

In 1963, with ten years left as a baseball player, Mays was the subject of a feature article by Arnold Hano in *Sport* magazine. Hano captured the triumph and the torment of Mays' Hall of Fame career. He described Mays as "this strangely troubled, strangely alone man who has crested his peak and who will start downhill any year now, and whose success story is in many ways a horror tale, and in many other ways one of the brave sagas of our time."

But the memories of Willie, the Say Hey Kid, the one fans thrilled to and hailed, are the ones that endure. That was the Willie Mays who told *This Week* in 1954, his first year back from Army duty, that the best feeling he had "is every day, just before I go to the ballpark. Sort of like I can't wait to get there to put on my uniform and run out on the field."

He said the feeling reminded him of a tap dancer he saw in a show who enjoyed his work so much he told his audience, "It's a shame to take the money."

"Of course," Willie went on, "he said it to get a laugh, but I could tell he meant it all the same. And it's sort of the way I feel about baseball."

WHAT OTHER PLAYERS SAID ABOUT WILLIE MAYS

Bill Virdon—Mays was the best player I ever played against. He did everything to help beat you. He was just always in your hair. He could do just about anything he wanted to out there.

Del Crandall—He was just so dangerous. He swung so hard. If you didn't make about a perfect pitch on him, he'd have a good swing at it. He was more of a wild swinger than Aaron.

Al Kaline—Willie Mays might have been the greatest player who ever lived.

Bill Rigney—He had raw power. When he came up, it was just a question of time as to how many homers he would hit. If anyone were to make a run at Babe Ruth, I thought it would be him. He loved to play, was so strong and never got hurt.

Larry Jansen—I'm glad he was on my side. There was one guy who could do it all. He went from first to third on passed balls more than anyone I ever saw. He was popular with the players. You've got to like someone who did everything right.

Alvin Dark—When Willie came up, he was a real baby. He went 0-for-21 and was sitting in the corner crying. I hugged him and told him, "You catch the ball and throw it. Your hitting will come." I was close to him when he was nothing. When I later managed him, we had a peculiar relationship. I had to manage the player. The player didn't manage the manager. I had to get on Willie in Cincinnati once when he hit a popup and didn't run it out. It might have put a hair between us. I hope not. But I gave him hell. You can't have the best player not running it out. I saw most of the greats, but when it came to putting the uniform on every day, he was the best I ever saw.

Steve Garvey—I saw him toward the end of his career at San Francisco in that wind and cold. But he still found a way to get to the ball, try to climb a fence, and take what was usually a single and make it into a double. He still had that savvy that you knew came from a very special performer.

Enos Slaughter—Mays, to me, could have been under a lot of fly balls, in position to throw, when he would make those fancy basket catches. I didn't like it. When you play the game, you go out there and get in position to throw.

Gaylord Perry—The best player I ever saw was Willie Mays, and I was fortunate to be on the same team with him. He could do it all. It was always great playing Pittsburgh. Roberto Clemente was the best rightfielder I ever saw, and he and Willie would go at it. One day McCovey hit one off the wall and Mays was going to try to score. Clemente made a great catch off the wall and turned a made a beeline throw to the plate. Mays knew he would be nailed and went back to third. You don't forget things like that. He liked to play cards and was an excellent card player. I had some friends who would always come to San Francisco. He was great to my friends. He couldn't go to restaurants, so we would get a suite and order room service and play cards all night . . . . I pitched once when Mays played shortstop . . . . He could have played anywhere. He was awesome!

U.S. Senator Jim Bunning —He was a much tougher out with the tying or winning run on base. He was really competitive. Much more than with no one on. If you got the pitch up on him, he would really hit it hard.

Bobby Thomson—When he came up, he was just an innocent kid with all the tools and born to play the game. Defensively, he had his glove right from the start. All of us knew it would just be a matter of time.

Bob Feller—I saw a lot of him in spring training because we trained in Arizona and barnstormed home every year. He was just as good an outfielder as Joe DiMaggio but didn't have his arm. He was an actor. He either wore a hat that was too small or too big so he could run out of it. It was all part of his act. But he was a fine outfielder, probably nobody any better. I didn't have much trouble with him. I threw him fast balls tight on his hands between his belt line and his jock. He didn't hit me, but that didn't mean he didn't hit everybody else.

Warren Spahn—He loved to play and could beat you so many ways. A great, great ballplayer ....He was so quick through the strike zone, and that's what made him so dangerous. Sometimes it seemed he would hit the ball out of the catcher's glove just like Hank (Aaron).

Ernie Broglio—I don't know if I ever got him out.

Dick Groat—He was just a great hitter in every possible way. He could flat out play centerfield. He was the absolute complete player.

Frank Howard—The greatest all-around player I ever played against as far as doing it all is concerned.

Johnny Podres—Willie Mays! Are you kidding me! What can you say about a guy who is so great? I'm pitching against the Giants in L.A., and I got them beat, 13-0, in the ninth and Mays is the last hitter. So I get him two balls and two strikes and I throw him a big, slow curve. And he sees the pitch coming ... and he took it for strike three. I say to myself, "I got another pitch for this guy." The next time I faced him in Candlestick, I got two men on and two out. I got him three balls and two strikes, so I say, "This is the time to throw him that big, slow curve again." Well, it was a 3-run homer. I thought I was setting him up, but he was setting me up!

Johnny Callison—Willie Mays? The best I ever saw. He did everything great. He could run the bases better than anybody, and if he wanted to steal a base, he would steal it.

Billy Williams—I didn't see a lot of the great players of the early years, but when somebody asks me who was the best player I ever saw play Major League baseball, I don't hesitate at all to say Willie Mays. He was a player I idolized. I was excited just being on the same field with him. You saw some great things when he was out there. Catching, stealing a base, hitting a home run. He was an exciting player. He excited his teammates, he excited the opposing players, he excited the fans in the stands. He was a guy you would come to see play and you could stay there all day. He had such great instincts to play this game of baseball.

Ray Sadecki—He hit his share off me at home in that small Sportsman's Park—not that he needed a small park. But it was hard for him to drive that ball in Candlestick. The wind blew in from left field a lot.

Jimmy Piersall—Willie Mays was the greatest player I ever saw. I don't care about Ken Griffey, Jr. He couldn't carry Mays's jock. He is a good player; he is no Mays. He doesn't put them (fans) in the park like Mays did. He and Joe DiMaggio put more people in the park than anyone.

Vinegar Bend Mizell—I don't want to remember or talk about all the homers he hit off me.

Mudcat Grant—I think he showed he loved to play the game more than anyone I ever saw.

Ron Santo—Willie was the best all-around player I ever played against. When he moved from New York to San Francisco, he had to change his swing. Mays would have hit as many home runs as Aaron if he had been in any other ballpark but San Francisco. He was a righthanded hitter, and the wind blew in from left. It would literally move me at third base. It would push me in. And as a hitter, you always felt the wind was holding you back. He had to learn to take the ball to right center or right, where the ball would carry.

Bob Purkey—I think I probably got Mays out better than anyone in the league. Willie would tell you that today. I would stay in on him, but would slip (up) on him, and you know what would happen then! He was more mad at me than anything because I would stay in on him. It bothered his concentration, and he got frustrated because he couldn't hit me.

Wally Moon—The consummate ballplayer as far as I was concerned.

Frank Torre—Willie was another one who suffered big-time, home run wise, from playing in those big ballparks—the Polo Grounds and San Francisco's Candlestick Park. For the most part, Willie was a gap hitter, and those two parks were not parks for gap hitters. After three in the afternoon, you needed an M-1 rifle to hit it out of Candlestick. It was amazing. About the seventh inning of the ballgame, the temperature would drop about thirty degrees, and it was every day ... Defensively, the Polo Grounds were perfect for Mays. It was such a huge middle of the field that Willie was able to roam and make great catches.

Bob Friend—He was more of a wild swinger. I had pretty good luck against him early in his career, but he pretty well took care of me later on. He was an excellent triple hitter.

Bobby Bragan—He was the most exciting player ever to play the game. He was the only player I ever saw who would excite the crowd before the game even started. He loved to play ... Next to Mays, Joe DiMaggio was the best player I ever saw. Mays was Frank Sinatra, DiMaggio was Caruso. Willie was entertainment, and Joe was classic—Mays all emotion, Joe no emotion.

Willie Stargell—I just saw him do so many wonderful things ....You name it, he did it. You just marvel at him. Seems you can't keep your eyes off him. He did what everyone would have liked to duplicate.

Bob Gibson—Just about everything he did was right. There was a guy who could run full speed and look over his shoulder without missing a step. And he was so damn quick. He was the quickest person I ever saw. And if you decided to knock him down, hell, you couldn't hit him. He'd hit the ground and he'd be back up before the catcher threw the ball back to the pitcher.

Dean Chance—The greatest all-around player I ever saw—a ten in every department of play.

Orlando Cepeda—He wasn't a Hank Aaron. He was a different person. But he was the best all-around player to play the game.

Monte Irvin—When he first came up, Leo (Durocher) put him with me. I looked after him. He was shy, quiet and had all kinds of talent. He could do everything, and he was a natural doing it. All he needed was to get his confidence ...He had a certain style about him. Everything he did, you could tell he had that little extra.

Duke Snider—I think the world of Willie. Willie had longevity in that he never got seriously hurt during his career. He put up terrific numbers, and you can't put up terrific numbers without longevity and ability.

Bill Mazeroski—All-around, the best player I ever saw. He looked like he had fun playing the game ...like he really enjoyed it ...He went at it like he had fun all the time.

Ralph Kiner—He had such natural talent. I don't think Willie ever thought much about hitting. He was just so good at it, it seemed to come natural to him. One thing—he didn't like to be thrown at, but he could still hit even though he was bailing out. It must be great to be such a natural hitter that you don't have to think about it.

Don Newcombe—No doubt in my mind that he was the greatest all-around player I ever saw. The records he set, the things he did were a part of history and greatness. And he even missed a year (almost two, actually) in the Army. I don't believe he developed his skills—he was just born with them. I don't know where he got them from. God gave them to him, that's all I can think.

Gene Oliver—Willie Mays was the purest all-around player I saw next to Roberto Clemente.

Al Downing—Willie was the cream of the crop. Not taking anything away from the others, but the Willie Mays package is what every general manager is looking for ....He liked to decoy you. He liked to mess with your mind. He'd swing at a pitch and miss and you feel, "Okay, I got him set up for that," and you come back with it and it's in the centerfield seats.

Maury Wills—Mays and Roberto Clemente were the two best all-around players I ever saw. Mays could do it all, no question. But Mays could be intimidated at the plate. Don Drysdale would get Mays back on his heels.

Vernon Law—The most complete player I ever saw. He could beat you so many ways.

Ed Kranepool—The purest of the superstars on and off the field. To me he was Mr. Excitement on the field. He was the last of the superstars until Ken Griffey, Jr. came along.

Roger Craig—Willie and Roberto Clemente could hit anything. You could throw it in the dirt or over his head and he might go after it. He hit to right field as well as he could to left ... He was great in the clubhouse with the players, that high voice, and he talked all the time ... On the bench or on the field he reminded me of Roy Campanella's statement that you have to have a lot of the little boy in you to play baseball. He enjoyed playing the game as much as any player I've ever been around. He'd go out and take infield at shortstop and look as good as any Gold Glove shortstop. He could play any position he wanted to. He was just a great natural athlete—and always kidding with his teammates and opponents.

Don Zimmer—Willie Mays was to me the greatest all-around player I ever watched. People ask me that, and I don't hesitate ....He could have been an All-Star shortstop, that's how good an athlete he was ....He could run backwards as fast as he could forward.

Stan Musial—He was something. There wasn't anything he couldn't do. It was something that he, Mickey Mantle and Duke Snider all played in New York at the same time.

Juan Marichal—Willie Mays, to me, was the best ballplayer I ever saw in my life .... Nobody in the history of baseball is going to see anyone like Willie Mays. Everybody loved Willie in the clubhouse. Willie used to do a lot of things for different players, especially rookies. Willie used to take players to clothing stores to buy them clothes. Sometimes he would get free clothes, shoes and stuff, and give them to players. He was like the mother of the team.

Whitey Herzog—If Willie Mays hadn't been scared at the plate, he might have hit .600 every year. You pitched him close, his cap would fly off, his bat would fly in the air and he'd be down, and the ball didn't even come close to him. He just left the ground. He'd look like he didn't want to get back in the box, but he'd jump in there and hit the next damn pitch out of the park. In my lifetime, though, he was the best total picture for a ballplayer I ever saw. When you think about centerfield defensively and how he played and the flamboyancy and the crowd pleaser he was, I don't see how you could play the game over a long period of time better than he did.

Bill White—The best all-around player I ever saw. He knew more baseball than anybody I ever knew. The year I came up, he spent time with me talking about the pitchers and how to play first base.

Carl Erskine—Willie had no real weakness. You had to really bear down on the hitters ahead of him and keep them off the bases .... Mays and Mantle were such outstanding talents. The only difference between those two guys was you'd probably pick Willie because he was so durable. He was never out of the lineup. If Mantle had been as durable as Mays, it's hard to tell what kind of records he would have set.

Randy Hundley—Willie Mays was the best player I ever saw for doing everything that there is to do playing the game of baseball. Plus, he was the type of guy who really had fun playing the game .... He looked like a body builder, like he lifted weights all his life. Very muscular .... Just a very intelligent baseball player.

Doug Harvey—Willie Mays was the greatest ballplayer who ever walked on this earth .... The only man I ever knew who swung hard at the ball every time. Even with the winning run on third, he swung hard every time. A marvelous athlete. He was so strong, shaking hands with him was like gripping a sledgehammer.

Ron Swoboda—He was always talking to people. A smart ballplayer, smart outfielder, smart base runner, a smart hitter .... He had really smart insights on the game.

Harmon Killebrew—When you talk about ballplayers and who was the greatest player of all time, his name always pops up. I was in home run hitting contests with Aaron and him, and I can tell you, both of them could do it all.

Hank Aaron—Willie was probably one of the finest athletes and ball players who ever played the game, in every phase of the game. You have to put him 1-2-3-4 with the greatest players ever. He just did everything so naturally. When you had supreme confidence in yourself like he did, he could do some things that people dare not do because they didn't have that self-confidence.

Pete Rose—He's one of the top five of all time. He was as exciting and had as much charisma as any athlete ever. He was greater for New York than for San Francisco, I think.

Joe Garagiola—People ask me, "Who was the greatest you ever saw?" I would say I've seen a lot of "greatests," but if there was one guy and I had five dollars to go to a ball game, I would want to see Willie Mays. He could beat you every way there was and gave you that boyish enthusiasm. I played with him with the Giants, and Leo (Manager Leo Durocher) would heap nothing but praise on him. He'd tell our outfielders—Don Mueller, Monte Irvin and Dusty Rhodes—that if a ball was hit in the air in the Polo Grounds, just get out of his way. He played with such a flair.

THE MAYS FILE

Full Name: Willie Howard Mays, Jr.
Date and Place of Birth: May 6, 1931, Westfield, Alabama.
Nickname: "Say Hey"
Position: Center Field.
Major League Career: 22 years, 1951-1973 (missed most of 1952 season and all of 1953 because of military duty during the Korean War).
Home Runs: 660 (3rd).
Runs Batted In: 1,903 (7th).
Runs Scored: 2,062 (5th).
Lifetime Batting Average: .302.
Number of Hits: 3,283 (9th).
Walks: 1,463.
Strikeouts: 1,526.

Records: When he retired, Mays held league records for playing in 150 or more games (13 straight seasons), putouts (7,095) and for hitting three triples in one game. He has the third most home runs, fifth most runs, sixth most games played, eighth most times at bat, seventh most runs batted in, ninth most hits and the tenth highest slugging average.

Other Highlights:
— Led National League in fielding five times.
— Won 12 straight Gold Glove awards.
— National League Most Valuable Player twice, 1954 and 1965.
— National League Rookie of the Year, 1951.
— National League Batting Champion, 1954.
— Led League in home runs and stolen bases four times and total bases three times.
— Hit 50 or more home runs twice.
— Hit 40 or more home runs six times.
— Drove in 100 or more runs eight years in a row.
— Hit over .300 ten times.
— Hit four home runs in a single game.
— Played in 24 All-Star games, the most ever (Baseball played two All-Star games a year from 1959 through 1962).
— Most Valuable Player in 1968 All-Star game.

Elected to Hall of Fame: 1979.

9

WILLIE McCOVEY

What Was and What Might Have Been

Those who played with and against Willie McCovey say he was the best hitter of his time. They say he hit the ball harder than anyone else, harder than Frank Howard, harder than Mickey Mantle, harder than anyone. And they say if Willie hadn't been injured so much and walked so often, Mark McGwire and Sammy Sosa might have been aiming at *his* record in 1998 instead of at the 61 hit by Roger Maris.

McCovey was asked about that possibility early in his career, and his response showed a surprising amount of confidence. "I can answer seriously that it's possible to hit 60 homers (in one season)" he said, "because it's been done twice already in the other league."

McCovey, called "Stretch" because of his ability to catch errant throws at first base, was seldom free of injuries. He played in pain most of the time, dating from a game in Dallas when his career was nearly ended prematurely with a serious knee injury. After that it was a series of operations on the knee, arthritis, calcium deposits in his hip, a broken arm, blurred vision, a wrist injury, a dislocated shoulder, jammed wrists and thumbs, and foot problems.

As for the walks, McCovey drew 1,345 bases on balls, including a league-leading 137 in 1970. Opponents gave him pitches on the outside part of the plate as much as they could, usually on orders. Cincinnati Manager Sparky Anderson once ordered a pitcher to walk McCovey even though first base was already occupied. "He's the best hitter in baseball," Anderson told reporters later. "I'm not going to pitch to him if I don't have to. I'd rather take my chances with someone else. Why let him beat you?"

Walter Alston, the skipper of the Dodgers, topped Anderson. In what must rank as the ultimate compliment to a hitter, Alston ordered McCovey to be walked intentionally as the leadoff hitter in the ninth inning of a tie game, violating a cardinal rule: Never put the winning run on base intentionally, certainly not with no outs and none on in the ninth.

CHEERS, BOOS AND HISTORY'S CRUEL BLOW

McCovey was the seventh of ten children, the last of eight boys. At Central High School, he played baseball, basketball and football and ran track, but then dropped out of school and joined the Navy to see the world. When his mother heard the news, she immediately called the recruiting office and informed the men there that her son was only 16 years old. He was rejected immediately.

McCovey began playing baseball on the sandlots of Mobile, on the same diamonds where Hank Aaron, Willie Mays and Billy Williams began, only a few years after Jackie Robinson made history by becoming the first African-American to play in the major leagues in the 20th century.

"That was my inspiration," he said later. "I knew right then that a door had been opened wide, and I wanted to pass through it."

With a semi-pro team called the Hawks, McCovey was attracting attention because he was only 14 years old, the youngest player on the team, nicknamed, of course, "The Kid."

"My mother had to give permission for me to play because I was so young," he said later to Nick Peters in *The Sporting News*. "They had to promise to look after me, and I was the cleanup hitter. I looked up to players like Hank Aaron, Ted Williams and Stan Musial, but I was a Brooklyn Dodgers Fan. I would swing a bat in our back yard against imaginary pitches, thinking about hitting a winning home run at Ebbets Field in the World Series."

His glove "wasn't much. It was so worn out I had to stuff it with string for padding. The edges were so tattered they had to be sewed up once a week."

Alex Pompez, the owner of the New York Cubans of the Negro Leagues, who sent Willie Mays and Monte Irvin to the San Francisco Giants, gave McCovey his start after being tipped off by Jesse Thomas, a local "bird dog," a part-time scout usually not on the payroll who recommends prospects to professional teams. Pompez passed the word on to the Giants, and McCovey was invited to their spring training camp in 1955.

McCovey got off a bus in Melbourne, Florida, some wrinkled clippings about Jackie Robinson in his wallet as always, and immediately dazzled scouts and managers on his first day in camp. His reward was a contract with Sandersville, Georgia, of the Class D Georgia State League for $175 a month, plus a bonus of $500 for his mother, Esther. With his new wealth, the kid bought his first new baseball glove.

After tearing up the league and continuing his success at Danville, Virginia, of the Class C Carolina League, he was on his way, armed with wise advice from his manager at Danville, Salty Parker, who told him, "You're tall, so you're going to be the subject of attention. People will notice you. You're nonchalant, and people are going to criticize it. Don't change. Play your way. Be you."

His career-long struggle to overcome injuries began when he tore the cartilage in his right knee sliding home for Dallas of the Double-A Texas League in a game against Fort Worth. Later in the season he injured the same knee again, underwent surgery in the off-season and played for Phoenix of the Triple-A Pacific Coast League in 1959 with a heavy knee brace. His spectacular progress continued, with a .372 average and 29 home runs, plus two more homers en route to winning the Most Valuable Player Award in the All-Star game.

That was enough to prompt the Giants to put in a call to Phoenix. McCovey was on his way to "the big club" the next day. Few players ever broke into the big leagues with less sleep or more hits.

After a twi-night doubleheader that lasted late into the evening, McCovey stayed up all night. "I was too excited and afraid I'd miss the plane in the morning," he said. When he reported to Candlestick Park, he asked for, and received, the uniform number of his idol—Hank Aaron's number 44.

When he trotted onto the field for pre-game practice, Manager Bill Rigney asked him how he felt, never dreaming the rookie had been up all night. McCovey said he felt great.

Then Rigney told him, "Good. You're in there, and you're hitting third. And you know whose spot that is. I'm moving Willie Mays up to second today, so you know what we're expecting of you."

So there he was, a 21-year-old rookie on the 1959 San Francisco Giants, the same team with the great Willie Mays and hitting right behind him in the batting order, no sleep and—as if all that weren't enough—facing a future Hall of Fame pitcher, Robin Roberts of the Phillies.

When McCovey stepped up to the plate for his first time at bat in the big leagues, the Dodgers and the Phillies saw a 21-year-old rookie, but they saw more than that. They saw an imposing lefthanded slugger with 198 pounds packed solidly over his 6-foot, 4-inch frame.

He looked even bigger, with broad and powerful shoulders that made him look more like 6-7, with his weight concentrated more in the upper part of his body instead of in his hips or legs. His power came from his whip-like snap of his bat and those broad shoulders.

Willie singled in his first time up, then tripled off the scoreboard 410 feet away, lined a single to right field wall that he hit so hard it bounced all the way back to the infield, and finished off his sparkling debut with another triple.

The next day, Willie stepped up against Pittsburgh's Harvey Haddix in the bottom of the eighth inning in a tie game and with Mays on first base. Rigney suddenly bounded out of the dugout, prompting McCovey to think he was being lifted for a pinchhitter.

Instead, Rigney trotted to the plate and told McCovey, "If you're patient and take a couple of pitches, that guy at first will steal second for you and you can win the game." Sure enough, Mays stole second—and McCovey drove him in with the game-winning hit. In his first seven games, the Giants, who had lost four in a row when McCovey joined them, suddenly won six straight and vaulted back into first place, on the strength of Willie's three home runs, nine runs batted in and a .467 average.

The *San Francisco Examiner* promptly published a three-part story on his life, after he had been in the big leagues only one week, already calling him "the most discussed figure in baseball." His success continued —leading the revitalized Giants to a third place finish and winning the National League Rookie of the Year award with a .359 average, 13 homers and 38 RBIs in only two months.

But for McCovey, success at the Major League level was frequently interrupted, especially in his early years, by injury or some other form of misfortune. The man who played in the minor leagues for six years, longer than any of the other fourteen members of the 500 Club, ran into baseball's dreaded "sophomore jinx" in his next season, slumping to .238 with only thirteen homers and 51 runs batted in. And he was having trouble with popups in windy Candlestick Park. The Giants dropped to fifth place.

Rigney was fired as manager, then said of McCovey, "He hit .354 as a rookie and made me look like a genius. The next year, he hit .238 and got me fired."

Rigney's replacement, Tom Sheehan, began to platoon McCovey, saying, "He can't run, he can't hit and he can't field."

The reporters, after making him the toast of the town in his rookie season, were all over him in his second year. Columnist Charles McCabe wrote in the *Chronicle*:

> *"Giant management and ownership continue to stick by the misbegotten view that in first baseman Willie McCovey they have another Honus Wagner, or Ty Cobb, or Ted Williams. Since the first couple of weeks he was on the club in 1959, Willie has done nothing to justify any such assumption."*

Late in the season, McCovey suffered the indignity of being optioned out to Tacoma of the Pacific Coast League. He regained his batting stroke there in the final seventeen games of the '61 season and was back with the Giants to stay in 1962.

But all was not roses. The sensation who became a local favorite in his first season was now relegated to part-time duty, moved off first base by Orlando Cepeda and unable to crack an outfield that included Mays, Harvey Kuenn and Felipe Alou. He was booed regularly by the fans and made no favorites with the news media by displaying a moody attitude.

Still, McCovey was the central figure in a memorable finish to the 1962 season. He was an almost-hero in the seventh game of the World Series against the Yankees and the "M&M Boys," Maris and Mantle, after a season of one drama after another for the Giants. They chased the Dodgers in the National League standings, caught up with them, forced a play-off and won it in another comeback, then they caught the Yankees by winning the sixth game of a see-saw Series, forcing the maximum seventh game. Now it was the last half of the ninth inning at Candlestick, with the Yankees leading 1-0 behind a two-hitter by righthander Ralph Terry. Matty Alou led off the inning with an infield hit, but that hopeful sign was followed by two outs. Willie Mays breathed new optimism into the hometown crowd with a double.

With men on second and third and two outs in the ninth inning of the final game, McCovey came to the plate. Willie almost hit his second triple of the game, lining a 1-1 pitch foul into the right field seats. Then, with the tension of knowing he was only one strike away from ending the season for his team, McCovey ripped a vicious line drive smack at second baseman Bobby Richardson. The game was over, and so were the World Series and the season.

For McCovey, a chance to recapture the magic he enjoyed in San Francisco as a rookie had come and gone in a flash. Willie never received a chance to play in another World Series.

McCovey still remembers the play all too vividly. When he was inducted into the Hall of Fame 25 years later, he said, "I'd like to be remembered as the guy who hit the ball *over* Bobby Richardson's head, but that's not going to happen."

Richardson remembers it, too. He said he thought the liner was going over his head, but it had so much top spin on it, the result of McCovey's brute power, that the line drive dropped just enough for Richardson to catch it. Instead of benefitting from his power, McCovey was the victim of it. He didn't hit the ball well—he hit it *too* well.

Richardson said there was more to the story than most people know. He said he had been distracted just before the pitch by the second base umpire, of all people. Al Barlick asked him if he could have Richardson's hat after the game for his son. "I was thinking about that," Richardson said, "and wasn't really concentrating totally when McCovey hit the ball."

He made the transition back to the business at hand just in time to make the most important catch of his life, on what may be the most famous line drive in World Series history.

THE ROLLER COASTER

McCovey kept coming back, throughout his career, from injuries and other adversities, including that line drive. In '63, never one to let adversity keep him down, he came back with a flourish and had the San Franciscans cheering again. He tied his boyhood idol, Hank Aaron, for the National League home run championship with 44, scored 103 runs, drove in 102 and hit .280. He tied the Giants' team record with a hitting streak of 24 straight games.

Many opposing pitchers wanted to call in sick that year, as Mays and Cepeda added to the power of the Giants' lineup. Mays hit .314 with 38 home runs and Cepeda chipped in with 34. They had one of the greatest middle-of-the-lineup threesomes in history. Still, they could finish no higher than third place.

Adversity, never far from McCovey's door, returned in 1964 with the death of his father and recurring problems with the arch of Willie's left foot. He slumped to 18 homers, only 54 RBIs and an anemic .220 average. He seemed to be back on his roller coaster, unable to put two good years back-to-back.

The next season, 1965, provided a new opportunity when Cepeda injured his knee and was declared lost for the season. McCovey, playing in the outfield after his rookie year, was moved back to his more familiar first base by the Giants' newest manager, Herman Franks. Willie responded by belting 39 homers.

The Giants lost the pennant to the Dodgers by only two games.

It was the start of a six-year reign of terror for McCovey. He led the National League in home runs twice and in runs batted in twice. For those six seasons, he averaged 38 homers a year and 106 RBIs.

He wasn't just hitting home runs. He was hitting bazooka shots, what the players call "frozen ropes." He wasn't just defeating the Giants' opponents—he was scaring them.

Hall of Famer Al Kaline said flatly, "He might have hit the ball harder than any man who ever lived." His manager, Alvin Dark, was awed by McCovey's distance as well as his power. "He could hit the ball as far as any man living," Dark said. "He was just unbelievable with his power. He hit the longest home runs I've ever seen."

First Baseman Steve Garvey of the Dodgers said, "I was rarely fearful on the baseball field, but at San Francisco with wet astro turf and McCovey up, I tried to make myself as small as possible while holding a runner on first base."

Bill Mazeroski gave Willie as much distance as possible while still being able to handle the second baseman's position. "I played McCovey as deep as I ever played anybody," Maz said, "and he'd still handcuff me. In Forbes Field, I used to play him way out, about four steps back on the grass, and he'd still hit line drives. I think he hit the ball as hard as anybody, along with Frank Howard."

Ed Kranepool of the Mets gave his pitchers orders: "Willie looked like a big statue up there. I didn't like holding men at first base when he was up." Kranepool says he would go to the mound and tell the pitcher, "You'd better not pitch him inside, because if Willie doesn't kill you, I will."

It didn't make any difference who was pitching. One of his favorite meal tickets was the Dodgers' future Hall of Famer, Don Drysdale, another big man, an inch taller than McCovey at 6-5, and just as strong at 190 pounds. McCovey roughed Drysdale up for 12 home runs over their careers, and Drysdale never forgot it.

"He gave me as much trouble as anyone ever did," Drysdale said. "Those first few years, he just beat on me like a tom-tom, and I was bullheaded enough to keep trying to pitch to him. He wasn't hitting 1.000, so somebody had to be getting him out. But it sure wasn't me."

THE BOMBSHELL, AND THE GLORY THAT FOLLOWED

With the 1966 season barely a month old, the Giants dropped a bombshell, and McCovey was one of its innocent victims. They were afraid that off-season surgery on Cepeda's knee might be unsuccessful, so they traded the star to the Cardinals for a lefthanded pitcher, Ray Sadecki, a 20-game winner in 1964 but only a 6-15 pitcher in '65. The trade ignited a season-long explosion among Giants' fans.

Cepeda was a Candlestick Park favorite after giving Giants' fans seven outstanding years, averaging .311 and 32 homers a year while playing in almost every game. His outgoing personality made him even more popular.

Now it was a tandem of McCovey and Mays, a powerful combination even though the two never got along. McCovey even omitted Mays from mention when he listed the best hitters he'd ever seen. He said the two best he had seen were Dick Allen and Ted Williams. In an article in *Sport* magazine, he accused Mays of faking dizzy spells so he could get some rest. The team's doctors contradicted McCovey's statement, said the dizzy spells were real and they treated Mays for the condition.

Cepeda continued his stardom with the Cardinals, but Sadecki was a bust with the Giants, winning only three games in 1966 while losing seven. McCovey was booed throughout the season, not because he was McCovey but because he wasn't Cepeda.

"I've always been aware of those things ever since I started playing ball," he said. "I know by the letters I receive that most of the fans always have been with me. But, funny, it seems the negative things always have the loudest voice."

McCovey played through the fallout with a banner season, taking over Cepeda's role by hitting 36 home runs and driving in 96 runs with a .295 average, sparking his team to a second place finish only a game and a half behind the Dodgers of Drysdale, Koufax and company.

The home runs kept exploding off his bat. In 1967 he hit 31 more. Over the 1968-69 seasons he became only the fourth player to lead his league in home runs and runs batted in during consecutive seasons, joining Frank "Home Run" Baker, Babe Ruth, Jimmie Foxx and Bill Nicholson.

He homered 36 times in '68 and hit another 45 in '69. Home runs weren't his only accomplishment in 1969. He also hit .320, drove in 125 runs and was walked 126 times, 45 times intentionally, the Major League record. In the All-Star game at RFK Stadium in Washington, McCovey hit two home runs, powered the National League to a 9-3 win and was voted the game's Most Valuable Player. At the end of the season, he won both the National League Most Valuable Player Award and *The Sporting News* Player of the Year Award.

It wasn't just his hitting that solidified McCovey's status as a certified super star. In the process, he was also becoming one of the best first basemen in either league. His manager in 1969, Clyde King, called him the best first baseman in the league, and the greatest he had ever seen on handling bad throws, justifying his long-standing nickname of "Stretch."

King said, "He saved our infielders a great many errors this season. He pulled throws out of the dirt and grabbed them over the tops of runners' heads while staying on the bag. Our infielders realized Willie would catch throws that weren't perfect, so they had more confidence."

With his banner year and his MVP award, McCovey was winning more than awards, individual championships and games for his team. He was winning a personal victory, too. At the age of 31 and in his eleventh season, he had finally won over the fans through his enormous talent and his courage in playing through his frequent injuries. For years he had coped with monumental slumps, fits of depression, unmerciful abuse from the fans, inconsistency and almost constant physical problems. And through the early years, he didn't know whether the team considered him an outfielder or a first baseman.

He put most of that behind him, especially the fan abuse, with his dominating performances, capping them with 39 home runs in 1970, 126 runs batted in and a .289 average, plus a league-leading 137 walks. He had long since firmly established himself as one of the truly dominating hitters in baseball.

He did it all while wearing specially designed baseball spikes to cushion his bad arches. On many days he could barely make it to the ballpark. To run out a ground ball was sheer agony. Herman Franks once removed him from a game even though he had hit two home runs, saying McCovey needed the rest, and the opposition wasn't going to give him anything more to hit anyway.

McCovey spoke frankly about his injuries. "My job is to play," he said. "If I'm able to at all, I will. Some of these things like my hip and knee and feet have bothered me for years, so why talk about them? I was injured my whole career. It would have been strange for me to play without some kind of pain."

LAST HURRAHS

McCovey was part of a unique experience in 1972, when not one but three stars—Willie, pitcher Juan Marichal and Willie Mays—were able to stage their last hurrahs on the same team at the same time. For Willie, it meant he might get to play in the World Series again.

With a new manager, Charlie Fox, and new faces Bobby Bonds, Chris Speier, Dave Kingman and Tito Fuentes, the Giants bolted out of the gate with an 18-5 start and beat out the Dodgers by a game to reach the National League playoffs. McCovey contributed to the Giants' success with 18 home runs and 70 runs batted in, Mays added 18 homers and 61 RBIs. Marichal won 18 games.

For the playoffs, the picture looked bright for the Giants. They had defeated their opponents, the Pirates, nine times in 12 games that season, then beat them in the first game of the playoffs, 5-4, when McCovey and Fuentes each hit two-run homers.

But the Pirates won the next three games and the first round of the playoffs. The 1971 season was over, and McCovey never came close to playoffs or a World Series again.

Still, Willie had one more good year in his bat, with 29 home runs in '73 and 75 RBIs. But things were coming to an end for McCovey as a Giant, at least for the next three seasons. Disagreements with Fox and the Giants' front office led to a trade which sent McCovey to the San Diego Padres after 15 years as a Giant.

He became a fan favorite in San Diego just as he had in San Francisco. The Padres, formed as an expansion team in 1969 and struggling with last place finishes in every one of their five seasons, had attracted only 611,000 fans in 1973. In Willie's first year there, he hit 22 home runs and attendance jumped to over one million, almost double the previous season, even though the team finished last again. Owner Ray Kroc, who also owned the McDonald's fast food chain, called McCovey "the original Big Mac."

In McCovey's second season as a Padre, 1975, he hit another 23 homers. The team finished fourth and drew 1.2 million fans. Fate stepped in again on August 30, 1976, when the aging McCovey, now 38 years old, was hitting a meager .203 with only seven home runs. Then he was traded again, this time back to the Bay Area, to the Oakland A's, where he hit only five singles in eleven games.

At his $500,000 hilltop home in Woodside, 30 miles south of San Francisco, with its sweeping view of San Francisco Bay, McCovey waited throughout the winter of 1976-77 for the phone call that never came. Then he swallowed his pride, contacted the Giants and asked for permission to attend spring training as a non-roster player in the hope that he could win a job as the Giants' left-handed pinchhitter.

He did better than that. On Opening Day 1977, Willie McCovey was the Giants' first baseman. When the public address announcer introduced the starting lineup, McCovey received a standing ovation which lasted almost five minutes and brought tears to his eyes. The storybook plot even had a storybook ending—Willie drove in the winning run with a hit in the bottom of the ninth inning.

The fairy tale continued on September 18, when he was honored on Willie McCovey Day at Candlestick Park, with his mother, Esther, by his side. A crowd of 27,043 fans gave him not one but two five-minute standing ovations, one before the game and one after it.

There was a good reason for the second one: He duplicated his Opening Day feat by driving in the winning run in the bottom of the ninth again, this time with a long single off Cincinnati's Pedro Borbon with two on and two out for a 3-2 Giants' victory. He was showered with gifts ranging from a new Cadillac to a basset hound puppy.

"The biggest thrill of my whole career was the day they had for me at Candlestick Park last season," he said in 1978. "Driving in the winning run in that game made it a perfect day."

His achievement was no temporary thing. He hit .280 in 141 games in '77 with 28 home runs and 86 runs batted in. He won the National League's Comeback Player of the Year award in a walk.

It helped that McCovey had followed good habits throughout his career. "I never was impressed by night life," he said. "I spent most of my time in my hotel room and at the movies. I couldn't wait to get to the ballpark."

Willie offered his own explanation for his rebirth, and an insight into his makeup: "I believe that no really good player ever loses his physical skills. What makes him start to fade is that he loses his desire. You get so you don't want to go to spring training and get into shape as good as you should. You don't have the drive to get up for every game. If you don't get that way, you could almost play forever. And I don't mind going to spring training. I haven't lost those desires."

In adopting that attitude as a way of life, McCovey was trumping the argument heard for years from front office officials: "A ballplayer doesn't look into the mirror and see what's really there. All he sees is what he wants to see."

In 1980, his twenty-second year in the Major Leagues, Willie reached two milestones. He became one of a mere handful of players who played in four decades. And on May 3, he hit the last home run of his career, off Scott Sanderson of the Montreal Expos. It was his 521st homer, tying him with Ted Williams for the Number Eight spot among all-time home run leaders, before they were passed by Reggie Jackson and Mike Schmidt.

When he looked back, McCovey said, "I wasn't unhappy about my career. I was unhappy about having had too much pain. But I've been fortunate. I've been able to live with it and perform, whereas a lot of guys would have been forced out of the game."

When he was inducted into the Hall of Fame on August 3, 1986, in his first year of eligibility, even the weather seemed to be a commentary on his career. When he began his acceptance speech after receiving the traditional replica of his plaque from Commissioner Peter Ueberroth, it was drizzling.

When he finished, the sun was shining.

WHAT OTHER PLAYERS SAID ABOUT WILLIE McCOVEY

Dave Winfield—When I came up, he was one of the pictures on my wall because I was big like he was. I was ecstatic when he joined the Padres. I then had a role model. It's important for a young player to have a role model, someone you can look up to and learn a lot from. He would let me tag along with him on the road when he went out and I learned a lot from him off the field as well as on the field—the way he always conducted himself. He was a gentleman, he played the game hard, he was awe-inspiring.

Fergie Jenkins—Of all the home run hitters I faced, I think I feared Willie McCovey the most. I didn't feel too safe just 50 feet away after you deliver the pitch. In 1969, we were staying at the Jack Tarr Hotel in San Francisco. I got a message when I came down for breakfast at nine that a limo driver had just arrived and was waiting for me to go to the ballpark for a day game. I found the driver, and he gave me this message: "I just want you to get to the ballpark early and safe, because I know I can hit you, and I know I'm going to get my hits." It was signed by Willie McCovey.

Gaylord Perry—He hit the ball so hard I felt sure he was really going to hurt somebody. He hurt a lot of pitchers' feelings. He was a hitter who was just awesome. Some times Willie Mays would hit an easy double but would stop at first so they wouldn't intentionally walk McCovey. The fans would think Mays wasn't hustling, but he was doing the right thing for the team. He (McCovey) was very quiet, but when he spoke, you listened.

Jimmy Piersall—The only guy to hit the ball quicker through the infield than McCovey was Ted Williams.

Ron Santo—He was definitely a pull hitter. He'd scare the hell out of first basemen.

Bob Purkey—Don't even ask me about McCovey. I'll tell you, the guy drove me crazy. I tried to pitch him on his fists, and if I made a good pitch, he was still strong enough to muscle that ball over the infield somewhere. And if I didn't throw him a good pitch—see you later!

Bob Friend—I had pretty good luck early on in getting him to chase the curve ball, but he started learning that strike zone a little better, and, boy, he was really a tough out. He hit two of the longest home runs ever hit off me.

Chuck Tanner—McCovey played for me. He could hit a single harder than anyone alive. It would sink because he hit it so hard. If he got on top of the ball a little bit, it would go over—like Niagara Falls.

Willie Stargell—He looked like such an intimidator. When I saw him, I was just floored by what I saw. I said, "Now if there is anybody I would like to emulate, it would be McCovey." Even if the game was out of reach in the final inning, he was the kind of exciting hitter that people would stick around to see. If he was the first hitter in the ninth and made an out, everybody would start leaving.

Orlando Cepeda—He was a lot like Hank Aaron to me. Same way. Great teammate, great baseball player. He never complained. He played hurt all the time. It was an honor for me to play with Hank and Willie.

Duke Snider—He hit the ball as far as anyone I've ever seen. He hit Don Drysdale like he owned him. Drysdale tried everything—spitters and all. He tried everything. Whatever he threw seemed to hit McCovey's bat and went even farther.

Tommy John—He hit me harder than any batter I ever faced. I'll tell you how much I respected him. I had a 3-1 lead in the ninth inning, two out and the bases loaded with McCovey up. If we win the ball game, we win the National League West. Lasorda came out and asked me what I thought. I told him in all honesty that I wanted to win, but I had a terrible time with McCovey. He brought in a chunky little lefthander who slopped three sliders up to the plate and struck out McCovey. And that was the year I won 20 ball games. I just had a hard time with McCovey.

Clete Boyer—The nastiest S.O.B. I've ever seen. He was nasty. I mean, you'd get two strikes on him and still be behind on him. You just never felt you had him. Willie McCovey, he scared you. He looked like he was on every pitch. Hank Aaron beat you, but McCovey scared you. He looked like he was playing with Little Leaguers.

Maury Wills—Just an awesome guy. I don't remember Dodger pitchers who were known for moving hitters back—Stan Williams, Norm Sherry and Don Drysdale—throwing at McCovey much. I don't think they wanted to mess with Stretch. I don't think they wanted him to come to the mound.

Roger Craig—He, Frank Howard and Mickey Mantle could get the ball out of the ballpark faster than anybody I've ever seen. The ball just jumped off their bat. Sometimes McCovey would take a swing and it would seem the ball would be out of the ballpark before he completed his swing.

Stan Musial—This guy hit some of the longest home runs I've ever seen.

Al Downing—There are only two guys who scared me when I was on the mound. When I say "scared me" I mean you worried about yourself physically. Most home run hitters hit long shots or line drive homers, but there were two—McCovey and Frank Howard— who hit the ball through the middle. McCovey would hit the most vicious line drives. He would just hammer those low fast balls. He'd hit those towering shots and just when you would forget about it, he would hit that liner right at you.

Phil Rizzuto—Oh, gad—I'll never forget that ball he hit for the last out of the World Series at Bobby Richardson.

Umpire Doug Harvey—He hit one in Philadelphia I thought was never going to come down. He hit it over a 45-foot scoreboard, and it was still climbing. I was at first base that night, and I said, "Willie, you sure hit that one." And he replied, "Douglas, that's as good as I can ever hit a ball." He was a great athlete, one of the finest, if not THE finest first basemen I ever saw. He was so tall you couldn't throw it over him, and he could scoop it up with the best of them. I remember I was traveling with the Giants in spring training, and he said, "Doug, what's my number?" I said, "Forty-four." And he said he was going to hit 44 home runs and steal 44 bases. (McCovey never stole more than four bases in a season.) He had a good sense of humor. I'd take Willie on any man's ball club.

Dick Stuart—When Mays would get on first base, he would hide behind me because McCovey was up and he was a strict pull hitter. Every time I would go to move, Mays would take his finger and hook it into my pants and he would hide behind me because I was a lot bigger than him. McCovey would hit a line drive at us, and we'd both fall to the ground at the same time. Danny Murtaugh (Pittsburgh's manager in Stuart's years with the Pirates) would say, "You're supposed to catch the ball," and I'd tell him Mays had a hold of me and I was trying to get out of the way of the ball. That's how I got my reputation as "Dr. Strangeglove." I told Murtaugh I would try to catch the ball if McCovey hit it a little slower.

Randy Hundley—He was a smart hitter as well. You had a tough time fooling him. You hard to work hard setting him up to get him out. There were a couple of years there when I thought he was the best hitter in baseball. My first big league game, I was a pinch-runner at first base in Wrigley Field. The sun had gone down behind the bleachers, and the first baseman is playing way behind because he's scared to death, and here I am ninety feet away with Willie McCovey hitting. I'm telling you, I was the sacrificial lamb that they put on first base in case he might hurt somebody. I can tell you, it was a frightening thing being that close with McCovey hitting.

Frank Robinson—McCovey was one of those guys you looked at and said, there's no way this guy could be a player. A tall, lanky guy who was slow moving basically, but very athletic. I just admired his swing. He kinda put everything into it without any real effort. What a powerful swing he had and what a dangerous hitter and outstanding clutch hitter. You did not want McCovey at the plate with runners in scoring position. And, for him, they were in scoring position if they were on first base! He'd score you from first base. Tremendous offensive player.

Steve Carlton—I had pretty good luck with him, being a lefthander, and I'd keep that ball down and away on him. He had a long stroke and therefore was vulnerable up and in, but that stuff down and in or over the plate—you couldn't get it by him.

Hank Aaron—I don't think there was a pitcher he couldn't hit—lefthander or righthander. You didn't want to play in the infield or be on the pitcher's mound with this guy up. He was so strong.

Pete Rose—A tremendous hitter. I used to fear him when I played second base and if I were holding a runner on. I don't think it bothered him, but he kind of lived in the shadow of Willie Mays.

Joe Garagiola—He was one of the easiest-going, hardest-hitting guys. I saw him hit home runs so high I thought they were going to come down with snow on them. That's how high he hit them. He was kind of an easy, lumbering type of guy until he got in the batter's box. Then, look out. I'll never forget that ball he hit at Bobby Richardson in the Series. I thought it was going to nail Bobby to the ground. It had overspin on it. It was really tatooed.

THE McCOVEY FILE

Full Name: Willie Lee McCovey.
Date and Place of Birth: January 10, 1938, Mobile, Alabama.
Nickname: Stretch.
Position: First base, left field.
Major League Career: 22 years, 1959-1980.
Home Runs: 521 (tied with Ted Williams for tenth place).
Runs Batted In: 1,555.
Runs Scored: 1,229.
Lifetime Batting Average: .270.
Number of Hits: 2,211.
Walks: 1,345.
Strikeouts: 1,550.
Records: National League records for most career grand slam home runs
(18), most career home runs by a lefthanded hitter(521), most hom-
ers by a first baseman (438), most seasons played by a first baseman
(21), most consecutive games receiving an intentional walk (11).

Other Highlights:
— Winner of awards for Rookie of the Year (1959), National League Most
Valuable Player (1969), National League Comeback Player of the Year
(1977).
— With Hank Aaron and Willie Mays, the only players to hit at least one
home run in 22 different National League parks.
— Hit three straight home runs in a game twice, also hit three homers,
but not consecutively, in another game.
— Played in four different decades.

Elected to the Baseball Hall of Fame: 1986.

10

EDDIE MURRAY

"Just Regular"

On the night Cal Ripken broke Lou Gehrig's streak by playing in his 2,131st straight game, he told almost 50,000 fans in Baltimore's Camden Yards and a nationwide television audience, "When I got to the big leagues . . . . Eddie Murray showed me how to play this game, day in and day out. I thank him for his example and for his leadership. I was lucky to have him as my teammate for the years we were together."

A week later, Murray told reporters, "It was a nice gesture on his part. I appreciate what he said and the few years we had together."

Ripken elaborated on his remarks of the week before, saying, "Advancing to the Major Leagues can be a lonely existence, because with each level you progress, fewer and fewer of your minor league teammates go with you. I think Eddie recognized that . . . .And he took me under his wing. We've become good friends since."

Murray, then with the Cleveland Indians, said, "I just told him it was a game he should love and play hard every day."

For Murray, the newest member of baseball's 500-homer club, who reached that Hall of Fame level in 1996, his was a career of consistency and contrast. The record shows that Murray:

— Never hit more than 33 home runs in a season, but hit 504 in his career.

— Led the league in homers, walks, and RBIs only once, never led in any other category but is the only man to drive in at least 75 runs for 20 straight seasons.

— Collected 3,218 hits but never reached 200 hits in a season.

— Had a career batting average of .416 with the bases loaded as a feared clutch hitter and hit .294 in three American League Championship Series but hit only .169 in three World Series and .091 in six All-Star games.

— Endured controversies with fans, the media and even his owner but was considered by his teammates to be a leader and a positive influence in their dugout and clubhouse.

Hall of Famer Al Kaline defined Murray's greatness by comparing him with Reggie Jackson. Kaline said, "I always thought he was the opposite of Reggie. When Reggie thrived on media attention and things like that, Eddie just went out and played baseball."

Kaline's teammate with the Tigers, Alan Trammell, said, "Not to short-change his 500-plus home runs, but I just think of him as 'Steady Eddie.' It fits him perfectly. He played every day, and when all is said and done, he is one of the greatest players of all time."

Wade Boggs said it differently but maybe best. In 1995, he told Michael P. Geffner of *The Sporting News:* "Eddie has just always been one of those 'lay in the weeds' guys. He comes out just long enough to really hurt you, then goes back into hiding again."

A CRISCO LID AND A GARAGE

Murray was introduced to baseball by his four brothers in a Los Angeles ghetto where bullets fired during the race riots in Watts in 1965 ricocheted off a water tower next door and onto the Murrays' lawn.

It wasn't the ideal atmosphere for a kid, but the place had a garage, and that became the spawning ground for the future Hall of Famer. The brothers used bottle caps, rolled-up pieces of aluminum, tennis balls and lids from cans of Crisco shortening as baseballs. Those Crisco lids were a favorite "ball" because the boys could make them curve, sail, dip or rise.

They stood deep in the garage to hit each others' pitches. Two rules of their kids' game had a lasting effect on the future star: If a ball hit the side of the garage, it was a strike, forcing the boys to develop an even, balanced swing and hit every pitch up the middle, disciplining young Eddie's swing at an early age. And the brothers pretended to be members of the starting lineups of Major League teams, so they had to hit both lefthanded and righthanded, depending on who they were pretending to be.

Thus was born one of the two greatest power switch hitters in the history of the sport, in the same class with Mickey Mantle.

The game was more than just fun—it worked. All five Murrays signed professional baseball contracts. Eddie's younger brother, Rich, made it to the Major Leagues too, for parts of two seasons with the San Francisco Giants at the beginning of the 1980s. Another played Triple-A ball, the highest level in the minor league classification system, and the other two reached Double-A.

Rich played with the Giants long enough to hit four home runs, which, with Eddie's 504, ranks them behind only the three DiMaggio brothers—Joe, Dom and Vince—and Hank and Tommie Aaron as the leading brother combinations in home run history.

AGENT MOM

In the early 1960s, the oldest Murray son, Charlie, was invited to try out for his high school team, but his mother, Carrie, said no. Eddie remembered later, "We didn't do anything without asking Mama, and Mama just said no, which was the way she usually reacted to something like that."

One of her brothers talked her into letting her son play ball anyhow. Charlie played baseball in his senior year, then signed with the Houston Astros when Eddie was eight, a development which carried a message for all three of the younger Murray boys.

"It opened our eyes to something we could do," Murray told *Baseball America.*

When he was still only ten, Eddie was playing on a team with 15-year-olds. A few years later, Locke High School achieved the unimaginable distinction of having four future Major League players in its lineup— Eddie and Rich Murray, catcher Gary Alexander and another future Hall of Famer, Shortstop Ozzie Smith.

Even as a high school player, Eddie was a study in contrasts. He was known to his friends as "Easy Ed" because he played the game with such ease, but that appearance made some scouts suspicious that he was nonchalant and not a hustling, hard-nosed player. The talent was there, and so was the size. Eddie was now six feet, two inches tall and 200 pounds. As a pitcher, he was blessed with a good fast ball and compiled a 7-1 record in his senior year. When not pitching, he played first base and impressed Locke's followers—including the scouts—with his hitting ability.

The Orioles weren't fooled by his demeanor and chose him in the third round of the 1973 draft. His mother handled the negotiations.

"She was the best negotiator I ever faced," according to the man who signed Eddie, Dave Ritterpusch, then the Orioles' scouting director. For Michael Geffner's feature article in *The Sporting News,* Ritterpusch said, "She's the only person I've ever seen as composed as Eddie. She was totally unflappable. As cool as could be. At one point, she just said, 'Well, if you don't really want to sign my boy, that's all right. It doesn't really matter. I'm going to send him to college anyway.'"

Ritterpusch finally signed Murray, but only after 17 visits to the Murray home over five weeks and a signing bonus of $25,000.

The Orioles gave Murray and their other prospects an exam of 190 questions to reveal their characteristics—intangibles such as motivation, desire and composure. The results showed that Murray was far from lazy or nonchalant, charges which would surface periodically throughout his career, just as they had during his days at Locke High.

Ritterpusch said Murray's test results showed he was "very high" in motivation and desire and "flew off the chart" on composure. The team's psychological profile of Murray, gauged shortly after his seventeenth birthday, said, "Murray is an extremely stable individual with exceptional emotional control. Regardless of how stressful the situation becomes, he will think clearly and concentrate on his objectives."

That strong feeling of composure contributed to his success on the field, and to his problems with the fans, the media and his owner off the field as his brilliant career unfolded.

SWITCHING AGAIN

Murray began his professional baseball career at Bluefield, West Virginia, in the Appalachian Rookie League in 1973, was promoted to Miami the next year and made the All-Star team in both leagues. Then something happened.

The Orioles promoted him again, this time to Asheville, North Carolina, and his hitting fell off to only .264. The problem was the same one that has ended the professional career of many baseball players before they reach the Major Leagues: the curve ball. Murray was hitting righthanded exclusively, and righthanded pitchers were getting him out on the curve that broke low and away.

Then the other Ripken—Cal, Sr.—entered his life as the Orioles' trouble shooter in the minor leagues. When he visited Asheville, he encouraged Murray to become a switch-hitter again, just like in high school and in his garage back home. Then those curve balls from the righthanders would break into him instead of away from him. He'd be able to reach them easier. Better yet, he might see more fast balls.

Over the next 14 days, Murray, batting lefthanded against righthanders, rapped out ten hits in 31 times at bat for a .322 average.

Now a full-time switch hitter, Murray exploded in 1976, his fourth year in the minors, with 23 home runs while dividing his time between Charlotte and the Orioles' top farm team, the Rochester Red Wings of the Triple-A International League.

In the Orioles' 1977 spring training camp, Murray turned heads by hitting .400 as a 21-year-old rookie. Like many rookies who prefer to spend their time in the batting cage, Murray devoted less time to his fielding at the start of his career. Later, as he applied himself diligently with the first baseman's mitt, he led the American League in fielding four times. Brooks Robinson, considered by many to be the greatest third baseman of all time, once said Murray was the best he ever saw in making the "3-6-3" doubleplay, from the first baseman to the shortstop covering second and back to first.

Murray opened the '77 season as Baltimore's designated hitter while slugger Lee May played first base. Just as he did in the minors, Murray jumped off to an exciting start, tied May for the team's home run leadership with 27, hit .283 and played in all of the Orioles' 160 games, a feat which he duplicated five other times. And he drove in 88 runs, starting that record-making streak of 20 straight seasons with at least 75 RBIs.

In his first game, the rookie who once had trouble hitting righthanded curve ballers in the minors singled off one of the best righthanded curve ballers in history, Bert Blyleven of Texas. He followed that on April 18 with his first home run, against Cleveland's Pat Dobson. He was earning $19,000 a year.

Murray continued his development by avoiding baseball's dreaded "sophomore jinx," when the league's pitchers, having pitched against a rookie for a year and learned his habits and weaknesses, begin to pitch differently against him, sending many sensations back to the bench—or to the minors.

Eddie matched his 27 home runs of his rookie season, raised his average two points to .285 and drove in seven more runs—95. He led the Orioles in hits, RBIs and runs scored and finished second in the American League in total bases. He was selected for the American League All-Star squad, the first of eight times he was named an All-Star.

In 1979, the Orioles won the American League pennant, helped in large measure by Murray's .295 average, 25 home runs and 99 RBIs. In the American League Championship Series, Murray led his team to victory over the California Angels with a .417 average, a home run and five runs batted in.

The World Series gave the season an unhappy ending, with the Pittsburgh Pirates overcoming a 3-1 Baltimore advantage to win the next three games. Murray reached base safely in seven of his first eight plate appearances in the first two games, but his big bat fell silent and he failed to get a hit in the final five games, an 0-for-21 drought.

Using a 36-ounce bat instead of the 32-ouncer of his first few seasons, Murray continued his pursuit of excellence into the 1980s, even though his team's success did not match his own. The Orioles missed their division championship by three games in 1980, two games in each half of a strike-split season in 1981 and by only one game in '82. Murray hit an even .300 in 1980 and topped the 100 mark in RBIs for the first time with 116. In September, he sparked his team with 30 RBIs but the Orioles, despite winning 100 games under Earl Weaver, lost to the Yankees.

Over the winter, Murray was rewarded with a five-year contract for $5 million, a shocking sum in those years before today's staggering salaries. After signing the contract, he had a jeweler make a necklace with two words on it: *Just Regular.*

"When somebody asks me what it's like to be a millionaire," Murray explained, "I point to the necklace. I like to think I'm the same as I was when I was playing ball for fun with my brothers back home in Los Angeles."

In 1981, Murray led the league in home runs and RBIs for the only time in his career in a strike-shortened season, but Milwaukee beat out the Orioles for the AL East title by a game. In 1982, it was more of the same, with the Orioles winning 94 games but losing to Milwaukee by one game again. Murray was still the model of consistent excellence with a .316 average, 32 homers, 110 RBIs and a club record of 20 game-winning hits. He finished second in the balloting for the American League Most Valuable Player Award behind the Brewers' Robin Yount.

Baltimore struck gold in 1983 under a new manager, Joe Altobelli, who replaced the retired Weaver. The Orioles beat the Chicago White Sox in the American League playoffs in four games, then won the World Series over the Philadelphia Phillies in only five games with Murray hitting two home runs in the final game.

It was Murray's greatest season. He led the team with 33 home runs and 111 RBIs, was second in the league with 115 runs scored and third in slugging and game-winning RBIs, fourth in homers and total bases and ninth in RBIs. He finished second in the MVP voting again, this time behind teammate Cal Ripken.

But Baltimore's glory days were over. Murray played five more seasons with the Orioles, but they finished fifth, fourth, seventh, sixth and seventh again before he was sent to the Los Angeles Dodgers in a stunning trade whose roots went back several seasons.

CONSISTENCY AND CONTROVERSY

Murray remained the model of consistency over that disappointing stretch, averaging .293, 27 home runs and 99 runs batted in during 776 games over five years from 1984 through 1988, an average of 155 games a season. His high-water mark came on August 26, 1985, against the Angels in Anaheim, when he slugged three home runs and a single and drove in nine runs.

At the same time, his teammates were looking up to Murray as their leader. Outfielder Mike Young said, "There's no way I can tell you how much I owe him. He has been like a brother and a friend to me." Pitcher Storm Davis said, "That man is our leader." Manager Earl Weaver obviously agreed. He made Murray the Orioles' first captain.

A nagging hamstring injury forced Murray onto the disabled list in July 1986, a first experience for him in his eight years with the Orioles. He missed 25 games and hit only 17 home runs, his career low. Then the fireworks exploded.

Owner Edward Bennett Williams, feeling the frustrations of another disappointing season, complained publicly, "Eddie Murray hasn't given us a good year. Look at his extra base hits. He's really hurt us. And his fielding hurt, too. At his age (30), he's got to work in the off-season. It's a full-time job."

Murray took offense at the remarks and did what professional athletes usually do in that case—ask to be traded. The feud went on for two years before Eddie got his wish after the 1988 season and was sent to the Dodgers for three players.

As the owner and his star duked it out in the news media, Murray remained the target of shots from different directions. The radio talk show hosts pounded him without letup, and so did some of the writers and fans.

Murray was paying the price for his career-long attitude toward the media. For years he had taken a standoffish stance toward reporters and broadcasters and encouraged the same attitude in his teammates in a negative approach to media relations. One reporter described him as "a cancer in the clubhouse," charging that Murray turned other players against the press. He added to his own problems by rejecting many requests for public appearances.

So when the owner and the player began feuding in public, Murray's past caught up with him. What did he do? Nothing. That wasn't his way.

Because of his self-imposed, career-long blackout with the media, other dimensions to the Murray makeup went overlooked or forgotten — his popularity with his teammates, his quick willingness to sign autographs for children, his purchase every season of 50 box seats for every home game for inner city kids, his financial support for the United Cerebral Palsy Fund and the American Red Cross and the Johns Hopkins Children's Center, or his donation of $500,000 to the city to finance a summer camp under one condition—that it be named in honor of his mother.

He continued just to play baseball, and to play it better than others. Once rated by many as the best player in the Major Leagues, he continued to perform at a high level. In his first ten years as an Oriole, he averaged 27 home runs and 101 RBIs while playing almost every game. Even after incurring Williams's wrath in 1986, he led his team in hitting for the sixth time with a .305 average and in RBIs for the seventh straight season. He was an automatic selection for the All-Star game. With most of the 1980s in the history book, Murray had more votes for the league's Most Valuable Player award than anyone else, although he never won it.

Also unmentioned: In an era when players' contracts were full of such niceties as interest-free loans, jobs for relatives, roundtrip limo rides to the ballpark, and private school tuition for a player's children, all Eddie ever asked for was a single room on the road, a common courtesy already being extended to veterans by that time.

Just before the 1986 season, Murray signed a contract that dwarfed his earlier one, this one for $13.2 million carrying him through 1991. That had at least one immediate effect: The fans booed him for that, too.

One of Murray's allies was Kansas City's star third baseman, Hall of Famer George Brett, who said, "If the guy goes out and puts the numbers on the board, I don't see how they can boo him."

The team's pitching coach, Ray Miller, stuck up for Murray, too. He told *The Sporting News,* "It's hard for people on the outside to understand Eddie. They might get the idea he's standoffish or even rude. But he really isn't like that at all. All you have to do is watch him when some of the kids come around the clubhouse—or when he's just kidding around with people in the front office. It seems like hardly a day goes by that he doesn't stop in the front office to talk to the people over there. And I don't mean the brass, either. The regular people. Eddie is very comfortable with them."

When Miller was named the Orioles' manager in 1998, one of his first moves was to appoint Murray as his bench coach.

BANNER SEASONS

As he continued to press to be traded, Murray hit 30 home runs in 1987 at the age of 31. He hit home runs from both sides of the plate two days in a row in Chicago's Comiskey Park, a feat which he has since called his greatest thrill.

He had another banner season in 1988, leading the Orioles in batting average, home runs and runs batted in, the fifth time he led his team in all three categories in the same season. His trade to the Dodgers came only two months later.

Pitcher Brian Holton, the key man in the trade for the Orioles, won only seven games for them in the next two seasons, while Murray was enjoying considerably more success with the Dodgers. Playing in front of family and friends, he stepped right into the Dodgers' cleanup spot on Opening Day and led the team in home runs, RBIs, runs scored and games played—while also leading the National League's first basemen in fielding.

In his second year as a Dodger, Murray reached the highest batting average of his career, .330, missing the league's batting championship by only five points. He was named to the All-Star team in 1991, when Los Angeles lost to the Atlanta Braves by one game in the race for the National League West championship.

In three seasons with the Dodgers, Murray averaged 22 home runs and 93 runs batted in a year. One of his biggest fans was his manager, Tommy Lasorda. "To me," Lasorda exuded, "the most amazing thing about him is, if you want to describe him in one word, it's 'professionalism.' He is a professional. He never takes a day off. He plays every day. That's what makes him the great player he is. He knows people pay to see him play, and he doesn't disappoint people. He's right there as the best to ever play for me, without question."

Then came another surprise. Murray became a free agent at the end of the '91 season and signed with the New York Mets, where his old difficulty, media relations, became a problem all over again.

He ran into more problems with the New York media. He kept them waiting for 45 minutes on the first day of spring training, then followed his tardiness with a warning that there would be "focusing" days for him during the season when he would be unavailable. He was an enigma to them, bantering with his teammates and opponents, going out of his way to make rookies comfortable and showing himself to be a friendly guest in radio and TV interviews. But he ignored the writers and gave the clear impression that he considered them the enemy.

The standoff continued during a milestone in his career when he could have been sitting on top of the world. He hit the 400th home run of his career in only his second month as a Met, against the Braves in Atlanta on May 3. The New York reporters rushed to the clubhouse and found Murray relaxing in a recliner and watching a Los Angeles Lakers basketball game on TV. He barely acknowledged their presence, eventually making his way to the food table, a standard feature in big league clubhouses, and disappeared into the trainer's room, off limits for the media. When he finally emerged, his only comment about hitting his 400th homer was, "It's a nice, round number."

Murray hit only 16 home runs in 1992, the first of his two years with the Mets, but he drove in 93 runs and led the Mets in games played, at bats, runs, hits, doubles and RBIs. On June 6, he drove in two runs at Pittsburgh and topped Mickey Mantle with the most runs batted in by a switch-hitter.

The Mets, who set the Major League record for the most defeats with 120 in 1962, their first year of existence, demonstrated a remarkable level of futility again in 1993 with only 59 wins, but it wasn't Murray's fault. He hit another 27 home runs and drove in 100 runs for the sixth time. He led the Mets again in batting average, games played, at-bats, hits, doubles and RBIs, even though he was 37 years old.

Murray took advantage of free agency again before the 1994 season by signing with the Cleveland Indians, who needed a respected hitter to hit behind their powerful slugger, Albert Belle, so pitchers wouldn't be able to "pitch around" Belle without fearing the hitter behind him. Now they had Eddie Murray to contend with in that spot.

MORE MILESTONES

The strategy worked. In another strike-shortened season, baseball's longest and most disastrous labor dispute, Murray hit 17 homers and drove in 76 runs. The presence of his productive bat right behind Belle forced the American League pitchers to pitch to Belle, and he responded with 36 homers and 101 RBIs in 106 games.

In Murray's first game as a member of the Indians, he became the all-time leader among first basemen in games played. Later in April, he established another milestone, passing Mantle again by homering from both sides of the plate in the same game for the eleventh time.

After he turned 39 just before the start of the 1995 season, Murray may have had the most productive season of his career, playing a key role as the Indians won their way to the World Series for the first time in 41 years. At the same time, he became only the twentieth member of the exclusive 3,000-hit club with a single to right field off Mike Trombley in Minnesota. The hit placed him next to Pete Rose as the only switch hitters with 3,000 hits.

When he reached first base, Murray smiled and shook hands with Coach Dave Nelson and Scott Stahoviak, the Twins' first baseman. Outfielder Dave Winfield rushed out of the Twins' dugout and congratulated Murray, followed by the rest of the Twins.

Murray's agent, Ron Shapiro, told Brad Snyder of the *Baltimore Sun,* "To see Eddie Murray smile on the field, which was something because he rarely lets his emotions get out, made me know there was a level of happiness that was unique. Two others in the Twins' ballpark that night joined in the applause—Eddie's wife, Janice, and their 10-month-old daughter, Jordan Alexandra."

On August 29, he was back in the milestone business, this time becoming the fourteenth player to drive in 1,800 runs.

Murray's numbers disguised his age. He hit .323, the second highest average of his career, with 21 homers and 82 RBIs while playing in only 113 games. Belle, with that kind of a threat behind him, slugged 50 home runs, drove in 126 runs and batted .317. Result: The Indians won 100 games, then swept the Boston Red Sox in three games in the divisional playoffs. Murray provided insurance in their second win with a 2-run homer in the eighth inning of a 4-0 victory.

Murray was a factor again for the Indians in the American League Championship Series, when they won the pennant by beating the Seattle Mariners. After the Mariners won the first two games, Eddie's three-run homer in the first inning of the third game launched Cleveland toward a 7-0 win. In the fifth game, with the Indians trailing, 2-1, Murray doubled and scored on Jim Thome's home run for a 3-2 victory. They won the pennant the next day and headed for Atlanta to take on the powerful, pitcher-rich Braves in the World Series, Murray's first in 12 years, since the Orioles defeated the Phillies in 1983.

The Cleveland bats were silenced, including Murray's as Atlanta won the Series in six games. The team hit .179 and lost three games by one run. Murray had a game-winning single in the seventh inning of the third game, but otherwise was a dud at the plate. The single and a solo home run were his only hits in 19 at-bats, adding up to only a .105 average.

Murray was 40 years old when the 1996 season began. He needed only 20 home runs to reach the magic number of 500, but expecting 20 home runs from a man 40 years old is asking a lot, especially from someone who has played almost every game of every season for 20 years in a row.

Still, Murray continued to chase immortality. Meanwhile, back in Baltimore, management was doing some thinking. Owner Peter Angelos wanted Murray to hit his 500th homer as an Oriole, so the team traded Pitcher Kent Mercker to the Indians on July 21 for Murray, who by then was within nine home runs of 500 and still swinging.

In his first game back in Baltimore, playing in the new, hitter-friendly Camden Yards instead of the old Memorial Stadium, Murray hit Number 492. On September 6, one year to the night after Cal Ripken broke Lou Gehrig's record, Murray tagged Detroit's Felipe Lira with a shot that sailed into the right field stands for the 500th home run of his career. He became only the fifteenth player in the history of Major League baseball to reach that monumental level.

With the same swing of his bat, he also joined Hank Aaron and Willie Mays as the only players to collect both 500 home runs and 3,000 hits.

Nor was he finished achieving distinction. Fifteen days later, Murray hit a grand slam home run, his second of the season, and the nineteenth of his career, powering him past Willie McCovey into second place for the most grand slams in a career, behind only Gehrig's 23.

By the end of this remarkable season, he had 79 more runs batted in, setting his record of driving in 75 or more runs 20 years in a row.

After 55 games in 1997, Murray called it a career, with 504 home runs. When he did, another slugger, who has since gained far more prominence than Murray, Mark McGwire, said, "The thing about Murray is: How do you get to 500 homers without anyone really taking notice?"

After Murray played his last game, Ken Rosenthal wrote in the *Baltimore Sun*, "His critics will argue that his achievements are merely a reflection of longevity. Actually, they're more a measure of his consistency, perhaps the quality treasured most by his managers and teammates."

WHAT OTHER PLAYERS SAID ABOUT EDDIE MURRAY

Robin Yount—He was the classic switch hitter, with power from both sides. He was one of the last guys you would want to see up there with the game on the line.

Dave Winfield—Eddie, to me, during the '70s and early '80s, was the best clutch hitter in baseball because he would blast you from either side. I never saw Mantle, but Murray was the best switch hitter I ever saw. From either side of the plate, you just hated to see him come up.

Gaylord Perry—He was very confident in his ability. He knew the game and was always talking baseball with the players.

Catfish Hunter—I never thought he would hit that many home runs, but he did .... He was so consistent he was overlooked a lot of times. You wouldn't think he was a home run hitter, but he was.

Joe Rudi—I played against Murray a lot. A very quiet man. I never heard him ripping on people. A class act .... He was one of those players who quietly did his job every day and didn't get a lot of notice until the end of his career, when people started realizing the numbers he was putting up.

Sal Bando—The one thing Eddie Murray had that a lot of young players don't have today is the desire to play every day and to perform at a consistent level.

Tommy John—He's a lot like me, Don Sutton or Phil Niekro in that a lot of sports writers say he attained his totals by being around so long, but that's part of being around so long. Eddie was a plugger. He was just one of those guys who plugged along.

Goose Gossage— ... the ultimate professional. A class guy who just went about his business. When the bell would ring, Eddie was there .... If you wanted a teammate, if you wanted to play with somebody, Eddie is one of the guys you would want on your team.

Don Zimmer—This guy put fear into the other manager, that's for sure. Very quiet. Just went about his business every day and, before you know it, there's all those big numbers. He was a great player.

Gorman Thomas—What he accomplished is a tribute to longevity. He was quiet, played the game hard and played the game well, day after day after day for a long time.

Phil Rizzuto—He was an amazing player. He wasn't a very likeable guy. Like DiMaggio (Joe), unless you knew him and he trusted you, he was miserable and sarcastic and mean. When Eddie came up, he had a lot of trouble hitting the off-speed pitches, but he learned how to hit them. He sure did! Steady, steady—every year, every year.

Randy Hundley—He was just a smart hitter who kept it real simple.

Umpire Doug Harvey—He was a fellow who was not happy very often. He could never accept my close calls. He's not what I would consider a real good guy. Give the devil his due: He could play. In my opinion, it's unfair they allowed him to get 500 home runs as a designated hitter. I don't think it's fair to the other men who achieved it without the DH.

Ozzie Smith— Along with Mickey Mantle, the greatest switch hitting power hitters of all time. I was very fortunate to have the opportunity to play with Eddie when he was growing up in South Central Los Angeles. Even then you could tell it was just a matter of time before he reached that point of greatness. He was so talented, and in basketball as well. He was a great athlete and came from a very athletic family . . . . He played the game from the old school. The mindset was totally different then than it is today. As an aside—he was the best man at my wedding.

Ralph Houk—Eddie was probably one of the most underrated hitters we ever faced. He had great power to all fields as well as being a great switch hitter. I think he was more dangerous righthanded although he hit more home runs lefthanded.

Chris Chambliss—Eddie was an amazing hitter. He had that great power and yet hit in the clutch so well. Not only did he have all those home runs, he was the kind of guy you'd want up there when the game was on the line, which is sort of rare with home run hitters because most of them strike out a lot. It's not that they are easy to pitch to, but there are a lot of pitches they overswing at and miss. But Eddie Murray was a real clutch hitter. A switch hitter and yet equally dangerous from both sides. He just didn't have a weakness from either side.

Boog Powell—What surprised me was he is quite a student of the game. He studies the game a lot more than people think. He studies pitchers a lot, and if a pitcher is tipping something off or giving something away, Eddie will spot it and give it to our hitters. He's definitely managerial material—no doubt about that.

George Bamberger—Eddie Murray was a great guy, an outstanding guy. Very quiet. Great tools. He did a great job, no doubt about it. To me, he was a leader by example. A fantastic talent. I never heard anything bad about him. A heads-up ballplayer. He knew what was going on all the time.

Ron Guidry—I didn't have much trouble with him at the start, but he got to be such a good hitter, a dangerous hitter and switch hitter from both sides. I never looked forward to facing him, especially with guys on base . . . . I always thought he was going to go on to become a very special player. He'll go into the Hall of Fame, and it will be a privilege because I know what it was like to pitch against him.

Dick Williams—To me, he's a cinch Hall of Famer when he is eligible. He's quiet, but he's a great team leader. Everyone I've talked to thinks the world of him.

Frank Robinson— A guy who just made himself into an outstanding hitter. The move to becoming a switch hitter late in his minor league career changed everything for him. You did not want the bases loaded when Eddie Murray came to the plate because they would become empty with one swing. And from either side of the plate. He was a little bit more consistent average-wise from the left side, but he could hit the ball out of the ballpark from either side. He was at team player without anyone knowing it but his teammates. He made everyone on that field better because he was into the game and let everybody know where they were supposed to be before the play came up. He would go to the mound and talk to the pitcher about the hitter. He wasn't given a lot of credit as a leader, but Eddie Murray was a leader on any club he played for.

Jim Palmer—He was a teammate. I think he got misunderstood later in his career, but he could play. A great switch-hitter. Turned himself into a real good first baseman. He was a natural righthanded hitter. He was very good at anticipating what a pitcher was going to throw. He was a lot like Reggie Jackson and Frank Robinson in that he could carry a team. He just showed up and played. He was a dominant player on our team.

Bert Blyleven—I gave up Eddie's first hit and really wasn't aware of it until he hit his 3,000th and mentioned it as one of his milestones — a base hit the other way. Anybody who hits third, fourth or fifth for his entire career has got to tell you he's a power hitter. Very disciplined at the plate and had a very good eye for a big man.

Umpire Don Denkinger—I umped a lot for Eddie Murray, and Eddie Murray was not an umpire's friend. He just had a bad attitude, and it got to the point I thought he had a chip on his shoulder when it came to umpires. He never changed. He was always the same. It was like he had an attitude against discipline or something. He had a mind of his own and hated us to call him out on half-swings, especially if there were men on the bases. He just couldn't stand it.

Joe Altobelli—He was the rare kind. He was kind of quiet. He was kind of like Joe DiMaggio to me. He went about his business as a real professional. He came to the ballpark to go to work. Everyone knew about his prowess as a hitter, but not that many realized what a good first baseman he was. I thought he played it as well as anyone I'd ever seen. It isn't that he doesn't know how to talk. He can hold a conversation, but he was one who just didn't like to talk.

Gary Carter—I played with him and, to me, he was the consummate professional. I mean, he wasn't the flashy type of player. He never won an MVP award or led the league or anything, but I'll tell you this guy went day in and day out. The guy was awesome. He just got the job done.

Hank Aaron—He was gifted. He was also underrated.

THE MURRAY FILE

Full Name: Eddie Clarence Murray.
Date and Place of Birth: February 24, 1956, Los Angeles,   California.
Position: First Base, Designated Hitter.
Major League Career: 21 years, 1977-1997.
Home Runs: 504 (15th).
Runs Batted In: 1,917.
Runs Scored: 3,255.
Batting Average: .287.
Hits: 3,255.
Walks: 1,333.
Strikeouts: 1,516.

Records:
—   One of only three men in history, with Hank Aaron and Willie Mays, to collect 3,000 hits and 500 home runs.
—   Holds Major League record for most times hitting home runs from both sides of the plate in one game (11).
—   Major League record for sacrifice flies (128).
—   Major League record for most games by a first baseman (2,413).
—   Major League record for assists by a first baseman (1,865).
—   American League record for most game-winning RBIs (117).

Other Highlights:
— Only player to drive in at least 75 runs 20 years in a row.
— Career batting average of .416 with the bases loaded.
— Led American League in home runs and RBIs in 1981.
— Hit .300 seven times.
— Led League in walks in 1984.
— Hit home runs from each side of the plate two days in a row in Chicago's Comiskey Park in 1987.
— Played in three World Series.
— Named to All-Star team eight times.

11

MEL OTT

"Master Melvin" In a Man's World

J ohn McGraw, the manager of the New York Giants, was sitting in his
office in New York's Polo Grounds one morning in mid-September of
1925. He was not in a good mood. After winning a record four straight
National League pennants, his team was fighting a losing battle to
make it five in a row.

Even on his good days, McGraw, an iron-fisted tyrant, was known
for being direct and sarcastic. But there was no arguing with his success.
In the past 22 years, he had become recognized throughout baseball as
the greatest manager in its history by winning ten pennants and finishing
second eight times.

There was a knock on the door. McGraw snorted gruffly, "Come
in."

A nervous, small kid of 16 entered. "Mr. McGraw," he said, "I'm Melvin
Ott."

It was the start of a saga and a relationship that nothing in the
annals of baseball would compare with, one that was equal to the most
creative fiction.

The kid, on the stocky side, was destined to spend the next 22
years with the Giants. When he retired, he ranked third behind only Babe
Ruth and Jimmie Foxx as the greatest home run hitter of all time, holding
the National League record for hits, home runs, runs scored, runs batted
in, total bases, extra base hits, slugging percentage, bases on balls and
most consecutive years with one team. In the process, he became the
first National Leaguer to hit 500 home runs.

And in one of those ironies that fate loves to inject into our lives,
Ott became manager of the Giants and occupied the same office where

he stood before the mighty McGraw on that fateful day in 1925, wearing his first pair of long pants.

Ott had been a catcher on his high school team back home in Gretna, Louisiana, across the Mississippi River from New Orleans, when he and the team's star pitcher were invited to try out for the New Orleans Pelicans, a team in the Southern Association. Young Mel had never worn anything but short pants or knickers, so his father bought him a pair of long pants on the indisputable reasoning that no high school kid still wearing short pants would have much of a chance of making a professional baseball team.

The president of the Pelicans, Alex Heinemann, signed the pitcher, one Les Ruprich, a senior two years older than Ott, to a contract. He took one look at Ott, the boyish teenager, and asked bluntly, "Exactly how old are you?"

Ott answered, "I'm only 15." Then he added quickly, "But I'll be 16 in a couple of weeks."

"Well," Heinemann said, "we don't need children in this league. But as long as you are the catcher for your friend, you can put on a uniform and work out for a few days."

When Heinemann saw Ott's disappointment at not being given a contract, he offered to help him land a spot on a semi-pro team in Patterson, 90 miles away. Heinemann called his friend, Harry Williams, a lumber baron who married one of the stars of silent movies, Marguerite Clark, "The Siren of the Silver Screen." Williams sponsored the Patterson Grays, an informal town team considered the best semi-pro team in southern Louisiana. He agreed to sign Ott for $150 a month, plus free room and board. He also paid bonuses for big plays, and when a player hit a home run, Williams allowed him to pass his hat around for a few more dollars. With a little luck, a heavy hitter like Ott could double his monthly take.

With that kind of dazzling future in front of him, Ott quit high school, a deep disappointment to his mother, and went to play for Williams. What the teenager didn't know was that Williams was more than the owner of a prosperous lumber company and sponsor of a baseball team. He was also a scout for McGraw.

THE "PHEE-NOM" SAYS NO

By the following season, Ott was the regular catcher for the Grays, and the word quickly got back to New Orleans and to Heinemann that the young "phee-nom," as they called bright baseball prospects in those days, was pounding the cover off the ball and was his team's best player. Heinemann sought to atone for his earlier rejection of Ott by offering him a contract for $300 a month, double his salary in Patterson, to come back to New Orleans and play for Heinemann's Pelicans.

The kid was elated and quickly told Williams his good news. But Williams, with no explanation, told Ott to forget it, that he had bigger plans and would discuss them with him on his return from a European vacation.

Ott, showing a degree of trust that few players have demonstrated in their owners, turned down Heinemann's offer. In the years that followed, Ott delighted in saying that turning down the first offer he ever got to play professional baseball was the luckiest thing that ever happened to him.

When Williams reached New York en route to Europe, he stopped at the Polo Grounds and excitedly talked McGraw into giving Ott a tryout. He didn't mention that Ott was still only 16 years old.

Before he boarded his ship, Williams sent Ott a penny postcard telling him to report to McGraw at the Polo Grounds on September 1 and wishing him luck. When Ott read it, he thought someone was playing a joke on him and threw the card away.

When Williams returned from Europe a month later and found Ott still in Patterson and two weeks late for his tryout in New York, he personally took Ott home to pack, then drove him to the railroad station. He told the teenager to tell McGraw he was the kid Williams had told him about.

Wearing his first suit and carrying a cardboard suitcase, young Melvin rode the train from New Orleans to New York for a day and a half, checked into the Hotel Ansonia because he'd heard that's where the players stayed, then headed for the Polo Grounds. When he asked a police officer for directions, saying he was going there for a tryout with the Giants, the cop laughed. The confused kid, a thousand miles from home and alone, took a subway to the Coney Island area of Brooklyn by mistake and arrived late for his tryout. He was disappointed again when the staff at the Polo Grounds told him the Giants were on the road and wouldn't be back in New York for another ten days.

That was the background ten days later as young Melvin stood in front of McGraw in his office on that September day in 1925 and presented his letter of introduction from Harry Williams. McGraw, whose dictatorial personality had earned him the nickname "Little Napoleon," chastised the kid for being two weeks late, wondering at the same time why Williams, a good judge of baseball talent, had sent him this 16-year-old with legs shaped like beer barrels. He told Ott to get into a uniform and take a few swings in batting practice.

For McGraw, it was love at first sight. After only a few swings by Ott, McGraw was convinced he was looking at a future star. He saw what everyone who ever saw Mel Ott swing a bat saw—a stance and swing that violated some of the most fundamental rules of hitting. A lefthanded hitter who stood five feet nine inches and weighed only 170 pounds—easily the smallest of the 500-homer hitters—the kid raised his right foot off the ground and above his left knee in an exaggerated goose step, then balanced himself on his left leg like a ballet dancer before shifting his weight forward into the pitch. Ott always maintained that the lifted leg played an important part in putting every ounce of his body into his swing.

FOR McGRAW, FINALLY SOME GOOD NEWS

The two, the gruff manager with the dazzling string of pennants and world championships and the polite kid from the Deep South, formed a closeness that endured until McGraw's death nine years later.

By the time of Ott's arrival in his office, McGraw was ready for some good news. The 1925 season had been a trying one for the manager. His team failed to win the pennant after those four straight championships, and a reserve infielder plus one of McGraw's coaches were barred from baseball for life for offering a bribe to an opposing player. The episode affected McGraw's spirits and his health. He was absent from the Giants' dugout for several weeks because of illness.

McGraw got a longer look at Ott during spring training for the 1926 season. Noticing his unusually heavy legs with their bulging calves and heavy thighs, McGraw suspected his young prospect would not last long as a catcher because the constant squatting behind the plate would make him muscle-bound. He asked Ott if he'd ever played the outfield.

Ott, who had just turned 17, answered, "Yes, sir—when I was a kid."

McGraw became such a strong believer in Ott's future as a hitter despite his unorthodox stroke that he refused to send the boy to the minor leagues because he thought Ott's swing, as unusual as it might have been, was nevertheless one of the smoothest, most rhythmic swings he'd ever seen. He didn't want any minor league manager trying to change it to a more conventional stroke. Ott is one of only two among the 500-homer hitters who never played an inning of minor league ball. The other is Ernie Banks.

Casey Stengel found this out the hard way. He was managing Toledo of the American Association that spring when he approached McGraw and suggested that a year in the minors might help to develop "this young fellow—what's his name—Mel Ott?"

The fiery McGraw exploded, informing Stengel in the clearest language that neither he nor any other minor league manager was going to fool with that kid. McGraw took the additional step of ordering Ott to sit next to him on the bench—a tactic which paid rich rewards later—and arranged for the kid to room alone on the Giants' road trips.

McGraw was determined to keep a close eye on "Ottie." He didn't want the youngster exposed to veterans who were known to drink, smoke, play cards and chase the ladies. When he found young Mel playing poker with a few older players, he told the kid he was too young to play poker and fined him a hundred dollars. The fine stuck. But when Ott checked his final pay envelope of the season, he found a "bonus" inside—for a hundred dollars.

With his protege next to him in the dugout, McGraw told Ott to keep his eyes and ears open to everything that was going on. He pointed out the different pitching styles and explained why they threw certain pitches in certain situations, reminding Ott to bear these conditions in mind when he would be the hitter.

It was June before the kid got into his first game, as a pinch hitter against the Reds in Cincinnati, and the pitcher was no patsy. It was no less than Pete Donohue, a 20-game winner that year for the third time in four seasons. He disposed of Ott quickly on strikes.

But it wasn't long before Mel got his first hit—a single off the great Grover Cleveland Alexander of the Cardinals, already a 300-game winner on his way to tying Christy Mathewson with 373 victories, still the all-time National League record for a righthander.

McGraw's plan to nurse Ott along slowly eventually paid rich dividends. Used mostly as a pinch hitter in his rookie season, Ott hit a stunning .383 in 1926. Ironically, the same slugging star who was to hit 511 home runs in his career didn't hit any in his first year. In 1927, with Babe Ruth hitting 60 home runs for the Yankees, Ott hit .282 and led the league with 46 pinch-hitting appearances.

THE BABE AND MASTER MELVIN

While Babe Ruth was thrilling the whole country by breaking his own record with 60 home runs, the teenager, who was now called "Master Melvin," hit his first. It came on a low line drive to center off Hal Carlson of the Cubs, and it was less than a classic blow. Outfielder Hack Wilson, one of the most powerful sluggers in baseball at the time, tried for a shoe string catch, slipped on wet grass and let the ball get by him for an inside-the-park home run. It was Ott's only homer of the year.

Ott made it as a Major Leaguer in 1928, playing in 124 games and hitting .322 with 18 home runs. Ruth continued to dominate the headlines with 54 more homers, but Ott could no longer be ignored as an established star hitter.

He added to his standing in 1929, the season that ended just before the stock market crash. He proved his high batting average of the year before was no fluke, raising it six points to .328. He also solidified his credentials as one of the power men in the game by finishing second in the National League in both home runs and runs batted in—42 homers, only one behind Chuck Klein of the Phillies, and 152 runs batted in, only seven fewer than Hack Wilson. As if all that weren't enough for a kid who turned 20 the month before the season started, he also led the league in walks with 113, the first of six times he topped the National League in that department.

Early in spring training before the 1930 season, on March 2, Ott surprised and scared McGraw at breakfast by confiding in him that when he woke up that morning, a man was in his room. McGraw, still protective of his prodigy, jumped to his feet and asked quickly, "Who was it?"

Ott said, "Me. Today is my twenty-first birthday."

He had been in the big leagues for four years, two as an established star, before reaching the voting age of that time.

With his gag at McGraw's expense, he was showing the same effervescent attitude that prompted his teammates on the Giants to give him a second nickname—"Little Sunshine."

Ott continued as a star that year and the next with a .349 average and 25 home runs in 1930 and another 29 homers in '31 even though his average dipped to .292. The Giants finished third both years, but when they won only 17 of their first 40 games in 1932 and were mired in sixth place, the unmatched managerial career of the great McGraw came to an end. Tired and discouraged, he had lost his desire to win and agreed it was time for a change. Two years later, at the age of 60, he died.

One of Mel's teammates and one of the biggest star hitters in the Major Leagues, first baseman Bill Terry, was appointed to succeed McGraw. He dazzled the baseball world two years earlier by hitting .401, the last time a National Leaguer has hit .400. In one scorching streak, he drove in 100 or more runs for six seasons in a row, hitting over .349 or better four straight times.

Terry was almost the opposite of McGraw as a manager. Instead of being a tyrant, he was quiet, almost sullen, a contrast to the always cheerful disposition of "Little Sunshine." But it was during Terry's years as the Giants' player-manager that Ott reached his full potential and his greatest glory.

Ott led the National League in home runs three times in those years and tied for the title in two other seasons while driving in 100 or more runs six times. He sparked his team into the World Series three times, compiling career Series totals of four home runs and 10 runs batted in during 16 games. In their only world's championship during that stretch, over the Washington Senators in 1933, Ott hit .389, won the first game with a two-run homer and blasted another in extra innings in the deciding game.

When the '33 World Series hero returned home to Louisiana for the winter, he was honored by his neighbors in Gretna with a high school diploma, the one he hadn't stayed around to get when he headed for New York and the Giants in the middle of his junior year eight years earlier.

He led his Giants to two other World Series, in 1936 and '37, both against the Yankees and both ending in defeat. Throughout the decade of the 1930s, Ott was what today we call a "superstar." He hit over .300 seven times in those ten years, including that .349 in 1930, led the league in home runs five times, in walks four times and slugging average in 1936.

The kid who was still only 21 when the 1930s began was performing these feats against a bumper crop of stars and future Hall of Famers—competing successfully against fellow hitting stars like Chuck Klein, Bill Terry, Hack Wilson, Johnny Mize, Gabby Hartnett, Ernie Lombardi, Lloyd and Paul Waner, Arky Vaughan, Dolf Camilli, Joe Medwick and Enos Slaughter.

And the pitchers he was hitting against with such consistent success included Carl Hubbell, Dazzy Vance, Burleigh Grimes, Freddie Fitzsimmons, Paul Derringer, Dizzy Dean, Lon Warneke, Claude Passeau, Bucky Walters and Johnny Vander Meer, every one of them an All-Star or a Hall of Famer.

Ott showed no signs of slowing up in 1938, after their second loss to the Yankees in the World Series. He hit .311 with a league-leading 36 home runs (his fifth homer title, with his sixth to come in 1942), 116 runs batted in and the same number of runs scored. He continued to be productive for seven more full-time seasons, but he never again drove in 100 runs and hit just over .300 only twice. The Giants didn't win another pennant until 1951, when Bobby Thomson hit his "Shot Heard 'Round the World."

THE "LITTLE GIANT" AND HIS GIANT-SIZED NUMBERS

When his playing days were over, Ott could look back on a stellar career as "The Little Giant." He compiled a lifetime batting average of .304, hit those 511 home runs and drove in 1,861 runs while collecting 2,876 hits. If he hadn't had such a keen batting eye and been so selective while drawing 1,708 walks, the sixth most in history, he easily could have joined the elite 3,000-hit club.

Throughout his Hall of Fame career, "Master Melvin" ruled the Polo Grounds. Giants fans were drawn to him by his heroics and his engaging personality. They worshipped him. He was more than just a home run hitter. He became an expert at fielding balls off the tricky right field wall. Despite his lumbering running style, he had his own knack for getting a good jump on the ball and had one of the league's strongest throwing arms, one of the fringe benefits from his high school years as a catcher. In 1929, he threw out 26 base runners from his position in right field, the most in the National League.

His admiring fans called the seats where his home runs landed in right field "Ottville. He could do no wrong, even in Brooklyn. The Dodger fans hated the Giants and poured it on the New York players with verbal abuse when the enemy dared venture into Ebbets Field. But they made an exception for Ott. "Ottie's different," they would say. "He don't count."

The Giants' fans roared their approval for Ott's every move, especially the 323 home runs he hit at home out of his career total of 511. Early in his career he perfected the knack of pulling the ball into the short right field stands at the Polo Grounds, only 257 feet down the line from home plate, the shortest distance in the Major Leagues.

When Ted Williams, a fellow member of the 500-homer club, wrote *The Ted Williams Hit List*, he rated Ott the sixteenth greatest hitter of all time. Williams wrote, "He was a real slugger, and I think that of all the hitters in baseball, Ott probably best adapted himself and his style to conform to his abilities. He could pull the ball, but his greatest skill was being able to conform to the greatest advantage to the park he hit in. And that's where his detractors come in."

And yes, he did have detractors. Ott easily hit more home runs at home—63 percent—than any of the other 500-homer hitters. After his playing career, Ott admitted he never would have hit over 500 homers if it hadn't been for that close fence in right field, what the players call a "short porch".

Baseball writer John Tattersall conducted a study of Ott's home runs and said it showed that two seasons—1943 and 1945—offered convincing evidence of the advantage Ott enjoyed in the Polo Grounds. Tattersall's analysis showed that all 18 of Ott's homers in 1943 came at home, and so did 18 of the 21 he hit in 1945.

Even some of Ott's contemporaries, while admitting his greatness, make the same point about his advantage in the Polo Grounds. Former infielder and manager Bobby Bragan said, "Ott was in the right park . . . He could pull on anybody. I mean, he could hit them out, but that park was made for his swing. He raised that right leg higher than anyone I ever saw. If you were in front of the centerfield clubhouse 500 feet away from the plate, you wouldn't have any trouble identifying Ott . . . . He would have hit 500 in Ebbets Field, Wrigley Field, Crosley Field . . . Master Melvin could hit."

Outfielder Jo-Jo White said, "He really didn't have a weakness . . . . The Polo Grounds, with that short rightfield fence, was made for him. But he could really hit them anywhere."

Ott tied or led the National League in home runs six times, and he might have made it seven if it hadn't been for the Phillies in 1929, when he hit 42. Master Melvin was tied with their Chuck Klein at 42 when they faced off in a doubleheader. Klein hit his forty-third off Carl Hubbell in the first game, so in the second game his pitchers conspired to protect his lead. They walked Ott four times, once with the bases loaded even though it forced in a run. Ott grounded out twice trying to reach outside pitches. The news media rained criticism down on the Phillies all over the country—but their boy Klein won the home run championship.

THE MANAGERIAL YEARS: "NICE GUYS..."

For Bill Terry, the bloom came off the rose as the 1930s ended. After winning three pennants in his first five years as their manager, Terry's Giants slipped to fifth, sixth and back to fifth in 1939-40-41, back to the low-rent district called "the second division" in those years of two eight-team leagues. It had been 39 years since a Giants team finished in the second division for three straight years.

Terry—sour and caustic and never popular with players or reporters even in the good times—was replaced by the always popular Ott, who started his managerial career the same way Terry did, as player-manager. Despite Ott's enduring popularity, skepticism greeted his appointment, and the one-time "Master Melvin" was alert enough to know it, so he tried to blunt it at the press conference announcing his appointment.

He promised to be "a fighting leader." He said he wouldn't just be Mr. Nice Guy any more. He had a job and he was going to do it and silence his critics while occupying the same office as the man he never called anything but "Mr. McGraw."

Ott seemed to be making good on his prediction, with the Giants finishing third in 1942. But when Ott had been named manager in December 1941, something else had happened: Five days later, the Japanese bombed Pearl Harbor. The Giants were hit hard by the military draft. For the next four seasons, how well your team did depended on how many players you lost to military service.

The Giants plunged to last place in 1943 and were able to rebound only as high as fifth place twice during the wartime manpower shortage that produced a hit song in which a young lady voiced the same complaint that baseball's owners were facing: "They're Either Too Young or Too Old."

His managerial fortunes produced at least one fringe benefit for Ott: He got to meet America's favorite hero of the war, General Dwight Eisenhower, before a rainy game at the Polo Grounds just after Ike's return from Europe in 1945. Ott and the Boston Braves' manager, Bob Coleman, presented Eisenhower with baseballs autographed by their teams, and Ott added an autographed bat.

The future president told the managers and his host for the day, Mayor Fiorello LaGuardia, about his boyhood ambitions to become a big league player and of his summer of playing semi-pro ball under an assumed name so as not to jeopardize his football eligibility at West Point. When reporters asked Ott what he said to the war hero in response, Ott said he couldn't remember. "I was too nervous. Boy, my hands were shaking."

In 1946, despite the return of the pre-war stars, the Giants dropped to last place again, their problems compounded when a wealthy Mexican business executive, Jorge Pasquel, lured several American stars to play south of the border with big-bucks contracts. The Giants and the St. Louis Cardinals were among the hardest hit teams.

But Johnny Mize, back from Navy duty in the Pacific, hit 51 home runs for the Giants in 1947, Willard Marshall hit 36, Walker Cooper had 35 and Bobby Thomson blasted 29. They climbed back to fourth place—the first division—with 221 homers, a National League record.

The clouds grew dark for the Giants again as the 1940s ended. In 1949, the Yankees began a string of five straight pennants under their new manager, Casey Stengel, while the Dodgers landed a team of future Hall of Famers and All-Stars—Duke Snider, Jackie Robinson, Carl Erskine, Roy Campanella, Don Newcombe, Pee Wee Reese and the rest—and came within two losses of duplicating the Yankees' feat. Only losing the last game of the 1950 and '51 seasons prevented the Dodgers from winning five pennants in the same years the Yankees did, from 1949 through 1953.

That kind of competition was too stiff for the Giants, and specifically for Ott. As early as the middle of the 1948 season, the Giants, the same team that set the home run record the year before, were last in the league in hitting. Their attendance showed it. Nearly one-third of their attendance came in the eleven games they played at home against the Dodgers.

It wasn't just Ott's team that was having problems. He was, too. He was often out of the lineup because of difficulties with his eyes, which forced him to wear glasses, and leg problems. He hit the last home run of his career on Opening Day in 1947.

With his team's performance matching his own, Ott was fired just after the 1948 All-Star game. It was a double jolt for Giants' fans: The man hired to replace the beloved Ott was the hated Leo Durocher, the Dodgers' manager. The man who acquired the nickname of "Leo The Lip" — and he earned it—was everything that Ott wasn't—brash, loud, cocky, vulgar and foulmouthed.

Giants fans were shocked beyond belief. Durocher? Satan himself! As if the Giants didn't have enough reasons to despise the man, he had enraged them even more after a reporter asked him why he couldn't be a nice guy for a change. Durocher pointed across the infield to the dugout of the Giants, who were in last place. He nodded toward Ott, their manager, and scornfully uttered one of the all-time sports insults: "Nice guys finish last."

Two years later, the Giants, under Durocher, won the pennant.

Some of the players from that time agree today that Ott may, in fact, have been too nice to be a manager, and maybe too indecisive. Former manager Bill Rigney said, "I came to the ballpark early one morning, the first to arrive. I was going good and playing every day. He was sitting there in the clubhouse with four empty quarts of milk and a pile of cigarettes. He had been there all night. 'Do you think this would be a better ball club if I quit?' he asked. I told him we just had to play better, but I remember thinking you just have to get on these guys' butts once in a while. A month later he was replaced by Leo Durocher."

Pitcher Larry Jansen, another member of Ott's team, said, "He couldn't make up his mind quick enough on decisions like whether to hit and run. By the time he made up his mind it was too late. He was just too slow making up his mind. He always had to question his coaches before he decided."

Outfielder Bobby Thomson: "You couldn't compare him with Leo Durocher as a manager. Hell, he just let the guys go out and play."

When Ott was in his early days as the Giants' manager, owner Horace Stoneham said, "If I fired Mel, my mother and sister wouldn't speak to me." When Stoneham did it anyhow, Ott had two years left on his contract. The owner made the announcement with tears in his eyes.

Ott spent his remaining two years by helping his old friend and teammate, Carl Hubbell, who was then in charge of the Giants' minor league system. He managed Oakland in the Pacific Coast League, became a weekend broadcaster for the Mutual radio network and later for the Detroit Tigers, then moved out of baseball and back home to Louisiana.

Before he left the big city, the New York baseball writers made him a lifetime member of their organization, the first non-writer so honored. The Giants gave him the highest tribute any team can bestow—they retired his Number 4.

Four years after his playing career ended, he was elected to the Baseball Hall of Fame in 1951.

TEN YEARS LATER, A FOGGY NIGHT

On November 14, 1958, ten years after his dismissal as the Giants' manager, on a wet and foggy night near Bay St. Louis, Mississippi, Mel Ott and his wife, Mildred, left the Flamingo restaurant after dinner, climbed into their station wagon and headed toward Route 90 and the trip back to their home in the New Orleans suburb of Metairie.

Because of the heavy fog rolling in from the Gulf of Mexico only a few blocks away, Mel drove with extra caution as they pulled onto the highway. Suddenly, out of the fog, a car crossed the center line and smashed head-on into their wagon. The driver of the other car, a father of seven, was killed instantly. Mel and his wife were both critically injured. Mel had two broken legs, innumerable cuts and possible internal injuries.

The doctors, after waiting until the next day because Ott was in shock, operated and were optimistic, but Mel took a sudden turn for the worse with kidney problems. Another operation followed, as baseball fans across the country prayed for him. But it was too late. Officially, he died of uremic poisoning a week later, at 2:30 on the afternoon of November 21. His wife survived.

Tributes poured in from teammates, opponents and dignitaries. Leo Durocher called a friend and cried while saying that Ott was the nicest guy who ever lived.

At his family's request, Mel Ott was buried quickly, without the company of the many baseball greats and unknowns who would have paid their final respects. Forty years later, former Mets' star Ron Swoboda, said this year, "His tomb is right on the corner of Metairie Cemetery in New Orleans. You can actually see it as you drive by there. No one visits it anymore. Melvin Ott. Nobody keeps it up or puts flowers on it or anything."

Cecil Travis, an All-Star shortstop and third baseman with the Washington Senators in the 1930s and '40s, described Mel Ott completely. "He lifted that leg in an odd way, but he had a pretty swing and he was a good hitter. And he was a nice fellow with it."

WHAT OTHER PLAYERS SAID ABOUT
MEL OTT

Ralph Branca—The only hitter I've ever seen who could lift his leg the way he did and hit as well was Sadaharo Oh (the home run king of Japanese baseball).

Frank Torre—I was a Giant fan when I was a kid. I used to go up to the Polo Grounds by train. He'd kick that leg up and pull the ball right down the rightfield line. Even though that was a monster ballpark, if you hit down the line you would hit home runs. He mastered the knack of doing that.

Bobby Bragan—As a manager he was too easy going, too laid back. But there is another angle. When you're the manager and you have to face that pitcher four times, you're not as apt to get on somebody if they look bad against that pitcher.

Jo-Jo White—He really didn't have a weakness . . . . He was all over the plate, and he could reach that outside pitch better than most. He wasn't that big a guy, but he had that power for a small man . . . .He was the real family man type. He managed the Giants for a long time, but good people don't make good managers. You have to be like Durocher to be a good manager.
I thought he was a good manager, but you have to have people who can do what you ask them to do, and he didn't have enough of those.

Claude Passeau —I remember he beat me with a home run in Philly, and it was the only one he ever got off me—but it beat me in a ball game in extra innings.

Harry "The Hat" Walker—He was a pretty good outfielder. You had to watch him. If you rounded first base too far, he would nail you. We learned that if you ever rounded first a little too far, just keep on going.

Don Mueller, Giants Outfielder—He was the manager of the Giants. That's why I signed with New York. He was my favorite player.

THE OTT FILE

Full Name: Melvin Thomas Ott.
Date and Place of Birth: March 2, 1909, Gretna, Louisiana.
Date and Place of Death: November 21, 1958, New Orleans, Louisiana.
Nickname: "Master Melvin"
Position: Right Field (also second base and third base).
Major League Career: 22 years, 1926-1947.
Home Runs: 511 (14th).
Runs Batted In: 1,861 (8th).
Runs Scored: 1,859 (9th).
Lifetime Batting Average: .304.
Number of Hits: 2,876.
Walks: 1,708 (6th).
Strikeouts: 896.
Records: When he retired in 1947, Ott held the National League records for the most hits, home runs, runs scored, runs batted in, total bases, extra base hits, slugging percentage, bases on balls and most consecutive years with one team.

Other Highlights:
— Played in three World Series, defeating the Senators in 1933, losing to the Yankees in 1936 and 1937.
— Led National League in slugging average in 1936, led league in home runs six times, runs scored twice, runs batted in once, bases on balls five times.
— Hit over .300 eleven times, including .349 in 1930.

Elected to the Baseball Hall of Fame: 1951 (with Jimmie Foxx).

12

FRANK ROBINSON

Underrated?

I t's hard to imagine that a player with 586 home runs, the fourth highest in history behind only Hank Aaron, Babe Ruth and Willie Mays, could be considered underrated, yet that's what many of his former teammates and opponents say about Frank Robinson.

When Bob Allen interviewed players for this book, the claim that Robinson was underrated and never given the amount of recognition his accomplishments deserve was a continuing theme. His manager with the Cincinnati Reds, Birdie Tebbetts, was emphatic: "He will go down as the most underrated player in the history of the game. He could do anything. What was there for him to do that he didn't do?"

Pitcher Mudcat Grant said, "Frank Robinson was the most underrated player of all time." Third Baseman Clete Boyer of the Yankees agreed: "The most underrated ballplayer I ever saw ....He never got the credit he deserved." Hall of Fame Pitcher Robin Roberts called him "the most underrated player of all time, in my book." Catcher Bill Freehan offered a clarification from the players' viewpoint: "Frank may have been underrated by the fans, but not by us."

Robinson himself has always been aware that he is often overlooked when the elite among baseball greats are listed. One writer suggested that Robinson didn't have the nicknames of affection and admiration given to other players—Babe, The Mick, Stan The Man, The Yankee Clipper, The Splendid Splinter, Mr. October, Say Hey or The Duke. Instead, he was known simply as "Robbie," a nice enough nickname but not one that suggests greatness as a dominating star.

Whatever the reason, Robinson told Doug Brown of *The Sporting News*, "I don't want people to say Mickey Mantle, Willie Mays and Hank

Aaron in one breath and then, in the next breath, Frank Robinson. I want them to say Mantle, Mays, Aaron and Robinson in the same breath."

His record justifies such mention. When he retired after the 1976 season, "Robbie" had more than just the fourth highest number of home runs in history. He also was tenth in runs scored and had the seventh most World Series home runs and the fourth highest Series home run percentage.

He could look back on a career in which he captured the American League's "Triple Crown," the first player in either league to do it since Mickey Mantle ten years earlier, by winning the league's hitting, home runs and runs batted in championships in 1966. That was his first year with the Baltimore Orioles, when he led his new league in six offensive categories and became the only player in history to win the Most Valuable Player award in each league.

COMPETITIVENESS AND PENCILS

Robinson commanded attention throughout his career as one of his sport's fiercest competitors. Catcher Del Crandall called him "a tremendous competitor." His namesake with the Orioles, Brooks Robinson, said, "Frank Robinson was one of the toughest competitors you will ever run into." Frank Howard said he was "probably the most competitive player I ever played against." Duke Snider said, "He was a fierce competitor and would do anything within his power to beat you one way or another."

Centerfielder Paul Blair, who played next to Rightfielder Robinson in the Orioles' outfield, ranked him as "the most intense ballplayer I ever played with." Don Zimmer said, "He was about as tough a competitor as a ballplayer could be." Even the umpires admired his desire. Shag Crawford was driven to repetition to emphasize his point. He called Robinson "a tough competitor—a tough, tough competitor."

That sense of competition came at least in part from Robinson's start in life as the youngest of 11 children in Beaumont, Texas, where his parents separated when he was a baby. Robinson later credited the size of his family with helping him as a baseball player. He told his audience in Cooperstown when he was inducted into the Baseball Hall of Fame in 1982 that people used to ask him how he had developed such quick hands for fielding and hitting. His answer was, "When you sit down at the table to eat with ten kids, you'd better be quick."

Like many fathers, Frank's bought him a baseball glove, ball and bat when he was three. Three years later, his mother, Ruth, moved her brood to Oakland, California, to live with one of her older daughters. Frank later lost his glove and ball, as boys do, but he dragged that bat with him wherever he went.

At Tompkins Grammar School in West Oakland, he became known as "Pencils" because of his thin legs, inherited from his father. But he became known as something else—a superb natural athlete who told everyone he was going to be a big league baseball player when he grew up.

He continued to attract attention at McClymonds High School as a fullback who scored six touchdowns in his only season and as a basketball teammate of another future Hall of Famer, Bill Russell. In baseball, young Frank excelled. He was all-city as a third baseman and led his school to successive city championships. He played American League ball at the unheard-of age of 14 and paced his Legion team to the national championship at 15.

"Pencils" was still conscious of his skinny legs. He wore an extra pair of socks and pulled his baseball knickers as low as he could. Another characteristic distinguished him from his teammates—his shyness. He was unusually quiet, seldom saying a word, a trait that he still exhibited even during his first seasons in the big leagues.

As often happens in the stories of players who achieve greatness, Robinson was discovered when a scout was looking at somebody else. Bobby Mattick of the Cincinnati Reds was scouting a young catcher, J.W. Porter, but followed Robinson closely during his last two seasons in high school, attracted by Frank's quick bat.

Mattick eventually signed both high schoolers, Porter for a bonus of $65,000, Robinson for $3,000. Porter played in the big leagues for six years. Robinson played twenty-one years and made the Hall of Fame.

NICE TRY, BRANCH

The 17-year-old Robinson was sent to Ogden, Utah, in the Pioneer League to begin his career as a professional baseball player. In his first time at bat, he hit a 412-foot triple. The next day, he cleared the fence at the same spot for a home run. He never let up for the rest of that 1953 season. As a rookie "phee-nom," he hit 16 home runs in only 72 games and drove in 83 runs with a .348 average. His career as a third baseman ended in a hurry, after he committed two errors in his first two games. After that, he was an outfielder.

His dazzling debut season attracted the eye of Branch Rickey, who built the St. Louis Cardinals and then the Brooklyn Dodgers into pennant winners and was now assembling future championship teams for the Pittsburgh Pirates. Recognized as one of the keenest judges of talent in baseball, Rickey was discussing a deal which would send Second Baseman Danny O'Connell to the Reds for four players. He mentioned their names to the Reds. Then, trying to make it look like an afterthought, he suggested the Reds throw in a young outfielder. He said he couldn't remember the player's name, only that he was "some kid in Utah."

The Reds remembered the kid's name—and didn't fall for Rickey's smoke screen.

HARSH FACTS OF LIFE

The Reds promoted their budding superstar two grades, to Columbia, South Carolina, of the South Atlantic League, from Class C to the Class A "Sally League," where he continued his success by hitting .336 with 25 home runs and 110 RBIs.

That season may have been more influential on Robinson's maturity as a young man than as a baseball player. The league covered the Southeastern portion of the United States, and for the first time, Frank experienced the harsh facts of life that confronted a black person in the South in the early 1950s.

Robinson spent his formative years in a poor section of Oakland, among fellow African-Americans. On a team in the South, however, he heard insulting language and threats. He ate on the team bus while the white players dined in restaurants. He stayed in hotels almost uninhabitable while his teammates were quartered in far nicer accommodations.

Things reached his boiling point when young hecklers hollered continued racial epithets at him during a game. He headed for the stands, armed with a bat, but was intercepted. The experience, however, had a lasting effect on him and influenced his thinking and actions for years to come.

Fate threw Robinson a curve in 1955, when he came down with a sore arm while playing winter ball in Puerto Rico. There was concern both on Frank's part and management's when the arm refused to respond to treatment. But fate intervened again and the ailment miraculously disappeared just as suddenly and mysteriously as it had appeared.

Robinson became the sensation of the Reds' 1956 spring training camp. Birdie Tebbetts took one look at the kid and immediately proclaimed him his left fielder after the Reds had tried ten players at that position in the previous two seasons.

Robinson responded with one of the greatest rookie seasons in big league history. He hit 38 home runs to tie the 76-year-old National League record for most home runs by a rookie, led the league in scoring with 112 runs and in game-winning hits, was the starting left fielder in the All-Star game, hit .290 and drove in 83 runs. He was the *unanimous* choice as the league's Rookie of the Year.

Almost single-handedly, Robinson reversed the Reds' fortunes. They jumped from fifth place in 1955 to third, and their attendance spiked from 700,000 to 1,125,000.

Robinson avoided baseball's "sophomore jinx," when the league's pitchers catch up with a rookie by learning his weaknesses at the plate. He increased his average 32 points in 1957 to .322, third behind only Stan Musial and Willie Mays, even though his home run total dropped to 29. Another award followed—Sophomore of the Year—and attendance at Crosley Field topped a million again.

Despite the excitement he was causing and the success he was spawning for his team, Robinson remained an enigma. Birdie Tebbetts couldn't figure him out, and neither could anyone else. He was becoming disliked for his hard, aggressive style of play, but that was about all anyone knew about him.

One of his teammates, Outfielder Jerry Lynch, said in later years, "You can't say Robbie is the most hated player in the National League, because in order to hate somebody, you have to know him. Not many players on the other clubs know this guy . . . . If he's the most anything, he the most *unknown* player in the league."

While Tebbetts and Robinson's teammates were having trouble figuring out his strangely quiet conduct, opposing pitchers were having problems of a different sort. Robinson stood unusually close to the plate as a hitter—too close for the pitchers' comfort. In his rookie season, he was hit by the pitch 20 times, the most in the league.

The closer he stood, the more of a threat he became because he could reach the strike on the outside corner and still pull the inside pitch. Vinegar Bend Mizell, a flame-throwing lefthander with the Cardinals, said, "He got hit a lot. It wasn't like they were throwing at him. He just crowded the plate, and you couldn't afford to get that ball out there away from him. We pitchers called him 'Magnet Head.' He kind of drew that baseball to him, like a magnet."

Another flame thrower, Camilo Pascual of the Washington Senators, took exception to Robinson's habit of leaning over the plate, foiling the pitcher's attempts to throw strikes while avoiding the hitter's power. He hit Robinson with a pitch in an exhibition game in Portsmouth, Ohio, just before the start of the 1958 season. The ball struck Robinson in the left temple, just below his batting helmet. He was carried off the field on a stretcher and was hospitalized briefly.

Frank had headaches for a month. "That won't bother Frank," Tebbetts said. "He's been hit in the head before." Later Tebbetts told *Sport* magazine, "That's one of the things that makes Frank so great. He isn't afraid to take a toehold. He's no guess swinger. He hangs in there until the last second. He's got the guts to stay with a pitch. Nothing scares him."

Pitcher Tommy John once asked Robinson why he crowded the plate, and Robinson had a ready answer. He said, "I stand on home plate because if you can make three perfect pitches on the inside corner, you can get me. If you throw too tight, you hit me. If you miss over the plate or make a mistake, I hit you. So I stand over the plate, and there are three things that can happen—and two of them are bad for *you*."

When Robinson came back, he was gun-shy, backing away from the plate, and the National League's pitchers spotted it. By the All-Star break, Frank was struggling with a .247 average and only eight home runs and

23 RBIs. "I kept telling myself I wasn't afraid," he said, "and in a sense I really wasn't. But still I couldn't keep from flinching."

Then the Robinson competitiveness reasserted itself. He got mad, decided he didn't care if he got hit or not, and went on a tear, hitting 23 home runs and driving in 60 runs in the next 80 games. He also won a Gold Glove as the best fielding left fielder in the league.

With his new and daring presence near—and over—the plate, Robinson reached new heights in 1959 with his best all-around season yet—36 homers, 125 RBIs, 106 runs scored and a .311 average. In 1960, he refused to cool off, with 31 homers, 83 RBIs and a .297 average. That performance turned out to be a prelude for his—and his team's—memorable performance in 1961.

He wasn't winning friends or influencing people among the National League's pitchers by crowding the plate. Don Drysdale of the Dodgers didn't like Robinson's habits or Robinson himself. The Hall of Fame righthander once told teammate Duke Snider, "Alston (Walt Alston, their manager) told me to walk him intentionally, so I hit him with the first pitch. I figured why waste three more pitches?"

MARIS AND MANTLE

The year 1961 was an electrifying one in America, and baseball helped to make it so. John Kennedy was stirring the country with his activist New Frontier. The Russians were rattling their sabres in the Cold War again, this time by building a wall literally overnight to separate their East Berlin from the Allied sector, denying their citizens the freedom to cross into West Berlin.

Even before the baseball season started, Robinson made news in a brush with the law. He and two friends got into an argument at a sandwich shop after a pickup basketball game in February. Frank and the cook exchanged heated words, and when the cook waved a butcher knife, Frank produced a gun.

He was found guilty of carrying a concealed weapon, after explaining to a grand jury he carried the weapon because he often came home late, frequently carried large amounts of cash and lived in a dimly lit apartment complex. He was fined $250 but paid a far heavier price in negative national publicity.

Frank said in later years, however, that the incident was "the best thing that could have happened to me" because it taught him a valuable lesson in his responsibilities to his team, the Reds' management and, especially, his young fans.

In 1961, the New York Yankees hit home runs in the tradition of Ruth and Gehrig. Roger Maris broke Ruth's seemingly unbreakable record by hitting 61 homers, and Mickey Mantle added 54 of his own as the Yankees won the American League pennant by eight games over the Detroit Tigers.

In the National League, the personality transplant administered to the Reds by Robinson paid the ultimate prize—the pennant, by four games over the Los Angeles Dodgers thanks to a "career year" by the now-feared Robinson. Frank powered his team to its first pennant since 1940 with 37 home runs (third in the league) and 124 RBIs (second) and by leading the league in slugging average with .611. He was fourth in total bases, third in doubles, third in stolen bases and third in home run percentage. To the surprise of no one, he was voted the National League's Most Valuable Player.

The Yankee powerhouse, which included 25-game winner Whitey Ford, was too much for Cincinnati, with New York winning the World Series in five games. Robinson could manage only a .200 average, but he hit a home run and drove in four of the Reds' 11 runs. He was to have a better World Series five years later.

As good as he was in 1961, he was even better in '62, with career highs of 51 doubles and 134 runs scored. He had the league's second best batting average, .342, only four points behind Tommy Davis of the Dodgers. He led the league in slugging average for the third straight year and hit 39 home runs, third highest in the league.

The Reds were better, too, winning five more games than they did in '61—98—but they finished third behind San Francisco and Los Angeles.

While Frank was giving pitchers sleepless nights, he was having the same effect on infielders. He was earning a reputation as a fierce base runner, reminding some of Ty Cobb. Even today players remember his hell-for-leather aggressiveness.

Tommy John says, "When he got on first base, he was probably the hardest slider I ever saw going into second." Second Baseman Bill Mazeroski has the same memories. "He always teed me off because he came in sliding hard at second," Maz says today. "He was one of the hardest sliders and always came after you with more determination than other base runners. He'd knock you into left field if he could . . . . I had respect for him because he played so hard."

Base-stealing champion Maury Wills, a shortstop who had to deal with Robinson too, called him "the most terrifying base runner I ever played against . . . . If you didn't like him, you'd say he slides dirty with his spikes up, trying to hurt you, but if you liked him, you'd say he is a hard-nosed, rough-and-tumble ballplayer."

Robinson never denied his aggressiveness and instead was proud of it, admitting to *Sport* that he sometimes intentionally roughed up infielders in a doubleplay situation, even if he saw he wouldn't be able to break up the play.

"Oh, yes," he said. "It serves a purpose. If you can't break up a doubleplay, knock the man down anyhow. Make him think a little the next time you come around. I've seen ballplayers slide into a base and never touch the infielder, even when it's a close play. Not me! I'm going to nudge him, bump him, something—even if I'm out by 15 feet. I've always said I'll do it. They know it. I make myself do it, because I feel like it's good baseball, like that's my job."

For the first time in his eight years in the big leagues, Robinson ran into a slump in 1963. His averaged dropped 83 points to .259 and his home run total dipped to 21. The disappointing year ended the way it went all year—he was spiked sliding into second base, needed 20 stitches and missed part of September. The doctors feared his season was over, but in true Robinson fashion, he was back in the lineup in ten days.

Then a funny thing happened. Robinson continued to terrorize pitchers, with 29 and 33 home runs in 1964 and '65 and averages of .306 and .296, but the Reds' president, Bill DeWitt, Jr., openly shopped him around at the winter meetings in Florida. On December 9, he traded his star to the Orioles for pitcher Milt Pappas and two other players, with the explanation from DeWitt that Robinson was "an old thirty. He is certain to slow down dramatically one of these days because, as a young man, he led a fast life as a bachelor." DeWitt was saying this about a man who routinely got ten or more hours of sleep a night to make sure he was rested for the next day's game.

The move puzzled many observers, but convinced almost everyone of one thing: DeWitt had just won the 1966 American League pennant for the Orioles. "I didn't mind the trade," Robinson said. "I honestly didn't, but I was shocked and I was hurt at first, because that was the first time I felt like I had failed. And I really took a while to recover from that."

Far from failing, in his ten years with the Reds, Robinson averaged .302 with 32 home runs and 100 runs batted in per year. Before he arrived, the Reds had finished in the second division, among the bottom four or five teams in the eight and ten-team leagues of those years, 11 straight times. Led by "Robbie," they finished in the first division seven times, winning a pennant and appearing in their first World Series in 21 years. With Robinson as their chief drawing card, the Reds averaged 900,000 a year compared to just over 600,000 before his arrival.

In his first year away from Cincinnati, the Reds dropped 300,000 in attendance and sank to seventh place.

CIGARS AND "A PSYCHOLOGICALLY IMPORTANT HOME RUN"

When the trade sending Frank to the Orioles was completed, Pitcher Jack Fisher of the Mets made a bet with Pappas. "I bet Milt five cigars that Robinson hits 25 homers," he said during the season, "five (more) if he hits 30, five on 35. I'm going to be cigar-rich." By the end of the season, Pappas owed Fisher 25 cigars.

Robinson said that when the trade was made, "I felt like really I had something to prove. Not on the baseball field—and not to myself, and not to the fans of Cincinnati, and not to the fans of baseball. But to Bill DeWitt."

Boog Powell still remembers Robinson's first game as an Oriole, in the 1966 spring training season. "He hit the first pitch over the palm trees," Boog says today, "and I was standing in the dugout with Andy Etchebarren (Baltimore's catcher), and I said, 'Andy, it's all over. We have just won the American League championship.'"

It didn't take the other Hall of Famer named Robinson—Brooks—long to make up his mind about Frank either. He told *Sport* magazine, "We waited for him that spring. Well, we'd heard about him, but you know how it is. You say, 'Well, here comes the guy with the reputation. Well, show me.' He showed us all right. He's got to be the best hitter I ever played with."

He showed everyone else, too, leading the American League in six categories and winning the coveted Triple Crown by outslugging everyone else in home runs with 49, runs batted in with 122 and a .316 batting average. Frank was also tops in three other categories—slugging average, home run percentage and runs scored. Only Ty Cobb, Jimmie Foxx, Lou Gehrig, Ted Williams and Mantle had won the Triple Crown in the American League. And only Carl Yastrzemski has done it in the 33 years since.

To top off his individual recognition, Robinson was voted the league's Most Valuable Player and remains today, 33 years later, the only man ever to win the MVP award in both leagues.

He started his American League years in typical Frank Robinson style. No, not with a home run—by getting hit by the pitch in his first at-bat. Brooks followed with a home run, and Frank added one later in the game, an ironic beginning to a season in which the World Series began almost the same way.

The Orioles started with a bang, winning 12 of their first 13 games. By the end of May, Frank had ten home runs and was hitting .348.

One of those home runs was the only one ever hit out of Baltimore's Memorial Stadium, a 540-foot blast that cleared the fence and came back to earth in a parking lot. It happened on May 8, and Boog Powell, who hit 339 home runs himself including some gigantic shots of his own, remembers that one, too: "It was off Luis Tiant, and I was on deck, and it was probably the most impressive home run I've ever seen."

Robinson himself remembers that homer. "I knew it was gone," he told Arthur Daley of the *New York Times* five years later, "but I lost sight of the ball as I ran the bases. When I reached the dugout, they told me I had just hit the first ball ever knocked out of the ballpark. 'You gotta be kidding,' I said."

Robinson saw another significance to the mighty blast. "The thrilling thing to me, though," he said, "was that I got a standing ovation. It meant a lot to me. I was with a new team in a new league. They seemed to say to me, 'You are one of us now. You have it made.' It therefore was a psychologically important home run."

By mid-June, the Orioles were 12 games ahead of the Yankees, and the 1966 American League pennant race, three years before the start of the playoff system, was all over. Baltimore was not only winning the pennant, but the O's were doing it over a Yankee team that only two years before had completed a string of five pennants in a row from 1960 through 1964. In 1966, the Yankees, with Maris and Mantle still in the middle part of their batting order, finished last for the first time since 1912—in tenth place.

REMAKING AN ENTIRE LEAGUE

Frank Robinson didn't just make the grade in a league new to him in 1966. He re-made the league.

That's the opinion of lefthanded pitcher Al Downing, a 10-game winner for the Yankees that season. "Frank revolutionized the American League when he came to Baltimore," Downing claims. "You look at the Baltimore Orioles before Frank came there, and the Baltimore Orioles after Frank had been there—two totally different organizations.

"Before Frank, they were a ball club that resigned itself to the fact the Yankees were tops and they were sliding along. After Frank got there, it was 'Hey, we're the team to beat.' That was the attitude, and that's what Frank brought to them. He had a persona of a warrior, of a champion."

As evidence, Downing mentioned a spring training game when Robinson slid into Bobby Richardson at second base and "cut his foot off, almost. And you say, 'Hey, this is just spring training.' That's the impact he had on his ball club."

Beyond that, Robinson had an impact on the entire league, according to Downing. "Frank was a force to himself," Downing says today. "Seems to me the American League was a kind of quiet league until Frank got there. Not too many knockdowns or breaking up double plays."

Downing says Robinson "brought a different temperament to the American League .... Until then, the Baltimore ball club had a lot of talent but was sort of laid back, and you could all of a sudden see the guys stick their chests out. You could see that Frank Robinson brought a whole different attitude toward playing the game."

When he barreled into Richardson in spring training, the Yankees literally sat up and took notice. "In the dugout," Downing says, "we kind of sat up and said, 'Where did this guy come from?' It just brought a different temperament to the American League after the story got around. Until then, everyone sort of conceded the pennant to the Yankees and played for second place. His attitude was, 'We're going to be the team to beat.' He couldn't understand how a ball club with so much talent could accept being second. All that changed very quickly."

Paul Blair has the same kind of memories. He said, "No question—he was the leader of our ballclub .... He was so determined to win. He just showed you what was required and demanded of you to win and stay at the top as long as we did. And to him that meant that every time you walked on the field, you gave 100 percent. He wouldn't accept anything else. He led both by example and the way he talked to you."

GOOSE EGGS AND A CORVETTE

That example led the Orioles into the 1966 World Series against the heavily favored Los Angeles Dodgers of Don Drysdale and Sandy Koufax. Frank and Brooks started the Series almost the same way they started the season, with back-to-back home runs off Drysdale in the first inning of the first game to spark the Orioles to a 5-2 win. For Frank, the home run was extra sweet because it came off Drysdale, his old National League tormentor.

When starter Dave McNally got into trouble, Manager Hank Bauer lifted him with one out in the third inning, and that turned out to be virtually the end of the World Series. At the start of what many baseball students rate as the greatest team pitching performance in Series history, Moe Drabowsky slammed the door shut on the Dodgers, striking out eleven, six in a row, and shutting them out the rest of the way.

Shutting them out is exactly what the rest of the Baltimore pitchers did, too—Jim Palmer in the second game nine days before he turned 21 years old, Wally Bunker in the third and McNally in the fourth. The Dodgers never scored a run after Drabowsky took the mound in the third inning of that first game. For the Series, they scored only those two runs in 36 innings and collected only 17 hits, barely four a game.

To add to the storybook finish, Frank won the final game with another home run, also off Drysdale, in the fourth inning for the only run of the game as Drysdale and McNally dueled each other with a pair of four-hitters. Each pitcher went the distance.

Dick Williams, a big league manager for 21 seasons, understood the significance of those two home runs by Robinson against Drysdale. "He and Don Drysdale couldn't stand each other," Williams says. "Don would knock Frank down, and Frank would get up and hit one nine miles off him."

Robinson experienced another satisfaction after the World Series. *Sport* magazine awarded him a new Corvette convertible as the outstanding player in the Series.

A SLUMP, A COMEBACK AND EARL WEAVER

The Orioles slumped into a tie for sixth place in 1967, tied with the expansion Washington Senators, when their pitching fell apart. Robinson, however, continued his success in his second year in the league, this time with a .311 average, 30 homers and 94 RBIs.

Things weren't much better for the team midway through the '68 season, but then Earl Weaver came on the scene, with no experience in the Major Leagues either as a player or a manager. The Orioles named him to succeed Bauer, and signs of improvement set in. Baltimore played 14 games over .500 in the last half and finished second. Robbie slumped with the rest of the team, hitting only .268 with 15 homers and only 52 RBIs, his lowest numbers in his 13 years so far in the big leagues.

But then the Orioles set out on a stretch of success that lasted over the next three years, winning the pennant each year with 109, 108 and 101 victories respectively in 1969-71. They joined the fabled Philadelphia A's of 1929-31 under Connie Mack as the only team to win 100 games three years in a row.

In 1969, the first year of the League Championship Series, the Orioles swept the Minnesota Twins for the American League pennant but ran into a team of destiny in the World Series, the "Amazin' Mets," who defeated the O's in five games.

A strong team effort led them to the 1970 World Series. Powell was the league's MVP with 35 homers and Frank hit .306 with 25 home runs and 78 RBIs to get the Orioles to the playoffs. Three members of the pitching staff became 20-game winners—Mike Cuellar, Dave McNally and Jim Palmer. Again they swept the Twins in three games in the League Championship Series.

Robinson—Brooks, not Frank—led Baltimore to baseball's world championship in what is still called "the Brooks Robinson World Series." They faced Frank's old team, the Reds, in the early years of their "Big Red Machine" of Johnny Bench, Pete Rose, Tony Perez and Lee May.

But the Orioles defeated them, with Brooks hitting .429. The O's made quick work of the Reds. The Series lasted only five games. Brooks had nine hits, with two doubles, two home runs, five runs scored and six driven in while also making several brilliant plays at third base on hot smashes, especially from Bench and May.

Frank did his part with six hits including two homers, five runs scored and four RBIs.

With their talent and Frank's driving leadership, the Orioles won the 1971 American League East title by twelve games over Detroit. Robinson hit .287 with 28 homers and 99 RBIs, followed by Powell's 22 homers and 92 runs batted in and Brooks's 20 round trippers and 92 RBIs.

The pitching staff topped itself with four 20-game winners instead of the three of the year before—McNally, Cuellar, Palmer and Pat Dobson —the first time one staff had four 20-game winners since the 1920 Chicago White Sox.

The mighty Orioles again swept the league championship series, knocking off the Oakland A's. After three years of the new playoff system, only one team—Baltimore—had won the league series, and the Orioles still hadn't lost an ALCS game, with three-game sweeps against the Twins in 1969 and '70 and the A's in '71.

The O's won the first two games of the World Series against Pittsburgh before the Pirates rallied to win four of the last five and the Series.

Frank achieved a personal high point that season. In a doubleheader against Detroit in September, he hit the 500th home run of his Hall of Fame career, only a few hours after the thought of it entered his mind.

"I hit 499 off Mike Kilkenny in the first inning of the opener," he said. "Between games I suddenly began thinking of 500 for the first time, and I kept wanting it more and more .... When the ninth inning (of the second game) arrived, I didn't expect to get to bat. I was the fifth hitter, and two men went out. But Curt Motton doubled off Fred Scherman, and Boog Powell singled through the shortstop hole of an overshifted infield. Much to my surprise, I was at bat again. Then I connected with a Scherman pitch.

"I knew immediately that it would be a hit, maybe a single or maybe a double. But I didn't think the ball would do what it actually did do, ride all the way into the stands for a home run. It was not one of my best, but I file no complaint. It was 500."

As luck would have it, the feat—coming in the ninth inning of the second game—was too late to make the morning papers.

OTHER SHOCKS

Only three months later, after leading the Orioles to four pennants in his six seasons with them, Robinson was traded back to the National League, to the Dodgers. In what might have been a bittersweet experience for Robinson, the Orioles retired his number 20, the first time a team retired a player's number while he was still active.

With the Dodgers, Frank never got untracked, starting with a jammed wrist early in the 1972 season. In and out of the lineup, he hit only .251, the lowest average of his career, with 19 homers and only 59 RBIs.

A change to the crosstown rivals, the Angels, brought a change in Robinson's fortunes. He raised his average 15 points, hit 30 home runs and drove in 97 runs. In '74, he hit 22 homers before being surprised again, this time when he was traded to the Cleveland Indians, where destiny was waiting for him.

He was named the first African-American manager in Major League history, as a player-manager replacing Ken Aspromonte after the Indians finished in fourth place in 1974. In his first time at bat in that historic role, he showed his sense of the dramatic again in the best way he knew how, with a home run against the Yankees as 56,204 fans cheered.

He guided the Indians to two more fourth place finishes before meeting every manager's ultimate fate by being fired himself in 1977. His performance as manager draws high marks from veteran baseball executive Roland Hemond, who was the Orioles' general manager several years later when Robinson was their field manager. "I thought he was a hell of a manager," Hemond says. "I really enjoyed working with him in the front office. He's a real good judge of talent. He knows what it takes to put a team together."

Dick Williams, who managed in the American League at the same time as Robinson, agrees. "I'm glad he got a chance to be the first black manager,"Williams says. "He did a hell of a job. He's a great baseball man."

One of Robinson's pitchers on the Indians, Gaylord Perry, said, "I played for him in Cleveland when he was the first black manager, and I disagreed with him on only one thing: He didn't put himself in the lineup enough, because he was still a great hitter."

Others make that same point, adding that if Robinson had inserted himself into the Cleveland batting order more times, he would have hit over 600 home runs instead of 586. That would have made him one of only four players to top 600, joining Aaron, Ruth and Mays. He also might have reached the 3,000-hit level, which would place him with only Aaron, Mays and Eddie Murray in the exclusive category of 3,000 hits and 500 home runs.

Frank served as a coach for the Angels in 1977, managed the Orioles' farm team at Rochester in '78 and returned to Baltimore as a coach in 1979 and '80. He made another managerial stop with the Giants for four years, was out of uniform from 1985 through '87, then returned to the Orioles again, this time as their manager for three and a half seasons. In his eleven years as a manager, Robinson's teams finished in the first division five times, with the Orioles reaching second place in 1989.

In 1982, Robinson received the ultimate tribute. The members of the Baseball Writers Association of America elected him to the Hall of Fame with another member of the 500-homer club, the leader himself — Hank Aaron.

The writers, like the players, were not underrating Frank Robinson.

FRANK ON FRANK, AND OTHERS ON FRANK

Frank Robinson never lacked for candor, even while describing his own personality. Despite his quiet, sullen manner in his first years in the big leagues, he later opened up, a man who enjoyed his teammates and was popular with them.

He was a jokester in the clubhouse, later presiding as the judge of the Baltimore Orioles' "Kangaroo Kourt" when players were fined petty amounts for silly violations, with the money donated to charity at the end of the season. Judge Robinson would preside in the clubhouse after each win, with a mop on his head as his judicial hairpiece. After a loss, "kourt" was not in session.

He was always willing to spend time with his teammates, especially rookies, on their personal or professional problems, especially hitting. His attitude toward opposing players wasn't so friendly. They were the enemy.

He refused to fraternize before games the way stars like Musial, Banks, Mays and Mantle did. He didn't make small talk with opposing infielders while he was on base. He kept to himself on the field and off and was one of the movie industry's favorite customers. He was known to see four different movies in one day.

He led his team's charge from the dugout at the start of each game with "Let's go!" He shouted encouragement from the dugout, got on his teammates for mistakes or loafing, and showed them his respect.

He was viewed by many as a chronic trouble maker, but he said, "You can't go into second base to break up a double play like you're having dinner together after the game. If so, you're letting your teammates down. I don't care. This isn't a popularity contest. Some players are afraid of losing their friends. Not me. I'm not out there to win friends. Just ball games. I'll do that any way I can."

Don Zimmer mistook that fierce determination to win as a mean streak to hurt people. He said, "Some players play to win, others play to hurt someone." Later, when they became teammates, Zimmer corrected the record. "I was wrong," he said. "He's just a hell of a competitor."

Robinson once crashed into the Braves' Eddie Mathews at third base with spikes high (see Mathews chapter), igniting a brawl in which Mathews clobbered him, leaving Robinson with bandages and bruises on his face. It was a doubleheader. Frank came back in the second game looking like a fugitive from "ER," his right eye swollen almost shut and still bleeding, and won the game with a home run and a double and robbed Mathews of a two-base hit with a diving catch.

Mathews said, "I have great respect for him. He had it coming, and took it like a man."

Robinson surprised his teammates by saying he won the confrontation. "I got even the best way," he said, "by winning the second game."

WHAT OTHER PLAYERS SAID ABOUT
FRANK ROBINSON

Bill Virdon—I thought he was the best RBI man in an RBI situation who ever existed. With men on base in scoring position, he invariably hit the ball hard somewhere.

Brooks Robinson—When he went out on the field, he was all business. You could see that from the way he stood up on top of the plate. He just dared the pitchers to try to get inside, and consequently he was hit many times. With him, it was just a fact of life. He was going to stand up there, and if you made a mistake, he was going to hit it out. It helped him that most mistakes by pitchers are made inside rather than outside. He came to Baltimore from Cincinnati with some wraps on him. He had something to prove, and he did it. He fit in perfectly. The two of us got along great. He was a force and led by example.

George Kell—I never thought of Frank Robinson as a 500-home run hitter, but I always thought he just might be the best all-around player I ever saw. He just did everything. A great competitor.

Bobby Thomson—I never liked him. I never liked guys who beat us.

Herb Score—At one time I think he might have been the best player in baseball.

Dick Groat—A teammate of mine, Jerry Lynch, played with Frank at Cincinnati and said Frank Robinson at times would just pick up that Cincinnati ballclub on his shoulders and just carry them. He was a great, great player—a complete player.

Milt Pappas— I got traded for him. After the trade, a photographer came up to me and asked if he could take a picture of me with Frank. I said yes, but Frank refused. I bided my time . . . about six years later, I finally faced him and the first time up I knocked him down and struck him out. The second time, I knocked him down and struck him out. The third time I knocked him on his ___ again and struck him out. He started yelling at me, that I was going to kill him. The fourth time up, I knocked him down again, and he popped it up. I won the game, 5-0, and got even with him. But he was a hell of a player, a real battler.

Lew Burdette—Robinson was the greatest streak hitter I ever saw. When he was going good, you couldn't get him out . . . . I remember when he slid into third base and cut Eddie Mathews. Eddie hit him five times before he hit the ground. But Frank came back the second game (of a doubleheader) with his eyes and eyebrows taped and beat us in the ball game. He earned my respect that day.

Catfish Hunter—He was the only home run hitter I could get out. I always threw him my fast ball . . . . I never even showed him my breaking ball—until one day I was pitching and, you know, a pitcher always starts a-thinking. Ninth inning. I'm thinking, "I've always been throwing him my fast ball, and he'll be on it. I'd better throw him a slider. So I threw him a slider, low and away, exactly where I wanted it—a double off the wall.

My manager, Dick Williams, walked out to the mound and said, "Man, that was a good fast ball, wasn't it?"

I didn't say a word.

He said, "That was a fast ball, right?"

I said, "No, it was a slider."

He said, "What! You mean to tell me you threw him a slider and you've been getting him out on fast balls all your life?"

He threw his hat straight up in the air, and when it came down he said, "Go take a shower."

He told me later, "When a pitcher starts thinking, that's when he gets into trouble."

That's what I remember about Frank Robinson.

Hank Bauer—When he came to Baltimore, he was the missing link in the spoke. I was the manager, and he challenged me one time, and that was it. We got over that hurdle in a hurry. He was some player for us!

Bobby Bragan—He was almost defiant at the plate. He just couldn't be intimidated with the inside pitch.

Joe Rudi—I remember him as a very stern-looking guy. All business. He kind of intimidated young players. In my first year, he scared me to death.

Bob Gibson—He was not afraid of getting hurt, and I don't care how many times you hit him, you could not get him away from that plate. He stood right up on top of it. I'm just sorry I never got him good enough to discourage him.

Orlando Cepeda—That guy, he belongs in the category of Mays, Aaron, Clemente, Banks. That guy was a gamer. He played every game, he played hard, he broke up double plays. That guy was awesome.

Duke Snider—When he came up, you could just sense that he was going to be a very good competitor because of the way he approached the game. He was very serious, and you could tell when he came out on the field he was there to beat you. His attitude was exceptionally good in that respect. He was a fierce competitor and would do anything within his power to beat you one way or another.

Sal Bando—I was a rookie in Kansas City, and he made that ballpark look like Fenway Park. From the day I first saw him, I thought he was one of the most intelligent players, to go along with his fabulous ability. There was very little he couldn't do—and there were very few Frank Robinsons ever to play the game.

Tommy John—I considered him the hardest guy I ever faced. Not only was he a good home run hitter, he was a good hitter. I hated to face him.

Jim Lonborg—Once in Baltimore …I ended up knocking him down so bad there was dust and bats and helmets flying everywhere ….Well, he dusted himself off, put his cap back on, picked up his bat, got back in the batter's box and the next pitch, I made a perfect pitch on the outside corner and he drilled it to dead center field over the fence. That was the last time I ever knocked Frank Robinson down.

Don Newcombe—He's in that group of the greatest players. He could do everything. The thing I respected about him was he could move from one position to another. He could play center field, right field, first base, third base. He could really adapt if the team needed him to do that. He probably could have caught if he was asked to, but because of his greatness, they'd never put him behind the plate.

John Briggs—We were in Cincinnati, and we brought Grant Jackson in with the bases loaded and no outs. He was a lefthander who could really throw hard. He was really bringing it and struck out the first two guys and threw two quick ones by Frank. The next one he hit over the left center field wall and it's still going. I'm telling you—that was one of the hardest balls I've ever seen hit …and Grant was throwing it by everybody. When he threw two past Frank, everybody thought he was going to strike out the side. And BAM!

Dick Radatz—We used to call him "The Rattler" because his hands were so quick, like a snake. I'd put him in the category as one of the five best hitters of all time.

Umpire Doug Harvey—Maybe the reason he never seemed to get the credit he deserved was he was not liked. Frank Robinson was the most unfair ballplayer I ever umpired for. Once I called him out on three plays at first base that were close but not really what I would call real close. Normal calls. I had to argue with him all three times, but luckily I didn't have to eject him.

He came up to the plate the next day in Cincinnati. It was a day game and it was hot. And those were the days we had to wear our coats. The league insisted on it. And we were in all black in that heat. And he comes up and stands outside the batter's box. And he's mumbling and I could just make out what he's saying: "Damn umpires. Don't know their butt from a hole in the ground."

I said, "Frank, I don't know what your problem is, but let's get going —it's hot out here." He said he didn't give a damn if it was hot or not and backed away. I told him I was not going to stand out there and melt and told him, "Let's go." He said he would get in the box when he wanted to. I told the pitcher to pitch the ball. Boom!—strike one. Next pitch, boom! —strike two. He went berserk.

Shag Crawford came in from first base, listened to Frank's beef and told him if he didn't get in the box by the time Shag got back to first base, he'd run him (eject him) himself. Frank said, "I always thought you were a fair shooter, but you're a _____ too." And Shag runs him. This is typical of Frank.

Another time, in the Astrodome, the game's over and they lose and he stands in the dugout waiting for us and says, "And you, Harv — you are the biggest _____ of anybody." I told him the report was going in, and I suspected he would be fined. He never forgives anybody for anything. He keeps it all in.

Roland Hemond—He had no fear at the plate, no fear on the field, in any aspect of the game. He accomplished everything a player could, one of the greatest clutch hitters of the game. A lot of people don't know him. He used to be a little distant, but that's the barrier he put up for all the celebrity status he has. He's really a fine and talented guy.

Joe Garagiola—His MVPs in both leagues say volumes. If there was one word that would describe Frank in the batter's box, it would be "fearless." He would crowd the plate, knew he was going to get hit when the pitchers tried to move him back, and he knew it was the price he had to pay. He'd just run down to first and it was business as usual. When you talk about tough — he was tough to pitch to and tough everything else.

Jim Palmer—he year he came to us, he showed up at spring training just a little late because he was getting a house in Baltimore. We were having an intrasquad game and a pitcher named Steve Cosgrove threw him a fabulous curve ball down and away in his first at-bat, and he hits it with one hand and hits it off the wall. I turned to the guy next to me and said, "We just won the pennant."

Harmon Killebrew—When you talk about home run hitters, his name doesn't come up as much. He was a rare power hitter who hit for average, which is unusual, and he did it in both leagues....And I can't think of anyone who was a greater competitor. Easily one of the greatest players I ever saw.

Bill Virdon—I really thought Frank was the best RBI man in an RBI situation who existed. Playing center field against him, I thought that with men on base in scoring position, he invariably hit the ball hard somewhere. He didn't always get a hit, and sometimes he'd hit it at somebody, but he always put the ball in play with authority.

Umpire Don Denkinger—When I umped behind the plate, I was totally amazed at his ability to hold up on a pitch and check his swing. You'd see the bat go and you say, "Well, gee, he had to swing at it," but if you blinked your eye for just a second he'd hold it back. Not many could do that.

Hank Aaron —He was really underrated. He had a way of carrying a winning attitude on the field at all times and with every club he played on. He did anything I could do, that Willie (Mays) could do and he did everything that anybody else could do. That man could do a lot of things for a ball club, and I mean a lot of really good things.

Pete Rose—I played with him for three years. He was the workaholic type, very knowledgeable, very smart, a great leader. You couldn't intimidate him. If you tried, it would backfire.

THE ROBINSON FILE

Full Name: Frank Robinson.
Date and Place of Birth: August 31, 1935. Beaumont, Texas.
Nickname: "Robbie" and "The Judge"
Position: Right field, left field, first base, third base designated hitter.
Major League Career: 21 years, 1956-1976.
Home Runs: 586 (4th).
Runs Batted In: 1,812 (10th).
Runs Scored: 1,829 (10th).
Lifetime Batting Average: .294.
Number of Hits: 2,943.
Walks: 1,420.
Strikeouts: 1,532.
Highlights:
— Only man to win Most Valuable Player Award in each league.
— First African-American manager in the Major Leagues.
— Fourth leading home run hitter in history.
— Triple Crown winner in 1966.
— Led league in slugging average four times.
— Led league in runs scored three times.
— Hit over .300 nine times, from .306 to .342.

Elected to the Baseball Hall of Fame: 1982 (with Hank Aaron).

13

BABE RUTH

The Greatest of Them All?

In his 1948 autobiography, written with New York columnist Bob Considine, Babe Ruth said, "If my home run hitting in 1920 established a new era in baseball, and helped the fans of the nation to forget the past and the terrible fact that they had been sold out, that's all the epitaph I want."

Indeed, it became his epitaph, figuratively, only a few months later.

Ruth's home runs, in fact, did save the sport immediately after the infamous Chicago "Black Sox" scandal of 1919, when eight White Sox players were accused of conspiring to "throw" the World Series when they lost to the Cincinnati Reds.

What Ruth did before and after hitting an unimaginable 54 home runs in 1920 did more than save baseball, no small feat in itself. His deeds from his arrival as a lefthanded pitcher in 1914 until his retirement 22 years, 94 victories and 714 home runs later, plus the overpowering force of his personality, stamped him as the most dominating figure in the history of American sports.

He established himself as the best lefthanded pitcher in the American League for the Boston Red Sox beginning in 1914, then became baseball's brightest star of all time with his home runs for the New York Yankees starting in 1920.

His daughter, Julia Ruth Stevens, now in her eighties and dividing her time between New Hampshire's summers and Arizona's winters, remembers her father's great pride in his pitching success. "With all those home runs and his great deeds as a hitter and an outfielder," she told Bill Gilbert in a lengthy interview in 1997, "Daddy was proudest of his pitching. He never failed to talk about his pitching records." Then she added with a chuckle, "If somebody else didn't mention them, he would."

John Drebinger, the baseball writer for the *New York Times,* expressed the same sentiments in a 1973 story on his memories of The Babe. "Great hitter that he was," Drebinger wrote, "he rarely discussed his astounding home run feats. He sort of felt that was something he was expected to do and what's there to say about it? But pitching or great defensive play, ah—that's something he would talk over by the hour."

THE GREATEST ATHLETE OF ALL TIME?

Marty Appel, a respected author and former public relations director of the Yankees, was asked by Gilbert a few years ago whether Ruth might even have been the greatest athlete of all time.

"I think he was the greatest baseball player who ever lived," Appel reasoned, "and if baseball players are more gifted because of the skills required in their game, then clearly he was the best athlete America ever produced. Certainly by the force of his personality, he was the most important athlete ever produced in America."

Michael Jordan? Certainly one of America's most superb athletes, but he showed he couldn't hit a minor league curve ball. Jim Thorpe? Talented and versatile, but a .254 hitter with seven home runs in six Major League seasons. Muhammad Ali? Fast and strong, but could he have hit 714 home runs with a .342 batting average over 22 years and been the best lefthanded pitcher in the American League, too?

Ruth's enormous popularity was worldwide and, outside the U.S., was strongest in Japan beginning with barnstorming trips there in the 1930s. His popularity among the Japanese endured even during World War II. In an interview for a video cassette, "Babe Ruth Remembered", a Japanese baseball writer and historian, Kazuo Sayama, told Gilbert, "He's been a big hero for us. And even in the war time, we felt very friendly feelings toward him. The impression of him was so strong upon us. He was always a hero..."

Any claims about Ruth's greatness on a baseball diamond are strongly documented by the record books. "The Babe" did all these things and more:

— Set a record for the most home runs in one season, 60, which lasted until one of his successors in right field for the Yankees, Roger Maris, broke it 34 years later.
— Set the record for the most home runs in a career, 714, which lasted until Hank Aaron broke it 39 years later.
— Hit over .370 six times, including .393 in 1923, and won the American League batting championship in 1924 with .378.

— Achieved the highest slugging average, percentage of home runs per times at bat and number of walks in history.
— Hit the second most home runs, behind only Hank Aaron.
— Stole 123 bases.
— Accomplished the tenth highest batting average in history, .342, according to the *Baseball Encyclopedia*, only two points behind Ted Williams and topping such other Hall of Fame hitters as Bill Terry, George Sisler, Lou Gehrig, Nap Lajoie, Stan Musial and Joe DiMaggio.
— Won 94 games in only five full seasons as a pitcher, including two 20-win seasons.
— Set pitching records for the most consecutive shutout innings in World Series competition which lasted 43 years. Against the man considered by many the greatest pitcher of all time, Walter Johnson, Ruth won six 1-0 games.
— Holds the highest won-lost percentage for World Series games, a perfect 1.000, with three victories and no defeats.

ST. MARY'S, AND BROTHERS MATTHIAS AND GILBERT

None of this seemed to be in his future while Ruth was surviving the first seven years of his life as a street urchin named George in Baltimore while the nineteenth century unfolded into the twentieth. The oldest of eight children, he was born on the ground where today's Orioles play. He and his sister, Mamie, were the only ones who survived infancy in the family of George and Katie Ruth.

The elder Ruth installed lightning rods for a living before buying a saloon, which became young George's hangout and the source of some of his early problems. In the saloon, he sipped the same booze that the workers from the docks nearby slugged down, acquired their vocabulary and chewed tobacco.

"I chewed tobacco when I was seven," Ruth said years later. "Not that I enjoyed it especially, but from my observations around the saloon, it seemed the normal thing to do."

By the time he was seven, his parents were claiming he was "incorrigible" and had him admitted to St. Mary's Industrial School for Boys, a Catholic institution operated by the Xaverian Brothers. In the terms of the day, Ruth described St. Mary's as "a reform school," but whatever it was, young George met two men there who changed his life.

He stayed for 12 years, except for occasional breaks when his parents brought him back home, but never permanently. Some accounts of his boyhood say Ruth's parents never visited him at St. Mary's. His mother died when he was 15 and still living at the school.

At St. Mary's, where every student was taught a trade, Ruth was trained to be a tailor. He also learned something else—baseball—from two teachers, Brother Matthias and Brother Gilbert.

Brother Matthias, described by Ruth as "the greatest man I ever met" and "the father I needed," commanded immediate respect on the basis of his appearance—six feet, five inches tall and 250 pounds. To make the picture complete, Brother Matthias was the school's disciplinarian.

"He seldom raised his voice," Ruth said, "a sharp contrast to what I had known at home and in my neighborhood. But when he spoke, he meant business."

Brother Gilbert introduced Ruth to baseball, and George—still not known as "Babe"—became the team's lefthanded catcher. When he criticized his pitcher during a game, Brother Gilbert dared him to try to do better. With that challenge, George soon became a star pitcher.

On the times when Ruth went back home for family visits, with approval or not, he was frequently greeted by Brother Matthias at the gate of St. Mary's on his return. "I shouldn't be glad to see you, George," Brother Matthias would say, "but to tell you the truth, the team needs you."

Ruth developed into a genuine star, prompting Brother Gilbert to write to Jack Dunn, owner of the Orioles, then a minor league team in the International League. On February 14, 1914, eight days after the former street urchin's nineteenth birthday, Dunn signed him to a contract sight unseen for $600 a month. He left shortly for the Orioles' spring training camp in Fayetteville, North Carolina—his first time outside Baltimore and his first ride on a train. As the one-time "incorrigible" walked through the gates of St. Mary's into the uncertain life ahead of him, Brother Matthias told him in reassuring tones, "You'll make it, George."

Over the years of stardom that began in his immediate future, Ruth never forgot St. Mary's or the brothers, especially Matthias. When his wild ways got him into hot water, the team would put in a trouble call to Matthias. In appreciation, Ruth often left tickets for Brother Matthias at the gate and even bought him two Cadillacs.

"I believe it is customary for a man whose education was acquired as mine was to look back on those days either with scorn or a wish to conceal the facts," Ruth said in later years. "I look back on St. Mary's as one of the most constructive periods of my life. I'm as proud of it as any Harvard man is of his school ... "

"BABE"

Ruth turned heads immediately with his performance in spring training. Dunn wrote to Brother Gilbert, "That fellow Ruth is the greatest young ballplayer who ever reported to a training camp. If he doesn't let success go to his head, he'll become the greatest ballplayer of all time."

With success came Ruth's new, and permanent, nickname. According to Brother Gilbert's memoirs, a scout named Steinman learned that Ruth had suffered a spill while riding on a borrowed bike in front of the team's hotel. Steinman was moved to say, "If Manager Dunn does not shackle that new babe of his, he'll not be a Rube Waddell (one of the top pitchers at the turn of the century) in the rough. He'll be a Babe Ruth in the cemetery."

A reporter, Rodger Pippen, heard the comment and called George "Babe" in his column the next day, March 19, 1914, the first time the name "Babe Ruth" was heard or published. In later years, he was also dubbed "The Bambino" and "The Sultan of Swat."

With his new name and his new life, Ruth became one of the Orioles' stars and won a 50 percent pay raise to $900 a month after only one month. After the second month, Dunn gave him another raise, to $1,300 a month.

The Orioles were burning up the league, in first place by 17 games, but attendance by the fans didn't match the team's performance. After only 17 people showed up one afternoon, Dunn felt compelled to sell off some of his stars to relieve the financial problems which were piling up. He sold Ruth, pitcher Ernie Shore and catcher Ben Egan to the Red Sox for $8,500—$2,900 of it to buy Ruth.

"Babe" joined his new team on July 8, a Major Leaguer already, only a half-season out of St. Mary's. By the start of the 1915 season, he was making $3,500 a year. At the same time, he was taking on his mature appearance, filling out to 190 pounds distributed over his six-foot, two-inch frame.

As a rookie sensation, Ruth pitched the Red Sox to the American League pennant, winning 18 games and losing only eight. He had the league's third highest won-lost percentage, the second fewest hits allowed per nine innings and one of its best earned run averages, only 2.44. To make his year complete, Ruth hit .315 with four home runs, only three behind the league's leader in the final years of the "dead ball era."

He was deprived of a chance for success in the World Series when Manager Bill Carrigan went with a pitching rotation of three veterans. The strategy worked, and the Red Sox defeated the Philadelphia Phillies in five games. The man destined to hit the second most home runs, score the third most runs and drive in the fourth most in Series history was limited to one unsuccessful pinchhitting appearance against Grover Cleveland Alexander.

In 1916 and '17, "The Babe" won 23 games, then 24. His two-year totals were exceeded only by righthanders Alexander and Johnson, establishing Ruth as the best lefthanded pitcher in either Major League. In 1916, still only 21 years old, he led the league in earned run average (1.75), games started (41) and shutouts (9).

He topped off his season by getting into the World Series in dramatic fashion, holding the Brooklyn Dodgers to six hits while going the distance in a 14-inning, 2-1 victory in the second game, the longest in Series history. The Red Sox defeated the Dodgers in five games.

Ruth's victories dropped to thirteen in 1918, although he still posted a respectable 2.22 ERA and lost only seven games, but he shocked fans and writers by winning the league's home run championship with 11. He also hit an even .300 and, every bit as incredible as his home run total, led the league in slugging percentage—while playing in only 95 games as a pitcher, first baseman and outfielder.

It was the first year he won the league's slugging title, and then he made a habit of it. He won the title for seven years in a row and 13 seasons of the next 14.

All of this paced the Red Sox to another World Series berth, this year against the Chicago Cubs. Babe won two games and set a pitching record as the Sox became baseball's champions again, in six games. He shut out the Cubs, 1-0, in the opening game on six hits, then pitched seven scoreless innings in the fourth game, giving him a streak of 29 and two-thirds straight shutout innings stretching back to the 1916 Series. The record lasted until another Yankee lefthander, Whitey Ford, broke it in 1961.

But it was his hitting that caused America to sit up and take particular note of this pitcher with a bat in 1919, the year of the Black Sox scandal. Ruth became the most talked-about athlete in the nation. While playing the outfield more often between pitching starts so he could hit more home runs and drive in more runs, Ruth suddenly caught fire.

With the season only half over, he broke the American League record of 16 homers. In September he passed the National League mark of 25, then boomed his way past an obscure record of 27, set in the 1880s. He finished with the unheard-of total of 29 home runs, a record achieved in only 130 games.

As a pitcher, with his starts down to 15, he won nine games, lost five, and pitched 12 complete games.

While they experienced success on the diamond, the Sox were falling on hard times at the bank. Owner Harry Frazee was squeezed for cash because he still owed $350,000 on his purchase of the team only two years before. Meanwhile, the Yankees had not won a pennant in their first 17 years, a record compounded by the success of their rivals, the New York Giants, who won six pennants and finished second seven other times over the same period. To make matters worse, the Yankees lacked a stadium of their own and had to play their home games in the Giants' ballpark, the Polo Grounds.

BRIGHT LIGHTS AND KIDS

Frazee, a New York theatrical agent who knew the value of a marquee name, sold Ruth to the Yankees for $125,000 and a personal loan of another $350,000. The sale set the Yankees on their historic path of success. For the Red Sox, it started a famine in which they have never won a World Series since, a Boston marathon which Sox fans call, painfully, "the curse of The Bambino."

For the Yankees, acquiring the man who had led the Sox to three pennants in his five full seasons with them, it was the start of the most famous dynasty in the history of American sports—seven pennants in Ruth's 15 years with them and four World Series championships, followed by other dynasties in the DiMaggio and Stengel eras.

For Ruth, the switch was followed by immediate, sensational accomplishments—a .376 average in 1920, fourth highest in the league, with 54 home runs. He broke his one-year-old record of 29 homers by mid-season and the Yankees doubled their attendance record. Ruth's deeds were almost beyond measure. Those 54 homers were more than the number hit by 14 of the other 15 *teams* in the big leagues. The runnerup behind Ruth in the American League was George Sisler, one of the greatest hitters of all time, with 19. Ruth left him in the dust, 35 homers behind.

The Yankees gave him a raise of $10,000, to $30,000 for the 1921 season. In return, Ruth kept outdoing himself. In his second season as a Yankee, he broke his record again, this time with 59 homers while hitting .378, the league's third best average, and adding the head-shaking total of 171 runs batted in, 177 runs scored and 457 total bases, all three of them career highs. He showed that he brought versatility as well as greatness to his performances by stealing 17 bases and winning two games as a pitcher.

In the World Series, against the Giants of all people, Ruth had four singles and one homer and missed two games with arm problems. The Giants won baseball's crown, five games to three. History repeated itself in 1922, with the Yankees winning the pennant again and losing the Series to the Giants again.

But Ruth won something else—a "mascot." He was captivated by the sight of a three-year-old boy playing baseball with his father in a park near Ruth's apartment on Riverside Drive along the Hudson River, so he invited the two to visit him the next day at the ballpark.

The boy, named Ray Kelly, showed up at the Polo Grounds the next day with his father. Sure enough, Ruth had left word at the players' entrance that the boy and his father would be coming to the game. "When we got there," Kelly was remembering a few years ago, "we were escorted right into the Yankees' dugout, and that's the way it started."

Kelly became Ruth's "mascot" for the next ten years, with the senior Kelly's permission. He sat with Ruth in the dugout and even accompanied him on road trips. The relationship may have been a reflection of Ruth's troubled boyhood, but whatever the reason, it was clear evidence of The Babe's continuing love affair with kids everywhere.

"He was more than a hero to me for the ten years I spent with him," Kelly remembered. "He was almost like a father. What more than that can I say? . . . . He always acted around me like a big kid. He was a jovial individual, loved everybody, particularly loved children. He never had a bad word to say about anybody in my presence. He was just a wonderful human being."

His love of children was radiated everywhere he went, including overseas. When he went to Japan in 1934 on a barnstorming trip against Japanese teams, that love was evident the minute his ship arrived at the dock in Yokohama.

Kazuo Sayama remembers, "When he came to Japan in 1934, the first thing he did was to see grandchildren. They were lining up at the pier .... They were lining up in baseball uniforms. And the first thing Babe did was to walk to them, shook with them, you know, and carried them in his arms. And not only that, he encouraged other baseball players, American players, to do the same. The first—the first point he showed, you know— the love for the children, the love for the Japanese, and we all loved him."

Ruth soon became known for his fondness for the bright lights as much as for his home runs. His roommate, Ping Bodie, said he didn't really room with Ruth. He said, "I room with his suitcase."

Bob Considine, his pal during their New York years before becoming Ruth's biographer, said The Babe "thought every night was New Year's Eve." Paul Derringer, an All-Star pitcher with the Cincinnati Reds, said he once saw Ruth's prowess at the table on a train when The Babe downed a breakfast of porterhouse steak, four fried eggs, fried potatoes, toast, a pint of bourbon and ginger ale and a pot of coffee.

His daughter offers an explanation for Ruth's excesses. "When Daddy was beginning his baseball career and maybe overdoing some things from time to time were the very same years when he was enjoying certain experiences for the first time," she said.

"The sportswriters covering the Orioles in Daddy's first spring training season wrote that he spent a lot of his spare time riding a bike, like a kid. Well, he never had a bike when he was a kid. When he started earning enough money to buy nice clothes, he was seeing them for the first time. When he began to eat the good meals that professional athletes had always eaten, he was experiencing fine foods for the first time. When he stayed in swanky hotels with the Orioles and then with the Red Sox and the Yankees, it wasn't just the first time he stayed in swanky hotels—it was the first time he stayed in any kind of hotel. When he bought sporty cars, it wasn't the first time he owned *sporty* cars—it was the first time he owned any kind of car, new or used, sporty or otherwise."

Ruth's behavior once brought a sharp rebuke, in public, from Jimmy Walker, then a state senator and later the mayor of New York. Walker, no stranger to fun himself, stood up at a baseball writers dinner at the Elks Club of New York on November 15, 1922, and said directly to Ruth, "Babe, are you once again going to let down those dirty-faced kids in the streets of America?"

The new Yankee star stood and said, "So help me, Jimmy—I'll go to the country and get in shape." He lost 20 pounds that winter.

By 1923, Ruth was earning the princely sum of $54,000 a year. Management could afford it. His home runs were packing them in all over the American League, so much that the Yankees could cut the cord with the Giants and the Polo Grounds by building their own ballpark. They began the 1923 season in what has become the most famous sports facility in the world, Yankee Stadium.

The landmark has another name, acquired after Opening Day of 1923, when Ruth hit a home run to help win the game. In his report the next day in the *New York Evening Telegram*, Fred Lieb described the majestic new athletic monument as "The House That Ruth Built," a name still used today.

Ruth never let up that year. He finished with the highest average of his career, .393, ten points behind Detroit's Harry Heilmann, and led the league in seven offensive departments—41 home runs, 151 runs scored, 131 RBIs, 399 total bases, .764 slugging average, 170 walks and a home run percentage of 7.9. Small wonder he was voted the American League's Most Valuable Player—unanimously.

Small wonder, too, that the Yankees left the Tigers 16 games behind in second place. Then they got their revenge against their rival Giants by defeating them in the World Series, four games to two. Ruth hit .368 and belted three homers.

The Washington Senators snuffed out any Yankee hopes for a repeat performance in 1924, but not before the Yankees won 18 of their last 22 games. Ruth won the batting championship with a .378 average and led the league in home runs—for the fifth time—with 46. For the second straight year, he led the league in seven departments.

"THE MIGHTY MITE"

Ruth continued to gain fame across the country and the world for his achievements, but in 1925 he won recognition for his stomach instead of anything he did on the field. Coming north by train from spring training, he devoured what some estimates said were 25 hot dogs during one stop and ended up in a New York hospital with acute indigestion in what quickly became known as "the stomach ache heard 'round the world."

The episode was a forerunner for the season. Ruth hit only .290, a drop of 88 points in his batting average, with only 25 home runs, barely half of his '24 total. The Yankees plunged to seventh place in the eight-team league.

The year included another explosive development near the end of the season. Ruth was hitting only .246 when the Yankees traveled to St. Louis, where, by his own admission, "I had a lot of high-living friends." He said he "forgot to come home to my room in the Chase Hotel for a couple of nights, and I didn't get away with it."

When he showed up at Sportsman's Park badly hung over, he ran afoul of the Yankee manager, Miller Huggins, a small but stern man called

"The Mighty Mite," who stood only five feet, six inches tall and weighed only 140 pounds.

When Ruth noticed a look of fury on Huggins's face, he tried to head off any trouble by apologizing before Huggins had a chance to speak. The following exchange took place:

"I'm sorry I'm late, Hug. Had some personal business to attend to."

"You've had too much personal business lately. And what's more, don't bother dressing today."

"Why not?"

"You know damn well why not! What's more, I'm fed up with your excuses. This time you've gone too far. You're suspended indefinitely, and I've got some more news for you—you're fined five thousand dollars."

"Why, you little runt! If you were 50 pounds heavier, I'd knock your brains out!"

"It's a good thing for you I'm not 50 pounds heavier!"

"You can't do this to me! I'll go to New York and see Ruppert (Colonel Jacob Ruppert, the owner of the Yankees) and—"

"That's what I want you to do. And I'd like to be there when you burst into Ruppert's office, carrying that .246 batting average and telling him I'm picking on you."

Ruth made good on his threat and met with Ruppert, but the fine stuck and so did the suspension. Ruth was ordered to make a public apology, which he did, and missed ten games. When he came back, he raised his batting average 44 points by the season's end the following month. Huggins later told Ruth he admired a man who could triumph over a lot of tough opponents but he admired a man even more who could triumph over himself.

After vowing to come back stronger than ever in 1926, Ruth spent the off-season working diligently to get himself into peak condition and then ignited the Yankees on a streak of three straight pennants and two World Series championships. Even with the record-breaking success of the 1998 Yankees under Joe Torre, their 1927 team is still considered by many observers to be the greatest team of all time.

They won 110 games, the American League record until the Cleveland Indians broke it in 1954, and ran away from a great Philadelphia A's team that won three pennants in a row beginning in 1929. Ruth dazzled the sports world, and the non-sports world too, by hitting 60 home runs, the record that lasted 34 years. He added a .356 average, drove in 164 runs and led the league in runs scored, total bases and slugging average.

Under the pressure of chasing his own record of 59, Ruth hit more homers in September than Cleveland's starting lineup hit all year.

It's hard to believe, but his new partner in power, Lou Gehrig, matched The Babe's overall performance with 47 homers, a league-leading 175 RBIs and 52 doubles and won the Most Valuable Player Award. Together they formed the strongest one-two punch baseball ever saw until Hank Aaron and Eddie Mathews gave the Milwaukee Braves of the 1950s and '60s baseball's most powerful tandem ever.

As Ruth and Gehrig slugged the American League's pitchers for the next decade, comparisons between the two became inevitable despite the differences in their personalities—the bombastic Ruth and the quiet Gehrig.

Over their ten years until Ruth's departure from the Yankees after the 1934 season, Gehrig was a terror himself with a bat in his hand, but he always played in Ruth's shadow, hitting in the cleanup spot behind Ruth's number three position—and was content to remain there.

Columnist Joe Williams wrote in those years, "Half of the time Gehrig is at bat, the customers are still cheering Ruth. He (Gehrig) has been a sort of afterthought with Yankee Stadium crowds since he has been with the Yankees."

Gehrig had no problem with that arrangement. "I could never be another Ruth," he said, "if I lived to be 500 years old."

Together they demolished the Pittsburgh Pirates in four straight games to win the '27 Series, the only Series that may have been won before the first game was played. Ruth hit an even .400 with the only two home runs for either team, four runs scored and seven RBIs.

The New York Baseball Writers selected The Babe as their Player of the Year. He said later, "They didn't give it to me because I had hit 60 home runs and helped the club to a four-straight World Series by getting the only two homers of the Series. They told me they were giving it to me because of the comeback I had made after my terrible season of 1925, when a lot of them figured, and wrote, that I was all washed up."

HOW TO WIN A WORLD SERIES BEFORE IT STARTS

Before the Series started at Forbes Field in Pittsburgh, the Pirates decided to sit in the stands and get a look at their opponents. It was a costly mistake. As Ruth said, their manager, Donie Bush, "should have insisted that they go right home."

Ruth, Gehrig and others pounded the batting practice pitching with one long blast after another into the outfield seats. "You could nearly hear them gulp while they watched us," Ruth said. "We really put on a show. Lou and I banged ball after ball into the right field stands, and I finally knocked one out of the park in right center. Bob Meusel and Tony Lazzeri kept hammering balls into the left field seats. One by one, the Pirates got up and left the park. Some of them were shaking their heads when we last saw them."

In all the talk in 1998 about whether the Yankees of that season were better than the '27 edition, everyone forgot the other powerhouse of the 1920s, the Philadelphia A's. They had six Hall of Famers including their owner-manager, Connie Mack, and reeled off three consecutive seasons of 104, 102 and 107 victories beginning in 1929. They won the pennant by 18, eight and 13 and a half games.

But Ruth and Gehrig were still baseball's most potent punch, even in the A's three-year string of successes. The Bambino averaged 47 home runs over those seasons, 157 RBIs and a .359 average. Gehrig averaged 41 homers, 161 RBIs and a .340 average.

As the nation staggered under the stock market crash of October 1929 and the world-wide economic depression which followed, Ruth was earning more money than ever—$70,000 in 1929, followed by his demand for $80,000 for 1930. When it was pointed out that he was making more money than the President of the United States, Herbert Hoover, Ruth responded with, "Well, why not? I had a better year than Hoover."

Huggins died unexpectedly at the end of the '29 season at the age of 50. When Ruth asked Colonel Ruppert for the job, Ruppert passed him over, afraid that the managerial responsibilities might interfere with his productive bat. It was the beginning of Ruth's biggest disappointment in life, his inability to be hired as the manager of a big league team.

Still, The Babe continued to enjoy life. John Drebinger described the Ruth of those years as "warm and friendly, with an almost outrageous sense of humor." Drebinger wrote, "He seemed to have only one major aim in life, to enjoy every minute of it and help others do the same. I never met another man who was so uninhibited. There never was any acting."

Not even when it came to calling people by name. Ruth was the league's worst at remembering names, so he simply called every young player "Kid" and every veteran "Doc." When one of his closest friends, and his teammate for ten years, Waite Hoyt, was traded to Detroit, Ruth said an emotional goodbye, then added, "I'm going to miss you, Kid. Take care of yourself—uh—uh—Walter," as the whole Yankee dressing room exploded in laughter.

THE "CALLED SHOT"

One of the best remembered moments of his career occurred in the 1932 World Series when he hit his "called shot" home run against Charlie Root of the Cubs at Wrigley Field when Ruth was 37 years old. It was the climax to a Series-long feud, sparked when the Cubs voted only a half-share of the players' Series money to former Yankee Mark Koenig. Koenig, an infielder, came to the Cubs in a trade with Detroit and played 33 games for them, hitting .353 and providing the drive that propelled the Cubs past the Pirates and into the Series.

Koenig had been on the great Yankee teams of 1925-30 and still had many friends on the team, all of whom felt the Cubs had short-changed their old teammate. The New York players called their opponents "cheapskates" and taunted them from the start of the Series.

They beat the Cubs in the first two games in New York, then moved to Chicago for the next three games. Before the first game there, Ruth pumped nine balls into Wrigley Field's stands during batting practice and loudly informed the Cubs in the other dugout that he'd play for half his salary "if I could hit all year in this dump."

The Cubs answered by insulting the overweight Ruth for his "pot belly," a charge to which The Babe was vulnerable. He had gained considerable weight, including an ample stomach which, combined with his spindly legs, prompted one writer to describe him as "a balloon on toothpicks."

Ruth one-upped his opponents with a three-run homer in his first time up. The jockeying from the Cubs' bench continued and was still going strong when Ruth stepped to the plate in the fifth inning with the score tied, 4-4.

He took two called strikes from Root, holding up first one finger, then two, calling out, "That's one!" And then, "That's two!" Then he made a gesture that is debated to this day. He seemed to point to dead center field as if to predict that he would park the next pitch there, then did exactly that.

Did he really point to that spot and say he was going to hit the ball there? Players and opponents disagreed. Ruth's own testimony, to Chicago writer John P. Carmichael, was, "No, I didn't point to any spot, but as long as I'd called the first two strikes on myself, I had to go through with it. It was damned foolishness, sure, but I just felt like doing it, and I felt pretty sure Root would put one close enough for me to cut at, because I was showing him up, too, wasn't I? What the hell, he had to take a chance as well as I did or walk me. Gosh, that was a great feeling."

Ruth admitted, "Yeah, it was silly. I was a blankety-blank fool. But I got away with it, and after Gehrig homered behind me, their backs were broken. That was a day to talk about."

Another day for him to talk about occurred the next season, in the first All-Star game ever played. He hit the first home run of baseball's summer classic, revisiting Chicago to do it in Comiskey Park. The blow provided the winning margin as the American League defeated their National League rivals, 4-2.

It was his latest example of his ability to do what needed to be done. Like the time the Yankees and the White Sox were tied, 1-1, in the bottom of the fifteenth inning in Chicago. New York's traveling secretary, Mark Roth, was worried because he had booked the team on an early train for New York, and the railroad was warning him the train could not be held much longer.

As Ruth walked past Roth's box seat on his way to the plate, he asked, "What's the matter with you? Sick?"

Roth said, "Yes. If you bums don't win this game in a hurry, we'll blow the train."

Ruth said confidently, "Take it easy. I'll get us out of here."

Then he went up to the plate and hit the first pitch into the right field seats to take the lead. They retired the White Sox in the bottom of the fifteenth, made a quick change in the clubhouse and were sped to the train in a fleet of taxi cabs.

As they were getting on board, Ruth said to Roth, "Why the hell didn't you tell me about that before?"

MANAGER RUTH?

Ruth's unsuccessful struggle to become a manager entered a second chapter in 1934, when the Tigers invited him to come to Detroit to discuss the possibility of becoming their skipper, Ruth said he was leaving the next day for Europe and the Orient and would contact them on his return. The Tigers didn't wait. They hired Mickey Cochrane instead.

Ruth, who also turned down opportunities to manage in the minor leagues, was signed by the Boston Braves for the 1935 season, the last year of his playing career. He made the mistake of telling a press conference he would probably become the Braves' manager the next year and that Manager Bill McKechnie would be elevated to the position of general manager. The prediction did not sit well with management. Ruth hit only six home runs that year, and retired as a player after 28 games. McKechnie kept his job as manager.

On May 25, 1935, Ruth hit three home runs in one game. His last traveled an estimated 600 feet, the only ball hit over the right field wall at Pittsburgh's Forbes Field. It was the Babe's 714th home run, and his last. A few days later, he retired.

Following his retirement as a player, Ruth continued to hope for a chance to become a Major League manager. The criticism against him after his various scrapes with management was that he couldn't be expected to manage an entire team if he couldn't even manage himself, but Ruth had an answer.

"Nobody knows what kind of manager I would have made," he said in 1946. "Today I'm not sore at anybody, but I still think I should have had my chance. Speaker and Cobb had theirs, and I guess it was natural that I should expect a crack at managing some day. But I didn't, and that's that."

Julia Ruth Stevens agrees with her father. "He would have been good," she told Bill Gilbert. "He deserved the chance as much as some of the others who were named managers. And if he fell flat on his face, then that would be it. But he might have been a really good manager."

Mrs. Stevens applied more than just a daughter's loyalty in justifying her opinion. She cited specific reasons, saying, "He was so baseball wise. That's the reason I think he would have been a good manager. And I think the players would have enjoyed him so much. He would have been what baseball people call 'a player's manager,' and his players would have wanted to win for him. And that's what makes a manager successful."

Despite his disappointment and the nagging feeling that baseball had deserted him—at least at the big league level—he remained active in the sport, making numerous personal appearances and working with kids in a program sponsored by the Ford Motor Company.

He followed the sport too, and knew the teams and the players. He told his daughter that he rated Ted Williams as the best player of the generation that followed his. He told Julia that Williams was "the greatest natural ball player I ever saw." Today she points out, "He wasn't just talking about Ted's greatness as a hitter. He was talking about Ted's all-around ability."

During World War II, he made countless visits to troops stationed almost everywhere and lent his support to "the war effort" by encouraging Americans to buy war bonds to finance the fight against the Axis nations of Germany, Italy and Japan.

After pitching some mementoes from the Japanese people out his window on the night of the attack on Pearl Harbor—they landed in Riverside Park, 14 floors below—The Babe faced Walter Johnson one last time in a benefit game at Yankee Stadium in 1942 and hit a "home run" into the right field seats.

He made a surprise appearance at Griffith Stadium in Washington as the grand finale to an exhibition game that featured earlier appearances by Bing Crosby and Kate Smith. The occasion, the brainchild of Shirley Povich of *The Washington Post*, raised two million dollars in war bonds, enough in those days to pay for building a Navy warship.

A WORLD-WIDE TRIBUTE TO AN AMERICAN HERO

Ruth was stricken with throat cancer in 1946 and fought the disease for two years before his death on August 16, 1948. But he never knew he had cancer. The New York writers and broadcasters never reported it, although they knew.

After his death, Jack Lait of the *New York Daily Mirror* wrote, "Every newspaperman in New York knew for years that Babe Ruth had cancer of the throat. Yet that was never written. We knew he did not suspect and feared that the dread word would break him down."

When he was hospitalized, he received 30,000 letters. Two special days were held in his honor in the last two years of his life. The first was celebrated in every ballpark in the Major Leagues in 1947, by order of Commissioner Happy Chandler. The second was a salute from his old team at Yankee Stadium four months before he died. As he leaned on a bat belonging to Bob Feller of the Cleveland Indians, the day's opponents, Ruth whispered hoarsely into the microphone at home plate, next to announcer Mel Allen, "The only real game in the world, I think, is baseball." He left the field with tears streaming down his face.

Even while suffering from his fatal illness, The Babe made a contribution to society. He was treated with injections of a new drug, teropterin, as one of the first human patients to receive it. "In the early months of treatment last year," a 1948 newspaper article reported, "the drug produced what doctors described as a 'remarkable' improvement in Ruth's condition, although it did not seem to be so effective in other cases."

The article continued, "There was great excitement in the medical profession at the time, and doctors throughout the nation came to know of Ruth as medical science's best example of teropterin therapy in cancer. His improvement gave the medical profession the world over hope that cancer could be combatted successfully by the simple administration of a drug."

When he died, the magnetism of his personality, his greatness as an athlete and his stature as a world figure all were reflected in the global reaction to his passing. Eighty thousand fans filed past his open casket as he lay in state in the rotunda of "The House That Ruth Built." The line lasted all night, from five o'clock in the afternoon until seven in the morning. Five thousand mourners jammed St. Patrick's Cathedral on Fifth Avenue for the funeral the next day, while another 75,000 filled the street in rainy weather.

In Japan, every baseball game in the country was halted for one minute. President Truman issued a statement. Truman's only living predecessor, Herbert Hoover, told reporters he once signed his autograph three times for a boy because the boy said he could keep one and "trade the other two for one of Babe Ruth."

As his pallbearers carried his casket out of the Cathedral, one of them, Joe Dugan, Ruth's old teammate, feeling the August heat and humidity, said quietly to another teammate and pall bearer, Waite Hoyt, "I'd give my right arm for a cold beer."

Hoyt replied, "So would The Babe."

At the time of his death, Ruth held 56 Major League hitting records, plus ten American League marks. As a percentage of total homers in the league, a player today would have to hit 150 home runs to equal his 60 in 1927. Every time Ruth stepped to the plate, he was 20 percent more likely to hit a homer than Ralph Kiner, the next best, and 40 percent more likely than Hank Aaron. In 16 years as an everyday player, Ruth averaged 43 home runs a season compared to Aaron's 32. He won 12 home run championships. Mickey Mantle, Willie Mays, Ted Williams and Aaron won four each.

The Yankees erected a monument in Ruth's memory in center field at Yankee Stadium, next to ones for Lou Gehrig and Miller Huggins. At their home opener in 1949, the spring after Ruth's death, his widow, Claire, walked out to center field with Governor Thomas E. Dewey, Mayor William O'Dwyer and every member of the Yankees and the Washington Senators. Mrs. Ruth pulled the cord that lowered the veil from the monument. On the facing was a plaque which read:

George Herman "Babe" Ruth. 1895-1948.
A great ballplayer. A great man. A great American.
Erected by the Yankees and the New York Baseball Writers.
April 19, 1949.

Maybe an even more telling tribute was the one written by the immortal Grantland Rice. On the morning after The Babe's death, his new three-stanza poem, "Game Called", appeared in newspapers all over America. The first stanza said:

Game called by darkness—let the curtain fall.
No more remembered thunder sweeps the field.
No more the ancient echoes hear the call
To one who wore so well both sword and shield.
The Big Guy's left us with the night to face,
And there is no one who can take his place.

WHAT OTHER PLAYERS SAID ABOUT BABE RUTH

Frank Crosetti—Hell, he did more for baseball than anybody ever did or ever will do. After the Black Sox scandal, he brought people back. People think something is crooked and they're not going to go, right? Then along comes this guy hitting home runs and the people listen to him on the radio because there's no TV then and they finally said, "Let's go see this guy hit those home runs."

He once told me, "Every time I go to bat, I try to hit a home run, because I know the people come out to see me hit a home run." That's why he struck out a lot. And when he would strike out, I mean he really struck out. And the fans would get just as big a charge out of that as when he hit a home run. He stood out like a great big rose atop a rose bush. He had more color than any player ever had or will have.

As far as Ruth pointing before hitting that famous home run at Wrigley Field against the Cubs—he didn't point. The only thing is, the writers wanted to make a big story about it—that he pointed. And the next day in the dugout, Ruth said, "If the writers want to think that I pointed, let them. I don't care." I was standing there right next to him when he said it.

Mel Harder—You had to be careful with him on everything you threw. I tried to pitch to spots and go in and out. You couldn't repeat a pitch. He used a 38-40 ounce bat, and when he hit it, it looked like a golf ball. I faced him for the last time in Cleveland. All our infielders played way around on him, because he was such a pull hitter. But he never tried to pull on me all day. He just tried to meet the ball and drive it to left. He did it all day long. He aimed for the open space in left and had five singles. He didn't hit the ball hard at all, and the fans booed him.

Stan Musial—I met him once in Rochester, New York, just before I went to the big leagues, when he was giving a hitting exhibition. I was just a kid, but I got a ball signed by him. It was about five years after he retired, but at least I got a chance to get that ball signed. Of course, he wouldn't have known then who I was, but it was a real thrill, something I've never forgotten. I still have the ball.

Phil Rizzuto—Did I ever see Ruth? Are you kidding? When I was a kid, my Uncle Mike used to take me to Yankee Stadium and then I got to meet him many times on his way out. He'd come to Yankee Stadium a lot and sit on the bench and talk to us. When he was young, he had a nice shape, but as he got older, he got top heavy—he had the big chest and stomach but very thin legs. He was a hell of an outfielder with those small gloves. I could never believe that no one ever gave him credit for being a great outfielder. He would come and sit and tell stories. Geez, everybody got around him. Oh gee, everyone looked forward to him coming around.

Jo-Jo White —No one compared with him. He was for the fans— very accommodating for the fans. He wasn't the type to make excuses.

Cecil Travis—I saw him toward the end of his career, but he could still hit that ball. Looking at him, you wouldn't think he could do it with that kind of odd build of his. He was a different kind of hitter. He'd hit them about a mile high. Everybody sort of looked up to him . . . idolized him, you know. He was a hero of mine growing up, and almost everybody else too. Also, he had a great arm. He was well worth the money he got.

Al Lopez—I'm not knocking the other guys, but I think if I had to pick the one player that I think was the greatest player of them all, I'd have to take Babe Ruth, because he not only was a great outfielder and a home run hitter, but he would have been a Hall of Famer as a pitcher. He was a great pitcher—the best in the league at the time.

Harry "The Hat" Walker—My brother, Dixie, was kind of like a caddy for Ruth in his first four years. When Ruth would go out (of the game), he (Dixie) would go in. And he always said that Ruth had the best instincts playing the game as anybody. When he got the ball, he knew where it had to go. Dixie said the man was uncanny, and that he ran a lot better than people thought. You know, he stole 123 bases. This man was the greatest ballplayer who ever played, in my book.

THE RUTH FILE

Name: George Herman Ruth.
Date and Place of Birth: February 6, 1895, Baltimore, Maryland.
Date and Place of Death: August 16, 1948, New York, New York.
Nickname: "Babe" also "The Bambino" and "The Sultan of Swat"
Position: Pitcher, Right Field, First Base.
Major League Career: 22 years, 1914-1935.
Home Runs: 714 (2nd).
Runs Batted In: 2,211 (2nd).
Runs Scored: 2,174 (2nd).
Lifetime Batting Average: .342 (10th).
Number of Hits: 2,873.
Walks: 2,056 (1st).
Strikeouts: 1,330.
Records: When he retired, Ruth held 56 Major League records and was tied for four more. He also held ten American League marks and was tied for five others.

Other Highlights:
— Led the Major Leagues in home runs 11 times.
— Led the American League in homers 12 times.
— Led the League in runs batted in six times and in runs scored eight times.
— American League's Most Valuable Player, 1923.
— First player to hit 30, 40, 50 and 60 home runs in a season.
— Highest home run percentage in history—a homer every 11.7 times at bat.
— During his 15 years with the Yankees, Ruth averaged 44 home runs, 131 runs batted in, 123 walks, 130 runs scored and a .349 batting average. In World Series play, he has the second highest home run percentage, the second most homers, the second highest slugging average, the second most walks, the third most runs scored, the fourth most runs batted in, the tenth most hits and the tenth most games played.
As a pitcher, he holds the best won-lost percentage (3 wins and no losses, for a perfect winning percentage of 1.000) and the third best earned run average (0.87 earned runs for every nine innings pitched).

Elected to the Baseball Hall of Fame: 1936, in the first class, with Walter Johnson, Ty Cobb, Christy Mathewson and Honus Wagner.

14

MIKE SCHMIDT

The Impossible Dream?

I f you wonder how much more Mickey Mantle might have achieved if he hadn't played his entire career on two bad legs, you have to wonder the same thing about Mike Schmidt.

Near the end of his career, after winning his third National League Most Valuable Player Award, Schmidt told a reporter his knees were "extremely bad, but they are extremely good considering how bad they are." He added, "I've learned to live with creaky knees. But they have deteriorated a great deal. There's a lot of arthritis, a lot of pain in them."

A Hall of Fame baseball career looked like the impossible dream when Schmidt damaged the cartilage in his right knee returning a punt for Fairview High School near Dayton, Ohio, then damaged the cartilage in his other knee the next season. Doctors said he knee problems might have started even earlier, when he fell 30 feet to the ground while climbing a tree in his back yard at age seven.

As he fell, he grabbed for the first thing he saw—a live wire carrying a charge of 4,000 volts. He let go of the wire and dropped to the ground as the charge went through his body and came out at his shins.

In a 1977 interview with Ray Kelly of *The Sporting News*, Schmidt said, "The doctors think there could have been a weakness in my knees from that high-wire accident."

None of that stopped Mike from a successful high school sports career. He played football, basketball and baseball for Fairview and became an all-city shortstop. However, scouts knew about his knees and the two operations he'd had on them—scouts always know about such things —and showed little interest in him as a professional prospect. He was also afflicted with that fatal baseball shortcoming: He had trouble hitting the curve ball.

Still, he persisted. How much determination did he have? When his high school coach called off baseball practice in early March because of snow, Mike called his teammates, told them to bring their shovels to the field, then called his coach to tell him practice was back on.

He always wanted to be a big league baseball player, from the time he started playing catch with his father. When he enrolled at Ohio University, school officials told him their insurance plan wouldn't cover him, but he continued to hope for a career in baseball while planning to study architecture, just in case.

He worked to build up the strength in his knees with weights, starting with only five pounds. Eventually he was lifting 90 pounds with his knees, with the continued encouragement of his biggest booster, his grandmother, Viola Schmidt.

By the time of his sophomore year, Mike was Ohio's starting shortstop. He began to attract the attention of those scouts by leading his team to the finals of the College World Series in his senior year and being named a college All-American as both a junior and a senior. He set a conference record with 27 home runs and school records for runs scored and runs batted in.

And he made a decision that had ramifications for the rest of his baseball career. He took the advice of his coach, Bob Wren, and abandoned his plan to make himself into a switch-hitter because he thought he would be able to hit the curve ball better that way. During his 18 years with the Philadelphia Phillies, Schmidt said that listening to his coach was the most important change he made in his career.

"A WAGONLOAD OF PUMPKINS"

A second-round draft choice by the Phillies, Mike established a reputation for his hitting, including home runs, and his strikeouts. While playing for Eugene, Oregon, in the Class AAA Pacific Coast League, one of the toughest minor leagues in the country, Schmidt attracted the attention of the Phillies' brass with 26 home runs, 91 RBIs and a .291 batting average. He also struck out 145 times.

When the Phillies brought him up to "the big club" for a look during the last month of the 1972 season, they might have been wishing they hadn't. Schmidt, 23 years old that September, hit an anemic .206 in 13 games, with one home run and three RBIs. But the statistic that attracted the most attention was 15 strikeouts in only 34 times at bat.

When a reporter asked Manager Danny Ozark if Schmidt had a future with the Phillies, Ozark answered, "I'd trade him for a wagonload of pumpkins."

Cooler heads prevailed, however, and the Phillies placed a sizeable bet on Mike's future by trading their slick-fielding starting third baseman of the past four seasons, Don Money, to the Milwaukee Brewers and handing the third base job to Schmidt.

Ozark might have been looking for a wagon load of pumpkins again, because Schmidt, after being touted in the spring as a future Hall of Famer, hit only .196 and averaged more than a strikeout per game, fanning 136 times in 132 games.

Like many young players, Schmidt pressed as his hitting slump continued. Every at-bat became a life-or-death crisis. He became indecisive, confused, disgusted. As hit hitting problems mounted, his fielding also began to suffer.

The Phillies fans began to boo him. Young Mike tried to hide his disappointment behind a show of supreme confidence, which only compounded his problems. When he tried to act cool and cocky, he came off as unemotional, nonchalant and impersonal, with something of a so-what attitude.

When the subject of his 1973 season came up in an interview with *The Sporting News,* Schmidt said, "I can't even bring myself to talk about it. There is no way I could hit .196 with 136 strikeouts."

Under the experienced eye of a former Phillies star, Bobby Wines, Schmidt played that winter in Puerto Rico and fulfilled the hopes of the Phillies that the bright prospect would stop thinking too much about his disappointing performances and work on his hitting away from the spotlight of spring training.

He helped his Caguas team win the championship while concentrating on relaxing at the plate and letting the game come to him. He worked on making contact, on hitting the curve ball and the change-up along with the slider and other off-speed pitches. Slowly, his confidence began to return.

THE HOLE IN HIS SWING

In 1974, Schmidt displayed a complete reversal of form. He led the league with 36 home runs and a .546 slugging average. He still had what players call a "hole in his swing" and led the league in strikeouts for the first of four times with 138, but he also hit .282, finished second only to Johnny Bench in runs batted in with 116 and in total bases with 310, drew 106 walks and even stole 23 bases. All of this helped to jump-start his team from sixth place to third, only eight games behind the champions of the National League's East division, the Pittsburgh Pirates.

In 1975, Schmidt led the league in home runs again, with 38, the first time a slugger led the majors in home runs in consecutive seasons since Harmon Killebrew accomplished the feat in 1963-64. Schmidt also drove in 95 runs, scored 93, walked 101 times and stole 29 more bases.

Strikeouts continued to be his demon. He struck out 180 times, the fifth most in the history of either league. Despite that depressing figure, Schmidt's hitting helped to power the Phillies to six more victories and moved them up another step in the National League East's 1975 standings, to second place and two games closer to the Pirates, who repeated their championship of the year before.

By the time the '76 season started, Manager Ozark wasn't thinking of trading Schmidt for a wagonload of pumpkins.

The season was barely underway when Mike hit home runs in four consecutive times at bat in Wrigley Field. His success that day told Schmidt something about his approach to playing the game of baseball.

"I had not hit too well up to that game," he told the *Philadelphia Daily News*. "I remember Dick Allen teasing me in the locker room right up until National Anthem time about losing the ability to have fun while I was playing the game. He said he wanted to see a smile on my face, that he and I were just going to go out and have fun."

Others offered the same advice from time to time, but he was never completely able to make the adjustment. "Some people think I made it hard on myself," he said at the end of his career. "Some people think that if I had the Gary Matthews approach to life and had fun every day at the ballpark, been more outgoing and interested in other people, had more fun, that I would have played the game better." Matthews was a big league outfielder for 16 years and Schmidt's teammate on the Phillies in 1981-82-83.

"But," he reasoned, "I've always contended I would have been a mediocre player if I'd had a lot of fun. It was my obsessive personality that took me beyond being pretty good."

The Phillies won 50 of their next 63 games in 1976 after Schmidt's 4-homer explosion in Wrigley Field, won 101 games overall and passed the Pirates to win the National League East title by nine games, the first of three consecutive division championships.

For the third straight year, Schmidt stood at the top of the list of the National League's home run hitters, with 38. He also drove in 107 runs, collected 100 walks—and led both leagues in strikeouts, now with 149.

His fielding was also winning high marks. He led the league in assists for third basemen for the second straight season, and people began mentioning his name in the same breath with Brooks Robinson's.

All of this combined for another dramatic turn in Schmidt's career when the Phillies made him the highest paid player in Major League history before the start of the 1977 season. They rewarded his stardom with a $3 million contract for six years and, at Mike's request, included a no-trade clause covering the next four years.

GOD

Just before being rewarded with his big, new contract, Mike Schmidt turned to God. He said he was shooting baskets outside his house one winter day, "and I just stopped and asked myself, 'Why me?' It occurred to me that I had no idea how these things happened in my life. I knew there had to be more."

Later he said, "The one thing people should realize, and the thing I am beginning to realize, is that if I am out there giving 100 percent, whether I go 4-for-4 or 0-for-4, in Christ's eyes I am a winner. I don't care if the whole stadium is booing or cheering. It doesn't matter anymore."

Would that much money become a distraction and affect his performance on the field? He told *The Sporting News,* "I love to play baseball. I never think of the money once I put that uniform on, and I never played a game in my life that I didn't give it 100 percent."

His history-making contract, however, had a different impact. If it didn't affect Schmidt, it affected his boo-birds. The Philadelphia fans—some people say they would boo Santa Claus and the Pope—made Schmidt their favorite target almost from the beginning of his career. Now they had more fuel for their fire.

Reports on the air and in the Philadelphia papers accused him of refusing to sign autographs, of rarely having anything to do with rookies, of refusing to autograph one of his bats for a rookie who was being farmed out because, Schmidt allegedly said, "I get $100 dollars for those." His problems were made worse because he did not go out "with the boys" after road games.

The fans accused him of being unable to hit in the clutch, of caring only about hitting home runs, and worst of all, of not being a winner.

The fans were overlooking Schmidt's contributions to their team. Instead, they remembered that the Phillies were defeated in the playoffs three years in a row, 1976-78, without reaching the World Series—and in two of those playoffs, Schmidt's batting averages were .063 and .200.

In contrast, Schmidt was accorded respect in every other ballpark in the league because of his greatness. Second Baseman Tom Herr of the Cardinals, who became Schmidt's teammate on the Phils in 1988, said, "I can remember many times sitting in the Cardinals' dugout and wondering, 'What do they want from him?' In St. Louis, the players are all heroes. If Mike had played there, he wouldn't have been treated that way (the way he was in Philadelphia)."

Another turning point in Schmidt's career occurred on December 5, 1978, when the Phillies won a fierce bidding battle and signed free agent Pete Rose. He was 38 years old but was still going strong, coming off a .302 season and 198 hits in his sixteenth season with the Cincinnati Reds.

The Phils dropped from first place to fourth in 1979, but it wasn't Rose's fault. He kept right on hitting—a .331 average with 208 hits. The skid wasn't Schmidt's fault, either. He hit 45 home runs and drove in 114 runs. Unfortunately for the Phillies, their pitchers didn't have the year their hitters did.

That season started Mike Schmidt on a journey for the balance of his career that elevated his standing from All-Star to Hall of Famer. He said, "Pete Rose taught me what I needed to be great. He was consumed by the game. I'm not sure I was totally consumed by baseball until I met Pete."

A Phillies coach, John Vukovich, agreed. "His approach to the game changed in '78 when Pete came," Vukovich said. "I don't think there's any reason to believe it's a coincidence that Schmitty had his big years when Pete was there. He hit 45 home runs the first year, and he hit 48 the next year."

The record bears out Vukovich's testimony. Five of Schmidt's eight National League home run championships came after Rose joined the Phillies.

THE MVP AWARD, AND A DEDICATION

Rose's second year with Philadelphia dramatized his effect on Schmidt and on the entire team. Schmidt's 48 homers led the league and set a record for the most home runs by a third baseman. He also led the league with 121 runs batted in, a .624 slugging average and 342 total bases. He was a hands-down winner of the league's Most Valuable Player Award, which he dedicated to the memory of his late grandmother.

Rose wasn't the only reason for Mike's success in 1980. Mike deserved some of the credit himself for a basic change in his batting stance. He moved back in the batter's box and began striding into the pitch, a small but important adjustment which enabled him to hit to all fields and raise his average 31 points above his career mark to .282. He raised it another 34 points in 1981, to .316.

Still, Schmidt had at least one more monkey on his back—the charge that he couldn't deliver when the chips were on the line, a charge that lingered from his dismal batting averages in the '77 and '78 divisional playoffs. The boo birds ignored his .308 performance in 1976 when the Reds swept the Phillies in three games.

"You like to think you can handle it," he said in an interview, "but for me it's hard. Heck, I'm not trying to fail. I'm concentrating every second I'm on the field, on doing my best, on doing the right thing. I want it for myself, for my kids, for my wife, for my teammates, for the fans, and for the good Lord. But how do you convince people of that?"

In 1980, he established new credentials for himself, beginning with three games left in the regular season. The Phillies traveled to Montreal in search of two wins to clinch the division championship. Mike hit a home run to win the first game. In the second game, the pressure reached the boiling point with a three-hour rain delay and a game that went into extra innings.

Against that kind of pressure, Schmidt smashed a 425-foot three-run homer in the eleventh inning to advance his team into the National League Championship Series against the Houston Astros. It was his fourth home run in four games, all of them with his team's season on the line.

In a five-game series which included only one home run, by the Phillies' Greg Luzinski in the first game, and none by the Astros, Rose offset Schmidt's .208 average by hitting an even .400. Then Mike came back to life for the World Series.

His eighth inning double helped to win the first game. He scored the tying run in the fifth game to push the Phillies out in front in the Series, three victories to two, then drove in two runs in the sixth game in front of the Philly fans to win the game, 4-1, and the Series.

It was one of those World Series whose climactic moments remain etched in the memory of the fans who were there or who saw it on television, with relief ace Tug McGraw almost flying off the mound after the last out, his arm piercing the air as fans everywhere remembered his battle cry of that season—*Ya gotta believe!"*

Schmidt's stats showed a .381 batting average, six runs scored, seven runs batted in, eight hits in the six games, a double and two home runs. For that, he was selected as the winner of the Most Valuable Player Award —and a new Corvette.

His momentum from 1980 was stalled by a players' strike early in the '81 season, causing baseball's first "split season." Mike had 14 home runs before the strike and seventeen after, 31 in only 107 games, tops in the league for the fifth time. He achieved the highest batting average of his career, .316, the league's fourth best, while also leading the league in six other departments—total bases, runs scored, RBIs, slugging average, walks and home run percentage.

There were no raised eyebrows when he won the National League's Most Valuable Player Award for the second time.

"THE GREATEST"

After a near-miss in 1982, when the Cardinals beat them out by three games despite Mike's 35 homers, 87 RBIs and .280 average, the Phillies were in the thick of things again in 1983. After acquiring Joe Morgan, the Phillies fielded a lineup that sparkled with three future Hall of Famers in the infield—Schmidt at third base, Morgan at second and Rose at first.

They won their fifth divisional title in eight years, with Schmidt supplying the power with a league-leading 40 home runs—while the fans were voting him the "Greatest Phillies Player Ever."

The Phillies dispatched the Los Angeles Dodgers in four games, with Mike hitting .467 and winning the first game with a homer in the first inning, the only run of the game. His .467 average led all hitters on both teams.

Hopes were high in Philadelphia when the Phils won the first game of the World Series, 2-1, over the Baltimore Orioles on home runs by Morgan and Garry Maddox, but the Orioles stormed back to win the next four straight, the last three in front of the Phillies' home fans. The Philadelphia offense was anemic, a mere .195 team batting average and only nine runs in the four games.

The biggest disappointment was Schmidt himself, with only one hit—a single—in 20 trips to the plate and an average of .050.

It was more bird seed for the boo birds, who were aware that without his MVP Series in 1980, Schmidt's numbers in 25 post-season games added up to one home run, seven RBIs and a .204 average.

Strikeouts continued to plague him, as he fanned 148 times in 1983. He was candid on the subject, once admitting, "There's no reason in the world why a guy should strike out over 100 times a year."

But he did. "I can't seem to control my adrenaline when I get to the plate," he said in frustration. "Instead of just trying to put the ball in play, I'm overswinging, trying to hit it too far."

The Phillies did not recover from their loss to the Orioles in the final years of Mike's career. They finished fourth the next season, 16 games behind the Cubs, and placed higher than fourth only once in Mike's last six years in the game.

SELECT COMPANY

Mike received new recognition for his performance in 1986. Even though his team finished in second place, 21 and a half games behind the New York Mets, he was voted the league's Most Valuable Player for the third time on the basis of his 37 homers, 119 RBIs, .547 slugging average and a strong .290 batting average. His homers won him his eighth and last home run championship.

With his MVP selection, Schmidt joined select company, becoming only the seventh player in history to win the prestigious award three times, along with Stan Musial, Roy Campanella, Jimmie Foxx, Joe DiMaggio, Yogi Berra and Mickey Mantle.

Good things continued to come his way. In 1987, he joined the game's immortals with his 500th home run, after hitting his 499th in Pittsburgh the day before against Bob Patterson. On a hunch, he called his wife, Donna, and suggested she come to Pittsburgh for the game the next day.

It happened on April 18, 1987, when Mike connected against Don Robinson on a 3-0 fast ball with two men on base in the ninth inning to give the Phillies an 8-6 victory. Stepping out of his reserved character, the supposedly unemotional Schmidt jumped with joy at home plate, then pumped his arms into the air in exultation on his way down the first base line. He was mobbed by his teammates at home plate while the crowd of 19,361 fans gave him a standing ovation. When he trotted to third base for the start of the bottom of the ninth, the Pittsburgh crowd gave him its second standing ovation.

After the game, he expressed relief that No. 500 came so quickly after 499. "I was elated that it happened to fast," he said. "It's a big relief to have it out of the way. Now we can get back to baseball and the business at hand."

He also told reporters he wasn't really trying for a home run. "I knew we didn't need a home run to win the game," he said. "I hit the home run as a result of trying to hit a hard line drive. You've got to keep the game in mind."

Mike didn't celebrate with his teammates. Instead, he had dinner with Donna and the team's broadcasters.

That was Schmidt's last big season. He finished with 35 home runs, drove in 113 runs and—here's the good news—reduced his strikeouts to eighty while hitting .293.

An arm injury in 1989 required surgery and kept him out of the lineup for the final third of the season. By the start of the '89 season, things were different for him. The arthritis in his knees was worse, and he was bothered by elbow and back problems. The team had slipped to sixth place in 1988 and lost 96 games. There were a lot of new, young players, and Mike did not feel at ease around them.

After 42 games of the '89 season, Mike was struggling both at bat and at third base. He was burdened with a .203 average and only six home runs, with only two hits in his last 41 times at bat. He had the most errors on the team—eight—and booted a ground ball with two runners on base in a Sunday game in San Francisco. Will Clark, the next hitter, followed with a grand slam home run to beat the Phillies.

As the Phillies prepared to catch their chartered flight down the West Coast to San Diego for their next series, Mike told his teammates he was retiring. The next day, at age 39, he told a crowded news conference at Jack Murphy Stadium, "I left Dayton, Ohio, with two bad knees and a dream of becoming a baseball player. Thank God it came true."

Then he broke down and cried for several minutes. When he regained his composure, he continued: "Over the years of my career, I've set high standards for myself as a player, and I've always said that when I feel I can't perform up to those standards, it would be time to retire. I feel like I could ask the Phillies to keep me on to add to my statistics, but my love for the game won't let me do that. My skills to do the things on the field, to make the adjustments to hit, to make the routine play on defense and to run the bases aggressively have deteriorated. I look for signs and reasons every night to continue as a player, but I just couldn't find them."

In one of the most convincing tributes ever paid to an athlete, the National League fans elected him to the All-Star team even though he had retired six weeks earlier.

Ironically, six months after Schmidt concluded that his skills had deserted him and dictated his retirement, *The Sporting News* chose him as its Player of the Decade for his years of unsurpassed excellence in the 1980s: the most home runs by any big league player (313), three MVP awards, two World Series appearances, six Gold Gloves, eight All-Star teams, eight straight 30-homer seasons and 929 runs batted in, all in those ten years.

After his retirement, Schmidt expressed his desire to become a general manager or to serve in some other executive capacity in baseball. He never received an offer. Today he practices golf diligently, has a scratch handicap and at times has entertained hopes of joining the seniors tour.

As he works on his drives, his irons and his putting game, Schmidt can remember a long litany of special moments: 548 home runs—the seventh most in history—those four home runs in one game in Wrigley Field, another homer in Chicago to win a 23-22 game in the tenth inning, his three Most Valuable Player awards, those ten Gold Gloves for fielding excellence, his World Series MVP award, a triumphant ride down Philadelphia's Broad Street and 100,000 screaming fans at JFK Stadium after winning the 1980 World Series and, finally, his 500th home run.

Schmidt told Philadelphia baseball writer Rich Westcott about his innermost thoughts on that night in San Francisco when he told his teammates he was retiring. "Only a few athletes have ever felt what I felt that night," he told Westcott. "The love that was felt in that room was unbelievable."

Then he said, "I am secure in knowing now that every time I had an injury and played, every time I spoke my piece in front of the team, every time I stayed up until the wee hours of the morning thinking about the game, every time I stood at third base and wondered if all this was actually worth it, I know now it was."

WHAT OTHER PLAYERS SAID ABOUT MIKE SCHMIDT

Dave Winfield—He was another player who had lightning-quick wrists. So many times, the ball would just be on him and he would flick those wrists and the ball would jump. He was a formidable opponent. He and Hank (Aaron) had the quickest wrists I saw.

Steve Garvey—He started slow and slowly got a feel for the game. He learned to hit through the ball and generate back swing. He was a complete player. The Philadelphia fans didn't really give him his due for years. He was more appreciated in visiting ballparks. Maybe early in his career he had trouble responding to the fans and they didn't seem to sense his respect for them. There was some love lost for a long time. At the end of his career, it turned into a honeymoon.

Al Oliver—Mike was such a great athlete and things came so easy to him that he appeared to the fans that he didn't give 100 percent or wasn't hustling. He wasn't flashy, just appeared to be nonchalant, and that didn't go over with the fans. But if you knew him, you knew that wasn't true.

Jay Johnstone—I roomed with him with the Phillies, and he was a real worry wart. He was an incredible third baseman. Everyone considered Brooks Robinson the best, but Mike has such great range, fabulous reflexes and a superior arm to Brooks, and he was playing on astroturf. He was his own worst enemy. He wanted to hit home runs, but he wanted to bat .340 too. Heck, Ted Williams named him as one of the top 20 hitters of all time. He's not the kind of guy to go out and meet the public every day, but one-on-one is best for him. He is a caring guy but just doesn't know how to express himself. He'd give you the shirt off his back, but he kind of kept to himself and just didn't have great relations with the fans.

Ron Santo—I played with Mike at the beginning of his career. You could get him out inside. It looked like he wasn't going to stay in the big leagues. Then, all of a sudden, he made an adjustment and ended up hitting 548 home runs. He just all of a sudden started laying off the bad ball, and if they made a mistake inside, it was gone.

Chuck Tanner—Now there's a player, one of the greatest of all time. In Philadelphia, they would boo the Pope. The fans would get on him, and it would really hurt his feelings because he played so hard. He thought, "How can they do this to me?" When he came up, he would chase that curve ball out of the strike zone. He was so eager to do well.

George Foster—He got off to a slow start, but I think his confidence really began to come when people like Joe Morgan and Pete Rose were asking him if he realized how good a hitter he was.

Ralph Garr—He was a gamer. The guy that really helped Mike over the bump was Dick Allen, and I'm sure Mike would tell you that. He needed a veteran like Dick to take an interest in him.

Tommy John—When he came up, he had a big hole in his swing. He worked hard at plugging that hole. Mike hit mistakes. If you made a mistake, he would kill you. He'd just hammer it.

Ed Kranepool—He was one of those guys who really struggled for a while, but he could hit it as far as anyone in the game once he got going. He had such a great swing you would wonder in the early years, "How did he swing at so many balls and miss them?" Then the next game, he would put one or two in the upper deck. In his last ten years, he was really outstanding.

Roger Craig —One time I was managing, and I intentionally walked him in the first inning . . . . I had a base open, and he was red hot, so I walked him.

Don Zimmer—He was awesome up at the plate, no doubt about it.

Gorman Thomas—He's the reason I wore number 20. When I got sent down to the minors in '77, I would photograph his times at bat on television with my camera . . . . He's just a hell of a guy, and he didn't change once he made the Hall of Fame. As far as the fans getting on him, some players wear their emotions on their sleeve. Some don't. And he didn't.

Al Downing—When he came up, everyone knew he had hit a lot of home runs in Triple-A ball, and he looked like a ball player—like an athlete. He walked with a little bit of a swagger and looked confident, but he struck out a lot. Mike Schmidt had the ability to hit, but his confidence level wasn't there yet. And coming up to Philadelphia didn't help. They aren't very patient over there. But he finally made some adjustments. I remember someone once asked him what made him turn the corner, and he said Dick Allen took time to really talk hitting with him, and those talks turned it around.

Juan Marichal—He was the guy who really hit that ball. And really played that third base, too. He had the power, he had the glove, he had everything.

Whitey Herzog—When you look at all the third basemen in the history of the game and you look for the complete guy—I mean the best defensive third baseman I ever saw was Brooks Robinson, but when you look at the total package, Schmidt was the best all-around third baseman I ever saw, and I managed George Brett, who was a pretty good ballplayer. He (Schmidt) was a superstar among superstars.

Don Money—I was with the Phillies when Mike came up, and he had 18 home runs that year but hit only .196. He was striking out one out of three at-bats, and I told everyone he would never make it if he kept that same stance. He stood open a little bit, pulled away from the ball, and he was subject to the sliders and the curve balls low and away. That's why he struck out so much. But when he hit it, he was strong enough to hit it to any part of the ballpark. Later he backed off the plate, closed his stance and went more into the ball and started to become a great hitter.

Randy Hundley—I didn't think Mike Schmidt was going to make it, period, when I first saw him. You could say, "We're going to throw you a slider," and he would have trouble with it. He would strike out three-four times a game. I just didn't think this guy was going to make it. But he was intelligent to make several adjustments.

Umpire Doug Harvey—I would place Mike Schmidt with the great ones—the great ones! Because he could play third base as good as anybody. And when he had a hot bat, I don't give a damn where you threw it —I mean in his eyes or at his ankles—he's going to hit it out. Actually, he has one more home run than he's given credit for. In the Astrodome one night, they'd had a boxing match the night before and somebody forgot to take the speaker down, and he hit a blast to center field and I didn't even move from second base, because I knew it was going to be out, but it hit the speaker, bounced back on the field, and the ball was in play and he got a double.

Nobody—I mean nobody—matches Mike Schmidt for offense and defense. The fans got on him in Philadelphia, but he stuck it out, and in Philadelphia, that's a tough thing to do. They get on you back there. They don't let up.

Ozzie Smith—Mike has definitely set himself apart from the rest by being a part of that elite group that hit 500 home runs. Playing shortstop against him, I didn't have to worry. If, at any time, he hit the ball to me, it was an accident because he was always trying to hit the ball out of right center field. He stayed on the ball a long time and hit it a long way. He was a great hitter. Anybody who saw the enthusiasm which he displayed when he did hit the 500th . . . anybody who doubted whether or not it meant anything to him . . . I think that's the moment that should stand out more than any.

Dick Williams—He got off to a really bad start when he came up to the big leagues. Once he caught fire, you couldn't get him out and couldn't stop him defensively. He was a great ballplayer. The fans there in Philadelphia would boo their own mother, and they got on Mike, but they are good baseball fans. Once he learned to hit the curve ball and the offspeed pitch, there was no stopping him.

Frank Robinson—he was the kind of guy that shows you you never give up and never judge someone on the first impression and say can't cause Mike Schmidt struggled at first and it looked like he didn't ever belong in the big leagues but he continued to work hard on his defense and he made himself an outstanding third baseman and worked on his hitting until he became an outstanding hitter. He could have quit; it would have been easy for him to quit but he didn't. He's a perfect inspiration for young people in that if there is anything worth having it's worth working for.

Bob Horner—He was really a streak hitter. He would get hot, and when he got hot, he could carry a team on his back as long as his streak would last. He'd get cold and have the opposite problem. But when he was hot—just get out of the way. He'd hit balls up around his neck and down around his ankles. When he was hot, he was as dangerous a hitter as you would want to find.

Eddie Mathews—He was a hell of a hitter. I'm honored to be compared to him.

Ernie Banks—He was one of the few players in the "500 Club" who played in a city where people had high expectations of him and expected him to hit a home run every time up. It was a joke.

Harmon Killebrew—I didn't see that much of him, but what I saw I would have to say I would put him in the same class as Brooks Robinson as a third baseman. And if that's true, my hat's off to him because Brooks is the greatest third baseman I ever saw. His (Schmidt's) record speaks for himself as one of the great power hitters of all time.

Gary Carter—To me he was the ultimate player. Not only was he a great hitter and a great home run hitter, but he was also a great third baseman. With the game on the line, to me he was the best. I will always remember him as the guy I didn't want to have at the plate when the game was on the line. It was a shame the way the fans got on him. He was the type of guy who had a way about him as a player. He was known as "Cool Schmittie," the reason being that was his style of play. Maybe he didn't endear himself that much with the fans, but, I'll tell you what, he was a great player.

Steve Carlton—Schmittie, to me, was a lot like Hank Aaron as a hitter—his wrist ability to flick that bat real quick, a lot of similarities in their two styles. There wasn't anything he couldn't do as a third baseman. As far as the Philadelphia fans, it's something you have to live with just about anywhere on the East Coast. He could have been fourth on the all-time home run list. He could have easily hit 600 if he had gone over to the American League as a DH. He could have probably hit another 100 to 150 home runs. Too bad, because he denied American League fans the pleasure of seeing him hit home runs. That's what he was—a home run hitter.

Joe Garagiola—I thought his description of playing third base was one of the great ones. He said, "You're really a hockey goalie there, with the only difference being you have to make a throw." He was another guy who knew what he had to do and went out and did it.

Pete Rose—For most of his career, he was pretty much misunderstood in Philadelphia. The fans misunderstood him, and he misunderstood them. But it ended up a pretty good love affair with him and the town. I don't think Mike knew how to handle the press in his early years, but both the press and the fans grew to realize what a great player he was. He had a hard time expressing himself.

THE SCHMIDT FILE

Full Name: Michael Jack Schmidt.
Date and Place of Birth: September 27, 1949, Dayton Ohio.
Position: Third Base, First Base, Second Base, Shortstop.
Major League Career: 18 years, 1972-1989.
Home Runs: 548 (7th).
Runs Batted In: 1,595.
Runs Scored: 1,506.
Lifetime Batting Average: .267.
Number of Hits: 2,234.
Walks: 1,507.
Strikeouts: 1,883 (3rd).
Records: When he retired in 1989, Schmidt held or shared fourteen Major League records and eighteen National League marks. He had the seventh most home runs of all time and the third most in National League history behind only Hank Aaron and Willie Mays. He led the National League in home runs a record eight times. In the field, he won ten Gold Gloves as the League's best third baseman. Schmidt also set League records for the most chances, assists and double plays at his position.

Other Highlights:
— National League's Most Valuable Player for 1980, 1981 and 1986, tieing Stan Musial and Roy Campanella as the only National Leaguers with three MVP awards.
— *The Sporting News* Player of the Decade for the 1980s.
— Voted by the fans the "Greatest Phillies Player Ever."
— Voted to All-Star team 12 times.
— Played in two World Series and five National League Championship Series.
— World Series Most Valuable Player, 1980.
— Uniform Number 20 retired by the Phillies in 1990.

Elected to the Baseball Hall of Fame: 1995.

15

TED WILLIAMS

The Greatest Hitter Ever?

When he was beginning his professional baseball career, Ted Williams used to say his ambition was to walk down the street after his playing days were over and have people point toward him and say, "There goes the greatest hitter who ever lived."

They do, including even Joe DiMaggio. "He was the greatest hitter ever," DiMag told reporter Steve Kornacki, "and I have a lot of respect for him."

To the many writers and fans who said Williams achieved his immortality because he was a natural hitter, Ted has a surprising answer: "There's no such thing as a natural hitter. I've heard people say Joe Jackson was one. Maybe so, but I find it hard to believe. I became a good hitter through hard work and practice. You can't get too much of that."

BASEBALL PLAYER OR FIRE FIGHTER?

Ted's high school coach in San Diego, Wes Caldwell, liked to say he always heard Ted from two blocks away before he saw him. People who knew him in his growing-up years at Herbert Hoover High School described him as loud, impulsive and free-spirited. They also said he could hit a baseball better than anybody in town.

From the start, Williams had to make his own way. His father, Samuel Williams, worked long hours in a photo lab and was nowhere to be found when he wasn't working. His mother, May, was a captain in the Salvation Army and was known around San Diego as "Salvation May." Ted and his brother, Danny, were on their own most of the time.

For Ted, all that time alone meant the ball field and the chance to play baseball 365 mornings, noons and nights a year thanks to San Diego's warm, sun-kissed weather. When he graduated from high school, his yearbook described his activities with one word next to his picture: "Baseball."

His baseball wasn't confined to playing for Hoover. He also played semi-pro ball for two dollars a game. Much to his mother's dismay, his team was sponsored by a liquor store.

Williams began his career as a pitcher with his hometown team, the Padres, in the Pacific Coast League after he and his mother failed to convince a New York Yankees scout he was worth a bonus of $1,000. The league was a fast one, at the Triple A level, only one notch below the Major Leagues. Williams was earning $150 a month.

His dream immediately became a nightmare. In his first game, he allowed two runs, two hits and a walk in only an inning and a third. When Manager Frank Shellenback came out to the mound, Williams told him, "I think you've got me playing the wrong position." Shellenback agreed and made him a lefthanded-hitting outfielder. Then Eddie Collins and Bobby Doerr entered his life.

Collins, a .333 hitter over one of baseball's longest playing careers, 25 years, had spotted Williams while scouting Doerr for the Boston Red Sox. He sent glowing reports on the skinny kid, but the Red Sox were unenthusiastic because he was a lefthanded hitter, the wrong side of the plate for Fenway Park, a ballpark better suited for righthanded hitters. Collins persisted long enough that his bosses in Boston eventually caved in and invited Williams to their 1938 spring training camp. They asked Doerr to accompany him.

On the train to Sarasota, Florida, in those days before plane travel became so popular, Doerr described the Red Sox slugging star, Jimmie Foxx, another 500-homer hitter. Doerr told Williams with excitement, "Wait till you see Foxx hit."

The confident kid responded, "Wait till Foxx sees *me* hit."

Doerr continued, "Then when we got to Sarasota, I remember taking Ted in to meet Joe Cronin, the manager. And I said, 'Ted, this is Joe Cronin,' and Ted says, 'Hi, Sport.' I don't think that went over too well with Cronin."

In spring training, Doerr remembers, "Ted was high-strung and full of pepper and vinegar. He was hitting some balls pretty good and popping off. He was a handful. All he did was hang around the batting cage. He didn't have much interest in working on his outfield play. That irritated the veterans."

Boston's starting outfielders—veterans Ben Chapman, Joe Vosmick and Doc Cramer resented the young pop-off and made their displeasure known. When the decision was made to farm Williams out to Minneapolis, they were delighted to see him go. They hollered, "Goodbye, busher," or words to that effect. He heard them and paused long enough to predict to clubhouse manager Johnny Orlando that one day he'd make more money than all three of them combined.

At Minneapolis, Manager Donie Bush found Williams to be a problem. The last straw came when Bush spotted him sitting down in the outfield during batting practice, legs crossed, while others shagged fly balls. Bush called the Red Sox and demanded that they send Williams somewhere else. The Sox responded by pointing out that Williams was hitting .350, and if anyone left, it would be Bush.

The manager suffered through the rest of the season, which Williams finished with a .366 average, including 43 home runs and 142 runs batted in, numbers strong enough to make many managers put up with a budding young star, especially one who can hit like that.

In Boston, the Red Sox had languished in the second division in 17 of the previous 19 seasons, so when Williams arrived at the start of the 1939 spring training season, his powerful, run-producing bat was welcomed warmly.

Williams hit .327 with 31 home runs and led the American League with 145 runs batted in, topping the likes of Foxx, DiMaggio and Hank Greenberg. His average was the second highest on the Red Sox behind only Foxx's .360 as the rookie helped to lead his new team to the dizzying heights of second place, behind only the all-powerful Yankees of DiMaggio, Joe Gordon, Red Rolfe, Tommy Henrich, Bill Dickey, Red Ruffing and Lefty Gomez, who won their fourth straight American League pennant.

During a trip to New York that season, Williams received some prophetic advice from Cronin. "Ted," his manager told him, "you're a great ballplayer and you're with a great team, but you'll never be as famous playing with Boston as you would be if you were here in New York. Just remember that and you'll understand a lot of things."

Later in his career, Williams said, "He was right."

The Boston fans loved Ted and their team's new success. Doerr remembers that Williams was a big Fenway favorite as a rookie. "He played right field," Doerr says. "The fans were crazy about him. He would tip his hat and wave to them. The next year, they moved him to left field because there wasn't as much area to cover and you didn't need the arm you did in right field."

Doerr says the transfer to left field was the start of Williams's troubles with the fans. "A few loudmouths really got on him, and he took about so much. He came in one day after the game, and the sportswriters were all gathered around him, and he said something like, 'Those smart so-and-sos out in left field. I'll never tip my hat to them again.' And he never did."

It didn't help that Williams had a unique sense of hearing. He admitted, "I believe I have the best pair of 'rabbit ears' ever developed in Major League baseball. There might be 30,000 people in the stands, some of them cheering and some of them talking to their neighbors, but if there are a half-dozen people giving me the old razoo, I can spot them in a matter of seconds. I know who they are before a half-inning is over."

His long, loping stride in the outfield, from his 6-3 frame and his skinny build, fooled the fans into thinking he was loafing on balls hit into his area. "The writers," Doerr says, "made a big deal about it, and it just got worse."

The writers became as much of a problem in Ted's life as the fans in left field did. Ted's friend to this day, the man who played center field next to him, Dom DiMaggio, told about his memories of the Boston writers in his book about the 1941 season, *Real Grass, Real Heroes*. DiMaggio, brother of both the Yankees' center fielder, Joe, and the Pirates' center fielder, Vince, said, "A big part of the problem in Boston was simply that we had so many newspapers ... ten newspapers with 40 members of the Baseball Writers' Association, and that doesn't even count the radio broadcasters. We had reporters falling all over themselves, and the competition among them for stories often led to the kinds of problems that Ted and others encountered."

Williams said, "I don't give a damn about the writers ...They knew where they stood with me right from the start. I'm certainly not going to play politics and soft-soap them so they'll write nice things about me."

He added, "Most of the trouble doesn't come from the guys who cover the team and have to come into the clubhouse every day to look me in the eye. It comes from columnists like Dave Egan and Austen Lake, who don't come in here twice a year."

Early in the 1940 season, in typical Williams fashion, he livened things up even more with some surprising comments to a reporter after a game when he struck out, then made an error in the next inning. The fans in left field let him have it, and Williams lashed back.

After the game, he talked of being traded because Boston "wasn't one of the cities I had wanted to play for in the first place." Then he dropped a bomb shell by telling Harry Grayson, sports editor of the NEA Service, that he was thinking of quitting baseball. Starting only his second year in the big leagues, already one of the biggest stars in either league and obviously destined for greatness, he said, according to Grayson, "he would like to quit baseball and be a fireman."

Grayson quoted the young star as saying, "I'd quit tomorrow if I knew where I could get another job." Grayson wrote, "Williams tells teammates he'd take the examination as a fire fighter at once if assured he wouldn't have to wait too long for an opening."

Grayson put the comments in the proper context by writing, "Williams's talk is ridiculous, of course, but officials of the Boston club are alarmed at their prize's present attitude."

Williams had other problems that year as well. The Red Sox moved in the right field wall, hoping he might one day break Babe Ruth's record of 60 home runs in one season, but his home run and runs batted in totals dropped to 23 and 113.

Some writers hinted that maybe Williams wasn't giving 100 percent. One of them wrote that he was a grown man with the mind of a juvenile. Another called him the all-time heel ever to wear a Boston uniform. Others charged that he wasn't a team player. Williams, understandably, reacted with scorn.

Williams continued to amaze players, fans, reporters and broadcasters. He raised his rookie average seventeen points to .344, third in the league behind Joe DiMaggio and Luke Appling, led the league in runs scored, finished third in total bases and slugging average and was fourth in doubles and triples. The Red Sox proved that their second place finish of 1939 was no fluke. They finished among the American League's elite again in the first division, this time in fourth place but only eight games behind the champion Detroit Tigers.

Then Williams accomplished something that no one in baseball has done for the past 58 years.

1941

Every baseball fan above the age of reason knows that Williams—by then called "The Splendid Splinter" or "The Thumper" or "Teddy Ballgame" or "The Kid"—broke the .400 barrier in 1941, hitting .406, the first Major Leaguer to top .400 since the Giants' Bill Terry's .401 in 1930.

There was more than that to the 1941 season. Historians have called it baseball's greatest season, a claim that might survive the challenges of the drama-filled 1998 campaign. The 1941 season has credentials of its own as baseball's most historic season:

— Williams hit .406, a feat unmatched since.
— Joe DiMaggio hit in 56 straight games, something else that hasn't been equalled since.
— Williams hit the most dramatic home run in the history of the All-Star game.
— Lou Gehrig died at 37, only two years after ending his streak of playing in 2,130 games, an achievement that lasted 56 years.
— In the most famous "strikeout" in baseball history, Tommy Henrich reached first base in the World Series when Hugh Casey's 3-2 pitch with two outs in the ninth inning eluded Catcher Mickey Owen and enabled the Yankees to win the game that day and the Series the next.
— The war in Europe threatened to erupt into World War II, causing fears that baseball may be discontinued because of a possible manpower shortage.
— The Brooklyn Dodgers, Washington Senators and others were beginning to play some of their games at night—night baseball—after Larry MacPhail pioneered the practice in Cincinnati in 1935.

That event-filled season began for Williams with, of all things, an injury. He chipped an ankle bone while sliding into second base in spring training and spent the first two weeks of the season recovering and seeing only limited duty. His absence cost him an unknown number of additional hits, but it also spared him the threat of getting off to a slow start playing full-time in Boston's cold and wet spring weather. He used the time to sharpen his skills by having a curve baller, Joe Dobson, pitch batting practice to him every day, valuable practice that might have contributed to his .406 average.

When he returned to the lineup on a full-time basis, he was a slugging terror. By June 6, he was batting .436, and the exciting prospect of hitting .400 wasn't his only thrill that year. On July 8 in Detroit, he hit his historic home run with Joe DiMaggio and Joe Gordon on base with two out in the bottom of the ninth and the American League trailing, 5-4.

The Chicago Cubs' respected righthander, Claude Passeau, was the victim, on a waist-high fastball. Ted's hit was not only historic in its drama but also in its dimensions. It soared to the third level of Briggs Stadium—now Tiger Stadium—and struck the facade, a three-run shot that won the game, 7-5.

After the game, Williams told reporters, "I just shut my eyes and swung. I had a feeling that if I got up there in the ninth, I'd go for the downs. Boy, I feel great! There's nothing like hitting a home run!"

In later years, Williams said, "I was so happy, so charged up, that I grabbed Joe's hand really far too hard. That was my greatest thrill."

Enos Slaughter of the St. Louis Cardinals, playing right field for the National League in his first All-Star game, remembers the homer as well as Williams does. From his home in North Carolina, he said, "The ball bounced back on the field. I picked it up and stuck it in my pocket and kept it for 44 years."

When he was inducted into the Hall of Fame in 1985, Slaughter gave the ball to Ted. Williams had Slaughter autograph it, and today the ball is in Cooperstown, with Slaughter and Williams.

Williams was hitting .397 just after the All-Star break when another injury threatened his season, on a walk. As he was trotting down to first base in Detroit after a light rain, his spikes caught in the soft dirt and he injured the same ankle again. This time, he was out for ten days except for four tips as a pinch hitter. His average dropped to .393, hardly grounds for concern—unless you're trying to hit .400.

THE LAST DAY

Williams rallied and was hitting .3995 on the morning of the last day of the season, when the Sox were to play a doubleheader against the A's in Philadelphia. One writer described him by saying, "The swing was long and perfect, the stance tall and upright, and the wrists were oiled like the workings of a fine watch."

Cronin asked him if he wanted the day off, which would have guaranteed him an even .400 for the season when his average was rounded off, or did he want to finish the season in the lineup?

In his best John Wayne determination, he snapped, "You're damned right I want to finish."

Williams was swinging one of the lighter bats in the league as a result of his emphasis on "bat speed," which he discovered when he accidentally used teammate Stan Spence's bat and liked the lighter feel. Ted was one of the first preachers of that gospel, and Bobby Doerr could testify that Williams knew what he was talking about.

Bobby remembers that Williams was one of the first sluggers to use a lighter bat and the first to order a set of postal scales for the clubhouse so he could weigh his bats precisely.

"We used to think that with a heavier bat you had a better chance of getting a base hit out of it," Doerr says, "but Ted's theory was that with a light bat, you had better bat speed and better control."

Tommy Henrich, one of three stars in the Yankees outfield in 1941 with Joe DiMaggio and Charlie Keller, makes a telling point about the way Williams was hitting in 1941. In his book, *Five O'Clock Lightning*, Henrich says, "I have one vivid memory of playing against Ted in 1941: I don't think he ever hit a fly ball to me. He hit plenty of shots at me all right, because he was a lefthanded pull hitter and I was the right fielder, but the only fly balls in my general direction were over my head and into the seats."

Tommy continued, "Everything was hit hard: line drives that landed in front of me for singles, drives up the alley in right center between DiMaggio and me for doubles, and ground balls that scorched the earth on their way between Gordon and Johnny Sturm for more singles."

Henrich joked, "Between DiMaggio's rocket shots and Ted's, 1941 was no year to be a baseball."

Williams heard from two unexpected sources as he stepped into the batter's box for the first time on that last afternoon of the season—the umpire and the catcher. Umpire Bill McGowan, one of the greatest of all time, dusted off home plate, saying to Williams without looking up from his whisk broom, "To hit .400 a batter has got to be loose. He has got to be *loose*."

Philadelphia's catcher, Frankie Hayes, looked up at Williams through his mask and said, "Mr. Mack told us if we let up on you, he'll run us out of baseball. I wish you all the luck in the world, but we're not going to give you a damn thing."

Williams singled sharply to right off righthander Dick Fowler on his first time up on, then hit a home run off Fowler. Against a lefthander, Porter Vaughn, on his third trip, Williams singled up the middle. He singled over first against Vaughn on his next trip, then reached first on an infield error—four for five. Refusing another offer from Cronin to sit out the second game, Williams added a single and a double—six for eight and a final season's average of .406, the first of his six American League batting championships.

The Red Sox were becoming a team to be reckoned with every season. After finishing second in 1939 and fourth in 1940, they finished second again in '41, but a distant 17 games behind the Yankees, who were propelled to the pennant on the wings of DiMaggio's 56-game hitting streak.

Williams also won the first of four home run titles that year, with 37. His roommate on a road trip that season, Pitcher "Broadway Charlie" Wagner, saw Williams strive for power firsthand.

In St. Louis, the Red Sox were staying at the Chase Hotel when Ted was swinging a bat in front of a mirror between his and Wagner's twin beds. He accidentally hit the bedpost on Wagner's bed and broke it, sending Broadway tumbling to the floor.

Charlie said Ted's only reaction was to say, "Call down and see if you can get another bed." Wagner said it didn't occur to Williams to apologize because with Ted, the swing was the only thing he was interested in.

Instead of apologizing, Ted just said, "Man! What power!"

THE DURATION: "WHAT IF?"

Williams followed his history-making season with one in 1942 which some historians argue may have been even better. He won the Triple Crown—leading the league in batting average, home runs and runs batted in—joining Ty Cobb, Jimmie Foxx and Lou Gehrig as the only American Leaguers to achieve that feat to that time. He hit .356 with 36 home runs and 137 RBIs. To add to his accomplishment, he led the league in slugging percentage, runs scored, walks and home run percentage—hitting a homer every 14.4 times at bat.

But controversy still managed to stalk Williams. Some were starting to question his patriotism during that first full year of America's involvement in World War II. He was granted a deferment for the 1942 season as the sole support of his mother, but he silenced his critics by enlisting in the armed forces at the end of the season. Like everyone else, he faced the prospect of being gone for "the duration and six," the duration of the war and up to six months after.

Williams could have spent the war playing baseball for the Marines, which many players did as their assignment, with the generals and admirals feeling that seeing their prewar baseball heroes would improve the morale of the GIs. Williams, however, signed up for pilot training and became a fighter pilot in the Marine Corps.

He was gone for three full seasons, rejoining his team along with the other 500 returning prewar Major Leaguers for the start of the 1946 season. Since then, the question has been asked: What if there hadn't been a World War II? What more would Williams, DiMaggio, Bob Feller and others have accomplished in their baseball careers?

A computer expert in Seattle, Ralph Winnie, has the answers, based on projections he developed by feeding the figures for the prewar players into his computer. Using their last three years before the war and the first three seasons after their return, Winnie developed a report called, "What If?"

It showed that Williams, also allowing for almost two full seasons back in the Marines during the Korean War, would have become the all-time runs batted in champion without his two terms in military service and would have hit 222 more home runs. That would give him 743, ranking him right behind Hank Aaron's 755. Instead, he hit 521 and ranks tenth.

Williams shrugs off such speculation. In talking about his absence during World War II, he told us, "The three years that I lost—hell, there were nine billion guys who contributed a lot more than I did."

THE WORLD SERIES

On his return, it was as if Williams had never left and had been swinging a Louisville Slugger all along. This time, instead of leading the Red Sox to simply another respectable finish, he led them all the way to the American League pennant. They topped Detroit by 12 games and their prewar rivals, the Yankees, by 17.

Ted immediately returned to the top of the American League himself, leading the league in slugging average, runs and walks while finishing second behind Mickey Vernon with a .342 batting average. He drew 156 walks, the second season in a stretch when he led the league in that department six straight years and eight times in all. Twice he walked 162 times. He ranks second in walks, only 37 behind Babe Ruth, creating speculation on what his totals might have been had pitchers not walked him 2,019 times.

"I kept applying myself," Williams said after his career ended, "kept improving myself, and pretty soon I became a good hitter. There is no secret to hitting. It takes work—damn hard work."

One of the highlights of his season—and of his career—came in the All-Star game, played in Fenway Park, when Ted rapped out two home runs, scored four times and drove in five runs with a perfect 4-for-4 day. But the achievement that left everyone talking came when he did what had been considered the impossible—he hit a home run off Rip Sewell's "blooper ball."

The pitch was a change-up that floated up to the plate at a peak height of 25 feet and then finished its flight in a downward arch like a softball at the company picnic. Williams took a couple of steps toward Sewell and timed his swing precisely. The ball landed in the right field bullpen. Hitting a pitch that had no power of its own, Williams generated enough power by himself to send the ball 400 feet.

"I figured he would toss me one of those high, arching pitches just to kid me and give the crowd a laugh,"Williams said. "I took sort of a hop, skip and jump forward as he let the ball go and practically ran out of the batter's box. I put all my weight behind it and it went into the right field stands. I laughed my way around the bases, and I think Sewell was as surprised as I was."

As his career continued to unfold with his spectacular hitting achievements, Manager Lou Boudreau of the Indians devised a new strategy that year to stop him—"the Williams shift." In the second game of a doubleheader, after watching Williams drive in eight runs so far for the day, Boudreau saw his opportunity with the bases empty. He moved his whole defense to the right side of second base except for his left fielder.

Boudreau explained,"I can't stop this guy from hitting home runs, but practically all his base hits are to the right of the diamond. I can sure cut into his doubles and singles."

Hall of Fame hitter Al Simmons immediately predicted,"Well, that's the end of Williams—he can't hit to left field." Williams hit 11 home runs and batted over .400 against the Indians that year. He admits, however, "There is no doubt that the shift hurt me later on."

Something less positive happened later that year. The Red Sox first baseman, Rudy York, confronted Williams in the clubhouse in front of their teammates and accused him of loafing on a ball hit to him in left field. He told Williams the team had a chance to win the pennant if every member played hard.

One of the ways Ted played hard was by hitting a special kind of home run to win the last game and the pennant for the Sox. Against Cleveland's Red Embree, he hit a fly ball to deep left field over the head of Pat Seerey, the first inside-the-park home run of Ted's career. It was the only run of the game, the only one Tex Hughson needed to bring the Sox their first pennant since 1918.

Exploits like that enabled Ted to win the first of his two Most Valuable Player Awards.

The Red Sox lost to the Cardinals in the World Series in seven games when Harry Brecheen won three games and Enos Slaughter scored all the way from first base on a double by Harry Walker. The Series matched Williams against Stan Musial, who won the second of his seven batting championships that year with a .365 average.

Neither future Hall of Famer starred at the plate in the Series. Williams hit an even .200 with five singles in 25 trips, two runs scored and one batted in. Musial managed only a .222 average. Neither hit a home run.

However, Joe Garagiola, a 20-year-old rookie catcher with the Cardinals that year, remembers something that history has forgotten. "Terry Moore made two great catches off him," Garagiola said,"and Harry Walker one. He hit the ball hard each time. He really did."

If those three shots had dropped in for hits, Williams would have had eight hits in those 25 times at bat instead of five, and rather than a .200 batting average, he would have hit .320.

For Williams, the disappointment hurt. He had seen his first World Series game in 1939 and, watching the Yankees and the Cincinnati Reds, became convinced that he could hit in World Series competition, even though he considers hitting in the Series harder to do than during the season.

"It is usually played in cooler weather, for one thing," he said later. "You play half the games in a strange park and usually against pitchers you never saw before."

In later years, Williams said the '46 Series "ended in a frustration that grew, like the importance of the .400 season, to a terrible dimension as the years passed. Who was to know at that time I would not get another chance? The first World Series Ty Cobb played in, he batted .220 (actually .200), but he got two more chances. The first World Series Stan Musial played in, he batted .222, but he got three more chances. That was it for me."

Two other factors contributed to the poor performance by Williams. In a practice game before the Series, he was hit on the tip of the elbow by a pitch from lefthander Mickey Haefner of the Senators. "It went up like a balloon," Williams said. "It turned blue. The World Series was to begin three days later, but I didn't get any batting practice for two days."

As the train carrying the Red Sox rolled from Boston to St. Louis to start the Series, Williams's harshest antagonist in the Boston press corps, Colonel Dave Egan, broke a story claiming the Red Sox were about to trade him to Detroit for star pitcher Hal Newhouser. "There was never any foundation to the story whatsoever," Williams said, "but there it was in the papers, and how do you think that made me feel?"

On the trip home from St. Louis after his disappointing showing, "I went into my little compartment on the train and didn't come out until about 10:30. When I got in there and closed the door, I just broke down and started crying."

Then, Williams said, "I looked up, and there was a whole crowd of people watching me through the window."

Just as he had done in 1942, following his .406 season with another dazzling year, Williams followed his 1946 return to stardom with another starring season in '47, winning his second Triple Crown with a .343 average, 32 home runs and 114 RBIs.

Only one other player in either league, Rogers Hornsby of the Cardinals, had won the Triple Crown twice. Williams now stood unchallenged as the most feared hitter in all of baseball, yet the baseball writers voted to give the Most Valuable Player Award to the more popular DiMaggio. The margin was one vote.

The Sox dropped to third place that year, and Manager Joe Cronin was replaced by, of all people, the manager of the rival Yankees, Joe McCarthy. The winner of eight pennants and five second place finishes in sixteen years as the Yankees' skipper, McCarthy was known as a disciplinarian, a member of the old school way of doing things.

Speculation was rampant all over Boston and throughout baseball about how the disciplinarian and the temperamental, fiery star would get along. McCarthy put that question to rest in his first days on the job, when a reporter asked him about Williams and his go-it-alone attitude, most obvious in his stubborn refusal to wear neckties in those days when players always dressed in coat and tie for their public appearances and on their train and plane trips.

Except Williams. A sport shirt open at the collar was his style, and his trademark. When McCarthy showed up at Spring Training in an open-necked sport shirt himself, he told a reporter, "Any manager who can't get along with a .400 hitter is out of his mind."

That was good enough for Williams. In 1948, his first year under McCarthy, he proved that the two would get along just fine. He won the American League's batting championship for the fourth time by hitting .369, his highest average since his .406 seven seasons earlier, and hit 25 home runs. He led the league in slugging average, doubles and walks.

After the traditional holiday doubleheaders on Labor Day, the Red Sox led the American League by four and a half games over the Cleveland Indians, but the Indians overtook the Sox and were leading the league by one game on the last morning of the season. Detroit's Hal Newhouser shut out the Indians, and Williams took care of the rest. He cracked two doubles to lead Boston to the first playoff game in the history of the league, on the momentum of a three-game winning streak during which Ted had six hits in his last eight trips to the plate.

A flip of a coin determined that the game would be played in Boston. Cleveland won behind Boudreau's leadership—two home runs and two singles, scoring three runs and driving in three. Williams had a single in four at-bats.

The Sox experienced another bitter disappointment in 1949. They swept a three-game series from the Yankees, stretched their winning streak to nine in a row and sat atop the American League standings with a one-game lead over New York as the season entered its last week. For the second straight year, fate frowned on the Sox. The Yankees won the last two games of the season, and Boston again came up short.

For Williams, the year, and its finish, were remarkable. He homered in each of the last four games in Boston's winning streak and lost the batting title by the slimmest of margins to Detroit's George Kell. Both hit .343, but Kell won when the average was carried out to four places after the decimal point instead of the conventional three.

Williams had plenty of other achievements to take pride in despite losing the batting championship to Kell. He put together the greatest slugging season of his career by leading the league with 43 home runs, 159 runs batted in, 150 runs scored and 368 total bases. All four numbers remained his career high-water marks. He also led the league with 39 doubles and proved himself to be an iron man. He played in 155 games in those years of the 154-game schedule. All of this produced Ted's second Most Valuable Player Award.

HOT WATER AGAIN, THEN A FANS' SALUTE

With the 1950 season only 59 games old, Joe McCarthy resigned as manager of the Red Sox at the age of 63 after 24 years as a big league manager, replaced by jovial Steve O'Neill, but that wasn't Ted's biggest development that year. He broke his elbow in the All-Star game at Comiskey Park in Chicago while making a spectacular catch of a ball hit by Ralph Kiner.

The injury came, as injuries often do, at the worst possible time for the team and himself. Williams already had 97 runs batted in and 28 home runs in only 89 games. He was out for the season, after doctors removed seven bone chips from the elbow. He has said he was never the same hitter again.

"The balls never really flew off the bat they way they had before," he said. "The next year, there was enough weakness in the elbow for me to know that I wouldn't be hitting with authority for a long time."

He was right. After hitting 31 or more homers six times in his first eight years, Williams hit 30 or more only twice in the remaining ten years of his career.

The Sox finished in third place in 1950, only four games behind the pennant-winning Yankees and one game behind Detroit. Without his injury and those losses at the end of the '48 and '49 seasons, the Sox would have been described as a dynasty with a string of four pennants in five years.

If his elbow was better for the 1951 season, his unsteady relationship with the fans in left field was not. He got into hot water with them again, this time in a doubleheader against the Tigers—in both games. After dropping an easy fly ball in the first game, his constituents in left field let him have it with boos. Williams responded by putting his hands to his ears and wiggling them like a donkey's. The boos subsided later in the game when he hit a grand slam home run.

In the second game, with the Red Sox winning, 3-1, in the eighth inning and the bases loaded for Detroit, Williams charged a base hit by Vic Wertz, trying to scoop it up and hold the tying run at third base. But the ball got by him and rolled to the wall, the "Green Monster." Williams only jogged back to retrieve the ball. All three runs scored.

This time, the bleacherites knew they had justification for their boos and rained their displeasure down on Williams. As he trotted to the dugout at the end of the inning, Ted made an obscene gesture. In his defiance, he did it three times.

Fenway Park was jammed the next day, with fans primed to unload on Williams again, but he foiled their intentions by issuing an apology before the game. The uneasy truce continued for the balance of the '51 season, as Williams led his team again with 30 home runs and 126 RBIs while topping the league with 295 total bases and 144 walks. The Sox finished third as the Yankees won their third straight pennant under Casey Stengel.

By now Williams had driven in 1,261 runs in nine and a half seasons, an average of 133 RBIs a year, but that wasn't good enough for some fans and writers. They charged that Williams didn't drive in the important runs, the ones that win games. Williams, as always, knew what they were saying.

He told two New York writers, Joe Reichler and Joe Trimble, "It gripes me when some writers say that I don't win important games, that I don't hit in the clutch. That's a lot of rot. Any guy who drives in over 100 runs, scores over 100 runs and hits over .300 year after year must win more than his share of games, I don't care who he is."

The Sox were ready for another challenge against the Yankees when Williams jumped off to a torrid start for the 1952 season, with a .400 batting average in his first six games. But everything was different in America. We were at war again, this time in Korea, and Williams, an officer in the Marine Corps reserve, was recalled and assigned to combat duty.

Ted was 33 years old and had already served those three years in World War II. There was widespread resentment across the country, with many Americans charging that the Selective Service was trying to prove it wasn't afraid to recall celebrities and was using Williams as a case in point.

This was one time when the fans were on his side. The Sox staged a day for Ted before he left and gave him a new Cadillac. But better than that, he received a good luck message from the fans, signed by 500,000 of them. The Fenway Park crowd serenaded him with "Auld Lang Syne". Then the departing Marine pilot threw a party at the Kenmore Hotel for his favorite people including bellhops, cab drivers, bat boys and police officers.

"I was singled out for sympathy because I was called up twice," he said. "In my heart, I was bitter about it, but I made up my mind I wasn't going to bellyache."

Williams remembered, "The day I left to go to Korea as a jet pilot, one hometown paper took note of my departure with these words: *goodbye, and good riddance.*"

As part of the United Nations force in Korea, Williams was assigned to the same fighter squadron as future astronaut John Glenn and flew 39 combat missions before being grounded because of an ear problem. One of those flights almost cost him his life. His plane was hit by small arms fire. Approaching his landing field with his engine on fire, his instruments not working and his wheels stuck in their wells, he "bellied in" at 200 miles an hour and slid 5,000 feet before screeching to a halt. As flames and smoke engulfed his war plane, Williams jumped out, lucky to be alive.

FENWAY'S FAVORITE

Just as he did in 1946, Williams returned to the baseball wars with gusto midway through the 1953 season, after considering his baseball future extensively. Joe DiMaggio retired after the 1951 season, and it weighed heavily on Williams. The Yankee Clipper had been a great athlete and retired because he didn't want to embarrass himself as he grew older.

Williams didn't want to, either, but, as he neared his 35th birthday a month later, he decided to work relentlessly, get himself into top baseball condition and resume his professional career. He rejoined the Red Sox on July 29, two days after representatives of the U.N. and North Korea signed a truce agreement ending the shooting in Korea.

Ten days later, Ted made his first appearance at the plate and popped up. The old Williams flair for the dramatic returned the next day, when he hit a home run off Cleveland's Mike Garcia as a pinch hitter. Playing regularly for the last month of the season, he astonished fans, writers, players and everyone else. He hit .407 in 37 games, with 13 home runs and 34 runs batted in. His highest slugging average had been .735, but for that month it was .901.

With his career starting for the third time, his history of injuries and illnesses returned, too. On the first day of spring training in 1954, he dived for a ball hit by Detroit's Hoot Evers and broke his collarbone. Later he came down with pneumonia. Playing in only 117 games, he hit .345 and led the league with 136 bases on balls and a .635 slugging average as Cleveland set an American League record with 111 wins that lasted for 44 years, until the Yankees broke it in 1998.

Back problems bothered him in 1955, limiting him to 98 games, but still he hit 28 home runs and led the league with 17 intentional walks. In '56 a bad foot kept him out of the lineup, this time for a month, but he still hit a healthy .345 with 24 home runs. He continued to produce his own excitement in All-Star games too, launching a towering homer against the National League that soared to the bullpen in right center field in Washington's Griffith Stadium.

In 1957 a chest cold sidelined him for three weeks, but that didn't keep him from achieving what may have been his greatest all-around season in a year when he turned thirty-nine in August.

He caused heads to shake all around baseball by hitting .388 at that advanced age, was walked intentionally 33 times, hit 38 home runs and drove in 87 runs. His average led the league and was the highest for a full season since his own .406 in 1941. One statistician figured out that if Williams, running on his 39-year-old legs, could have legged out five more hits, he would have had his second .400 season. Over the second half, he hit .453. Twice he hit three home runs in one game.

First baseman Mickey Vernon, a two-time batting champion himself, had some fun with Williams that year, kidding him that "the only reason you're hitting so well is you want to break my record of being the oldest player to lead the league." When Vernon won the American League batting title in 1953 for the second time, he was 35 years old.

"That's the farthest thing from my mind," Williams shot back. "My only thought is *always* to lead the league."

Something else was happening that year in Boston. The fans were solidly in Ted's corner. He was becoming a Fenway favorite, except for the two times when his old temper flared and he spat at the fans and the writers. He was fined on both occasions.

Nor did his new popularity prevent him from getting into controversy with his remarks to reporters. This time he popped off when Pitcher Johnny Podres of the Brooklyn Dodgers was called by his draft board. Williams, who criticized "gutless politicians" more than once in his career, teed off on the Marines and Senator Robert Taft of Ohio, a candidate for the Republican nomination for president only five years earlier. He later apologized—to the Marines.

After his incredible performance in 1957, his popularity was solidified in the voting for the Most Valuable Player Award, but not in the way you would expect. Twenty-four writers were eligible to vote. One of them placed Ted ninth on his ballot, and another voted him tenth—last place.

The fans knew the explanation: Those writers didn't like Williams and voted him far down on their ballots to deprive him of the MVP award. It worked. The award went to Mickey Mantle.

But Williams was winning something far more significant, according to his friend, Richard Cardinal Cushing, the Archbishop of Boston. "He is fighting and winning the greatest battle of them all—the fight against himself," Cardinal Cushing said. "He has had battles all the way. I've seen him grow. I think he's winning this battle."

To prove he was no fluke in becoming the oldest man to win a batting championship, Williams did it again the next year, 1958, with a .328 average and 26 more home runs. He was 40 years old.

A subpar season in 1959 caused in part by a neck injury suffered while fishing during the off-season left him with an average below .300 for the first time in his career, .254, and only ten homers and 43 RBIs. In typical Williams candor, he voluntarily took a pay cut of $35,000 down to $90,000.

He faced the inevitability of retirement, but he fought off Father Time once more with a .316 average in 1960 at age 42, including 29 home runs and 72 RBIs in 113 games. He became one of a handful of men who played in four different decades.

He hit his 500th home run that year. Then, on the last time at bat in his career, he went out in typical Ted Williams drama—with a home run off Jack Fisher of the Orioles. He rounded the bases with his head down as usual. When his fans called and yelled and cheered his name, he still didn't tip his cap, not after 20 years of stubbornly refusing to do it.

Williams was a manager for four years as the skipper of the Washington Senators and the Texas Rangers. After leaving the Rangers following the 1972 season, he has devoted a considerable portion of his working time to the Jimmy Fund in Boston, which raises money for children with cancer and other terminal illnesses. Williams himself has raised millions for the Fund and has donated sizeable amounts of his own money.

On December 15, 1995, Ted was on hand for a special occasion in Boston—the dedication of the Ted Williams Harbor Tunnel. Recovered from two strokes and using a cane, the 77-year-old immortal cried as the tunnel was dedicated in his honor.

But the most telling tribute to him came four years earlier, on May 12, 1991, Ted Williams Day at Fenway Park. His son, John Henry, Ted's business manager, was with him. "The fans just went wild," John Henry said, "and there was so much emotion and so much feeling there. It just broke him up."

Williams had a tribute of his own to pay to the fans that day. At the end of a moving speech, he told them how much it meant to him "knowing you guys really did love me."

Then he pulled out a Red Sox cap—and tipped it to his fans.

WHAT OTHER PLAYERS SAID ABOUT TED WILLIAMS

Bobby Doerr—He was so sharp. One day we were playing a day game in Boston and a little cloud comes over. The shadow the cloud caused was awfully small, but he stepped out of the box for a couple of seconds ....He's got three personalities. One you just love. Then he's got one you kind of want to walk away from and dislike, and then he's got another one—you'd like to kick him right in the tail end.

Birdie Tebbetts—He is the greatest hitter in the history of the game. One year Lou Boudreau was leading him by three or four percentage points. We were dressing for the game and I said, "The Frenchman's got you by four." On the field, he walked past me and said, "He won't be." He got a hit, then he got another hit and then a third hit. Before he went up to the plate for his final at-bat, he said, "The first three were for the Frenchman. This one is for me." And he hit a home run.

Yogi Berra—I liked to talk to the hitters. One day Ted stepped into the batter's box and I asked him if he had been doing any fishing lately. He said, "Shut up, Yogi!" He was all business. He was the greatest I ever saw.

George Kell—No doubt, Ted was the greatest I ever saw. He absolutely could play a tune with that bat. I remember one night when I was with Boston .... He had jammed his hand and could hardly grip the bat, but it was a big ball game, with Whitey Ford pitching for the Yankees. In a cab I asked him if he was going to play. He said, "I'm going to tell you exactly what I'm going to do tonight, George. I'm going to line the ball to left field four times. I might get four hits, and I might not get any." He was two for four, and they were all shots into left field.

Bob Feller—He could hit anybody. He made the ball be over the plate. He, Rogers Hornsby and Stan Musial were the greatest hitters I ever saw. He was single-minded. I remember someone asked him to play in a charity tennis game in Florida .... Ted figured it would be easy and said yes. He couldn't hit the ball and made a fool of himself. The next day, he hired a pro to give him lessons. That was Ted for you.

Warren Spahn—The most disciplined hitter of them all.

Al Kaline—He was the greatest hitter I ever saw. If the ball was half an inch off the strike zone, he wouldn't swing at it. He'd take a base on balls. If he hadn't played in Fenway Park, there's no telling how many home runs he would have hit. And those years in the service—he never complained. Boy, when they play that Marine Hymn, tears come to his eyes. He loves the Marines.

Bob Lemon—In his era, day in and day out, he was the toughest hitter any of us ever faced .... I think he could still hit today.

Lou Boudreau—He was the greatest hitter I played against. He could go to left field but didn't want to concede that any pitcher could make him go the opposite way.

Herb Score—He was just the greatest hitter .... a fierce competitor. It seemed like he'd always rise to the occasion. If he had played in Detroit or New York, he would have hit a thousand home runs. He played in the toughest ballpark in the American League for a lefthanded hitter.

Jay Johnstone—When I was a rookie, I idolized Ted Williams. I wrote him a letter asking his advice and he wrote me back a four-page letter on hitting. I still have it.

Dave "Boo" Ferriss—I could talk to you all day about that guy... His work habits were incredible. He never took for granted that he had such God-given ability. He took that ability, worked hard and made it even greater. I can see him now—he'd sit out there and watch that day's pitcher warming up. In those days, they did so right in front of the dugout, and there would be Ted—staring a hole through him and looking for some little thing that would give him an edge.

Minnie Minoso—With all due respect to other hitters, the best hitter I ever saw was Mr. Ted Williams.

Milt Pappas—Ted Williams, by far, was the greatest pure hitter I ever faced in baseball ....When he took batting practice, it seemed like 90 percent of the other team would be out in the dugout watching him hit. That's how great he was.

Don Larsen—I think he had such great eyesight that the umpires let him call his own game. I think he really influenced the umpires.

Mudcat Grant—Unfortunately for pitchers, he had a choice of what he wanted to hit at. You couldn't get a called third strike on Ted Williams. The umpires were of the opinion that if Ted didn't swing at it with two strikes on him, it was a ball.

Rocky Colavito—Ted knew what hitting was all about. He was the greatest hitter I ever saw. I played a lot of games against him, and I never saw him look bad at the plate. Never.

Tony Kubek—The greatest hitter of all time. No question. He may have hit more homers than Aaron if he hadn't spent four and a half years in the service.

Virgil "Fire" Trucks—He was the only hitter I never liked to face. I was glad to hold him to a single or double. The best chance for me to get him out was to walk him and try to pick him off first base.

Bill "Moose" Skowron—He's the only guy I feared with a man on first base and no outs. I had to play in front of the baserunner, and I said, "Please don't hit the ball to me."

Clete Boyer—I thought there was only one great hitter. I think everybody would tell you that, even Hank Aaron and Willie Mays. I played against him (Williams) for two years, and I couldn't believe him—the guy was that good. I don't think anybody ever said there was a better hitter than Ted Williams.

Stan Musial - The greatest hitter of our time, no question about that. He led the league six years, but you have to wonder how many batting titles he would have won if he hadn't been gone those five years.

Whitey Herzog—I never saw a hitter come close to what he can do. I bet as a Marine pilot he didn't need radar, his eyes were so incredible. Stan Musial was my idol when I was a kid, but Ted Williams with a bat in his hand was the best hitter I ever saw.

Bobby Richardson—I consider him the best hitter of all time. Not only was he a great hitter, but he could look at a young ballplayer and tell him how he could be a better hitter.

U.S. Senator Jim Bunning—I pitched my first complete game win in the big leagues in Fenway Park in 1957, and I struck him out three times and he flew out once. I think it was the first time anybody struck him out three times in a game. They tell me he got out a schedule and circled the next time we would face each other. That was in Detroit. He hit two home runs off me.

Al Lopez—You couldn't strike him out. Very seldom did you see Ted Williams strike out. He always got a piece of the ball.

Elmer Valo—He was a better all-around player than people made him out to be.

Sam Mele—I had him for dinner one night in Quincy, and the kids in the neighborhood heard about it and swarmed to our house. I was trying to shoo the kids away, but he signed autographs for an hour and a half. I'll never forget it.

Eddie Yost—Had he not gone into the service those two stretches, he would have broken Babe Ruth's record.

Eddie Mathews—I didn't see that much of him, but from what I did see, he was the greatest hitter—I mean hitter—I ever saw.

Harmon Killebrew—When I was a kid just coming into the American League, Ted took special interest and time to really talk to me an awful lot, and I got to know him real well. I once went on a hunting trip with him and, of course, we talked a lot about hitting. There wasn't anyone who knew more about the mechanics of hitting than Ted and, to me, he was the greatest hitter I ever saw and maybe the greatest of all time. Even today, despite all his physical problems, when he talks hitting, he still gets that look in his eye.

Hank Aaron—I didn't see much of Ted, but I didn't have to. All I had to do was hear people talk about him. He's just like E.F. Hutton — you know, people listen. Ted was a rare breed. He didn't steal a base. He didn't have to. He created excitement just because he was at the plate.

Joe Garagiola—In 1946, I got out of the service, joined the Cardinals and we went to the World Series against the Red Sox. The first time I saw Williams come into the batter's box, I was awestruck. I didn't know whether to give a signal or get his autograph. He came up there and he would squeeze the hell out of the bat. It was a habit of his. When he took batting practice, everyone would stop and watch him. Three of us got four hits in a game to break or tie a record, and I couldn't wait to buy a Boston paper the next day to read about something I was a part of—and all it talked about was "WILLIAMS BEATS SHIFT WITH BUNT!" I said, "Boy —that's when you're a great hitter. Bunt the ball and you're in the headlines!"

THE WILLIAMS FILE

Full Name: Theodore Samuel Williams.

Date and Place of Birth: August 30, 1918, San Diego, California.

Nicknames: "The Splendid Splinter", "The Thumper", "Teddy Ballgame", "The Kid".

Position: Left field.

Major League Career: 19 years, 1939-1960, with time out for military service, 1943-1945 and 1952-1953.

Home Runs: 521 (10th).

Runs Batted In: 1,839 (10th).

Runs Scored: 1,798.

Lifetime Batting Average: .344 (7th).

Number of Hits: 2,654.

Walks: 2,019 (2nd).

Strikeouts: 709.

Records: Only player to hit .400 since 1930, second most walks in history, oldest player to win batting championship, seventh highest lifetime batting average, second highest slugging average, fourth highest home run percentage.

Other Highlights:

— American League's Most Valuable Player twice, 1946 and 1949.

— American League batting champion six times.

— American League home run champion four times.

— American League RBI champion four times.
— Led league in bases on balls eight times, six years in a row.
— Never struck out 50 times after age 24.
— Struck out only 27 times while hitting .406 in 1941.
— Hit over .300 in 18 of his 19 seasons, missing only when he was 41 and injured, but returned to hit .316 in his last year, at age 42.
— Led league in various offensive departments 45 times, according to the *Baseball Encyclopedia.*
— Oldest player to win league batting championship, hitting .328 in 1958 at age 40.
— Military service came during prime years, from age 24 to 27 and when he was 33 and 34.

Elected to the Baseball Hall of Fame: 1966.

16

MARK McGWIRE

Who Knows How Many?

Mark McGwire's development both as a big league superstar and as a person can be divided into two stages—before 1991 and after. That was the defining season for him in baseball and a decisive year in his life.

"That was the turning point in my life as a person and a professional ballplayer," he told *Sport Magazine*'s William Ladson in 1997. After a disastrous '91 season left him in a depressed state, he underwent professional counseling. He said it "made me the person I am today. It made me find out what I'm all about. I'm a much happier person . . ."

He said that with assistance he was able to look at himself in the mirror and say, "I like myself," and that was when he turned the corner in his life. "My psychiatrist taught me a lot of things about life and myself," McGwire told Ladson. "I really believe that anyone who confronts his problems succeeds, and the ones who keep failing, you'll never hear from again."

CROSSROADS

That 1991 season is what drove McGwire to open up to himself and to his professional counselor. After setting a record for the most home runs by a rookie with 49 in 1987 and winning the Rookie of the Year award, and after blasting 156 homers by the time he was 27, he dropped off the radar screen in 1991. He hit only 22 home runs, 10 below his lowest number in his first four full seasons, drove in only 75 runs, 20 below his previous low, and hit .201, a disappointing average even for a good-field-no-hit infielder and a stunning one for someone who had always been rated a star hitter.

McGwire realized as early as his drive down the California coast from Oakland to his home in the Los Angeles area after the '91 season that he was at more than just a low point in his career. "I was at a crossroads in my life," he told *Sports Illustrated*'s Rick Reilly late in the 1998 campaign as he drew a bead on the record of 61 home runs in a season set by Roger Maris in 1961.

"I was so down . . . I just decided that there wasn't any room for pouting or complaining or anything but doing my best."

That's when he decided to call a therapist and talk to him. He talked to him for the next four years. "It took failure for me to understand myself," McGwire admitted. He added that "everybody needs therapy. It brought so many things to my life. I can face the music now, I can face the truth."

As a result, McGwire has put together a career as one of the brightest superstars in the history of baseball, and no one seems to know the limits of his greatness, if there are any. He keeps topping himself, breaking other people's records and then his own. First the question was whether he would break Maris's record. Then the question became whether he would break his own record. Now another question is whether he'll break Hank Aaron's record of 755 home runs in a career. If he does, the question automatically will become: How many more will he hit?

Not even Mark knows.

RIGHT FROM THE START

Home runs came early and often to Mark, right from the start. He hit one in his first time at bat as a Little Leaguer. But he wasn't a first baseman. With his father as his coach, young Mark was an overpowering pitcher. Today his father can't remember that their team ever lost a game when Mark was the pitcher. He does remember, however, just how hard Mark threw. How hard? While playing an innocent game of catch in the back yard, Mark broke his father's thumb.

By age 10, Mark already had hit 18 home runs in 30 games. As he grew into his teen years, his homers became accompanied by tales that would make Babe Ruth proud. One of his home runs actually sailed out of the county. Playing in Los Angeles County, the budding star hit a long fly ball over a fence 350 feet from home plate, over a cluster of cypress trees and across the street- into San Bernardino County.

One of five sons of Dr. John McGwire, a dentist, and his wife, Ginger, in the Los Angeles suburb of Claremont, Mark continued pitching and homering at Damien High School. His coach, Tom Carroll, says, "I've had kids that have had talent, but they're not willing to pay the price. Mark never worried about that."

Mom and Dad continued to feed their young giant. All five McGwire boys grew to at least 6 feet, 3 inches and well over 200 pounds and became varsity athletes. The Cardinals' 1999 media guide lists Mark at 6-5 and 250, with 17-inch forearms and 19-inch triceps, prompting some to nickname him "Popeye."

With five young and strapping athletes around the table, his mother "had to double and triple recipes," he remembers today. "She had to go to the store twice a week and it cost her a couple of hundred dollars each time she went."

After stardom in high school, despite an attack of mononucleosis in his sophomore year, Mark was drafted by the Montreal Expos but turned down their offer of $8,500 so he could go to the University of Southern California instead. In his freshman season, he won four games and lost four, with a 3.04 earned run average in 20 games. In 47 innings, he struck out 31. As a 19-year-old sophomore, he led the Trojans' pitching staff with a 2.78 E.R.A., better than his teammate, Randy Johnson. He also hit 19 home runs in 53 games, a USC record. He was USC's starting pitcher seven times that season, but his coach, the respected Rod Dedeaux, never used him in that role again.

McGwire's bat was attracting at least as much attention as his pitching. As a junior, and after a summer as a first baseman in Anchorage, Alaska, he became USC's first baseman at the urging of the team's hitting coach, Ron Vaughn. McGwire promptly hit 32 homers in 67 games, a career-high for the school. *The Sporting News* chose him as its College Player of the Year and a member of its All-America team.

Baseball became an Olympic sport in 1984, and McGwire was chosen as the U.S. first baseman, along with another big league first baseman and home run hitter, Will Clark. "It was exciting to be on the first Olympic baseball team," McGwire said. "That probably was the best amateur team ever."

"I'VE GOT TO QUIT"

By now the big league teams had him in their sights. With Mark passing up his senior year at USC, the A's selected him with the tenth pick of the 1984 draft and sent him to Modesto in the California League.

As happened so often in his amateur days and the first years of his professional career, Mark found himself locked in a struggle in his first days in the minor leagues. His former wife and onetime bat girl for USC, Kathy Williamson, with whom Mark has maintained a close friendship, remembers the nights when he would toss and turn in bed and say, "I can't hit the baseball anymore. I'm done. I've lost it. I've got to quit."

But he didn't. He made 33 errors as Modesto's third baseman, but he also hit 24 home runs and drove in 106 runs and was voted the league's Rookie of the Year. His reward was a promotion to Huntsville, Alabama, for the start of the 1986 season. After hitting .303 against Double-A pitching with 10 homers in 55 games, he was promoted again in June, this time to Tacoma in the Pacific Coast League, a Triple-A league, the highest level of minor league baseball. Only two months later, hitting .318 with 13 homers for Tacoma, he received the biggest promotion of them all, to the big leagues, in August, joining the A's in Baltimore—only to see the game rained out.

His first hit gave no hint of things to come. It was a single off Tommy John of the Yankees. He hit the first of his home run on August 25, 1986, in Detroit's Tiger Stadium off Walt Terrell, a 6-foot, 2-inch righthander who won 15 games for the Tigers that year. McGwire hit two more homers in those closing weeks of the season, but he also committed six errors in 16 games at third base.

"THE BASH BROTHERS"

In his first full season, when he set the rookie record with 49 home runs, McGwire played in 151 games, 145 of them as the A's first baseman. While he hit .289, his homer total led the American League and equalled Andre Dawson's pace-setting figure for the National League McGwire topped both leagues in slugging average and home run percentage, iust before his twenty-fourth birthday. He was second in the American League in total bases and third in runs batted in. Small wonder that he was selected for his second Rookie of the Year award. The vote by the Baseball Writers Association of America was unanimous.

His teammate, Outfielder Jose Canseco, chipped in with 31 home runs after winning the American League's Rookie of the Year award himself the previous season with 33 homers. Over the two seasons, Canseco drove in 230 runs. Together the powerful one-two punch of McGwire and Canseco was becoming known around the Bay Area and around the American League as "The Bash Brothers."

By 1988, that potent punch propelled the A's to the championship of the American League West, on the wings of Canseco's league-leading 42 homers and 124 RBIs. McGwire was third in the home run race with 32. The A's swept the Boston Red Sox in four games but then lost to the Los Angeles Dodgers in five games in the World Series. The most memorable moment of the Series came in the first game, when a limping Kirk Gibson hit a pinch-hit 2-run homer off relief ace Dennis Eckereley in the ninth inning to win it.

McGwire was experiencing post-season play for the first time. He had a .333 average in the American League Championship Series, although four of his five hits were singles. In the World Series, the Dodger pitchers held McGwire to only one hit in 17 trips to the plate—but it won a game. His home run in the bottom of the ninth inning of the third game carried Oakland to victory, 2-1.

The A's repeated as AL West champions in 1989 with McGwire leading the league again in home run percentage and finishing third in homers with 33. Oakland defeated the Toronto Blue Jays in the American League Championship Series in five games. McGwire hit .389 but connected for only one home run in 18 at-bats. Then came the World Series, which has since gone into the history books of baseball—and of the Bay Area. Ten years later it is still remembered as the Series that was interrupted by an earthquake.

It was the Battle of the Bay—the Oakland A's against the San Francisco Giants—with the first two games played in the Oakland Coliseum. The A's won both before the home fans, 5-0 and 5-1, and the Series moved across the Bay to San Francisco's Candlestick Park, or so everyone thought.

A devastating earthquake struck the Bay Area just as the teams were preparing to take the field for the third game. The Series was interrupted for ten days while the region tried to recover from the extensive damage, injuries and loss of life. Baseball Commissioner Fay Vincent authorized the Series to be resumed on October 27, as the sport faced the real possibility that the World Series would be played into November for the first time.

The A's resorted to their run-scoring power and prevented

that from happening. They outslugged the Giants, 13-7, as the two teams combined to break the World Series record for home runs in one game with seven. The next day they avoided the possibility of a World Series in November by jumping out to an 8-0 lead in the fourth game and then hanging on to win the game and the Series.

McGwire compiled another respectable batting average in the Series, .294, but only one of his five hits was for extra bases, a double. He didn't score a run and batted in only one That wasn't his only disappointment. The earthquake cast a pall over the city and the Series. When it was over, Mark felt that the A's had been deprived of the usual celebration because of the tragedy caused by the quake.

"We had to respect what happened to northern California," he said. "We didn't get to celebrate ... No champagne. No parade ... There will always be an asterisk next to our '89 championship."

MORE HOMERS, AND A GOLD GLOVE, TOO

The A's made it three AL West titles in a row in 1990, finishing nine games ahead of the White Sox with considerable help from McGwire'—39 home runs and 108 runs batted in. Between them, the Bash Brothers hit 76 home runs, drove in 209 runs and finished second and third—Canseco was second—in home run percentage. McGwire was becoming an excellent first baseman at the same time. He committed only five errors and finished the season with a sparkling .997 fielding percentage. For all this, the fans chose him as the starting first baseman on the American League All-Star team for the third straight time. Over the winter he expanded his trophy collection with his first Gold Glove, the annual Rawlings award to the league's best fielder at each position.

The A's post-season success continued, with a four-game sweep over the Boston Red Sox in the American League Championship Series. That sweep was followed by another in the World Series. Only this time it was the Cincinnati Reds who were doing the sweeping. The Reds managed to short-circuit the power of the Bash Brothers, holding McGwire to no home runs and Canseco to one. Between the two of them they had only two RBIs. McGwire outhit Canseco, but it was nothing to brag about. Mark hit .214. Canseco hit .083.

Then came McGwire's bottoming-out year, 1991, when he hit only .201 and had his streak of 30-homer seasons snapped at four. Canseco picked up the slack as much as he could, leading both leagues with 44 home runs and driving in 122 runs. McGwire's numbers, those 22 homers and 75 RBIs, placed him among the team's leaders, hut they were far below his usual level of performance.

That was when McGwire experienced his epiphany and vowed to seek counselling. He found himself through that process, and he found someone else too—his three-year-old son, Matthew. McGwire was going through a divorce. As part of that emotional transition, he began spending more time with Matt, establishing and solidifying a relationship that grows closer with each year.

It attracted the attention of the entire nation in 1998, when Matt, in his St. Louis Cardinals' bat boy uniform, became a familiar sight on network television, greeting Dad at home plate on the latest of his 70 home runs in one season.

McGwire frequently tells interviewers, "Everything I do in life and in baseball now is for my son." He's a bat boy when the Cardinals are at home and Matt is visiting from the home he makes with his mother in California, just five minutes from Dad. And Mark has it in his contract that there will always be a guaranteed seat for Matt on any of the team's chartered flights.

BACK ON TOP

As McGwire worked his way through his counseling and built a closer-than-ever relationship with Matt, things began to break his way again in 1992, even though the injury bug that plagued him for many of his early years struck again. He missed 20 games with a strained muscle on the right side of his rib cage in August, which cost him a chance at his second home run title. He finished with 42 round-trippers, 20 more than in '91 and only one behind the league's leader, Juan Gonzalez. McGwire led the league in slugging average, and the frequency of his home runs was also the best in the league, with a homer every 11.1 times he came to bat. To add to all this, he raised his batting average 67 points.

Counseling wasn't the only reason for his dramatic improvement. McGwire began to adopt a new attitude where stress was concerned, one that was especially valuable in his 1998 pursuit of the Maris record and the enormous pressure accompanying it.

In tense situations today, including the pressure-cooker years of '98 and '99, Mark says to himself, "'What am I getting so stressed about? The Man Upstairs knows what's going to happen.' I totally believe that, and that takes the pressure off."

During the 1992 season, McGwire gave evidence that he might be destined to hit his way into the 500 Home Run Club some day. On June 10 in Milwaukee, he hit the 200th homer of his career, off Chris Bosio, a 6-3, 230-pound righthander for the Brewers. There was still more significance to that blow. With it, Mark reached the 200-homer level faster than all but four other stars—Ralph Kiner, Babe Ruth, Harmon Killebrew and Eddie Mathews.

McGwire made another adjustment in 1992 that contributed to his renewed success. He accepted his role as a "slugger." He has since admitted he never liked that term because he felt it stereo-typed a player as one who hit a lot of home runs but couldn't do much else. McGwire has always taken pride in his ability as a first baseman and as one who hits singles and doubles too, not just homers. In 1992, however, he decided to accept the classification of slugger, while continuing to do everything else well, too.

The A's won the American League West championship for the fourth time in Mark's still-young career but lost the playoffs to Toronto in six games. McGwire belted a homer in his first time at bat in the playoffs. But finished with only two hits in his last 19 times up and only three RBIs for the Series.

McGwire's batting averages in three of his post-season ap-pearances are enough to make any hitter proud—.333 in the 1988 League Championship Series, .333 in the '39 ALCS and .294 in the '89 World Series. But his run production has never been McGwire-like, and his averages in his four other post-season appearances have sounded too much like the time of day in the early afternoon—.214, .154, .150 and .059.

His combined hitting statistics in 32 ALCS and World Series games show a .228 batting average, 26 hits in 114 trips to the plate, only four home runs and 13 runs hatted in. Over a full 162-game season, that works out to 21 home runs and 65 RBIs.

McGwire's performance during the '92 regular season won wide recognition. The fans elected him as the league's starting first baseman for the fifth straight season. They were rewarded in the pre-game home run contest, when Mark slugged 12 pitches out of the park in San Diego. He was also named to All-Star teams of *The Sporting News* and UPI. He finished fourth behind his teammate, Dennis Eckersley, in the Most Valuable Player voting, and UPI sa-luted him by naming him its Comeback Player of the Year.

The 1993 and '94 seasons brought serious setbacks for McGwire in the health department. An injury to his left heel and problems with his back cut his playing time drastically, to a total of only 74 games over the two years.

But, serious—student that he is, McGwire put the time to good use. He sat behind home plate with the big league scouts and studied the pitchers. He decided to abandon his practice of being a "guess hitter" and start to use his head instead, anticipating what the pitcher would be likely to throw next, and where. And he adopted some advice from the A's hitting coach, Doug Rader, as his personal creed of hitting: "Just take what they give you." '

INJURIES AND TAPE MEASURES

The injury jinx continued to stalk McGwire in 1995, and the worst strike in the history of professional sports shortened everybody's baseball season. Still, while his team was finishing last in the American League West, McGwire went on another of his hitting binges: 39 home runs in only 317 times at bat in 109 games, and 90 runs batted in. The fans voted him to his seventh All-Star game even though his injuries kept him out of the lineup.

He was placed on the disabled list twice. His injuries included being hit by pitches eleven times, a bruised foot and a sore lower back. After visits to the trainer and the doctor, McGwire hit the 269th home run of his career, breaking Reggie Jackson's record for the most home runs by an Oakland player.

Mark's homers weren't clearing the fences with only a few feet to spare, either. He was hitting tape-measure jobs, the way he always did. He has cleared the roof at Detroit's Tiger Stadium, caused $2 000 damage to the scoreboard in Phoenix and bounced a ball on the railing of a stairway on Waveland Avenue beyond Wrigley Field in Chicago.

He reached the players' parking lot at Coors Field in Denver, and the man who should know estimated the blast traveled a distance that could have covered two playing fields. That would be the Cards' batting practice pitcher, Dave McKay, who said, "That had to have gone 600 feet. Six hundred if it went a foot." McKay may he the world's foremost authority on baseballs hit by Mark McGwire.

He estimates he has given up 8,000 pre-game "home runs" to McGwire.

A NEW HEIGHT: 50 HOME RUNS IN ONE SEASON

The McGwire power was becoming legendary by 1996. Even after missing the first 18 games with a foot injury, he went on a season-long hitting spree that produced this long list of achievements:

— He became the 14th player in history to hit 50 home runs, leading both leagues with 52. That tied him at the time with three other players for the eleventh most homers in one season in Major League history and the most in the American League since 1961, when Maris hit his record-breaking 61 and Mickey Mantle slugged 54.

— He also led both leagues in slugging percentage and on-base percentage and equalled the Major League record he set himself the year before—one home run in every 8.13 times at bat.

— He led the A's in hitting with a .312 average, 60 points above his career percentage.

— He hit the 300th home run of his career on June 25 against Detroit's Omar Olivares.

— He hit a home run into the fifth deck of Toronto's Sky Dome.

— He reached 50 home runs in only 390 at-bats, breaking Ruth's record of doing it in 438 times up in 1921.

— And there was this hint of things to come: Over one span of 162 games stretching back to the previous season, the same number of -tames as a full season, McGwire hit 70 home runs.

A CARDINAL, THEN THE CHASE

With the speculation increasing that someone was surely going to break Maris's record and McGwire was the likely candidate, he added fuel to that fire in 1997, while switching teams and leagues. The A's surprised the baseball world by trading McGwire and his powerful bat to the St. Louis Cardinals of the National League for three pitchers on July 31.

As fans and the members of the media wondered how much trouble he might have adjusting to pitchers he'd never seen and ballparks new to him, he kept on swinging. By the time the season ended, McGwire had tied the record held jointly by Hank Greenberg and Jimmie Foxx for the most home runs in a season by a righthanded slugger with 58. The homers also made McGwire the only man except Ruth to hit 50 or more homers in consecutive seasons.

Five weeks before leaving the American League, he hit the longest home run in the history of the Seattle Kingdome—538 feet —off his old college teammate, 6-foot, 10-inch flame-throwing Randy Johnson. Then Mark answered the questions about his ability to adjust to a new team and a new league by hitting 24 home runs in a St. Louis uniform in only two months and breaking the team's record of most home runs in one month with 15 in September.

Of equal meaning to McGwire, he was chosen by *The Sporting News* as its Sportsman of the Year and by his fellow players as Man of the Year for his leadership and commitment on and off the field.

With two weeks left in the 1997 season, McGwire signed a three-year contract for $28 million, including a signing bonus of $1 million. One of his agents, Bob Cohen, said the St. Louis strong man could have commanded at least another million dollars a year by declaring himself a free agent, but he wanted to remain a Cardinal because of his fondness for the St. Louis fans.

At the same time, McGwire began donating a million dollars a year to a charitable foundation which he established to benefit sexually and physically abused children. At a press conference, he cried as he described his foundation, pausing for a full half-minute at one point to regain his composure.

Then he said into the cameras and microphones, "Let's just say children have a special place in my heart. I just really believe a guy in my position can really help out."

Then came 1998.

It started in typical McGwire fashion—a home run with the bases loaded on Opening Day against Ramon Martinez of the Dodgers. It didn't stop until he had stood the baseball world—and the world itself—on its ear by breaking Roger Maris's single season record of 61 homers by nine with his shortest homer of the season, a mere 341 feet over the left field wall against the Chicago Cubs in St. Louis.

There were predictions from every corner of baseball over the winter and in spring training that McGwire would break Maris's record in '98 the first time so many people predicted that the unthinkable would finally happen after the Maris mark had stood for 37 years. But no one ever predicted McGwire would do it by such a decisive margin.

While the nation was mesmerized by two chases in one, with both McGwire and the Cubs' right fielder, Sammy Sosa, slugging homers at a record pace, McGwire was piling up one achievement after another in his role as baseball's muscle man:

— He hit the 400th homer of his career on May 8 against righthander Rick Reed of the Mets in Shea Stadium, only the 26th player to reach that height and setting a record for doing it in the fewest times at bat.

— He hit the longest home run in the history of Busch Stadium in St. Louis, a 527-footer, on May 12, then topped that four days later with a shot that sailed 545 feet against the Marlins' Livan Hernandez. The ball bounced off a *St. Louis Post-Dispatch* sign in straightaway center field and then dropped into shrubbery below. "It's the best ball I've ever hit," he said. "I don't think I can hit one better than that."

— He became the host for 47,549 fans by becoming the first player to hit a home run into Busch Stadium's "Big Mac Land," a show place for advertising McDonald's fast foods restaurants. Thanks to Mark's homer, the fans were able to flock to McDonald's restaurants all over St. Louis the next day for a free hamburger.

— He became the first slugger to hit 25 homers before June 1, but Sosa wouldn't let him open up any wide gap between them. Sosa broke the Major League record for the most home runs in one month by rapping out 20 of them in June and electrifying fans all over the country with what had become an unimaginable assault by not one star home run hitter but two as both men chased the ghost of Roger Maris.

— He led the National League in the balloting for the All-Star game with 3.3 million votes, the sixth time he was voted to starting position and his tenth year as an All-Star.

— McGwire, after an 0-for-16 slump, broke the Cardinals' season record by hitting his 44th home run against the Rockies in Denver—and it was still only July 26.

— On August 19 at Chicago, less than an hour after watching Sosa hit his 48th homer to take over the National League lead in the fifth inning, McGwire tied the game with his 48th in the eighth inning, then won the game with No. 49 in the tenth to pass Sosa.

— The next day, against the Mets in New York, he became the first player to hit at least 50 home runs in three straight seasons.

— On September 1, McGwire broke Hack Wilson's National League record for the most home runs in one season with his 57th. Maybe even more significantly, his 128 homers in 1997-98 broke Ruth's record for the most homers in two seasons—114—which had stood for 70 years, since The Babe did it in 1927-28.

— He smashed his 60th home run of 1998 on September 5 off Cincinnati's Dennis Reyes in Busch Stadium in the team's142nd game, 12 games faster than Ruth and 17 sooner than Maris. They were the only three men to hit 60 home runs in a single seasonuntil Sosa joined them on September 12 as the two sluggers continued to chase each other in hot pursuit.

GENTLEMEN SLUGGERS

The whole nation followed the Cards and the Cubs on the evening news and in the increasing number of their games being televised by the networks. McGwire and Sosa were filling National League ballparks all over the country, even though only the Cubs were in contention to make the playoffs. In the village of Cooperstown—population 2,300—in upstate New York, the crowds that stayed away after the strike of 1994-95 came back. Attendance shot up and was still on the rise in 1999.

Their duel attracted more attention because of their own conduct. In this age of self-centered, seven-figure individualists, these two stars were actually rooting for each other. And they weren't afraid to display human emotions, with Sosa blowing kisses to his mother in the Dominican Republic and McGwire hoisting Matt high into the air with troth of them wearing their colorful Cardinals' uniforms and flashing grins almost as wide as Dad's bat.

With a two-man security detail protecting him everywhere he went, McGwire swung his way into even more historic territory on September 7 when he connected for a first-inning homer off the Cubs' Mike Morgan. The home run tied Roger Maris with 61. Mark reached that pinnacle in 144 games, 19 games sooner than Maris.

By now McGwire was attracting attention around the world. News of his 61st homer was the top sports story in baseball conscious Japan. The nation's largest newspaper, *The Yomiuri*, said, "All of America cheers the 'modern Ruth.'"

Sadaharu Oh, who hit 868 home runs as Japan's homer run star, told the *Kyodo News*, "It's great for him to hit such a number. Congratulations. I express my respect for him, particularly for his power of concentration."

In Europe, the *London Daily Telegraph* displayed McGwire's picture on its front page, showing him pumping his right fist into the air as he circles the bases. Next to the photo was a headline:

AMERICA STOPS AS SPORTING HISTORY IS MADE

The story below said, "McGwire has all of America on the edge of its seat and the whole country gives the impression of supporting him. But his run chase has not been without controversy, for he admits to taking a dietary supplement that contains steroids in order to maintain his muscle-bound bulk."

Indeed, McGwire had been taking androstenedione, an over-the-counter supplement banned by the National Football League, the National Basketball Association and the National Collegiate Athletic Association but permitted by Major League Baseball. In 1999, as he mounted another history-making assault, this time on his own record, he revealed he had stopped using the supplement.

One of the London tabloids, the *Daily Express,* ran a full-age feature article on the home run chase, written by its tennis correspondent who was covering the U.S. Open, The reporter showed a clear understanding of America's sense of values when he wrote, "America is totally transfixed. Bill Clinton's bedroom indiscretions? No. Wall Street's latest roller-coaster ride? Wrong again. In a nation preoccupied with sports and statistics, the race to break the number of home runs in one baseball season merits top place in the public interest polls."

The Sky Television Network broadcast footage and stories on McGwire's 61st home run, with a woman who was co-anchoring a newscast marvelling, "It's amazing. The ball is so small and the stadium is so big. How do they see anything?"

In Italy, the nation's leading sports daily, *Gazzetta Dello Snort,* published updates every day for two weeks as McGwire and Sosa closed in on Maris. Another publication, *Corriere Dello Sport,* said McGwire is now "entrenched in American history and given the same respect that is accorded Abraham Lincoln or Michael Jordan."

HOISTING MATT

McGwire slugged his way onto America's center stage the next night, September 8, with his 62nd home run off the season, against righthander Steve Trachsel of the Cubs in the fourth inning. The ball traveled a mere 341 feet to the left-field wall, puny by McGwire's standards and his shortest homer of the season. It cleared the wall 15 feet to the right of the foul pole. McGwire was as excited as any of the hometown fans in Busch Stadium, so much so that he missed first base and had to go back and touch it

The ball landed in a no-man's-land under the left-field stands where no fan could get it. It was retrieved by a member of the Cardinals' ground crew, Tim Forneris, who gave it to McGwire instead of yielding to the temptation of selling it. Collectors estimated he could have gotten a million dollars for it.

McGwire was mobbed by his admiring teammates at home plate as he hoisted Matt high into the night air in full view of the crowd and the millions watching on national television. Out in right field, sammy Sosa applauded with his hare right hand against his gloved left. Then he trotted into the area around home plate, hugged McGwire warmly and gave him an enthusiastic high-five.

Then McGwire added another of his unique touches, gestures that captivated the nation. He ran over to the box seats on the first base and hugged members of the Roger Maris family. As the sellout crowd remained standing, McGwire stepped up to a microphone provided by the Cardinals' staff and told his worshipping fans; "To all my family, my son, the Cubs, Sammy Sosa, it's unbelievable. Thank you, St. Louis."

Tim Forneris left his teammates on the ground crew, carrying the ball and its secretly coded markings, and joined the speechmaking in the infield. Passing up the opportunity to make a small fortune by selling the ball, he handed it to the Cardinals' star and said simply, "Mr. McGwire, I think I have something that belongs to you."

The celebration lasted eleven minutes, baseball's biggest and longest during-the-game celebration since Cal Ripken broke Lou Gehrig's consecutive games streak in 1995. When it was over, something else was over, too. For the first time in 78 years, since Babe Ruth hit 54 home runs in 1920, the record for the most home runs in one season was not held by a member of the New York Yankees.

The next day, the baseball hit by McGwire for his 62nd home run arrived at the Hall of Fame in Cooperstown, New York—autographed by Mark—along with the bat he hit it with, the uniform he was wearing when he hit it and his size 13 spikes. Hall of Fame President Don Marr said, "This is like Christmas. Mark McGwire has said these artifacts belong here. He's a man of his word. It was a spontaneous reaction by McGwire in the locker room. We didn't expect to be coming home with this."

For Marr, it was the end of a perfect trip. He had flown to St. Louis on the day McGwire was destined to break Maris's record and took with him the bat Maris used to hit his 61st home run in 1961. He showed the bat to McGwire, Sosa and the Maris family.

Marr said later, "Mark took Maris's bat, rubbed his chest with it, and said, 'Roger, you're with me today.'"

As Marr was returning to Cooperstown, McGwire did what he had been doing all year, playing for the Cardinals. He had spent a sleepless night because of all the celebrating, but when the Cards flew to Cincinnati and played the Reds before another sellout crowd, Mark was there. "When you've got 50,000 fans out there," he told reporters, "you've got to make some sort of showing."

"GET UP, BABY! GET UP!"

Sunday, September 27, was Fan Appreciation Day at Busch Stadium, and another capacity crowd showed up to express thanks to McGwire for his 68 home runs, hoping, of course, that he would thrill them just once more by hitting 70. In a season where nothing seemed impossible for him—when he broke the Maris record and even exceeded Matt's preseason prediction of 65 homers for his Dad—Mark had just kept on going. Now he was at 68. So why not 70? Besides, 70 sounds so much better.

That's what the whole ballpark was thinking. And that's what happened. Number 70 was a 370-footer off Carl Pavano of the Montreal Expos, at 3:19 pm, Central Time. It came in the seventh inning of the game, on McGwire's last swing of the season,

In the Cardinals' broadcast booth, announcer Mike Shannon, who played third base and the outfield for the Cards for nine years in the 1960s and '70s, yelled into his microphone:

"Swing and . . . Get up, baby! Get up! Get up! Get up! Home run! He's done it again! Seventy home runs! Take a ride on that for history. They'll be shooting at that one for years and years!"

Sosa finished the season with 66 home runs himself, an achievement that would have smashed the Maris record by five and would have made the Cubs outfielder the toast of the baseball world in any other year.

As McGwire rounded the bases for the 70th time, the Expos infielders shook his hand. This time the celebration lasted three minutes, through Brian Jordan's entire time at bat.

After the game, Manager Felipe Alou of the Expos told reporters he didn't want his pitchers to walk McGwire. "I left it up to God and the kid on the mound," he said. "I didn't want to tamper with history. Thank God the season's over, or he would hit 80 . . ."

McGwire's feat was unbelievable to everyone, most of all to Mark himself. "I can't believe I did that," he told reporters after the game. "It's absolutely amazing. It blows my mind. I am almost speechless."

He added, "I think it will stand for a while. I know how gruelling it is to do what I've done this year. Will it be broken someday? It could be. Will I be alive? Possibly. But if I'm not playing, I'll definitely be there."

It was, to borrow Hank Aaron's expression in the foreword of this book, a baseball Mount Everest, in more ways than one. Someone calculated that McGwire's 70 home runs went a total of 29,598 feet, almost 400 feet higher than Everest's peak. With 400-foot home runs still something to brag about, Mark's blasts sailed an *average* of 422.8 feet.

The season that began with a grand slam home run for McGwire ended with an even greater display not only of his power but also of his consistency. Under more pressure than any other hitter since 1961, when Maris broke Ruth's record, and 1941, when Ted Williams hit .406 and Joe DiMaggio hit in 56 straight games, McGwire closed out his season of history by hitting 23 home runs in his last 40 games, including five over the final weekend.

When he hit his 70th, the ball was recovered by a fan, Philip Ozersky of St. Louis, a 26-year-old research scientist who earns $30,000 a year—and he didn't give it back. He sold the ball for three million dollars at a New York auction. Arlan Ettinger, president of Guernsey's, the auction house that handled the bidding, said, "It's an extraordinary accomplishment to reach $3 million. It's 23 times the world record for any baseball ever sold and five to six times the record of any sports artifact."

By the time of his 70th home run, McGwire could look back on a season filled with all those accomplishments and even more:

— He drove in 147 runs, his career best, the third most in team history behind only Joe Medwick's 154 in 1937 and Rogers Hornsby's 152 in 1922.

— He led both leagues with a .752 slugging average, the second highest in league history, only four points below Hornsby's record in 1925.

— He broke his own Major League record by hitting one home run every 7.27 times at bat.

— By only one point, he missed adding a .300 season to all his other accomplishments with the bat, hitting .299.

— He hit a home run in 12 straight series, beginning in New York on May 8 and lasting until June 18 in Houston.

After America was finally able to exhale, McGwire amassed—long honor roll of recognition: Associated Press Player of the Year, Players' Choice Player of the Year—selected by his fellow Major Leaguers—Player of the Year for both *Baseball America* and *Baseball Weekly,* ABC Wide World of Sports Man of the Year and *Time* magazine's Hero of the Year, among other accolades.

During spring training at Jupiter, Florida, before the start of the 1999 season, McGwire was talking about his magical year to Peter Gammons, the respected baseball journalist for the *Boston Globe* and ESPN. He remembered standing in front of the TV cameras with his former wife and her husband after he broke Maris's record.

He asked Gammons, "You know what surprised me most? The fact that I heard from thousands of divorced parents . . . You can't believe how many people wrote or contacted me about that whole divorced parent problem."

McGwire has deep and strong feelings on the subject. He went on: "I feel very strongly that if adults cannot work things out, the kids come first. But I struck a chord . . . if it really impacted the well-being of some kids who are dealing with divorce, then it was all worth it."

ENCORE

Having accomplished the impossible in 1998, with both of them breaking Maris's record and McGwire then hitting 70, McGwire and Sosa then did the unimaginable in 1999—they reprised their act.

They were chasing each other again with more than 50 homers each in August, only this time they were chasing McGwire's record instead of Maris's. Mark, unbelievably, was running ahead of his '98 pace. The question was whether both men might top 70 this time, and whether the new record holder—if one emerged—might he Sosa instead of McGwire.

Mark wrote more history for himself on August 5 by becoming the 16th member of the 500 Home Run Club, against Andy

Ashby of the San Diego Padres at Busch Stadium. In right field, Tony Gwynn joined in the applause before entering the record book himself the next night with his 3,000th hit. McGwire's 500th homer came in the third inning. Then the man who often hits his home runs in bunches hit 501 in the eighth inning.

Just as he did on his 400th home run, McGwire also reached 500 faster than anyone else, getting there in only 5,487 times at bat compared to the 5,801 trips to the plate which Ruth needed.

Some more good news came out of that week. That was when McGwire told reporters he had stopped using androstenedione, the supplement banned by several other sports, four months earlier. He said he was concerned that kids might try to take it, too.

"I thought long and hard about it, and I don't like the way it was portrayed, like I was the endorser of the product, which I wasn't. I don't like how it's portrayed, but young kids take it because of me. I don't like that." The next day, the White House drug adviser, Barry R. McCaffrey, praised McGwire's decision.

TALKING AGAIN

Once again, America was talking about home runs. As early as Monday, August 23, *The Washington Post* ran a page one story by Richard Justice, who had been assigned to cover McGwire over the weekend against the Mets in New York. Justice and the *Post* got lucky. That was when McGwire, the only man to hit 50 homers in three straight seasons, became the only man to hit 50 homers in *four* straight seasons. He hit two home runs, his 49th and 50th, on Sunday, but he was trailing Sosa, who had 51 after homering twice on Friday and again on Saturday.

After McGwire's homers, Justice wrote, "For months, Mark McGwire said it would not, could not happen again, at least not like last season, when he and Sammy Sosa captivated a nation with their home runs, grace and goodwill. This afternoon, he showed he might be wrong."

McGwire's first home run that afternoon came against a rookie, Octavio Dotel, and actually dented the scoreboard at Shea Stadium 60 feet up and knocked out a light bulb. It was his longest homer of the year, measured by the Mets at 502 feet. McGwire himself admitted to reporters after the game, "That amazed me. That's as hard as I've hit a ball to the opposite field."

The Associated Press described it as "a gargantuan blast." The Mets' catcher, Mike Piazza, said, "I was as astounded as anybody. Wow! . . . Nothing he does surprises me anymore."

Just as he did in 1998, McGwire staged a strong finish in '99. After becoming the sixteenth member of the 500 Home Run Club, he passed Eddie Murray, Mel Ott, Ernie Banks, Eddie Mathews, Willie McCovey and Ted Williams to move into tenth place with 522 homers, just behind Jimmie Foxx and 14 behind Mickey Mantle.

In a head-to-head weekend duel against Sammy Sosa in St. Louis to end the season, McGwire won his fourth home run championship with 65 to Sosa's 63. Incredible as it may seem, both of baseball's premier sluggers duplicated their 1998 feats of topping Maris's 37-year record of 61 homers in a season. McGwire did even more than that. His powerful 1999 climax gave him 345 home runs in four years, an *average* of just over 61 a year.

McGwire homered six times in his last seven games, virtually duplicating his strong finish of 1998, when he hit five home runs in the last three games. "I'm pretty proud of myself as far as how I overcame a lot of things and to put up the numbers I put up this year," he said after the game ending the 1999 season. "It just goes to show you the mind is a lot stronger than people think."

WHAT NEXT?

Late in the 1998 season, as McGwire and Sosa were staging their first shoot-out, McOwire wrote in *Sports Illustrated* with Tom Verducci that he was looking forward to a coaching career after his playing days. "I want to coach." he said. "I have a lot to offer. I've been on top. I've been on the bottom. I've been injured. I've been through so much, I want to tell people you can overcome all this stuff."

But first there is this matter of home runs. "Somebody said I have a shot at .755, Hank Aaron's all-time career record," he said. "I think that's too far away for me. I will say this: how high my career total climbs comes down to my health. If I stay healthy like I have the past few years and I put up the numbers that I'm capable of, who knows how many more home runs I'll hit?"

THE McGWIRE FILE

Full Name: Mark David McGwire
Date and Place of Birth: October 1, 1963, Pomona, California
Positions: First base, third base, outfield, designated hitter.
Major League Career: 1986 to present
Home Runs: 522 (10th)
Runs batted in: 1,277
Runs Scored: 1,059
Batting Average: .265
Hits: 1,498
Walks: 1,185
Strikeouts: 1,400

Records:

— Most home runs in one season (70 in 1998).
— Only player to hit 50 home runs in four straight years, (1996-1999).
— Most home runs in two consecutive seasons (135 in 1998-99).
— Most home runs by a rookie (49 in 1987).
— Best home run percentage in a season (one homer every 7.27 times at bat, 1998).

Other Highlights:

— Has led his league in home runs four times, twice in the American League and twice in the National League.
— Has led his league in walks twice.
— With 1999 totals of 147 RBIs and 145 hits, he became the first player to finish a season with more runs batted in than hits.
— Member of All-Star team eleven times.
— Winner of Rawlings Gold Glove Award in 1990 as American League's best fielding first baseman.

17

"HEIGHTS BY GREAT MEN REACHED ..."

They played for teams with different names, these sluggers of historic dimensions, but they were all giants.
Not the New York or San Francisco kind but the kind
with the small "g"—Aaron and Ruth, Mays and Mantle, Williams
and Jackson and the rest. The mere mention of their names evokes
strength, muscle, power. Tension, excitement, drama. And greatness.

That's why the 16 men whose lives and exploits are chronicled
on these pages deserve this special book about them. There are
other exclusive categories of America's athletes, too—pitchers who
won over 300 games, hockey stars who scored the most goals, football greats who scored the most touchdowns and basketball players with the most points and the most rebounds.

But Mark McGwire and Sammy Sosa proved again in 1998
what Americans, even those who are not baseball fans, have known
all along—that home runs and the larger-than-life men who hit
them are a unique category of athletes and heroes.

Throughout this last century of this second millennium,
Americans have accorded home run hitters a special pedestal in
our lives—through two World Wars and others almost as bad,
through our worst economic depression and something called a
Cold War. We saw proof again in 1998, when the headlines about
McGwire and Sosa dominated the news of the day, frequently topping stories about an obviously less important subject, a presiden-

tial scandal, on our front pages and evening newscasts.

Who will be the next man to hit 500 home runs? Sosa? Ken Griffey, Jr? Jose Canseco? Or no one? Will these 16 be the only ones? Will today's athletes want to play long enough to try to scale that mountain, or will they take their seven-figure incomes to the bank and retire early, content with the good life and what they achieved but short of the magic 500 pinnacle?

Authors a hundred years from now may write another book about another 16 players like these supermen. Or maybe they won't have even one to write about.

That uncertainty serves to underline the greatness of what these men achieved, each against his own odds and his own obstacles. In so doing, each has given us a new definition of greatness. And each surely meets Longfellow's description:

> *The heights by great men reached and kept*
> *Were not attained by sudden flight,*
> *But they, while their companions slept,*
> *Were toiling upward in the night.*

Players interviewd by Bob Allen for this book

Hank Aaron
Joe Altobelli
George Bamberger
Sal Bando
Ernie Banks
Hank Bauer
Yogi Berra
Paul Blair
John Blanchard
Don Blasingame
Bert Blyleven
Bobby Bragan
George Brett
John Biggs
Ernie Broglio
Bob Buhl
Jim Bunning
Lew Burdette
Johnny Callison
Bert Campaneris
Rod Carew
Steve Carlton
Gary Carter
Phil Cavarretta
Chris Chambliss
Dean Chance
Rocky Colavito
Gene Conley
Roger Craig
Del Crandall
Shag Crawford
Frank Crosetti
Al DArk
Don Denkinger
Larry Doby
Bobby Doerr
Al Downing
Walt Dropo
Ryne Duren
Carl Erskine

Elroy Face
Bob Feller
Boo Ferriss
Rollie Fingers
Whitey Ford
George Foster
Bill Freehan
Bob Friend
Joe Garagiola
Ralph Garr
Steve Garvey
Bob Gibson
Alex Grammas
Mudcat Grant
Ken Griffey, Sr.
Ron Guidry
Mel Harder
Doug Harvey
Roland Hemond
Tommy Henrich
Whitey Herzog
Bob Horner
Ralph Houk
Frank Howard
Al Hraboski
Randy Hundley
Catfish Hunter
Monte Irvin
Reggie Jackson
Larry Jansen
Fergie Jenkins
Tommy John
Ernie Johnson
Jay Johnstone
Al Kaline
George Kell
Don Kessinger
Harmon Killebrew
Ralph Kiner
Ed Kranepool

Tony Kubek
John Kucks
Clem Labine
Don Larsen
Vernon Law
Bob Lemon
Johnny Logan
Mickey Lolich
Jim Lonborg
Al Lopez
Sparky Lyle
Juan Marichal
Marty Marion
Eddie Mathews
Charlie Maxwell
Willie Mays
Bill Mazeroski
Gil McDougald
Denny McLain
Sam Mele
Minnie Minoso
Vinegar Bend Mizell
Don Money
Wally Moon
Don Mueller
Bobby Murcer
Graig Nettles
Don Newcombe
Phil Niekro
Irv Noren
Blue Moon Odom
Tony Oliva
Al Oliver
Gene Oliver
Andy Pafko
Jim Palmer
Milt Pappas
Mel Parnell
Claude Passeau
Joe Pepitone

Gaylord Perry
Rico Petrocelli
Jimmy Piersall
Johnny Podres
Boog Powell
Bob Purkey
Dick Radatz
Bobby Richardson
Bill Rigney
Phil Rizzuto
Robin Roberts
Brooks Robinson
Pete Rose
Joe Rudi
Bob Rush
Ray Sadecki
Johnny Sain
Ken Sanders
Ron Santo

Hank Sauer
Mike Schmidt
Red Schoendienst
Herb Score
Bobby Shantz
Curt Simmons
Moose Skowron
Enos Slaughter
Ozzie Smith
Duke Snider
Warren Spahn
Willie Stargell
Ron Swoboda
Chuck Tanner
Birdie Tebbetts
Gorman Thomas
Bobby Thomas
Luis Tiant
Frank Torre

Alan Trammell
Tom Tresh
Virgil Trucks
Elmer Valo
Mickey Vernon
Bill Virdon
Harry Walker
Bill White
Jo Jo White
Billy Williams
Dick Williams
Ted Williams
Maury Wills
Dave Winfield
Wilber Wood
Eddie Yost
Robin Yount
Don Zimmer

The 500 Home Run Club

1.	Hank Aaron	755
2.	Babe Ruth	714
3.	Willie Mays	660
4.	Frank Robinson	586
5.	Harmon Killebrew	573
6.	Reggie Jackson	563
7.	Mike Schmidt	548
8.	Mickey Mantle	536
9.	Jimmie Foxx	534
10.	Mark McGwire	522
11.	Ted Williams	521
	Willie McCovey	521
13.	Eddie Mathews	512
	Ernie Banks	512
15.	Mel Ott	511
16.	Eddie Murray	504

VISIT OUR WEBSITE

AT

www.sportspublishinginc.com

ADDITIONAL TITLES FROM SPORTS PUBLISHING INC.

Tales from Baseball's Golden Age

By Gene Fehler

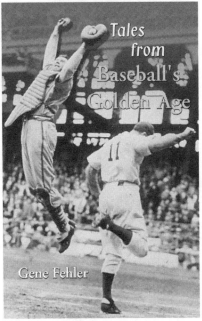

6 X 9 hardcover • 200 pages

Tales from Baseball's Golden Age is a collection of stories from ballplayers who played in the 1940s and '50s. Ralph Kiner, Bobby Thomson, Bill Virdon, Jerry Coleman, and Tim McCarver are just a few of the players who were interviewed for this book. Relive the best, worst, and most comical moments of the game from over 100 major leaguers.

$19.95

PERFECT BOOK FOR ANY BASEBALL FAN!

To Order: Call 1-877-424-BOOK (2665) or
For Savings, Service, and Speedy Delivery, Order On-Line At
www.sportspublishinginc.com